Reflections on American Exceptionalism

Edited by David K. Adams
and Cornelis A. van Minnen

RYBURN PUBLISHING
KEELE UNIVERSITY PRESS

First published in 1994
by Ryburn Publishing
an imprint of Keele University Press
Keele University, Staffordshire, England

© David Bruce Centre for American Studies
and Roosevelt Study Center

Composed and printed by
Ryburn Book Production
at Keele University Press,
Staffordshire, England

ISBN 1 85331 074 3

Contents

Foreword

European historians of the United States, working within the general framework of the European Association for American Studies, meet together at the biennial conference of EAAS in a session devoted to Historians' Shop Talk. This was originated by Professor Willi-Paul Adams of the Free University of Berlin at the Budapest Conference in 1986. At the London Conference in 1990 the idea of an historians' conference emerged, which was developed at the Seville Conference in 1992 with a decision to hold an inaugural meeting in 1993.

Professor David K. Adams of the David Bruce Centre at Keele University, United Kingdom, agreed to act as organizing secretary, together with Dr. Cornelis A. van Minnen, who offered the facilities of the Roosevelt Study Center in Middelburg, the Netherlands. Sponsorship for the meeting, which was held on April 21–23, 1993, was generously provided by USIS, The Hague, USIA, Washington, D.C., the Franklin and Eleanor Roosevelt Institute of Hyde Park, New York, the David Bruce Centre for American Studies at Keele, and by the Roosevelt Study Center.

The title of the Middelburg Conference, *American Exceptionalism in Comparative Perspective*, attracted a wide diversity of papers, ranging from intellectual and diplomatic history to popular culture. Fifty-five scholars from thirteen countries attended the conference and a total of twenty-four papers were delivered in plenary sessions. The selection for publication has been dictated by the desire to provide internal cohesion around the theme of democratic republicanism as expressed domestically, reflected externally and articulated in particular foreign policy exercises. As editors of this volume we have tried as far as possible to use a uniform system of spelling and annotation. The present collection of papers, however, reflects certain differences in national styles and also some of the inevitable problems of access to distant archival sources. Individual opinions expressed are those of the respective authors, they engage debate and are often controversial.

We are grateful to Leontien Joosse of the Roosevelt Study Center who typed all the papers with fidelity and good cheer and to Amanda Gautby at Keele for her technical skills. Publication has been made possible through the good offices of Richard Clark of Keele University Press, in a format designed to provide a forum for the work of European historians of the United States. The enthusiasm among the participants of the inaugural meeting in 1993 for a regular series of biennial conferences of Europeans historians of U.S. history, the expansion of research scholarship throughout the nations of Europe, and the existing pressure on established journals by the number of submissions, make it possible to envisage a continuing and flourishing series of volumes under the *EPAH* (*European Papers in American History*) imprint.

David K. Adams and Cornelis A. van Minnen
Keele/Middelburg, December 1993

1

The Turner Thesis Revisited[†]

Jan Willem Schulte Nordholt

Frederick Jackson Turner may have been rejected by the newer generations of historians of the West, but he certainly has not been forgotten. There is in itself nothing ungrateful or strange in that fate of the great historian. Turner himself rejected the ideas of his predecessors just as emphatically as his ideas are now contested by those who came after him. He actually pleaded for the study of the present and the recent past "as the source of new hypotheses, new lines of inquiry, new criteria of the perspective of the remoter past." History is, as Pieter Geyl has reminded us, "a discussion without end."

But there is also another more tragic aspect to the severe criticism of the great historian that he really was. Allow me to call it an American fate. For Turner might be called the American historian *par excellence*, who in his radical vision rejected not only the Teutonic theories of the renowned scholars of his time but the whole European background of American history; and who yet, at the same time, was deeply rooted in what I would like to call the innocent tradition. That is why I venture to call his fate a tragic one, as tragic as the history of America itself. For innocence and tragedy do belong together. The theologian Reinhold Niebuhr used another word for it, he called it irony, the word he used in the title of his perceptive essay: *The Irony of American History*.

There is still another word that we might use for the same problem, the word paradox. It is the paradox of a people who believe that they are able to make a completely new beginning in the history of the world, but who at the same time assert that they are the heirs of the cultural tradition of all mankind. Perhaps no one embodied this paradox better than Thomas Jefferson himself who, in a letter to his friend Joseph Priestley, proclaimed that it was no longer possible to say that there is nothing new under the sun [referring to the book Ecclesiastes]: "For this whole chapter in the history of our republic is new." But at the same time Jefferson as an architect imitated with eager enthusiasm the dictates of classical architecture, the Pantheon at

---

[†] This is the text of the inaugural address given by Professor Schulte Nordholt.

Rome, the Maison Carrée at Nîmes and of course the great Palladian villas. The most striking expression of this paradox is to be found in the famous *Letters From an American Farmer* by the French settler J. Hector St. John de Crèvecoeur. He was the first to ask the momentous question what kind of man the white colonist in the New World might be, and he emphasized that indeed the newness of the American settler was his most striking quality: "The American is a new man, who acts upon new principles; he must therefore entertain new ideas and new opinions." Yet in the same passage he wrote: "Americans are the western pilgrims who are carrying along that great mass of arts, sciences, vigour, and industry which began long since in the East; they will finish the great circle."

Crèvecoeur was referring to the old mythical metaphor that the development of civilization was following the sun, running from the East to the West. That theory became extremely popular in the eighteenth century, especially through the well-known poem of Bishop Berkeley: "Westward the course of empire takes its way." It remained common conviction in America during the nineteenth century, but it did of course imply the dilemma that Crèvecoeur so beautifully and naively formulated in his *Letters*. Americans struggled with it all through their history, and Frederick Jackson Turner was no exception to that rule. For he too was standing in the tradition of the admired Jefferson, proclaiming that America was making a completely new beginning. But by emphasizing the innocence of that miraculous, almost religious, new start in the western wilderness, he was at the same time continuing one of the oldest traditions of European civilization, the belief that man could renew himself by going back to nature, that there was something like a native innocence in man when he was able to find his way back to Mother Earth. That tradition extended all the way back to antiquity with its mythical tales of golden ages at the beginning of time or out on the western rim of the world. It was taken up again in the Renaissance by the first writers about the New World, Petrus Martyr, Amerigo Vespucci and the like. It was beautifully elaborated by the great Montaigne, who described the noble savages of the New World straight from Hesiod and Ovid. Rousseau carried it on in the eighteenth century, and in America Jefferson himself gave it a pastoral charm, when he confessed his belief that those who labor in the earth are God's chosen people. At the end of the century the innocent tradition evolved from classical attitude to romantic emotion, from culture to nature, which meant that the paradox became even more poignant in the resulting collision between material progress and nostalgic sentiment. That conflict dominated the cultural scene of America during the nineteenth century. Frederick Jackson Turner was its true heir.

All this may give the impression that he was more a poet than a historian, more a man of great visions than of careful analysis of the past. It can indeed be said that in many aspects Turner as an historian was an exception to the rules of the craft. He visited the archives, to be sure, but one gets the impression that he went to find what he already knew, what he saw in a vision before him. His primary interest was not in evoking the past "as it really was" (*wie es eigentlich gewesen*), to use the famous sentence of Leopold von Ranke, in the first place because he was not very fond of writing, but most of all because he found his true expression in provocative theses and suggestive phrases. Traditional history may dismiss such practices as "impressionism," a word which has, strange to say, become a term of abuse in our guild! But Turner, perhaps precisely because he was opposed to the scientific German-oriented school of history which dominated the universities of his day, liked the suggestive approach and his thesis gave a completely new impulse and perspective to America's past. The miraculous fact is that he became famous for an article of no more than thirty-eight pages (including the footnotes). It was a paper which he gave on July 12, 1893, at a meeting of the American Historical Association on the occasion of the World Exposition in Chicago.

Turner was fascinated by the question of the identity of American democracy and it was his idea that the answer to that question was to be found in the West, a region, as he believed, without a history, a virgin land. In the late nineteenth century American historical scholarship was dominated by a theory drawn after a German model – German because Germany was held to be the land of sound fundamental research. The theory was inculcated principally by the historical seminar at Johns Hopkins University in Baltimore. Its principal thesis was that American democracy had its roots in German antiquity. As Tacitus' *Germania* provided the evidence it was also called the "Teutonic theory." It held that the Germanic peoples who went first to England (the Saxons of the Anglo-Saxon invasion) and then to America had taken their local liberties with them. That too was of course a Romantic idea in origin, but it was developed with great methodical accuracy. Properly scientific researchers found striking parallels between the administrative systems of the ancient German village and New England towns (the famed "town meetings"). Their theories became known as the "germ" system, for they believed the "germ" of American democracy was to be found in the forests of Germany.

Frederick Jackson Turner, a Westerner himself, born in a small town in Wisconsin, was only thirty-two years of age when he announced his new theory at Chicago. His paper, entitled "The Significance of the Frontier in American History," was a direct assault upon the still respected "germ" theory. His thesis was that history had had an entirely new start in the New World and had developed on the "frontier." "Frontier," that was the magic word in his theory. He used it to describe the border between wilderness and civilization, a line that kept moving steadily westward. It was there that the colonist had learned the great lesson of the character of his new country. It was the frontier that had shaped him and made him into an American, a new man. "The wilderness masters the colonist. It finds him a European in dress, industries, tools, modes of travel, and thought. It takes him from the railroad car and puts him in the birch canoe. It strips off the garments of civilization and arrays him in the hunting shirt and the moccasin." For Turner that development was almost a religious experience. Every pioneer was confronted with it: "The Mississippi valley is asking, 'What shall it profit a man if he gain the whole world and lose his soul?'" The whole nation was involved: "Decade after decade, West after West, this rebirth of American society has gone on."

In the West the American became a new man, a democrat, a self-made individualist. "The new democracy that captured the country … came from no theorist's dream of the German forest. It came, stark and strong and full of life, from the American forest." That development had the greatest social consequences. For, according to Turner, the West acted as a safety valve; the dissatisfied worker in the East could always move to the West. This was why there was no labor unrest in the East and why socialism did not take hold in America.

Turner made the deepest impression upon his colleagues that summer day in Chicago, and for a time he seemed to dominate all American historical writing. In retrospect there is something a little strange in the excessive admiration Turner received, from historians most of all. When one reads the articles he wrote (his production remained very limited, a few dozen articles and two or three books), one is struck by the suggestive, not to say poetic, way in which he deals with his material and by the vitality and boldness of his assertions. Turner indeed gives the impression of a truly inspired Romantic poet. There is a sublime paradox in his appearance in Chicago: there he stood in the middle of a vast growing metropolis and proclaimed that the true American is at home in the wilderness!

But he also had a message, which is really what matters most in his work. At the very moment he was standing there in Chicago, Turner asserted, the westward movement, and with it the original impetus of American liberty and democracy, had come to an end. Perhaps, he said in an effort to comfort his audience, the nation would be able to find new sources of energy: "Since the days when the fleet of Columbus sailed into the water of the New World, America has been another name for opportunity." "But," he added as a warning: "never again will such gifts of free land offer themselves." The free lands that made the American pioneer have gone. The material forces that gave vitality to Western democracy are passing away."

Turner was troubled. In many articles he returned to his original theme, broadened it and refined it; he was seeking for elements of hope in a darkening landscape. Did not the West teach a lesson of solidarity, of hope, not only to the American people but to all mankind? "This new frontier should be social rather than individual" he wrote, but with "social" he did not mean any kind of solution imported from Europe like socialism or plutocracy. Not incidentally he issued that warning against the dangers of the Old World in the year 1914. America was and should remain innocent, close to nature, self-sufficient in its serene neutrality, an example to, not a part of, the evil world. It was this message which made him popular for he preached just what Americans were delighted to hear at a time when their familiar world was fundamentally changed by the rapid growth of industry and cities, so that the country ceased to be recognizable.

Essentially Turner was one of those historians for whom America was really the completion of history, at the same time that it stood outside history. He sounded so convincing, and he became so popular, because his message appeared to be so simple in its sweeping view of America's past as one great covenant, no longer with the God of the Puritans but with Nature's God, as revealed and adored in Jefferson's famous words. But exactly in his strength lay his failure. What he inherited was Jefferson's dilemma. For the progress that Jefferson had preached ended in the denial of all the values that Jefferson had stood for. Turner realized with regret that a revolution had been taking place: "The transformations through which the United States is passing in our own day are so profound, so far-reaching, that it is hardly an exaggeration to say that we are witnessing the birth of a new nation in America." All the dangers that Jefferson had been warning against in the beginning of the century had by 1893 become ugly reality. "The familiar facts of the massing of population in the cities and the contemporaneous increase of urban power, and of the massing of capital and production in fewer and vastly greater industrial units, especially attest the revolution."

The dilemma appeared to be unsolvable. Progress had defeated itself, innocence had been replaced by complexity, the simplicity of the West had turned sour. In the end Turner's vision proved to be inadequate and after his great victories came the devastating criticism of newer generations of historians. That criticism grew to a storm during the years of the great depression. How little meaning had his rural idyll in a nation wracked by unemployment and despair! After the Second World War Turner seemed to regain some of his stature, especially through the work of his follower Ray Allen Billington, who tried to save the remnants of his ideas. But new crises made Turner's theories even emotionally unattractive. As a modern observer remarked: "After Dallas and Vietnam it was hard to admire gunfighters and new frontiers." The present-day traveller in the West, who tries to be more than just a tourist impressed by the beauty of its national parks, realizes how little is left of Turner's dreams. Ian Frazier in his well-known book *Great Plains* expressed the disenchanted mood of our times when he painted a panorama of the West, past and present, which is almost an exact negative counterpart of Turner's idyllic myth:

We trap out the beaver, subtract the Mandan, infect the Blackfeet and the Hidatsa and the Assiniboin, overdose the Arikara; call the land a desert and hurry across it to get to California and Oregon, suck up the buffalo, bones and all; kill off nations of elk and wolves and cranes and prairie chickens and prairie dogs; dig up gold and rebury it in vaults somewhere else; ruin the Sioux and Cheyenne and Arapaho and Crow and Kiowa and

Comanche; harvest wave after wave of immigrants' dreams and send the wised-up dreamers on their way; plow the topsoil until it blows to the ocean; ship out the wheat, ship out the cattle; dig up the earth itself and burn it in power plants and send the power down the line; dismiss the small farmers, empty the little towns; drill the oil and natural gas and pipe it away; dry up the rivers and springs, deep-drill for irrigation water as the aquifer retreats. And in return we condense unimaginable amounts of treasure into weapons buried beneath the land which so much treasure came from – weapons for which our best hope might be that we will someday take them apart and throw them away, and for which our next-best hope certainly is that they remain humming away under the prairie, absorbing fear and maintenance, unused, forever.

Forgive the long quotation, it condenses so forcefully the modern reality of the West. It revolutionizes so completely the idyllic picture of the past. And here we might well consider the truth of an observation by a modern historian: "A romantic myth that is untrue for the present is probably untrue for the past as well." Some of the criticism of Turner's vision of the past has been long accepted. Obviously Europeans were not turned inside-out in America, and they did not discover their democracy in the American forests, for it was not be found there. Rather they came to America with their European ideas and European achievements, just as Crèvecoeur had described them; they took the ideas of Calvin and later of Locke, and added a whole stock of grandiose philosophical reflections upon society from Montesquieu, Hume and the Scottish school of Common Sense. Their American revolution was not conceived in the wilderness but, so far as theories were concerned, was based upon the philosophy of the Enlightenment, in particular of the so-called Real Whigs.

Modern criticism has not only rejected Turner's philosophical primitivism, but has left little or nothing of his other theses as well. That process has been very much accelerated in the last decade, perhaps, as I would suggest, in reaction to the blunt exploitation of the West by the conservative government of Reagan, a man who in a strange exhibition of innocence clung to all the clichés about the unspoilt West, and even personified them, while his own secretary of the interior allowed those same Western lands to be robbed by the private interests of big business. Exploitation had now finally come into the hands of the federal government itself, but it represented the old greed of the same men who had for a long time protested against the conservation policies of Washington and who of course had wrapped their avidity in pious words. They even had the impudence to call themselves the innocent victims of federal interference, and to compare themselves with the Indians, who had been robbed of their lands. For in the American myth innocence is a key-word and through Turner's plea it has been closely connected with the West, with Nature. O, the irony of innocence!

But the new critical historians – already distinguished as the school of the New Western History – of course did not start in a vacuum. They had their predecessors, and one of them must at least be mentioned here, Henry Nash Smith, who in his fine and highly original book *Virgin Land, the American West as Symbol and Myth* described how the development of the West was not determined by realities, but by mythical visions and dreams of innocence and progress. Turner's theories were based on lofty ideological conceptions and prejudices typical for his time. The new critics of today question all the theses of Turner. They attack his central idea of a moving frontier. They assert that it may be better to define the West as a special place, in the broadest terms the region beyond the Mississippi or, more restricted, the region west of the hundredth meridian. They object to the whole idea of a frontier as a boundary between civilization and wilderness, for in that way the original inhabitants of the West are already marked as savages, or, even worse, completely neglected. The term "frontier," writes Patricia Nelson Limerick, one of the most vocal of the new Western historians, is often nationalistic and racist (in essence the place where white people get scarce). So she proposes to replace the word "frontier" with the word "conquest."

The white settlers conquered a world which did not lie on some mythical rim of the world. It had a history of itself in which Indians and Spanish and Asian immigrants had played a great role, it had become the victim of brutal assault by the waves of white pioneers. Yet, as Mrs. Limerick wisely emphasized, the historians of the New West did not mean to paint the opposite picture of Turner's, to oppose his message with another one just as moralistic. "The intention is on the contrary simply to make it clear that in Western American history, heroism and villainy, virtue and vice, and nobility and shoddiness appear in roughly the same proportions as they appear in any other subject of human history."

The revisionists also contested the idea that the "frontier" as Turner had argued had ended around 1890. The trek of the white fortune-hunters to the mining and cattle areas of the West went on in full force until far into the twentieth century. Fault was also found in the safety-valve conception: was it not rather the other way around? Did not the people who failed on the land move to the big cities? What was worse was that Turner also had no eye for the evil aspects of the so-called march of civilization. In his writings there is not a single sign of embarrassment, not to say shame, concerning the harmful sides of Western development: "such aspects," to quote an older historian, Richard Hofstadter, "of Western development as riotous land speculation, vigilantism, the ruthless despoiling of the continent, the arrogance of American expansion, the pathetic role of the Indians, anti-Mexican and anti-Chinese nativism, the crudeness, even the near-savagery to which men were reduced on some portions of the frontier." Hofstadter's severe condemnation was published in 1968, the youngest generation of historians could only add to that catalogue of criticisms. It was about time, they asserted, that historians should pay attention to, as one of them, Donald

Worster, writes, "the ecological disasters and nightmares that have occurred in the West – the pillaging of public lands by oil companies and other energy and mining entrepreneurs, the pollution of coastal waters and pristine desert air, the impact of big-scale irrigation on the quality and quantity of water, or the devastation of wild-life habitat by the hooves and bellies of the fabled cattle kingdom."

The history of the West is not the mythical idyll that was painted by Turner. "The New Western History," as Donald Worster writes, "is now setting the agenda of the field." What it tries to do is to give a more realistic picture of the West in the hope that that region will "become a more thoughtful and self-aware community than it has been, a community that no longer insists on its special innocence but accepts the fact that it is inextricably part of a flawed world."

History should neither be mythical nor cynical. In America, especially in the West, there always has been a tendency to paint the past with mythical colors so that one observer, T. K. Whipple, even could write: "The story of the West is our Trojan war, our Volsunga saga, our Arthurian cycle, our song of Roland." It is understandable that the Americans when they started to build a nation in the wilderness, a nation which had no history, were inclined to myth making. But the wilderness has gone and America has become a part of the world for better and for worse. So in our time the revision of the past had to clear away many of the old optimistic myths. "Historians against history," David Noble has called the scholars who like Turner, tried to embellish the past.

Modern historians, influenced by the events of our tragic era, had to replace Turner's myth with the picture of a much more complicated reality. But interestingly enough in some ways they still admired him. First of all because they recognized his emotional involvement. His theories might have been wrong, or even, as Patricia Limerick claimed, irrelevant, but he had done what Western historians always had done, he had written with "emotion, subjectivity, point of view, and sympathy." They liked that because they themselves were deeply involved in the future of their region, and also because of the simplicity of his ideas. They were almost jealous of him. At a conference of the New Western Historians at Santa Fé in the fall of 1989 Richard White, one of the leading spokesmen of the movement, confessed with something of regret: "Let's face it, none of us will ever be as influential as Turner." The reason for that was given by another historian, Michael Malone: no "other single, overarching interpretation will ever hold sway the way Turner's frontier hypothesis once did."

Turner has not been forgotten. His hypothesis, his majestic myth of the rejuvenating innocence of the West, may have been more vision than reality, but it has stimulated whole generations of historians, who at least had to admit how alluringly beautiful the distortion of the past could be. That is exactly the problem we are dealing with. The irony of American history, which has been just as human, as full of hope and despair as all history, is that it has been embellished and been made into an eschatological myth, which obscured the bitter reality. So I could come back to Reinhold Niebuhr; but I think I had better finish my paper with an anecdote, for I am reminded of a story, as the greatest son of the frontier, Abraham Lincoln, was wont to say, a metaphor really, that came to the mind of that brooding man, who loved to think in similes: one day in the last year of the war, riding through a wood in Virginia somewhere behind the front-line, Lincoln and one of his generals were struck by the sight of an old oak tree which was completely overgrown with ivy. "Mr. President," the general said, "isn't that a wonderful view?" But Lincoln was not so enthusiastic. "Yes," he said, "it may be beautiful, but it reminds me of the habit of certain men. It decorates the ruin it makes."

Bibliographical note

The literature on Turner is immense. His own most important work, to be found in his lectures, is easily available.

An excellent collection is *The Frontier in American History*, ed. Ray Allen Billington (New York, 1962). A fine survey of his work is given by Wilbur R. Jacobs, *The Historical World of Frederick Jackson Turner, With Selections of His Correspondence* (New Haven/London, 1968). Jacobs also wrote a sympathetic essay on Turner as a teacher and writer in *Turner, Bolton, and Webb, Three Historians of the American Frontier* (Seattle/London, 1965).

Of the philosophical criticisms of Turner as a historian I must mention Lee Benson, *Turner and Beard, American Historical Writing Reconsidered* (Glencoe, Illinois, 1960), David W. Nobel, *Historians Against History, The Frontier Thesis and the National Covenant in American Historical Writing Since 1830* (Minneapolis, 1965) and Richard Hofstadter, *The Progressive Historians, Turner, Beard, Parrington* (New York, 1968).

The most important book in defense of Turner by Ray Allen Billington is *America's Frontier Heritage* (New York, 1966), which has a very helpful bibliography. He also wrote a well-known textbook *Westward Expansion: A History of the American Frontier* (fifth ed. together with Martin Ridge, New York, 1982). The book by Henry Nash Smith, *Virgin Land, The American West as Symbol and Myth*, originally published in 1950, is easily available in a paperback edition by Vintage Books (New York, 1957 and later printings).

Some of the most radical critics of the western myth from the New Left are Richard S. Slotkin, *Regeneration Through Violence: The Mythology of the Western Frontier, 1600–1860* (Middletown, Connecticut, 1973) and Richard Drinnon, *Facing West: The Metaphysics of Indian-Hating and Empire Building* (New York, 1980). A fine and much more balanced picture is given by Robert Athearn, *The Mythic West in Twentieth-Century America* (Lawrence, Kansas, 1986).

The most important books by representatives of the school of New Western History are Donald Worster, *Rivers of Empire: Water, Aridity and the Growth of the American West* (New York, 1985), ibid., *Under Western Skies, Nature and History in the American West* (New York/London, 1992) and Patricia Nelson Limerick,

The Legacy of Conquest, The Unbroken Past of the American West (New York/London, 1987).

A new textbook with a striking title has been written by Richard White, *"It's Your Misfortune and None of My Own," A History of the American West* (Norman, Oklahoma/London, 1991).

The best introduction to the whole movement is the collection of essays edited by Patricia Nelson Limerick, Clyde A. Milner II, and Charles E. Rankin, *Trails Toward A New Western History* (Lawrence, Kansas, 1991).

2

Concepts of Democracy and Republicanism in the Late-Eighteenth Century: America, France, Britain

Colin C. Bonwick

The character of the American Revolution remains as much a matter for debate among historians as ever. This is especially true when it is examined within a North Atlantic comparative framework. Jacques Godechot and R. R. Palmer have argued that the founding of the United States formed part of a much broader North Atlantic democratic revolution. Others, especially perhaps patriotic Americans, argue that American development was exceptional; given a unique opportunity to do so, Americans emancipated themselves from the shackles of traditional European society, customs and practices and created a new community grounded on different principles and providing a model for the rest of the world to emulate. Hannah Arendt, however, insists that by European standards the United States did not undergo a revolution at all, and was not a model for other countries.

Of the several approaches that can be taken towards the American Revolution, two are particularly illuminating when it is viewed in a comparative dimension. The first is to consider it as a democratic movement, that is to say, to examine its sources of legitimate authority, the extent of participation in government and the degree of social and political reform. It is not very useful to judge it by late-twentieth century criteria, but it is appropriate in this context to use Maximilien Robespierre's definition: "Democracy is a state where the sovereign people, guided by laws which are its own work, does by itself all that it can do well, and by delegates all that it cannot do for itself."[1] The second is to explore the meaning of its republicanism, that is to say, the relationship between the liberty of the citizen and the need for authority in government, and in particular the extent to which the government was allowed the necessary power to perform its proper duties without getting out of control and becoming tyrannous. The two elements are, of course, intertwined – especially in their dependence on the principle of the sovereignty of the people. Similarly, there are the two elements of the Revolution itself. Achieving independence from Britain was the most immediately obvious component of the Revolution, but by itself it was not sufficient. Founding the republic from 1776 onward was far more important and indeed literally vital.

I

There can be no doubt that use of democracy as a criterion by which to judge the American Revolution poses problems. Many historians have been very sceptical of claims that it was a democratic movement. In discussing the breakdown of the empire Louis Hacker argued that the struggle was not about political and constitutional principles or natural rights, but about the survival or collapse of English mercantile capitalism within the imperial system. Notoriously, of course, Charles Beard insisted that self-interest lay at the heart of the Revolutionaries' political actions and that the driving concern of members of the 1787 Constitutional Convention was a clash between possessors of real property and personalty. There are also historians who argue that even if the earlier phase of the Revolution – i.e. during the war – were democratic, the country underwent a "Thermidorian" reaction at Philadelphia and after.

Then, of course, there are those who argue that "no real" revolution took place at all. For obvious reasons the Daughters of the American Revolution have found the possibility that a revolution took place very embarrassing, and have preferred to insist that it was no more than a colonial rebellion. The greatest of all foreign commentators on American society, Alexis de Tocqueville, declared that social conditions and government were demo-cratic but that the United States had not had a democratic revolution. Similar views were expressed by both the consensus historians of the 1950s and the radical historians of the 1960s and later – though from very different stances. Daniel Boorstin argued that the "most obvious peculiarity of our American Revolution is that, in the modern European sense of the word, it was hardly a revolution at all." Instead, he insisted, it was a conservative revolution; the colonists were defending what they already had. The Revolution thus required no basic change, for it was in essence a kind of affirmation of faith in ancient British institutions.[2] As Sandos is quoted as arguing, the American Revolution was "a unique anti-modernist rearticulation of Western civilization; ... it was essentially restorative and retrospective."[3] In contrast, radical historians have complained that the revolution was not radical enough because no matter how central was the contribution of the lower orders, control remained in the hands of great white men. In their eyes, separation from Britain brought no more than a transfer of authority from one set of magistrates to another.

Further reinforcement of the view that the Revolution produced little change can be found in the fate of two major minority groups: African Americans and white women. And one might also add the original native inhabitants to this list of non-beneficiaries. Black, radical and feminist writers have compelled more traditional historians to acknowledge that the fifth of total population represented by blacks and the half of white population represented by women ought to be incorporated into any calculus of change. Both stories are at best disappointing, and at worst tragic. The movement to abolish slavery accelerated during the Revolution, but the disjunction between libertarian rhetoric and chattel slavery remained. The position was clearly shaped by the structure of each state. Northern states had begun to abolish slavery outright, but in the South, where 85 per cent of the slaves lived, there was little movement. Slavery failed to die the natural death suffered by white indentured servitude at the end of the eighteenth century but went on from strength to strength.

The second group arguably benefited even less from the Revolution. Recent feminist scholarship has conclusively demonstrated that the contribution of women to the success of the struggle for independence was very great indeed. Many performed vital support services such as nursing the sick for the army. The service of others was less direct but none the less substantial. In civilian life, according to Linda Kerber, the prime function of a republican mother was to train her sons for active citizenship. Women's political views were assumed to coincide with those of their husbands and they provided support for men otherwise engaged in public service. Thus Abigail Adams ran the family farm while her husband John attended Congress and served overseas. She urged him in a famous phrase to "remember the ladies" but her plea was ignored. According to Mary Beth Norton the effect of the Revolution on American women was felt in their private rather than their public lives – in familial organisation, their personal and their self-evaluation. If the Revolution did anything for white women, it took generations for the benefits to emerge. If the fate of the two major groups becomes the definitive criterion by which it must be judged, then plainly the problem of the American Revolution was that its great white male leaders failed to address their interests. The consequent implications do not need to be spelled out here.

But this leaves historians with a problem. If colonial America was undemocratic and Jacksonian America was, when did the change take place? Perhaps the time has come to brush the cobwebs off an old thesis and argue that a revolution really did take place during the final quarter of the eighteenth century. Certainly Gordon Wood has argued that American society as well as its institutions were transformed by what he describes in his recent book as "the radicalism of the American Revolution." He insists that the rebels did more than throw off their monarchical allegiance in 1776: "they struggled to find new attachments befitting a republican people, ... They eventually found new democratic adhesives in the actual behavior of plain ordinary people – in the everyday desire for the freedom to make money and pursue happiness in the here and now. To base a society on the commonplace behavior of ordinary people may be obvious and under-standable to us today, but it was momentously radical in the long sweep of world history up to that time."[4] He denies that it was essentially a conservative movement intended merely to protect or recover rights that had long been enjoyed, and that it was predominantly concerned with politics and constitutional issues. Similarly, he concedes that colonial

Americans were not an oppressed people, either politically or socially; nor did they have to endure the extensive violence of other revolutions. Nevertheless, he insists, American society was revolutionized. For, as he argued, "Far from remaining monarchical, hierarchy-ridden subjects on the margin of civilization, Americans had become, almost overnight, the most liberal, the most democratic, the most commercially minded and the most modern people in the world"; by the early nineteenth century democratized public opinion underpinned American government, society and culture.[5] When considered with his earlier book, *The Creation of the American Republic: 1776–1787*, Wood provides a sweeping interpretation on a grand scale; whether it is persuasive or not, it certainly restores the democratic thesis to the heart of modern discussion of the revolution. Nevertheless it leaves a number of problems, even for those who are sympathetic to his general thesis.

Part of the difficulty is a matter of terminology. It is not necessary to get involved in a philosophical definition of democracy, and better to take a more empirical approach; if the definition is too rigorous even modern Britain might not meet the criteria. The case of blacks and women must be conceded, but it must be remembered that the Revolution took place in the eighteenth, not the late-twentieth, century, and that it is doubtful whether any major revolution has achieved all its objectives at one time. It is therefore necessary to confine discussion to the largest single group of people outside the ranks of the elite, that is to say, adult white males. And even if one does not accept Wood's argument in full it remains possible to argue that the Revolution was progressive, and that although it was not in itself fully democratic in a more recent sense, it nevertheless had a powerfully democratizing effect. Secondly, it can be argued that the United States was largely successful in constructing a political system which permitted effective government without undue incursions into the liberty of its citizens. James Madison did not claim that the Constitution of 1787 was perfect, but he did argue that it was the best that could be achieved under the circumstances. Much the same can be said of early state governments (which were severely criticized by some people) and the Revolution as a whole. The point carries even greater weight when comparison is made with Britain and France.

II

The essence of the analysis can be set out fairly briefly. It starts with two reciprocal propositions and their associated problems. The first proposition is that colonial America had developed a particular theoretical basis for legitimacy, which may (or may not) have derived its intellectual under-pinnings from classical, renaissance, seventeenth-century commonwealth principles, puritanism and the Enlightenment. The problem, to use the terminology of political science, was how to operationalize that ideology. The second was the same problem turned upside down. Colonial America had developed a certain social structure and certain codes of social and political behavior. If the structures and practices changed, how could they be legitimated? Put differently, if one moral order failed, how could society shift beyond the Hobbesian world of all against all to construct a new moral order? What would be needed in such circumstances was a transforming event, experience or process which would trigger change and serve as a catalyst. In the circumstances of late-eighteenth century America the outcome was progressive democratization, that is to say, a major stage in the process of becoming democratic, or at least proto- or potentially democratic. Some historians, notably Robert and Katherine Brown, have argued that this was inherent in American society. If this is accepted the Revolution should be regarded as no more than a rite of passage, but the evidence clearly indicates that there were real alternatives, and that other more conservative paths could have been taken both within the empire before the Revolution and even after 1776.

The event round which the process of democratization turned was, of course, independence. Most commentators on both sides of the Atlantic assumed that sooner, or (more likely) later the colonies would become autonomous societies; as late as 1775 few if any predicted that it was imminent. The great climacteric took place between 1775 and 1783, but neither the war nor its outcome were certain or inevitable. Not that uncoupling the colonies from Great Britain was sufficient to democratize them fully, for the attainment of independence was primarily an enabling act which permitted the more important process of founding a republic to take place. Moreover, when colonial America became the United States, the British layer of society might have been shucked off like a snake sloughing off its skin, and the gentry could have been left in absolute command, ruling the lower orders in a traditionally unequal and hierarchical community. America could simply have changed one set of magistrates for another – and some scholars argue that that was exactly what happened. But this judgment is mistaken.

III

The source of the change can be located by looking briefly at the structure of American society on the eve of the war. In spite of the Browns' argument that it was already a middle-class society, the reality was that it was hierarchical. This is clearly evident from the uneven distribution of property if nothing else. The top ten per cent of population owned more than fifty percent of colonial wealth, while the bottom thirty per cent of the white population owned no more than three per cent. The extent of inequality varied from region to region, but the disparity between the wealth of rich merchants and the journeymen and dockworkers in Philadelphia, and the great southern planters and tenant farmers shackled to the cultivation of tobacco in Maryland was in each case stark. Nor was this hierarchy of wealth entirely accidental: even in New England the land in new townships was often distributed according to social status.

Great men and great families flourished everywhere, from the Livingstons of New York to the Randolphs of Virginia and Rutledges of South Carolina. Not surprisingly they dominated social and political life in every well-established local community and in each colony. These elites used a multitude of devices to impose their hegemony on their white inferiors, from public service on the bench and in assemblies to dress codes, high-stake gambling coupled with generous charity and seating by status in Anglican and Congregational churches alike. Some historians have argued that the rich in late colonial society were aristocratic. There can be no doubt that they aspired to be so. But whereas Alice Hanson Jones has estimated that the richest Americans possessed incomes of up to £9,000 per annum, their English counterparts such as the Dukes of Devonshire and the Earls of Derby had incomes of £30,000 or more. Even more important than their relative poverty, they lacked aristocratic status comparable to that of the Englishmen. They lacked the titles, privileges and above all the possession of high family status over many generations that gave automatic social prestige and political authority across the Atlantic. At best they were *nouveaux riches* and *arrivistes* by English standards.

The rich elites rationalized their supremacy by arguing that hierarchy encouraged stability and insisting that they possessed the eduction, talent and vision to enable them to pursue disinterestedly the public welfare; by contrast, they declared, the poor lacked these qualities, were entirely self-interested and could be "wound up by any hand who might first take the winch," to use Peter Oliver's phrase.[6] Moreover, this process of differentiation was if anything accelerating in the longer established areas: ironically the closer the colonies came to independence the more European they became in their social structures.

At the same time a number of dysfunctional processes were disturbing the prevailing social order, and in some colonies the supremacy of local elites was being challenged. Almost every province was affected and domestic tensions were aggravated by the worsening imperial crisis. There were land shortages in eastern Massachusetts, worsening poverty in the great port towns, and a tenant rebellion in the Hudson Valley. In Virginia the discovery that Treasurer-Speaker John Robinson had passed large sums of retired paper money to his cronies among the leading gentry instead of burning it as required by law raised challenging questions as to the trustworthiness of the elites who claimed so much. The potential threat to elite control also came from other directions. The Great Awakening and the spread of groups such as the Baptists in the Virginia backcountry were corrosive of traditional authority because they postulated intellectual and spiritual equality, and attached importance to individual responsibility, thus challenging the purported moral superiority of the elite.

These developments were accompanied by a significant increase in aspirations among the middling and lower orders which was spurred on by the argument with Britain. Urban artisans and mechanics began to claim the right to express broad political opinions, and as the Anglican minister Jacob Duché sourly remarked in 1772, "The poorest laborer upon the shore of the Delaware thinks himself entitled to deliver his sentiments in matters of religion and politics with as much freedom as the gentleman and scholar."[7] It is possible that these tensions might have evaporated had the colonies remained within the empire, but events that cannot be explored here precipitated an internal social and political crisis as well as the break with Britain.

The process of separation itself represented a substantial social revolution. At a time when American society was becoming more differentiated there remained a substantial gap between the self-perceptions of the rich elites and reality. For colonial America was indeed part of an aristocratic society, but the aristocracy was geographically displaced: it was located in England. Worse still from the perspective of their ambitions, even the most presumptuous Americans lacked the ultimate political control of their community that was the comfortable possession of the English aristocracy. Although they enjoyed extensive self-government within their own provinces, they were themselves subject to regulation by imperial authority: and imperial authority lay in the hands of the English aristocracy. And certainly the English aristocracy did not regard Americans as equals: at best they looked down on them with supercilious condescension. So when the Anglo-American dispute degenerated into war it became a rebellion of a local gentry against their metropolitan aristocracy. And in that respect even if no other the Revolution was a social revolution.

It could have stopped there but it did not. Unhappily for the newly independent American elites, their victory proved to be a mixed blessing for them. There is no doubt that they wished to retain control of their communities. For as David Ramsay pointed out in his *History of the American Revolution*, printed in 1789, "Revolutions in government are rarely patronised by any body of men who foresee that a diminution of their own importance is likely to result from the change."[8] But at the very moment of success against Britain, the American gentry committed ideological suicide. The explanation for this remarkable phenomenon goes a long way to explaining the progressive nature of the Revolution.

The critical factor was the definition of the term "people," for it was a vessel into which several meanings could be poured. During the struggle with Britain the elites had been obliged to postulate the existence of an American people in order to establish their position within the imperial system and defend it against parliamentary sovereignty and the doctrine of virtual representation. For somewhat different reasons the concept was also necessary in order to defend the citizen against government in that constant struggle to achieve a proper balance between liberty and power. At this point the process began to be progressive and democratizing. For when the lower orders became increasingly self-aware before the outbreak of war, they also became autonomous political actors for the first time. It would be mistaken to conceptualize this process in terms of class conflict, for it was much more subtle, but it did have important consequences. When the lower orders – artisans, small farmers, dockers and the like – used the term "people," they gave it a meaning which included themselves as equals rather than as subordinate members of societies ruled by their social superiors. Success in the political struggle with Britain in the 1760s, and even more during the War of Independence, depended on their active and autonomous support and reinforced their claims to admission to the world of active politics and government.

The consequence ran briefly like this. The defence of liberty implied the existence of a morally independent citizenry. But citizens could be independent only if they were equal, and equality implied democracy. The elites tried to retain their power, but the lower orders were sufficiently powerful and important to American society that they were able to capture a share of the authority previously held entirely in the hands of the elites. As yet the process was incomplete, but democracy is a reasonable description of the direction that American society was embarked on, and by the beginning of the next century it had become prescriptive as a system of American government.

IV

In breaking from Britain, the Americans were obliged to find an alternative basis for the exercise of legitimate authority. Within the empire the source of all legitimate authority had been the crown and it flowed in a downward direction through the colonial governors who (except in Rhode Island and Connecticut) were appointed or approved by the crown. Legislatures possessed limited local powers and could be – and were – overruled from time to time by Westminster. By the middle of the eighteenth century the colonists regarded the system of government as a manifestation of their rights, a principle that the British government refused to concede. Firstly the Declaratory Act of 1766 stated that Parliament possessed the right to legislate for the colonies in all cases whatsoever, and then in 1774 the government remodelled the Massachusetts charter on its own authority, thus contributing to the crisis which precipitated war. Put differently, ultimate authority in America was royal authority; it was exercised over the colonies rather than by their inhabitants colonies. This had ceased to be acceptable, nor was the principle of parliamentary sovereignty, since that was the very principle against they were rebelling. As colonials they had been willing subjects of the crown, but the reigning orthodoxy of prescriptive authority within an organic society seemed inappropriate and had little attraction for most Americans from 1776 onwards.

What replaced it was democratization and republicanism. The old monarchic regime had been characterized by deference, patronage and subordination, and an organic relationship between representatives and government on the one hand and subjects on the other. A heightened awareness of the conflict between the liberty of the citizen on one side and the power of government on the other, coupled with emancipation from the royal regime meant that Americans had to exchange the dependency of being subjects for the autonomy and self-responsibility of citizenship. This was coupled to the corrosive equalitarianism exemplified in Jefferson's Declaration of Independence, which insisted that all men were created equal and argued that they possessed certain unalienable rights.

Changed circumstances required a new source of authority to replace the prescriptive authority of the crown. Thomas Paine's reference to the "royal brute" in *Common Sense* struck a responsive chord. Beyond that almost the only thing that they agreed on was that republicanism was more than government without a king. What permitted continued change was the inescapable use of the word "people." The battle with Britain had been necessarily articulated in terms of the emancipation of the American people from imperial control, and it is hardly surprising that the rhetoric of early constitutionalism was couched in those terms. Application of republican principles came to rest on the doctrine of popular sovereignty, that is to say the doctrine that the people were the sole source of legitimate authority. In the words of the Virginia Declaration of Rights "All power is vested in, and consequently derived from, the people; ... magistrates are their trustees and servants, and at all times amenable to them."[9] This principle inverted the previous flow of authority and was replicated in other declarations and statements throughout the country.

It now became necessary to apply high rhetoric to the conduct of politics. After much huffing and puffing a model procedure was devised by which the sovereignty of the people was translated into a system of effective government. It reached maturity in the Massachusetts Constitution of 1780. A convention was elected on a universal male franchise with the sole duty of drafting a constitution. When drafted, the document was circulated among the state's townships for ratification. The constitution comprised a written set of rules, principles and restrictions and an apparatus for government machinery. Administrations elected under its authority were limited in their powers and subject to it; unlike Britain, only the people could change the constitution and the executive and judiciary as well as the legislature drew authority from them. Making government responsible to the community was in itself a revolutionary act, and Hannah Arendt is wrong in saying that "there is very little in form or content of the new revolutionary constitutions which was even new, let alone revolutionary."[10]

But the changes did not end there. It was also necessary to construct a system of national government which could resolve a number of complex problems while resting on the same general principles. James Madison described the new system in a nutshell. When advocating ratification of the United States Constitution in New York in 1788 he argued as follows:

> In a single republic [like the individual states], all the power surrendered by the people is submitted to the administration of a single government; and the usurpations are guarded against by a division of the government

into distinct and separate departments. In the compound republic of America, the power surrendered by the people is first divided between two distinct governments, and then the portion allotted to each subdivided among distinct and separate departments, hence a double security arises to the rights of the people. The different governments will control each other, at the same time that each will be controlled by itself.[11]

The constitutional system erected during the American Revolution was not perfect. It left many important matters open to interpretation, and did not avert bitter disputes in the future, including above all those which led to the attempt by many southerners to leave the Union in 1861. But it did provide a viable means of articulating a federal system based on the principle of the sovereignty of the people, and machinery which constructed a reasonably satisfactory balance between the legitimate needs of government on one side and liberty of the citizen on the other. It was both principled and pragmatic in character, and as such it reflected the character of its creators.

Simultaneously, American society – or at least the white adult male part of it – became increasingly if not completely democratic. But though the process was logically interlocked with the extension of republicanism, since it was also rooted in the sovereignty of the people, it encountered much difficulty. Part of the problem lay in the continuing ambiguity of the term "people." All members of the political community agreed that it referred to the nation and individual states as entities but beyond that there was room for significant disagreement. Elites continued to believe that it meant only community in the sense of "the American people" or "the British people" collectively; they did not intend it to imply equality of social status, political rights and political participation by the lower orders let alone majoritarianism. Having assumed that "the people" and "the community" were synonymous, they assumed that they could incorporate for themselves the authority previously exercised over the colonies by the British government and otherwise continue as before. Not surprisingly, the public debates of the next quarter century were peppered with sour remarks such as Jeremy Belknap's declaration "Let it stand as a principle that government originates from the people; but let the people be taught ... that they are not able to govern themselves."[12] Conservative elitist influence was clearly visible, especially in states like Maryland and South Carolina. The new constitutions continued to impose property qualifications on voting, membership of state legislatures, and eligibility for the office of governor, and just to make sure, most states inserted into their legislatures a senate which was *inter alia* intended to provide a bastion from which the propertied elite could maintain their influence and protect their interests.

At the same time as elites were struggling to retain command, the lower orders were moving in the opposite direction. It would be an over-simplification to describe the political debate as a class struggle, but there is no doubt whatsoever that men of different social standing saw themselves as having differing interests and that the lower orders were beginning to see their interests as in certain central respects opposed to those of their social superiors. The point was put with particular clarity by a writer identifying himself as "a leather-apron wearer" (i.e. a manual worker) when he asked in 1776:

> Do not mechanics and farmers constitute ninety-nine out of a hundred of the people of America? If these, by their occupations, are to be excluded from having any share in the choice of their rulers, or forms of government, would it not be best to acknowledge at once the jurisdiction of the British Parliament which is composed entirely of GENTLEMEN?[13]

The plain fact was that success in the struggle against Britain could not be achieved if the elites merely gave orders without making concessions. Rather it depended on the support of artisans, small farmers and the like as well as the generalship of great planters such as George Washington, and these lower orders were becoming increasingly autonomous in their actions. As the crisis deteriorated more and more people were mobilized. In New England artisans and others had long been active during the Stamp Act crisis and after; in Virginia mass meetings elected many men such as the lesser gentry and even yeomen who had not previously held office onto county committees of safety. Moreover, the Association ceased to be a semi-voluntary policy acceded to by consent and became the compulsory if extra-legal, authority of the majority. If anything, the process was even more evident in Pennsylvania where in the absence of firm leadership among the leading gentlemen of Philadelphia new men of lower social status were constantly brought into active politics through bodies such as the Committee of Privates. It was they who took the state towards independence in face of a divided elite and supported a coalition between town intellectuals and upcountry farmers which produced by far the most radical of the first state constitutions. The new machinery articulated popular sovereignty by making the executive and judiciary elective and giving predominant authority to a single-house assembly which was subject to annual election on a taxpayer franchise. This, Richard Ryerson has argued, was the beginning of modern American politics.[14]

The Revolutionary War itself quickly reinforced the trend for it immediately became a social process with social consequences as well as a military conflict. The two armies not only fought each other but struggled to secure the essential support of the civilian population. In the absence of professional soldiers, the Continental army and navy had to be drawn from a wide spectrum of the population. A very high proportion of the available population of service-aged men participated in active service, and the 24,000 service-related deaths gave the United States a death rate relative to population second only to the later Civil War. After due allowance is made for evasion of service and desertions, it is clear that successful prosecution of the war depended on the mass of the Patriot community as well as their political and military leaders. Nor was this all. The Continental army perpetually lacked sufficient "gentlemen" of high social status, and success depended on trawling deeper for officers and the consequence was that the social gap between them and other ranks narrowed considerably. All this created both political expectations and political obligations.

These processes and aspiration were matched by comparable processes in civil life. For several reasons the franchise expanded considerably during the Revolution, rising from perhaps 50 to 80 per cent beforehand to 60 to 90 percent of adult white males at the end. Property qualifications for voting and office-holding were lowered and, more importantly, electors increasingly voted for men of their own kind and there was substantial turnover in civil offices compared with the colonial era. In part, of course, these changes were a consequence of the expansion of the political system itself, the departure of loyalist office holders in some areas and an increase in the number of offices that required to be filled and could be filled only by drawing on new men. And to cap it all, the senates, which had been intended to preserve the power of the elites, failed to do so. Within a decade after the war, political divisions in most states ceased to run along horizontal lines between democratic lower houses and 'aristocratic' upper houses. Instead they ran along vertical lines between interest groups which were represented in both houses. The elite's efforts to retain control were in vain. Even Maryland, which had constructed the most conservative of all the early state constitutions, was forced to concede universal suffrage in 1802.

During the war years and for some time afterwards the states were obliged to devote most of their attention to the war itself and recovery from its dislocations. But the opportunity was taken to commence reforms which would reach full fruition in the following century. In particular every state eased discriminatory legislation directed against religious Dissenters, ecclesiastical establishments were dismantled everywhere except in Massachusetts and Connecticut, and in Virginia Jefferson's Statute for Religious Freedom was at last enacted in 1786. Blacks also benefited from the beginnings of emancipation in northern states, though sadly not in the South. There was limited redistribution of lands confiscated from Loyalists, though less than might be supposed; the great benefit for white men was an increase in opportunities deriving from expanding territories and a reviving economy.

V

The American Revolution took place primarily for domestic purposes. Nevertheless, many Americans were convinced that their actions had a wider purpose and significance. They hoped their Revolution would be a model and example for the rest of the world, and the available evidence makes it clear that many Europeans accepted this claim of universal significance if only because they shared many of the values and principles being implemented in the United States. There were undoubtedly many echoes throughout Europe, and particularly in Britain and France. But it is equally true that political processes had their own dynamics, and Europeans reluctantly acknowledge that if the United States was a model, the experiment took place in a highly favorable laboratory. The obstacles in the way of reform and the task of reformation were far more challenging in Britain and especially France. Little change took place in Britain but a major revolution took place in France and dominated the history of the ensuing century. It is tempting to take the easy way out by arguing that each process was unique and that the only thing they had in common was contemporaneity. But this would be a mistake. A brief comparison with the fate of democracy, republicanism and liberty in the two countries can indeed be illuminating.

It is first necessary to draw some limited comparisons with France. Many of the associations between the American and French Revolutions are obvious. French participation in the American War of Independence severely strained her national finances, even though France was a rich country with great economic potential. It also infected French public values, for the disparity between the new order in America and the *ancien régime* in France was glaringly evident. What was nominally an absolutist state but in practice was an ineffectually federal one staggered on until it collapsed. Whether reform was practical, as Jefferson and many English radicals believed and as some modern historians argue, is irrelevant here. Similarly, there is no need to examine the causal connections between the two Revolutions, though one point may perhaps be made. Thomas Jefferson, author of the U.S. Declaration of Independence, was still living in Paris as American minister during the early stages of the Revolution, and provided his friends with a detailed commentary until he departed for home in October 1789. He was an active advisor to the Marquis de Lafayette and the National Assembly, in particular in the composition of the Declaration of the Rights of Man, and optimistically believed the Revolution was complete before he departed for home.

According to one criterion, France achieved a much deeper democracy than did any American state before the end of the century. Where the United States metaphorically killed their king as a prerequisite to erecting their republic, the French literally executed Louis XVI as part of their republican revolution. The Declaration of the Rights of Man and Citizen, which was approved by the National Assembly in August 1789, affirmed the principle of popular sovereignty, although it attached far more centrality to the corporate entity of the nation than had the Virginia Declaration of Rights of thirteen years earlier. Throughout the Revolutionary and Napoleonic years, elections remained indirect, thus favoring middle or upper class candidates, and turnout diminished. But the electorate in France was far wider than in the United States, especially if male slaves are added to the American potential electorate. Most men were permitted to vote for the third estate of the Estates General in 1789, although the distinction between "active" and "passive" citizens contained in the Constitution of 1791 removed about one third of them from qualification. But this left a larger electorate than in almost every American state. Also, outside the National Assembly and Constituent, the Parisian *sans-culottes* exercised increasing direct political power, especially during the Jacobin republic, to an extent far greater than the Committee of Privates had done in Philadelphia.

In these respects American and French democratic republicanism had much in common. Neither had achieved the level of the following century, but both had made substantial advances since 1776 and 1789 respectively. But American republicanism had constructed a viable (if not perfect) balance between the liberty of the citizen and the authority of government. The French Revolution failed for many and complex reasons to balance the interests of liberty and power. In spite of their often valiant efforts, French radicals failed to establish governments by any means other than coercion, whether in Paris or the provinces. The American Revolution contained more political violence than is generally acknowledged, but it had no counterpart to the Terror as an instrument of government, nor did the United States endure the executions and *coups d'états* that characterized the 1790s. No doubt the difficulties facing France were far more acute than those facing the United States, but the country was unsuccessful in articulating the principle of popular sovereignty to the imperative of stable government which was essential if the benefits of the Revolution were to be enjoyed. In that respect, Napoleon, who brought efficient government as well as military adventurism, was the necessary concomitant of the Revolution.

In Britain the American Revolution undoubtedly encouraged radical demands for political change. Many radicals before the war became convinced that events on the two sides of the Atlantic were linked and that the British government was attempting to suppress liberty and establish an authoritarian regime throughout the empire. There was no truth in this, but it helped to revive long-dormant demands for parliamentary reform and an extension of the franchise. Demands grew increasingly more strident as the American War went from bad to worse between 1779 and 1781, but when peace was achieved without reform the majority of reformers faded away. One frequent argument for reform was that the United States had demonstrated that it could be safely implemented without risk of social upheaval. This argument was even more commonly used in support of the campaign to relieve religious Dissenters from discriminatory legislation including in particular the Test and Corporation Acts, but with similar lack of success. The impact of the American Revolution remained significant even during the 1790s, although it was largely masked by the example of the French Revolution. Symbolically, perhaps, the first part of Thomas Paine's *Rights of Man*, published in 1791, focused largely on France, but the second part, which infuriated the British government when it appeared in 1792, argued that America was the model for England.

One feature of English politics during the 1790s was the emergence of a working class movement. The influence of the American Revolution on it was substantial and different from that on radicals of the older – and socially higher-class – generation. The American model legitimated the empowerment of artisans in a way that the French example did not. Back in the 1760s artisans on both sides of the Atlantic had claimed that they had interests and rights different from those of their social superiors. In America during the Revolution such men went a stage further by exercising power particularly in Pennsylvania. And it was in good measure because men who previously had been excluded from the political world in England saw that America was admired as a refuge for radicals and other emigrants. Greater liberty, a broader extension of the active political nation were both attractive examples, and both had been achieved. Perhaps at least as importantly, artisan radicals were impressed by what they believed was the relative social equality of American society: a conviction that persuaded them that the United States had far more to offer them than did Britain in its current condition; indeed the American example contributed to the injection of a strain of virulent equalitarianism that had previously been lacking and which consequently caused the propertied classes considerable alarm.

In contrast, the success of the American Revolution convinced middle-class English radicals of the power and the safety of their proposals, particularly those relating to religious liberty, when set against the conservatism of Edmund Burke and the government on one side and extreme radicalism on the other. Crucially, the American experience provided prudential as well as theoretical support for their arguments. American government actually functioned effectively.

Unlike France, the new republic had achieved a satisfactory balance between the rights of the many and the interests of property, and between the liberty of the citizen and the authority of government. The position of the citizen was no longer defined by his obligation to public interest as defined by government; instead, his liberty was autonomous rather than privilege, and his political position was moving towards the individualism of the following century. It provided effective as well as representative government. And there was another thing which made America attractive where the French example so palpably failed in their eyes. The United States had successfully distinguished between constitutions and governments and had devised a system in which at last the executive had been curbed and controlled. At last the commonwealthmen's concern over the corruption of the House of Commons by the undue influence of the crown had found a viable alternative. In the United States the legislature and executive were separate and thus obliged to share power and collaborate, but neither could control the other in the manner that a British prime minister could – and still does – control the legislature. It imposed its authority, met its proper obligations, and promoted national interests – all without infringing the liberty of its citizens. It was indeed safe and prudent to embark on political change, and both theoretical and pragmatic benefits would follow reform. Thus it becomes possible to argue that the United States was a preferable model to France. The logic of the French Revolution leads to Napoleon; of the American Revolution to Andrew Jackson. No wonder nineteenth-century radicals continued to admire the United States.

What America, France and their Revolutions did not do was stimulate a revolution in Britain. Quite the reverse: the late-eighteenth century, and especially the 1790s undoubtedly brought a radical revival and an extension of the politically active nation to new classes of men, notably to urban artisans. But it also brought a conservative revival among the masses as well as the elite. Governments between 1789 and 1815 were as oligarchic as at any earlier time. The electorate remained low, and contested elections were fewer by the end of the century than in 1701. During the American War disillusion provoked demands for reform; after the outbreak of war in France in 1793 the opposite developments took place. Patriotism and loyalism spread widely, and radical insistence on natural rights, equality and popular sovereignty were dismissed as dangerous. Instead, it was argued with great success that the traditional values and stability benefited people of all classes. Reform in Britain had to wait for at least another generation. As far as that country was concerned, the American Revolution was indeed exceptional.

Notes

1. Quoted in William Doyle, *The Oxford History of the French Revolution* (Oxford: Oxford University Press, 1989), 272.
2. Daniel Boorstin, quoted in Edmund S. Morgan, ed., *The American Revolution* (Englewood Cliffs, New Jersey: Prentice Hall, 1965), 118.
3. Ellis Sandos, quoted in *Historical Journal*, 35, no. 2 (June 1993): 474.
4. Gordon S. Wood, *The Radicalism of the American Revolution* (New York: Alfred A. Knopf, 1992), ix.
5. Ibid., 4–7, 364.
6. Peter Oliver, *Origin and Progress of the American Revolution*, ed. D. Adair and J. A. Schutz (Palo Alto, California: Stanford University Press), 65.
7. Quoted in Daniel Boorstin, *The Americans: The Colonial Experience* (Harmondsworth, Middx.: Penguin Books, 1965), 349.
8. David Ramsay, in Morgan, *American Revolution*, 9.
9. S. E. Morison, ed., *Sources and Documents Illustrating the American Revolution, 1764–1788 ...*, 2nd ed. (Oxford: Clarendon Press, 1929), 149.
10. Hannah Arendt, in *The Reinterpretation of the American Revolution, 1763–1789*, ed. Jack P. Greene (New York: Harper and Row, 1968), 581.
11. James Madison et al., *The Federalist*, ed. Clinton Rossiter (New York: Mentor, 1961), 323.
12. Quoted in Richard Hofstadter, *The American Political Tradition and the Men who Made it* (New York: Vintage Books, 1958), 6–7.
13. Quoted in Philip S. Foner, *Labor and the American Revolution* (Westport, Connecticut: Greenwood Press, 1976), 165.
14. Richard Alan Ryerson, *The Revolution Is Now Begun: The Radical Committees of Philadelphia, 1765–1776* (Philadelphia: University of Pennsylvania Press, 1978).

3

Transatlantic Radical Liberalism: A Comparative Analysis of H. D. Lloyd and W. E. Adams

Owen R. Ashton and Alun Munslow

Introduction

A comparative examination of the life and work of W. E. Adams (1832–1906) and Henry D. Lloyd (1847–1903), British and American radical liberal journalists, illustrates the central features of a genuinely transatlantic late nineteenth century labor radicalism: notably the conflict between residual and producer artisanal individualism and the modernist idea of centralized state planning, cooperation and public control. The careers of both men reveal that labor leadership in the late nineteenth century in Britain and America did not necessarily have to be collectivist nor less socialist. By their specific contacts with surviving radicals and ex-Chartist emigrants, and their subjects of mutual concern, namely the removal of privilege and oppression, equality in race, class and gender, democratic social harmony, and an attack on imperialism as the focal point of the capitalist corporate state, their careers extend our understanding of transatlantic radical liberal connections.

Henry D. Lloyd and Transatlantic Radical Liberalism

While Henry Demarest Lloyd's radical liberalism emerged directly out of the established tradition of American radical democracy,[1] it was overlaid by his reading of the sources of European radicalism – notably the heritage in which Adams was steeped.[2] This heritage was a complex distillation of liberal theory garnered from the Enlightenment, Paineite secularism, early Victorian Owenite utopianism, John Stuart Mill's anti-majoritarianism, and the reciprocity of individual and society – that the self was a social self – all of which emerged through the influence of Giuseppe Mazzini with his emphasis on co-operative duties rather than individual rights. To this Lloyd added the American individualist tradition of Jeffersonian republicanism and the heritage of American transcendentalism.[3]

The context for the emergence of Lloyd's radical liberalism lies with the new industrial order in both the United States and Europe.[4] It was the attack on the tenets of American liberalism by the emergent and rapidly dominant corporate and imperialist classes that prompted the development of American radical liberalism.[5]

The hegemony of the new American business order was challenged by residual producer cultural groups like small-scale independent farmers, and the artisanal laboring classes moving increasingly into the burgeoning cities of the east and mid-west.[6] Such groups were led by men like Henry Demarest Lloyd. New York born Lloyd trained as a lawyer, but earned his living, like W. E. Adams did in England, as a journalist, most notably with the *Chicago Tribune* (1872–1885).[7] Usually read as an attack upon the corruption of railroad officers and the perversion of the free market in cereals, his radical liberal journalism at that time actually represents the first major effort by an influential commentator in support of a new definition of American equality.[8] His broad view was that if the tendency to combination was irresistible, control of it was essential and represented "the two great tendencies of our time: monopoly, the tendency of combination; anti-monopoly, the demand for social control of it... The first is capitalistic, the second is social."[9] In order to protect the great American principle of equality, therefore, in "the coming age of combination" a new morality that recognized the social character of humankind was essential.[10]

On an 1885 visit to Europe he met several reformer-radicals and quickly became a lifelong supporter of the cause of labor. In the wake of Judge Gary's gloatings after the hanging of five of the seven "anarchists" implicated in the Chicago Haymarket bombing, Lloyd was driven to respond with his most important lecture in February 1888, "The New Conscience or the Religion of Labor."[11] This represents the break that distinguishes the first phase of Lloyd's liberalism of the 1870s and 1880s from that of the second half of his career in the 1890s and early 1900s. The New Conscience idea focused his discourse of equality by shifting away from a purely statist route toward a broader social reconstruction which favored regulatory and positive government, thus pushing him, in comparison to Adams, toward a far more welfarist and collectivist or communitarian conception of society.

In the years from 1886 to 1895 Lloyd moved further away from his early Emersonian transcendentalism toward a more pragmatic assumption of the need to support equality, deny privilege and crusade for his new vision of an organic society of social harmony.[12] This very notion of idealism tempered by the empirical method seen in the specific relationship between the state and the individual was explored in his 1889 lecture "Mazzini: Prophet of Action" – in which he called for a new faith in the power of mankind to give effect to a new cooperative democratic commonwealth based on universal love and brotherhood.[13] This would, he was sure, pursue his three related discourses of equality, anti-privilege and social harmony.

The Italian patriot and political philosopher Mazzini was the model for Lloyd in his marriage of the transcendental spirit and the material world.[14] Lloyd imagined himself to be an American Mazzini – the spiritually inspired man of action. The action was, of course, to be directed toward social meliorism through both individual and state intervention.[15] But Lloyd felt the need to accommodate the new order in his radical liberal philosophy.[16] This meant acknowledging Mazzini's avowal of the collective over the individual while still leaving enough room for individual action. Here we have the confirmation of Lloyd's construction of man as the social creator with truth emerging by "its verification in the experience of individuals and mankind."[17] Mazzini's emphasis on individual duties rather than rights highlights Lloyd's radical liberal teleology and is significant for the transatlantic radical liberalism of the second half of Lloyd's life and work.[18]

Inspired by his Mazzinian world-view Lloyd came to the conclusion that privilege could only be abolished through the collective ownership of the production process. This should not, however, be read as Lloyd supporting socialism or in favor of the proletarianization of America. As he said "there are no classes in America."[19] Lloyd simply wanted the Golden Rule carried "into the market."[20]

The mature world-view that Lloyd possessed by the 1890s, summarized by him as "Man the Creator" and the religion of labor, tied together the three strands that made up the cord of his radical liberalism: a stronger anti-privilege discourse, a fresh emphasis on his belief in human equality, and a more certain commitment to a collective action productive of social harmony.[21] In the early and mid-1890s Lloyd lived through several labor upheavals but those experiences confirmed Lloyd's belief in the need for, and ultimate achievement of, urban labor and rural producer cooperation.[22] He argued that such cooperation actually heralded the New Conscience and the Golden Rule in action.[23] In part this summarizes the transatlantic cast of his "theory of progress," particularly his belief that co-operation was a major force in Britain and was becoming an equally potent force in America. Lloyd's pre-occupation with cooperativism in what was to be the last five years of his life did not preclude a continued attack on the stranglehold of the trusts on American life, and especially their international character.[24]

In respect of the United States's growing excursions onto the world stage Lloyd exhibited inconsistencies not unusual at that time among progressives and radical liberals.[25] Lloyd was a Monroe Doctrine imperialist at first endorsing Attorney General Richard Olney's application of the Doctrine to the Venezuelan boundary dispute with Britain in late 1895.[26] For Lloyd, patriotism was not a crime and he supported McKinley's 1898 Spanish-American War aims as stated in his message to Congress.

The dark side of war inevitably appeared and Lloyd was shaken from his *de facto* imperialism by the embalmed beef scandal when it was discovered that the beef trust provided tainted meat for the soldiers, and when it was revealed that the Winchester Arms trust cartridges used by American soldiers produced smoke by which the Spanish could locate their positions. Lloyd was also shocked by the dreadful conditions having to be endured by soldiers in the army camps.[27]

Lloyd soon turned completely against U.S. involvement abroad, referencing John Hobson's anti-imperialism as the bench mark and he concluded "Our war for humanity has unmasked itself as a war for coaling stations." [28] Nevertheless he still hoped that the great democracies of the United States and Britain would never subjugate "dependent peoples." [29]

In conclusion it was Lloyd who, perhaps more than any other, created a non-doctrinaire and conservative American radicalism largely in response to his life-long misgivings about the American Socialist party's doctrinaire Marxist class analysis. Any assessment, therefore, of Lloyd's radical liberalism must be informed by his decision – almost literally a deathbed conversion – to join the American Socialist party.[30] In his effort to enable America to come to terms with modern corporate capitalism and ensure his three key principles of equality, anti-privilege and social harmony, his organic conception of the state inevitably blurred the classic liberal distinction of the individual and group, the private and the public.

His pre-1886 bourgeois liberalism eventually gave way before a broader and more highly radicalized social ethic that cut across class boundaries. It was this faith that made it difficult for Lloyd to convert to socialism believing as he did in a value system that should be non-dogmatic and democratic. Nevertheless, his unshakeable belief in the primacy of the individual, though working within a social collectivity described in his notion of man the creator, was the shared essence of his and Adams's radical liberalism.[31]

W. E. Adams, Radicalism and Imperialism

William Edwin Adams (1832–1906) was an important figure in middle and late nineteenth century provincial radicalism in England; a man who mobilized opinion against the government's new imperialism. Much debate surrounds the issue of working class support for late nineteenth century British imperial expansion on a grand scale. Henry Pelling and Richard Price, for example, have argued that the working classes in Britain were indifferent to imperialism.[32] On the other hand, John Mackenzie has shown that from 1867 they appear to have shared an imperial vision whose key ideological components were a fervent, sometimes jingoistic patriotism firmly identified with conservatism, militarism, royalism and racism.[33] Between 1864 and the turn of the century Adams lived and worked as a journalist and editor-in-chief in Newcastle-upon-Tyne, at this time a city rivalling London as the epicentre of English radical republicanism.

He wrote two important works, his autobiography, *Memoirs of a Social Atom* (1903), and a travelogue *Our American Cousins* following a tour of the United States in 1883 which ranks as one of the first by a British working man on late nineteenth century America.[34] His employer was Joseph Cowen M.P., the leader of a "militant democracy" in the North and a great admirer of America as still "the beacon of freedom." Cowen's papers – the *Newcastle Daily* and *Weekly Chronicles* – were at the cutting edge of English radicalism. Adams at the *Weekly* left his mark in three ways: (i) troubling the authorities over what constituted freedom of speech, (ii) helping to get elected to Westminster in 1874 Thomas Burt the Radical Lib.-Lab. candidate for the mining constituency of Morpeth, the first working men's M.P., (iii) through an admiration for America and its radicals helping to cement closer transatlantic radical-liberal ties that stressed the importance of "community and citizenship," based on the discharge of duty as opposed to the more voguish upholding of rights in the modern political nation. For its content the *Weekly* attracted international praise. One competent American critic, Paul Carus, the positivist inspired editor in the 1890s of the *Open Court*, a Chicago journal with a high intellectual standard, described the *Weekly* as "the best paper in the world."[35]

In the late nineteenth century, Adams was active on many fronts. He was something of a proto-conservationist, campaigned for free libraries for the people and won a gold medal from the R.S.P.C.A. for his work against cruelty to animals. Yet it was in mainstream politics that he was best known, or despised, particularly with regard to his radical critiques of the new imperialism as a movement impeding the growth of the community of nations. The expanding influence of late nineteenth century socialism should not mislead us into thinking radicalism was a spent force. Many men, particularly skilled workers and the pit-men, shared Adams's tradition and vision which emphasized independence, self-help and self-education as strategies for life's endeavors, always accepting that "privileges" had been attacked and removed and that democratic government was in place. Socialism, the new political spirit of the age, appeared to deny, or at least downgrade, the importance of individual liberty and the freedom of working men and women to rise by their own initiative.

Adams personified some of the best traditions of the politically conscious and internationally-minded artisan. It was as a Chartist and printer in Cheltenham Spa that the young Adams first learnt about the character of England's warrior elite and satraps of empire. On retirement or completion of tours of duty such persons invariably returned to fashionable watering places like Cheltenham Spa, where their numbers swelled the ranks of the town's so-called politically influential "high society."[36] Their elite behavior helped define sharply an incipient Spa radicalism which held that, when the democratic, republican teachings of Thomas Paine and Giuseppe Mazzini which stressed duties as well as rights were fully implemented, then the politically unrepresented – those like Adams's poor and hardworking family – would no longer have to toil as white slaves to maintain the expectations of its parasitic rich and retired residents. Like fellow Chartist internationalists in Cheltenham, Adams therefore had no problem in the 1850s in aligning himself with the call for an immediate abandonment of the entire system of colonial government. In 1857 when in London Adams attended open air meetings of the National Chartist Association which passed resolutions of support (against the tide of opinion in the country) appealing for clemency for the Sepoys whose massacre of Europeans had sparked off the Indian Mutiny.[37]

Working as a journalist in cosmopolitan Newcastle-upon-Tyne also gave Adams a much greater and enduring appreciation of the consciousness of race, and it was as editor-in-chief of the *Weekly* that Adams, at Cowen's expense, came to know how the Irish lived and felt at first hand when he made a fact-finding visit in some of "the most disturbed districts of that unhappy country" in September 1875.[38] Given these perspectives, Adams, the advanced radical, was uniquely well-placed to comment on the momentous events which led from the annexation of Cyprus and Afghanistan to the establishment of imperialism as a new factor in British political life between 1878 and 1880.

1878 was a crucial year in the history of British imperial sentiment, language and action as Disraeli sought to project the image of a more "romantic" or glorified empire to the new and much expanded urban electorate.[39] Disraeli's ability to harness patriotic public opinion, in defence not only of the national interest but also of the new imperialism and royalist ideology, was achieved by a skillful handling of the famous outburst of bellicose jingoism against Russia in that year.

The Conservative government and its supporters received the acquisition of Cyprus with jubilation: it was a colonial gem gained without the loss of blood which would not only enhance the power and prestige of England's expanding empire, but, coming as it did at a time of economic depression, could also stimulate trade and industry in the form of railway projects in Asia Minor.[40] On the other hand Liberals rejected the Cyprus Convention in its entirety. For Gladstone, leading the wide-ranging attack, the agreement was "an insane covenant" which had absolutely no value to England.[41]

In his "Ironside" political column, and elsewhere in the *Weekly*, Adams agreed with all these liberal criticisms. He also stressed, like Gladstone, that he had no liking for British rule over alien races held in submission. Thus his life-long internationalist perspective led him naturally and prophetically to subscribe to the claims of the Greek Cypriots to be a constituent part of that Megali (Great) Idea whereby Hellenic aspirations would one day prevail in the Eastern Mediterranean.[42] The military occupation by Britain was therefore highly immoral. However, it was on three distinct issues, namely the government's gross mishandling of the occupation and the unhealthy living conditions subsequently endured by the troops, the association of imperialism with the monarchy, and Disraeli's personal political style, each in turn fuelled by the embroilment in Afghanistan, that Adams made in the best traditions of the powerful anti-statist strain inherent in 1850s Chartism and artisan radicalism generally his combative engagement with the imperialism debate. Like H. D. Lloyd, he feared the tyranny of a centralized state authority both emerging to "consume" the individual and bereft of accountability.

Between July 20 and the end of October 1878 the *Illustrated London News* published a series of artists' impressions which, in graphically depicting the nature and extent of the early military occupation, captured what was to become in effect some of the familiar themes and images of British superiority over indigenous peoples.[43] Yet the military occupation proved to be something of a hollow triumph. What was sensationally revealed was not, as the government had suggested, a beautiful and salubrious island but a fever bed and charnel-house. Adams seized on these findings and made ministerial incompetence and the health of the British troops in Cyprus an important issue in the *Weekly Chronicle*. For one thing, as a Chartist he had campaigned fearlessly behind Ernest Jones's call in 1855 for a "Soldier's Charter" of human rights – their brothers in uniform – during the misman-agement of affairs by the Whigs in the Crimean War.[44] For another, from the time of the hardships experienced by the troops in the Crimea, nurtured by the modernizing impact of the Cardwell Army Reforms (1868–1871), public esteem for the army in general, the lot of the ordinary soldier in particular and the perception of the regiment as a focus of civic pride or consciousness, had made substantial strides forward.[45] Consternation therefore grew in London and the provinces at the way the troops had been unnecessarily exposed to natural dangers.

By early August such was the public concern about the health of the British troops in Cyprus that Disraeli's Chancellor of the Exchequer, Sir Stafford Northcote, had to admit at Westminster "they had very little information about the island when they undertook charge of it."[46]

Judging by the extent of the baptism of fever the troops had undergone the government, acting on its limited information and imperfect knowledge, may well have sent the men without adequate supplies of quinine.[47] Other problems were now publicized, most notably the inability of the War Office to mount a major and co-ordinated landing between the Army and the Navy at Larnaca with the result that Adams noted:

Counter-orders succeed to orders, so rapidly that no one, from the admiral downwards, knows what is to be the next move, and a good deal of discomfort and some discontent is the result.[48]

However, what is highly significant in assessing the state of popular public opinion at this crucial time, judging by the revealing comments of Adams, is the degree to which hostilities in Afghanistan allowed Disraeli the opportunity to appropriate successfully to a degree working class patriotism to the national and imperial cause through calls for absolute loyalty to the state.[49] In his "Ironside" column Adams noted in this respect:

It is no doubt open to the opponents of war… to agitate against it. But if the advice were taken, we know what would be said of the patriotism of the agitators: for it has come to be a mark of patriotism that we must all subscribe to the immoral doctrine. Our country, right or wrong.[50]

Whilst the slippery trickster remained in power further damage would be done, Adams warned his readers, if they, like the country, were not eternally vigilant. Fortunately, Adams did not have long to wait: Disraeli was ousted by Gladstone in the General Election of April 1880.

Adams was also much troubled by Disraeli's identification of Queen Victoria as Empress of India with British imperial prowess in the national consciousness. Newcastle's radical Republican movement had strong traditions stretching back to the Chartist days.[51] By the early 1870s it was enjoying a renewed upsurge of popularity thanks nationally to the secularist, Charles Bradlaugh, and on Tyneside to the Radical M.P. Joseph Cowen.[52] There was nothing suddenly new therefore about his criticisms of the Queen after Disraeli had created her Empress in March 1876.[53] For Adams, the title was "tawdry" and the move part of a deliberate scheme to exalt the power of the crown as an accomplice to "a new form of Caesarism."[54] Pointedly, he warned that:

> Monarchy itself is not so sacred an institution that the English people will always be inclined to witness the subordination of popular liberties.[55]

Queen Victoria may well have been troubled by this kind of political discontent from amongst her Newcastle subjects. According to Nigel Todd, the biographer of Cowen,

> For "some years" during the 1870s she reputedly had a disdain for Newcastle-upon-Tyne, ordering "the blinds of her railway carriage" to be "drawn down" whenever she passed through Newcastle on her way to and from Scotland.[56]

The charge of personal rule became a prominent weapon in the Radicals' campaign against Disraeli in 1878.[57] Whilst difficult to measure, Adams's criticisms of the prime minister and his policies could rival the most acerbic and hard-hitting; and the emphasis could also be different. Adams, it must be remembered, displayed a natural and life-long antipathy towards Toryism, but Disraeli's attempt to introduce the "tawdry and meretricious dignities of Imperialism"[58] plumbed new depths of hostility in the language of dissent. For Adams, Disraeli was a "mosstrooper"[59] who had no qualms about encroaching upon popular rights and liberties both abroad and at home.

To what extent did Adams's trenchant views as editor-in-chief reflect popular public opinion, shape it, or do both perhaps simultaneously? Were the working classes of Newcastle-upon-Tyne able to withstand the pressures and processes of being insidiously hooked on to the dominant values of Disraelian-inspired Tory patriotism?

From evidence gathered from the contemporary press and printed sources it is clear that certain sections of the working classes in and around Newcastle, pit-men, engineering workers and Irish workers generally were particularly vocal in resisting Disraeli's Tory patriotism and its association with empire, militarism and royalism.[60] Around a number of core issues which men like W. E. Adams identified in the press and Thomas Burt articulated from the platform, namely opposition to Disraeli's style of one-man government and grandiose schemes for imperial military expansion, and the championing of one of its key agents, the common soldier as opposed to the incompetent aristocratic authorities who commanded them, we see the old traditions of radical, patriotic internationalism, republicanism and suspicion of the powers of the machinery of the State being vigorously upheld.

Events over the next twenty years tend to confirm how important the years 1878 and 1879 were as a watershed in the history of the language of resistance to right-wing patriotism. As the British Empire grew steadily in size and national standing working class people on Tyneside, as elsewhere, were impressed on all sides by "all-pervasive patriotic-imperial themes."[61] One particularly potent propaganda agency popularizing the empire-monarchy world view was the Primrose League which attracted many skilled engineers in the Newcastle munitions works.[62]

As the Empire grew rather than shrank in size Adams tried to take a more pragmatic view of the new imperialism, largely on the basis of the British template of what constituted "civilization." Thus he welcomed moves initiated in 1895 to put an end to slavery in the British East African Protectorates of Zanzibar and Pemba, and vigorously opposed the racist policies of the Boers in South Africa.[63] Yet he remained troubled by the fact that in India, for example, the British were still despots and ultimately ruled by exercise of the Sword. Whether his readers still shared his views in the 1890s is difficult to answer at this point with any degree of precision. If we are to believe Adams himself then this was unlikely. Increasingly disillusioned in old age he came to deplore in the Newcastle of the 1890s the working man's lack of political awareness both in the direction of radical liberalism and the new-fangled socialism. As far as Adams could judge, sport, gambling and drinking had taken over the individual's life. Working men were becoming obsessed by "more wages and more football."[64] Adams himself, like Lloyd in many ways, remained wedded to a radical individualist tradition which derived from Paine and from Mazzinian ideas about what constituted public duty and citizenship. In his *Memoirs* (1906) Adams's whole philosophy was summed up in words drawn from the poet Byron:

> I wish men to be free,
> As much from mobs as Kings, from you as me.[65]

Conclusion

Both men made a considerable contribution to the progressive mentality at the end of the nineteenth century, Lloyd who became increasingly pre-occupied with the Socialist vision, and Adams more and more concerned with the death of political liberalism as he understood it. For both men, radical liberalism was in practice less a program than a culture of opposition constructed out of broad feelings of moral outrage against the abuse of political power and great wealth, old and new corruptions, privilege and waste in any form and also dramatically opposed the burden of Empire.[66]

Lloyd established himself as a front rank American radical and Adams occupied the middle rank in Britain. Both shared common ideological roots and ultimately experienced the late nineteenth century tension in politics between individual liberty and public control with its emphasis on individual duties rather than rights. This derived from their joint view of community, inspired by Mazzini and Mill, as the continuing basis for true liberty. The words of the grandson of Thomas Burt, spoken at the cemetery in 1924 when his father's mortal remains were laid to rest beside those of his grandfather's, speak for both Lloyd and Adams and their shared project:

> Both had all their lives fought valiantly for freedom and justice for the working classes...[67]

The greatest irony of all is that the burgeoning Socialist movement at the close of the century presented itself as their final shared intellectual crisis.

Notes

1. Work on the intellectual roots of the American political tradition is substantial. The duality of social democracy and economic individualism has been at the centre of this tradition: see Bernard Bailyn, *The Ideological Origins of the American Revolution* (1967); Perry Miller has explored its origins in several important texts: *The New England Mind: The Seventeenth Century* (1939), *Jonathan Edwards* (1949), *The American Transcendentalists* (1950), *Roger Williams: Complete Writings*, (7 vols. 1963), *Life and Mind: From the Revolution to the Civil War* (1965). See also Charles M. Wiltse, *The Jeffersonian Tradition in American Democracy* (1935); Clinton Rossiter, *Seedtime of the Republic* (1953); Staughton Lynd, *Intellectual Origins of American Radicalism* (1968); Alfred F. Young, ed., *The American Revolution: Explorations in the History of American Radicalism* (1976); John Ashworth, *'Agrarians' and 'Aristocrats': Party Political Ideology in the United States: 1837–1846* (1983); Edward Countryman, *The American Revolution* (1985); Henry Steele Commager, *The American Mind* (1950); See also David Noble, *Historians Against History: The Frontier Thesis and the National Covenant in American Historical Writing Since 1830* (1965), 3–17; and David Hackett Fischer's, *Albion's Seed: Four British Folkways in America* (1990), 7; The continuing jeremiadic tradition acting as a culturally and politically hegemonic force remains significant, and has been emphasized by, among others, Sacvan Bercovitch in his *The Puritan Origins of the American Self* (1975) and *The American Jeremiad* (1978). The importance of the jeremiadic tradition is also briefly explored in Richard Ruland and Malcolm Bradbury, *From Puritanism to Postmodernism* (1991), 19–25; See also Richard K.

Matthews, *The Radical Politics of Thomas Jefferson: A Revisionist View* (1984).
A comprehensive introduction to the definition of American republicanism
as a development out of the jeremiadic tradition is provided by Isaac
Kramnick "Republican Revisionism Revisited," *American Historical Review*
87, no. 3 (June 1982): 629–664; See also Philip F. Gura, *A Glimpse of Sion's
Glory: Puritan Radicalism in New England, 1600–1660* (1984); John P.
Diggins, *The Lost Soul of American Politics: Virtue, Self-Interest, and the
Foundations of Liberalism* (1984); Joyce Appleby in *Capitalism and a New Social
Order: The Republican Vision of the 1790's* (1984) concludes that the central
strain of embryonic capitalism was free labor. See also Ann Kibbey, *The
Interpretation of Material Shapes in Puritanism: A Study of Rhetoric, Prejudice
and Violence* (1986) and Charles A. Miller, *Jefferson and Nature: An
Interpretation* (1988). A challenge to recent orthodoxy is offered in Frank
Bourgin, *The Great Challenge: The Myth of Laissez-Faire in the Early Republic*
(1989). The most recent study of the radical tradition is Christopher Lasch,
The True and Only Heaven: Progress and Its Critics (1991).
2.   J. O. Baylen and N. J. Gossman, eds., Introduction, *Biographical Dictionary of
Modern British Radicals*, vols. 2 and 3, (1984), 1–5 in each volume.
3.   No great difference of principle, for example, divided Lloyd's liberalism from
the Fabians of 1884 particularly with reference to his revision of American
liberalism's anti-anti-statist tenet. The role of the state increasingly for Lloyd
was one of regulation but a regulation constrained by maintaining the ideal
of individual freedom. The literature on American liberalism and its
antecedents is vast. See for example Claude G. Bowers, *Jefferson and
Hamilton: The Struggle for Democracy in America* (repr. 1972); Kenneth M.
Dolbeare, *American Political Thought* (1984); Henry S. Commager, *The
American Mind* (1950); Harry K. Girvetz, *The Evolution of Liberalism* (1963);
Richard Hofstadter, *The American Political Tradition* (1948); Louis Hartz, *The
Liberal Tradition in America* (1955); Charles M. Wiltse, *The Jeffersonian
Tradition in American Democracy* (1935); both David W. Noble in *The End
of American History: Democracy, Capitalism and the Metaphor of Two Worlds
in Anglo-American Historical Writing, 1880–1980* (1985) and James T.
Kloppenberg in "The Virtues of Liberalism: Christianity, Republicanism,
and Ethics in Early American Political Discourse," *The Journal of American
History* 74, no. 1 (June 1987): 9–33, argue that the essence of Jeffersonian
republicanism was autonomy and popular sovereignty, two forces that pre-
empted alternative world-views seductive to radicals like Henry D. Lloyd
notably socialism; Wiltse, op. cit.; Rossiter, op. cit.; Commager, op. cit.;
Lasch, op. cit.; Miller, *Jefferson*, op. cit.; Appleby, op. cit.; on transcendentalism see, for example, Perry Miller, *The American Transcendentalism*, op.
cit.; Henry A. Pochmann, *New England Transcendentalism and St. Louis
Hegelianism* (1948); Sherman Paul, *The Shores of America: Thoreau's Inward
Exploration* (1958); John L. Thomas, "Romantic Reform in America, 1815–
1865," *American Quarterly* 17 (Winter, 1965): 665–681; Joel M. Porte,
Emerson and Thoreau: Transcendentalists in Conflict (1966); John McAleer,
Ralph Waldo Emerson: Days of Encounter (1984); Sacvan Bercovitch "Emerson,
Individualism, and the Ambiguities of Dissent," *South Atlantic Quarterly* 89
(1989): 624–662, included in his most recent text, *The Rites of Ascent* (1993).

The most prominent feature of the new order was large-scale production and monopoly capitalism: the trusts in America, the cartels in Germany and the embryonic multi-nationals in Britain and its Empire. The social and cultural impact of the trustification of the American economy was immense, just as was the rise of large scale production in Europe. The forces of change were seen to operate at every level of society, in every institution, prompting among other things Robert Wiebe's famous summing up of the period in America as a search for order: Robert Wiebe, *The Search For Order* (1967).

America witnessed the trends of the modernization process in the shift from a primarily rural, individualist, free labor and laissez-faire society toward the emergence of the large corporation, mechanization and scientific management, accompanied by the complexities of an increasingly inter-ventionist and bureaucratic state apparatus. See Alan Trachtenberg, *The Incorporation of America* (1983), 3–10. All this represented a crisis of authority when extant power structures were challenged by new material and ideological forces. See David Noble, *The Progressive Mind, 1890–1917* (1970), 1–22.

Despite their highly distinctive national histories Liberals in the United States and in England shared a belief in the basic precepts of untramelled individualism, the free market, strictly limited government and a con-strained sense of the public interest.

4.   In both instances industrialism sundered established property and class relations and constituted new ideological frameworks. Where liberalism had placed the primary emphasis upon the individual in the construction of a natural rights polity and individualist property relations, its successor radical liberalism acknowledged the modernist revolution in patterns of property ownership and market relationships wrought by the industrialisation process, and revised notions of individualism although stopping short of collectivism. Martin J. Sklar, *The United States as a Developing Country* (1992), 38–40. In Britain, liberalism became radicalised in the 1830s and 1840s in the wake of the first phase of large-scale industrialism – an event not experienced in America until after the Civil War, where up until the 1870s industrialism was at best regional and small-scale. In Britain from the late 1840s following the success of the Anti-Corn Law League and the failure of Chartism, a lessening of the class cleavage was reflected in the development of mid-century radical liberalism as the state was seen to be less tyrannical and more reformist. The British Radical Liberals of the post 1850s often took their cue from John Stuart Mill and his fear of the tyranny of the majority, and collateral concern for the rights of minority groups like women. Consequently, British Radical Liberals were engaged by a diverse range of issues carried over from earlier days, that often carried with them a keen sense of dominant and subordinate class formations – female civil rights, trades union rights, Irish self-rule, anti-slavery, and racial equality, religious freedom (often couched as secularism), parliamentary reform, conservation, a foreign policy that ran from non-interventionism to interventionism on behalf of national self-determination. Thus Garibaldi and Mazzini aroused great support in Britain for the cause of Italian freedom. More often than not imperialism also presented Radical Liberals with a complex range of responses.

5. In the United States liberalism was the *idée fixe* of the Revolution derived from a strong anti-statism built on the Lockean idea of contract and law with a notion of freedom best described in the Bill of Rights' sense of prohibitions against arbitrary rule. In practice this translated as the natural rights philosophy of life, liberty and enjoyment of property. Finally the American stress on free labor equality emphasised its least contentious aspect, that of formal political equality and equality of opportunity. Expressly it did not highlight the idea of equality of condition. While maintaining a fundamental adherance to the principles of individualism and personal freedom and equality, the American Age of Reform produced a Radical Liberal wing which, despite the obvious differences between the two countries (Ireland, secularism, Parliamentary Reform in Britain, bossism, state conservation policies, the frontier experience, and the trusts in the United States), largely shared the manifesto of its British counterpart. The first major conflict within American liberalism lay in the battle between Alexander Hamilton (Washington's Secretary of the Treasury) and Thomas Jefferson (Washington's Secretary of State and later President). Hamilton represented a version of American liberalism that prioritized the practical development of a manufacturing and business economy cast within the political framework of an appropriately interventionist government. The social ramifications were simply that the entrepreneurial class would be allowed to maximise their opportunities, if necessary at the expense of the ordinary citizen. For Jefferson, sound economics and democratic politics depended on sustaining the individual whatever his rank (primarily farmers) within a free market, and maintaining an anti-statist or *laissez-faire* system of republican government which through its non-intervention would guarantee the public interest. For the first fifty or so years after the Revolution the term republicanism was employed to describe and summarize the basic principles of American liberalism which translated in practical terms as free, white labor, the protection of private property and representative government. This classic republicanism was largely endorsed by the egalitarian movements of the 1820s, notably the Workingmen's party, which also first demonstrated what was to be a growing antipathy to what later in the century was called socialism with their continued support for the protection of private property and equality of opportunity rather than condition. The anti-statism which lay at the heart of this republicanism, though challenged briefly in the 1830s and 1840s as westward expansion occurred and the role of government expanded, remained significant right through to the last quarter of the century. While the strength of American individualism was too great to allow the development at the national level of a British type Toryism, with an emphasis on the right of the community to restrict individual freedom, the South continued to be a bastion of political conservatism tied to chattel slavery. The growing *ante-bellum* sectional conflict was primarily a fight over the evolving definition of republicanism.

6. The literature on populism is vast. The most accessible introduction remains John D. Hicks, *The Populist Revolt* (1931). See also Richard Hofstadter, *The Age of Reform* (1955), Norman Pollack, *The Populist Response to Industrial America* (1962), Walter T. K. Nugent, *The Tolerant Populists*

(1963), Lawrence Goodwyn, *Democratic Promise: The Populist Moment in America* (1976), Bruce Palmer *'Man Over Money': The Southern Populist Critique of American Capitalism* (1980), Dewey W. Grantham, *Southern Progressivism: The Reconciliation of Progress and Tradition* (1983), Steven Hahn, *The Roots of Southern Populism: Yeoman Farmers and the Transformation of the Georgia Upcountry, 1850–1890* (1983), Barton C. Shaw, *The Wool Hat Boys: Georgia's Populist Party* (1984), and Norman Pollack, *The Just Party: Populism, Law and Human Welfare* (1987).

7. Chester McArthur Destler, *Henry Demarest Lloyd and the Empire of Reform* (1963), 122–143. The *Henry Demarest Lloyd Papers* are published in a Microfilm Edition by the Wisconsin State Historical Society (1972). Lloyd's papers have been the primary source for two major biographies of Lloyd. The first was by his sister Caro Lloyd, *Henry Demarest Lloyd, 1847–1903: A Biography*, 2 vols. (1912). The second, more critical but still highly complimentary was Destler's. During his lifetime Lloyd published five books, and his family undertook the posthumous publication of a pamphlet and five additional books. Lloyd's titles were *A Strike of Millionaires Against Miners, or the Story of Spring Valley. An Open letter to the Millionaires* (1890), *Wealth Against Commonwealth* (1894), *Labor Copartnership, Notes of a Visit to Co-operative Workshops, Factories, and Farms in Great Britain and Ireland, in which Employer, Employee, and Consumer Share in Ownership, Management and Results* (1898), *A Country Without Strikes. A Visit to the Compulsory Arbitration Court in New Zealand* (1900), *Newest England, Notes of a Democratic Traveller in New Zealand, with Some Australian Comparisons* (1900), and *The Chicago Traction Question* (1903). The posthumous works are *Man, The Social Creator*, ed. by Jane Addams and Anne Withington (1906), *A Sovereign People. A Study of Swiss Democracy*, ed. by John A. Hobson (1907), *Men, the Workers*, ed. by Anne Withington and Caroline Stallbohm (1909), and *Mazzini and Other Essays* (1910) and *Lords of Industry* (1910).

    The list of texts dealing with Lloyd and his impact on various aspects of American radicalism is not large. These include Henry Latchford "A Social Reformer," *The Arena* 10 (October 1894): 577–589, and rather more recently John L. Thomas, *Alternative America: Henry George, Edward Bellramy, Henry Demarest Lloyd and the Adversary Tradition* (1983), E. Jay Jernigan, *Henry Demarest Lloyd* (1976), Daniel Aaron, *Men of Good Hope* (1951), Chester McArthur Destler, *American Radicalism, 1865–1901* (1946). Texts which deal rather more obliquely with Lloyd include Sidney Fine, *Laissez-Faire and the General Welfare State* (1956), W. C. McWilliams, *The Idea of Fraternity in America* (1973), David W. Noble, *The Paradox of Progressive Thought*, (1958), H. Goldberg, ed., *American Radicals: Some Problems and Personalities* (1957), Howard Quint, *The Forging of American Socialism* (1953).

8. By the 1880s Lloyd's attention was increasingly turned to the great symbols of the new business order that threatened traditional notions of American equality – the railroads, the new class of powerful industrialists, and the trend toward the incorporation of society. Gradually Lloyd developed his answer to the emergent popular ideology of Social Darwinism and the *de facto* undermining of Jacksonian producer, workbench and free labor economics. In his discourse of equality Lloyd quite quickly minimized his

early 1870s anti-statist free trade and *laissez-faire* principles recognizing the potential reformism inherent in the expansion of state activity. See "The Story of a Great Monopoly" and "The Political Economy of Seventy-Three Million Dollars", published by the *Atlantic Monthly* in 1881 and 1882 respectively, and "Making Bread Dear" and "Lords of Industry", published in 1883 and 1884 in the *North American Review*; all four were eventually brought together in the posthumous book *Lords of Industry*.

9. Lloyd, *Lords of Industry*, 146.
10. John Clarke, *The Federal Trust Policy* (1931) quoted in Jernigan, 49.
11. "The New Conscience or the Religion of Labor," *North American Review* (September 1888): 325–339, repr. in *Man, the Social Creator*, 100–127 as "The New Conscience."
12. Destler, *Henry Demarest Lloyd*, 171–198.
13. Lecture before the Economic Conference, Chicago, February 23, 1889, repr. in *Mazzini and Other Essays*, 1–41.
14. Jernigan, 117–119.
15. In his applause for Mazzini Lloyd dispatched the Marxian alternative. As he said "For the formulas of [the] other school: 'To each according to his strength,' 'To each according to his needs,' he [Mazzini] substituted this: 'To each according to his love' – a law of distribution which no cunning of vested rights can evade," "Mazzini: Prophet of Action," 4.
16. Ibid., 11.
17. Ibid., 15.
18. Again quoting Mazzini Lloyd claimed there would be "'Education, the fatherland, liberty, association, the family, property, and religion [and all were] ...undying elements of human nature'" ibid., 18. That life was a mission Lloyd learned from the Italian revolutionary: "an expiation to be endured with resignation," ibid. It was with this 1889 lecture then that Lloyd first translated his broad Mazzinian world-view into a series of principles and consequent agenda for his radical liberalism. "Mazzini was above all a religious man 'Religion represents the principle; politics the application' [Lloyd quoting Mazzini]. And because he was religious he was a revolutionist." The principles of Lloyd's Mazzinian inspired radical liberalism were as he said "... the law of progress, a continuous revelation, humanity the sole interpreter of the law of God, no privileged middlemen between God and man, the divineness of earth, life a mission, [and] duty its highest law (p. 16)." Duties rather than rights were the bedrock for his practical Radical Liberal agenda which encompassed "... the equality of women, universal suffrage, public education, the abolition of all privilege, and the emancipation of labor (p. 17)." There would be no middlemen, no castes, no privileges, no proletariat and no aristocracy. In 1889, fired by his Mazzinian religion of labor, Lloyd became directly involved with the strike of miners at Spring Valley, and their efforts to retain union representation in the mine. From then until his death in 1903 Lloyd became centrally involved in American labor politics. The immediate result was the publication the following year of his first book *A Strike of Millionaires Against Miners* (May, 1890). See also "Servitudes Not Contracts," in the *Lords of Industry*, 148–158; and "The Labor Movement," in *Men The Workers*, 3–44.

19. Ibid., 23. The employer ideal of freedom of contract was rejected by Lloyd as not a real freedom at all. For him real freedom inhered in an equality of opportunity that was assured by the democratic control of the economic resources of society as a whole.

20. Ibid., 16. In addition to the book *A Strike of Millionaires Against Miners*, Lloyd also wrote two other pieces in 1890: "What Washington Would Do To-day" and "The New Conscience in Action", both of which further advanced and deepened his radical liberalism across the three discourses of equality, anti-privilege and social harmony. See "What Washington Would Do To-Day" an address before the Personal Rights League, Central Music Hall, Chicago, February 22, 1890 and included in *Lords of Industry*, 159–176; "The New Conscience in Action" an address at the Summer School, Deerfield, Massachusetts, July 29, 1890, and incorporated into *Man, the Social Creator*, as Chapter VI entitled "New Conscience in Industry," 128–152. 1894 is usually remembered for Lloyd's publication *Wealth Against Commonwealth*. Although several difficult years in the preparation and writing, when it was finally published it established his national and international reputation. Although ostensibly an examination of Standard Oil it was rather more a practical statement of his welfare philosophy. Its main contribution was not so much to the antimonopoly cause as to the ethical revival that was radical liberalism. In its text Lloyd continued to preach the New Conscience or religion of labor embodied in universal brotherhood, a testing of the tenets of Social Darwinism, and expression of a belief in progress and human perfectability. He was unwilling to surrender to a simple materialistic determinism, offering instead egalitarian mutualism as the foundation of a realistic welfare democracy.

21. Ibid., 300. Lloyd saw himself as interventionist intellectual, and this book was a long statement to that effect. This was recognized by contemporaries like Henry Latchford writing in 1894, when he described Lloyd's objectives as being to "… arouse the soul, heart and conscience of both employer and employed." See Henry Latchford, "A Social Reformer," *The Arena* 59 (October 1894): 577–589. Latchford saw Lloyd much as Lloyd saw himself, as an engaged reformer with a mission to change society through consciousness raising.

22. A collection of his jottings in notebooks called the "Manuscript of 1896" when posthumously published displays a mellowing optimism which was distinctly at odds with the turmoil he had lived through. Despite the collapse of the People's party in 1896 Lloyd remained stubbornly optimistic about labor cooperativism as the engine of wholesale social change. Lloyd also took an increased interest in the cooperative communitarian societies like the radical Julius Wayland's Ruskin Colony at Cave Mills, Tennessee. Lloyd was not alone in this preoccupation as many ex-Populists and free silver Democrats also evinced an interest in such developments as a means to effect social change. See Caro Lloyd, vol. 2, 45–93, passim; Jernigan, 124.

23. From the mid-1880s Lloyd travelled regularly in Europe to learn about labor relations, and was determined to pursue the new cooperative commonwealth founded on his New Conscience or religion of labor through a new program of travel and study. In June 1897 he was chosen as

the American delegate at the third congress of the International Cooperative Alliance to be held in Delft, Holland, later that year. At the congress he came across an active group of English delegates who preached a new kind of labor cooperativism – the building and operating their own factories. Lloyd went with them back to England after the congress and visited another cooperatist conference in Rugby, where he learned of the efforts to promote rural cooperativism. During his stay Lloyd visited several cooperative ventures and met several elder statesmen of the movement including George Jacob Holyoake. See Caro Lloyd, 74. The result of this tour was his third book published in January 1898 after his return to America – *Labor Copartnership*. See Jernigan, 125–126.

24. Published in the London *Progressive Review* in September 1897, and reprinted in *Lords of Industry*. Lloyd illustrated how American national politics had been taken over by the Sugar Trust in his article "The Sugar Trust and the Tariff," reprinted in *Lords of Industry*, 214–223. He described how Congress had held itself in obeisance to the sugar tariff lobby in the hysterical approach to the Spanish-American War. The Dingley Tariff raised rates on average by over 50% but on sugar by almost 100%.

25. Destler, *Henry Demarest Lloyd*, 447.

26. Lloyd argued that the United States had a to be a missionary of liberty in this instance. In a letter to the British reformer W. T. Stead, Lloyd denied there was a popular imperialism behind the Olney act, ibid., 447–448; Caro Lloyd, 127.

27. Ibid., 130–133.

28. Quoted by Destler, *Henry Demarest Lloyd*, 450.

29. Caro Lloyd, 133. However, Lloyd was unable to fully engage with the imperialist debate because in the winter of 1898/1899 he visited Australia and New Zealand to assess those countries' experiments with socialism, arbitration, progressive taxation, state welfare and pension systems, state sponsored land settlement projects, and state owned railroads. His study of these was published as his fourth and fifth books *A Country Without Strikes* published in May 1900 and *Newest England* published October 1900. Lloyd was very conscious of the speeding up of the American merger movement in the late 1890s which sharpened his radical interest in ways and means to combat it outside the United States. See Caro Lloyd, 133.

Whilst undertaking these tours he was also undergoing a personal ideological struggle with socialism. In 1898 he wrote to an English correspondent that he felt the world was moving "forward to a great crisis" and that he was "… profoundly impressed by the reactionary course which seems to be threatened in England, imitating America, with regard to trades unions," but this still did not convince him of the adequacy of the Marxian socialist answer which was to let the system become trustified and then "by a *coup d'économie*, change masters from monopolist to democracy." Ibid., 155.

30. In his discussion of what he calls the adversary tradition in American history John L. Thomas describes the American populist heritage as an adversary producer ethic that fell across the *laissez-faire*-interventionist boundary, the same might well be said of Henry Demarest Lloyd, Thomas, 313. Throughout his career Lloyd's anti-privilege and anti-monopoly discourses

meant that he urged a democracy of human welfare which from the mid 1880s was based upon universal love and the New Conscience expressed as the Golden Rule. When this failed to materialize in the alliance of farmer and urban worker in 1896 he turned to New Conscience communitarianism, which in its turn transmuted into a growing commitment to collective social action and cooperativism.

31. Lloyd believed in the power for change through the intellectual missionary, the individual who would work within the system to change it for the benefit of all. As he said close to the end of his life "My understanding of the true 'class consciousness' is anti-class consciousness. I stand for the people, and for the extinction of all tendencies that create class – whether a capitalist class or a working class" quoted in Destler, *Henry Demarest Lloyd*, 505–506. In his role of gentleman radical liberal Lloyd perhaps more than any other activist reformer realigned American thought from the age of Social Darwinism and its producerist response, toward the transatlantic age of corporatised welfarism. Lloyd's Mazzinian inspired radical liberalism emerged then from the social creator philosophy, which articulated the basic precept of democratic twentieth century American and European government: the creation of a society dedicated to the abolition of privilege, sustenance of equality, but which, paradoxically, might at best have only succeeded in achieving a dubious kind of social harmony. At the end of his life Lloyd had tried in his radical liberal discourse to combine several ideological positions, those of revolutionary, Fabian socialist, Socialist Christian, Christian, humanist, transcendentalist and pragmatician. It was this complex structure of values that constituted his radical liberalism.

32. H. Pelling, *Popular Politics and Society in Late Victorian Britain* (1968), particularly Essay 7 on "British Labour and British Imperialism," 82–100. R. Price, *An Imperial War and the British Working Class, London* (1972).

33. J. M. Mackenzie, *Propaganda and Empire: The Manipulation of British Public Opinion, 1880–1960* (1984), particularly the Introduction, 1–14.

34. W. E. Adams, *Memoirs of a Social Atom* (1903), 2 vols. repr. in one with an Introduction by J. Saville (1969). W. E. Adams, *Our American Cousins: Being Personal Impressions of the People and Institutions of the United States* (1883), repr. 1992 with an Introduction by Owen R. Ashton and Alun Munslow.

35. A. R. Schoyen, *The Chartist Challenge: a Portrait of George Julian Harney* (1958), 275.

36. For Adams's career in both Cheltenham Spa and Newcastle-upon-Tyne, see Owen R. Ashton, *W. E. Adams, Chartist, Radical and Journalist (1832–1906)* (1991), see generally. Hereafter cited as *W. E. Adams*.

37. *Newcastle Weekly Chronicle*, October 22, 1881, Ironside's Political Letters.

38. Ibid., September 18, 1875, Ironside on "Impressions of Ireland".

39. J. Sturgis, "Britain and the New Imperialism," 85–105, in C. C. Eldridge, ed., *British Imperialism in the Nineteenth Century* (1984).

40. For the impact of the Cyprus Convention on Liberal and Conservative public opinion see D. E. Lee, *Great Britain and The Cyprus Convention Policy of 1878* (Cambridge/Harvard, 1934), 112–131.

41. W. E. Gladstone, "England's Mission," *The Nineteenth Century* 4 (September 1878): 560–584, in particular 568.

42. *Newcastle Weekly Chronicle*, March 29, 1879, Ironside on Cyprus.
43. *Illustrated London News*, August 10, September 28, and October 12, 1878.
44. Owen R. Ashton, *W. E. Adams*, p. 53.
45. O. Anderson, "The growth of Christian militarism in mid-Victorian Britain," *English Historical Review* 86 (January 1971): 46–72.
46. E. G. Ravenstein, *Cyprus: Its Resources and Capabilities* (1878), 40.
47. That the government had bungled over the supply of quinine is strongly hinted at by the satirical magazine *Punch* (November 2, 1878) in an article entitled "Six Days of a Subaltern's Diary – Cyprus." We are particularly grateful for this information to the staff at the Levantis Municipal Museum, Nicosia, Cyprus.
48. *Illustrated London News*, August 24, 1878, "The British Occupation of Cyprus," and *Newcastle Weekly Chronicle*, August 31, 1878, "The Health of the British Troops."
49. H. Cunningham, "The Language of Patriotism, 1750–1914," *History Workshop Journal* 12 (1981): 8–33, particularly 20–21.
50. *Newcastle Weekly Chronicle*, November 30, 1878, Ironside on the Afghanistan War.
51. N. Todd, *The Militant Democracy: Joseph Cowen and Victorian Radicalism* (1991), 38–39.
52. Ibid.
53. *Newcastle Weekly Chronicle*, March 18, 1876, Ironside on The Queen's Title.
54. Ibid., May 11, 1878, Ironside on Imperialism.
55. Ibid., May 17, 1879, Ironside on the Prerogatives of the Crown.
56. N. Todd, *The Militant Democracy*, 80.
57. R. Koebner and H. D. Schmidt, *Imperialism, The Story and Significance of a Political Word, 1840–1960* (1964), particularly 154–159.
58. *Newcastle Weekly Chronicle*, July 20, 1878, Ironside on The Premier's Triumph.
59. Ibid., October 19, 1878, Ironside on Clouds in the East.
60. Ibid., January 12, January 19, May 18, and May 25, 1878 for Anti-War meetings in Newcastle and surrounding districts; and November 30, December 7, 1878, February 8, 1879 for Thomas Burt's campaigning against the Afghan War.
61. M. Pugh, *The Tories and the People, 1880–1985* (1985), 87.
62. Ibid., 127–128, 244. In Elswick, the home of the giant Armstrong munitions works, there were 700 members in 1891 and 1,500 by 1894.
63. Owen R. Ashton, *W. E. Adams*, 170–171.
64. *Newcastle Weekly Chronicle*, June 25, 1898, on the death of W. J. Linton.
65. W. E. Adams, *Memoirs of a Social Atom*, 227.
66. In practical terms a late nineteenth century transatlantic radical Liberal agenda included demands for programs of action to check and balance the corporatism of the new business order. This agenda revealed a pre-occupation with trades union organization, internationalist labor co-operativism, a welfare program for the masses *via* a measure of state regulation, anti-imperialism and anti-militarism, a women's rights movement, opposition to arbitrary government, and demands for a free judiciary. The function of radical liberalism both in America and Britain was at once to conserve the

political liberties which individualism originally enfolded and adapt them to the changes wrought in the modern phase of capitalism with its ideological buttresses, nationalism and imperialism, as well as the internal colonialism of great wealth and economic privilege. As a defensive response to the iniquities of capitalist industrialism both Lloyd and Adams acknowledged the arguments of the Oxford idealists, notably Thomas Hill Green, that individual liberty had to be tempered by social obligation and civil duties. See T. H. Green's Introduction to his reprint of Hume's *Treatise* (1874) and his chapters of criticism in his *Principles of Logic* (1883).

67. *Newcastle Weekly Chronicle*, May 3, 1924, "Some Recollections and Reflections" by Peter Burt.

4

James Bryce and Harold Laski: Two Views of American Political Culture

William R. Brock

Sixty years separated the two most ambitious books on America by British writers. James Bryce's *American Commonwealth* was published in 1888; Harold Laski's *American Democracy* in 1948. Neither are much read today but both deserve fresh appraisal as pioneers in the exploration of what is now called political culture and for their contrasting conclusions. For Bryce cultural change was an evolutionary process in which one must always look for better adaptation, but never discard principles that had stood the test of time. Laski diagnosed a conflict between capitalism and democracy that could not be resolved until the ideological defences of capitalism had been destroyed. Despite all the qualifications made necessary by changing times, intellectuals still fight from Bryce's or from Laski's corner.

Laski knew Bryce in old age, admired his work, and described the publication of the *American Commonwealth* as "a real event in the history of the relations between Great Britain and the United States," and the first work by a British author in which "the greatness of America was acknowledged in its due proportions." However the time was ripe for a new look at America and Laski worked intermittently for some ten years at the task before *The American Democracy* came off the press.[1]

Both men were well equipped for the undertaking. Both knew America well, had many close American friends, and enjoyed the relaxed atmosphere of American social life. Bryce made three long visits to the United States before he set to work on *The American Commonwealth*, and his wide circle of American friends included E. L. Godkin, the influential editor of *The Nation*, Charles W. Eliot, the celebrated president of Harvard, O. W. Holmes, Jr., the future justice of the Supreme Court, and Theodore Roosevelt. His correspondence seeking information was voluminous, and many friends read chapters in proof. Though his criticisms of American public life were numerous he was justified in claiming that all had been anticipated or endorsed by well-informed Americans.[2]

Laski had taught at Harvard as a young man and after his return to England kept contact with many American friends. Like Bryce he corresponded with O. W. Holmes and a selection of their letters has been published. His closest American friend was Felix Frankfurter, and he knew

Franklin D. Roosevelt well enough to write to him informally. Unlike Bryce he did not solicit the help of American friends when writing *The American Democracy*, but his liberal credentials were impeccable.[3]

Bryce and Laski were both radicals by the standards of their day. Bryce had entered politics as one of the contributors to a volume of essays supporting reform in 1867, was elected to Parliament as a Liberal in 1880, and actively supported Gladstone in the bitter controversy over Irish Home Rule. He would later be an anti-imperialist and a champion of the Armenians and other oppressed minorities. He reached the apex of his career from 1907 to 1913 when he was a very popular British ambassador to the United States.

Laski had won an international reputation as a professor of political science at the London School of Economics, where he exerted a powerful influence upon young men from the British Asian and African Empire who would go on to make new nations after the war. His political theory had developed from pluralism to Marxism, but in politics he had remained faithful to the Labour party as its leading theorist and in 1945 (the year of astounding victory) its chairman. He hoped that like Bryce he would be rewarded by being sent to Washington as ambassador, but Mr. Attlee, a man of few words, thought that Laski talked too much and ignored his request.

Bryce was the son of a Glasgow schoolmaster, Laski of a Polish Jew settled in Manchester. Bryce was not a member of the Church of England when this still counted for much in the English establishment; Laski had been brought up as a strict Jew but married a gentile and became an agnostic. Neither owed anything to birth but everything to their own intellectual efforts, and both were free from the upper-class prejudices that had marred so many English accounts of American life.

The baneful effect of equality on American manners had been a perennial complaint by English visitors, but for Bryce "equality of esteem" was the most attractive feature of American social life. Criticism of American materialism had been persistent, but Bryce could see how the spirits were raised in a land of opportunity. In the West, the "most American" part of America, he observed that

> all the passionate eagerness, all the strenuous effort ... is directed toward the material development of the country ... The passion is so absorbing, and so covers the horizon of public as well as private life that it almost ceases to be selfish – it takes from its very vastness a tinge of ideality.

Laski also distanced himself from the patronizing attitudes that still prevailed. American culture had "attained a richness and variety ... unsurpassed elsewhere," and the accusation of materialism was summarily dismissed as a myth.[4]

Both men gave America a unique and honored place in history. Despite all the faults recorded in earlier chapters, the closing sentences of *The American Commonwealth* declared that everyone who looked "not at the favoured few for whose benefit the world seems hitherto to have framed its institutions" must agree that "America marks the highest level, not only of material well-being, but of intelligence and happiness, which the race has yet attained." Consciously or unconsciously Laski began where Bryce had left off by opening *The American Democracy* with a declaration that in the past no nation had done "so much to make the idea of progress a part of the mental make-up of man ... [or] done more to make freedom a dream which overcame the claims of both birth and of wealth."[5]

Laski had an almost romantic vision of ordinary Americans. In 1940. anticipating Roosevelt's victory, Laski wrote "the people are superb. I know now why Lincoln had such ultimate faith in them." Meeting young American servicemen in England in 1943 he wrote that much could be forgiven when a nation produced such people – wisely led they would "fulfill the dream that America might be."[6]

Whatever the promise, reality fell short. Bryce wrote at length and critically of corruption and the spoils system, described municipal government as an outrageous failure, and delivered a scathing verdict on the parties. "Tenets and policies, points of political doctrine and points of political practice, have all but vanished ... All has been lost, except office or the hope of it." He regarded veneration for the Constitution as a sign of health, but did not hesitate to point out its shortcomings. For instance, the separation of powers had debilitated Congress and condemned its members to be "architects without science, critics without experience, censors without responsibility." Above all he found "the tone of public life ... lower than one expects to find in so great a nation." Exuberant national pride did nothing to raise the "worth and dignity of public office." Public opinion was "quick and strenuous in great matters [but] heedless in small matters, over-kindly, and indulgent in all matters." No one who looked back to earlier days could "repress a slight sense of disappointment" that America had not become "that which idealists have hoped for, and Americans have desired to establish."[7]

Laski called upon twentieth-century American historians to bear witness that their "half conscious preoccupation" had been "to discover what went wrong in the development of the American promise." No thinking person still took seriously "the legend of a special American destiny," or doubted that "an immense price had been paid by the farmer and the worker." Corruption poisoned the administration, the legislature, and the courts, and if the mass of the people failed to see what was wrong it was because their vision was obscured by false mythology.[8]

Inevitably the twentieth-century Socialist placed the blame on capitalism, but the nineteenth-century Liberal also saw the power of wealth as a greater danger than rings or bosses. Unscrupulous politicians could be defeated by resolute action, but the money power corrupted "sometimes the voter, sometimes the legislator, sometimes a whole party." There was "a strong element of plutocracy infused into American democracy."[9]

Bryce was by nature an optimist but dark clouds hung over the future. He foresaw "a struggle between two forces, the one beneficent, the other malign." As the land available for settlement shrank and the greater cities grew, the troubles of the Old World would strike America with added force. It would be "a time of trial for democracy." In similar vein Laski foresaw "no progress to greater well-being, but a struggle for the fulfilment of democracy in which the battles to be fought will be hard and long." [10]

Given these similarities, why was the reception of the two books in America so different? Bryce had feared that his criticisms might give offence, but found himself hailed as a prophet. At best he had thought that the book might "have some value as a collection of facts not elsewhere brought together" but had "no idea of the commendation it was to receive." A second edition was quickly called for and 1893 a third, revised and extended, was published and many times reprinted (passing 40,000 early in the new century). It was adopted as a text in innumerable colleges and universities (in either the full or an abridged edition), and had a marked influence upon the development of political science as an academic discipline. A fourth edition was published in 1910, and it was not until 1920 that the publishers finally decided that a new edition would require too much revision to make it worthwhile. Even this was not the end of the story: in 1959 a selection in paperback was published with an introduction by Louis M. Hacker.[11]

The fate of *The American Democracy* was very different. Laski died prematurely within two years of its publication, but there had been no demand for a second edition and no disciple took on the task posthumously. It is doubtful whether it was adopted in many university courses, and very few references to it are found in later works by political scientists. Even in the 1960s when radicals might have found its arguments congenial there was no revival – perhaps it was too long and too dense for impatient young people. In intellectual history *The American Commonwealth* has a firm place but *The American Democracy* can safely be ignored.

English reviewers gave *The American Commonwealth* a warm welcome. Frederic Harrison, regarded as one of the foremost intellects of his day, placed it "among the very small number of works on political and social science which are abiding possessions of the whole English-speaking world." Goldwin Smith, writing from Toronto after a spell at Cornell but formerly Regius Professor of Modern History at Oxford, described Bryce as "in everything except style and form … fully de Tocqueville's peer." The book would be "much in the hands of Americans and exercise a powerful influence over them for good." From America J. B. Thayer, a professor of law at Harvard, wrote privately that Bryce had placed "a whole nation under an obligation of gratitude." Lyman Abbott, editor of the *North Atlantic Review*, welcomed the third edition by telling Bryce that he had "furnished preachers and editors with a magazine of ammunition … [and] really started the reform movement." *The American Commonwealth* had "compelled Americans to think." [12]

Laski may not have expected so much but he got much worse. Arthur M. Schlesinger, Jr., the rising star in the liberal firmament, led off with a slashing review in the *New York Times*. He detected a split personality – a gifted political scientist, much admired as a teacher, and "a facile rhetorician and sentimental pamphleteer." At every stage in *The American Democracy* the political scientist started out but was "almost invariably stopped dead in the tracks by the iron abstractions of the pamphleteer." The book was "a desperate and doomed attempt by one of the most eminent of the last generation of socialists to adapt the aspirations of 1924 to the actualities of 1948." In England the anonymous reviewer in the *Times Literary Supplement* found "the excellence misplaced, the analysis abortive," and giving "as much insight into the mind of the observer as into the minds of those observed." The book was also too long, repetitive, and never used one word where ten would do.[13]

Other American reviewers were more charitable than Schlesinger. Most of them complimented Laski on his wide knowledge of America and his penetrating comments. In the *Annals of the American Academy of Social and Political Science* Roy E. Harvey praised it as the best study of American democracy by a foreigner since de Tocqueville and Bryce, but like others he was puzzled by the contrast between Laski's admiration for American people and his harsh criticism of the civilization that they had produced. He imagined Laski saying to himself, "I wish there were not so many facets of American democracy that I like."[14]

Other also found it hard to reconcile what seemed to be two sides in Laski's argument. At one point he was fully aware of the variety and complexity of American civilization, but at another all was fitted into a simple picture of domination by business. The contradiction was most apparent when he turned from diagnosis to prescription. Writing in the *Political Science Quarterly* Edward C. Lindeman thought that he developed the three great themes of America history – discovery, expansion, and optimism – "with skill, insight, and the benefit of a wealth of knowledge ... no other foreign critic possessed." He proved the utility of Marxist theory as an instrument for social analysis, but when he used it as plan of action it encountered so many "moral and logical difficulties that it was destined ultimately for that grave into which all dogmatic absolutes should be put to rest."[15]

Laski might complain that he had done no more than take recent American historiography to its logical conclusion. His text was liberally furnished with references to the social scientists and historians who were most honored in their own country. He admired Thorstein Veblen and quoted extensively from him. Vernon L. Parrington was his principal authority for intellectual history, and he praised Ralph Gabriel's history of American political thought. Turner's frontier thesis he thought exaggerated but praised the stimulus that it gave to American thinking. Charles Beard's economic interpretation of the making of the Constitution had "become part of the settled tradition of historians." When so many looked in the same direction, what was wrong with pointing out the destination to which they were bound?[16]

Moreover his Marxism did not advocate violent revolution, though he sometimes argued that revolution must come if capitalism became entrenched. According to his friend and biographer, Kingsley Martin, he "could never go the whole Marxist hog because he believed fundamentally in human liberty." The magnetic attraction that Marxism had for him was explained in an early pamphlet written when only half-converted. Marx had "perceived that a society dominated by business men had become intolerable." Was this not what Jefferson had implied, the anti-monopoly tradition affirmed, and Populists intended in their fumbling way? In all he had simply probed behind the corruption and vulgarization deplored by generations of decent Americans.[17]

This touched a raw intellectual nerve. Progressive historians and social scientists had shown the hollowness of much pretence, and one could read into their writings an agenda for radical change; but this was a transplant that they rejected. Laski wrote that modern reform had been "a pathetic and futile effort to meet the issues raised by monopoly capitalism with an ideology that was beginning to look old-fashioned in the Coolidge era." This was precisely the point at which his critics found it impossible to follow him.[18]

The reformers who welcomed Bryce were outsiders looking in; the academics who read *The American Democracy* were insiders looking out. They were not stuck in the Coolidge era, but had helped to make the New Deal. Many had been drawn into public life; all knew friends, colleagues, or former students who had been at the centre of things. This made all the difference.

Bryce had seen that a great weakness in American society was that the "best men" did not run for office, and bestir themselves when things went wrong; or, if they tried, were elbowed out by low-grade professional politicians (aided, perhaps, by corrupt wealth). This was what the literary men, academics, editors of high-class journals, and professional men, disconcerted by developments since 1865, wanted to hear.

The different receptions given to *The American Commonwealth* and *The American Democracy* were therefore a measure of the changed relationship between intellectuals and government. For his contemporary "best men" Bryce had opened a door of opportunity; sixty years later their intellectual heirs went on with little hindrance and a good deal of encouragement. Charles E. Merriam concluded a review of *The American Democracy* by inviting Laski to "come again and try again ... We will do our best to help you with the patterns, the meaning, the faith, and the constructive programs of emerging American democracy." No one was better qualified than Merriam to issue the challenge: he was a professor at Chicago, one of America's leading political scientists, an influential member of President Hoover's commission on recent social trends, deputy chairman of the

National Planning Board and of its successor agencies, and one of the authors of the Brownlow report on government reorganization. No one knew better what had gone on in the corridors of power since 1933.[19]

Laski had indeed called the New Deal "one of the most significant epochs in American history," but went on to say that it had failed to alter "in any profound way the fundamental characteristics of American state power." Merriam and others like him knew all about the limitations on what had been done – national planning had achieved little, reform of the Supreme Court had failed, social security went only half way, and government reorganization had been thwarted – but also knew that after the New Deal nothing would be the same again. As a then young New Dealer recalled in old age: "This was the spirit of the New Deal. We felt that we were going to change America and make it a better place. And we did, damn it, we did."[20]

There were other and deeper reasons why Americans welcomed Bryce and objected to Laski. Bryce saw America leading the way in advance of democracy and the displacement of traditional governing classes. Education was universal in the North and West, improving in the South. Every adult male could cast a vote. No social barriers prevented an able man from rising in the world. There was no privileged church. This was the system "toward which, as by a law of fate, the rest of civilized men are forced to move, some with swifter, others with slower, but all with unresting feet." There were failings that should serve as warnings but America had already "achieved many things for which the Old World has looked for in vain."[21]

Laski believed that America, once the best hope of mankind, now lagged behind. In a foreword to Denis Brogan's *American Political System* published in 1933 he wrote that in a land of opportunity it had seemed unnecessary to ask "those essential questions about the foundations of the State with which we in Europe have been so largely concerned." Material good fortune explained "the curious absence from American life of a socialist perspective to party action," but since the late nineteenth century America had "developed all the typical phenomena of European life," and must look to Europe for guidance.[22]

In his long final chapter of *The American Democracy* Laski argued that American civilization was politically immature. There had been momentous changes in social life but "the intellectual basis of the new Americanism has been incapable of the swift adaptation achieved in economic life." Men no longer lived as they had done in the past, "but the character of their minds and therefore of their expectations" changed too slowly or not at all. "Nearly all the effort to explain the social purposes of the new order was irrelevant to its character; it remained in large part at least half a century behind."[23]

In this way the twentieth-century Socialist revived in new guise the assumption of British superiority that had been so resented in the nineteenth century. Then upper class visitors had complained that America lacked refinement because it was too democratic; now it lacked intellectual muscle because it was not democratic enough. Conservatives had then seized upon de Tocqueville's tyranny of the majority to condemn democracy; now Laski believed that capitalism was tyrannical because democracy was too to represent the real will of the people.

This tyranny of the majority, with conformity as its obvious symptom, had to be confronted by every interpreter of American democracy, and both Bryce and Laski rejected it. Laski had a straightforward answer. In no capitalist democracy was "Marx's famous aphorism that 'the ruling ideas of an age are the ideas of a ruling class' ... more profoundly true than in the United States." The principal thrust of *The American Democracy* was to demonstrate the truth of this proposition in politics, religion, education, and the conventions of social life. Even organized labor was debilitated by accepting the social philosophy of its natural enemies.[24]

Bryce's answer to the tyranny of the majority was more subtle and introduced a concept that has never received the attention that it deserves. For external he substituted internal pressure, for social restraint personal psychology, and for the romantic belief that people were, everywhere in their hearts, struggling to be free a realization that for most of them the important thing was to live a quiet life. In organized society the natural inclination of most people was to accept authority, go with the herd, and look with suspicion on dissent. In his own words:

> This tendency to acquiescence and submission, this sense of the insignificance of individual effort, this belief that the affairs of men are swayed by large forces whose movement may be studied but cannot be turned, I have ventured to call the Fatalism of the Multitude.

This could be mistaken for tyranny by the majority but was something quite different. Admittedly there might be instances in which the general impulse to acquiesce was in conflict with an individual's wish to dissent, but in a democracy the person who disagreed with the majority was consoled by the knowledge that issues had been fully discussed and decided by fair votes. There was no tyranny by the majority when an individual decided voluntarily to accept decisions made by others who had the same political rights, were equally rational, and might be better informed.[25]

Public opinion was normally conservative, yet change occurred. There had been great reversals such as the shift from acceptance to condemnation of slavery, and a host of minor improvements in the quality of life. Bryce explained the process by examining the way in which new ideas were fed into the political system and gathered enough strength to achieve results. Laski believed that no change of lasting importance could be achieved until the power of the ruling class had been broken. Bryce believed that though conservatism must often yield ground it nevertheless deserved respect. What Americans wished to conserve were such basic principles as justice, fair play, and individual rights, on which beliefs they had built the rule of law, constitutional restraints, and acceptance of majority decisions. Laski also believed that the basic principles of Americanism should be preserved but that the superstructure had been erected to prevent their expression.

This was the parting of the ways and the differences are well illustrated by their treatment of higher education in America. Bryce was moved to enthusiasm by what he found. In America, as in Scotland and Germany, the universities and colleges were open to all who could pay modest fees, and students who had to support themselves by earning money were respected. There were also more and better opportunities for women. There were many small colleges with low standards, but even they "placed learning in a visible form, plain and humble indeed, but dignified even in humility, before the eyes of a rustic population." At the other end of the scale was the intellectually rarefied atmosphere of graduate schools in great universities. For undergraduates the choice was continually widened by more elective courses and new institutions endowed by wealthy benefactors or funded by State legislatures. In all, American universities and colleges were "supplying exactly those things which European critics have hitherto found lacking in America ... and were contributing to her political as well as to her contemplative life elements of inestimable worth."[26]

Laski saw the universities in a very different light. It had become their principal function to implant in the minds of future leaders in business and the professions the ideas of the ruling class. "Very few of the central issues which divide men in the world outside can be fully and fairly debated," or if discussed an easy victory for the conventional must be assured. The American student was shielded from doctrines that might disturb complacency and went out into the world without knowledge of the principles for which people elsewhere, rightly or wrongly, gave their lives.[27]

At Harvard, regarded by its alumni as the apex of the educational system, a faculty committee, charged with the task of defining the central purpose of university education, proposed "cooperation on the level of action irrespective of agreement on ultimates." In plain language: learn how to play with the team and forget ideals. Heeding such precepts the young university teacher began by taking no risks because he was uncertain and ended "by taking no risks because he has ceased, by use and wont, to have any convictions at all." In preparation for such a career a graduate student in history or social science was usually directed to time-consuming research on a subject that was trivial and safe.[28]

This deliberately unadventurous regime was sustained by a system of government that vested authority in trustees or politically appointed regents, in both cases normally including a majority of businessmen, and a president who wielded absolute power in his university. Academic freedom meant freedom to teach what the president permitted and the governing body endorsed. Members of the faculty might protest but no one was obliged to listen.

The account had a large grain of truth in 1948, and would soon have more than a grain, but also an element of caricature. It sat oddly with the tributes paid elsewhere in the book to the achievements of American scholarship. The idea that young Americans were the willing victims of indoctrination was wide of the mark. If they were so tame, where had the innovative young New Dealers come from? The criticism of university government was valid in some universities, but in others strong faculties were fully capable of making their voices heard in a way that could not be ignored.

Bryce discussed change by political action at considerable length and began by accepting public opinion as "the central point of the whole American polity," the sovereign to whose voice everyone listened, but whose expression was "vague, fluctuating, complex." At first impression this sovereign did not impress. The same opinions were encountered in all classes, stale platitudes were voiced as though they were original thoughts, and one quickly realized "how little solidity and substance there is in the political and social beliefs of nineteen people out of twenty." Moreover the conventional response to any new idea was to reject it.[29]

However, on reflection, this might not be all to the bad. "This conservative spirit sometimes prevents reform, but it assures to the people an easy mind and a trust in their future." If conventional public opinion took a poor view of radicals it liked rascals no more. American public opinion formed "a sort of atmosphere, fresh, keen, and full of sunlight, like that of American cities, and this sunlight kills many of those noxious germs which are hatched where politicians congregate."[30]

Nevertheless change occurred and could be explained at four levels: individual initiative, voluntary organization, political skill, and diffused but powerful changes in the intellectual climate. This approach drew upon the evolutionary theory that Bryce had accepted with enthusiasm as a young man though never with the implication that man was powerless to defy "nature." If nineteen out of twenty did not think for themselves, one in twenty did; and if the one thinking man or woman was respected in his community, others might follow. Once the seed was sown like-minded people organized, and with modern communications even small minorities could build up nationwide associations, and Americans displayed a quite unusual gift for this kind of voluntary organization.

They rouse attention, excite discussion, formulate principles, submit plans, embolden and stimulate their members, [and] produce that impression of a spreading movement which goes so far towards success with a sympathetic and sensitive people.

Provided that a movement so organized could strike some familiar chord in the public mind, it quickly gathered support.[31]

There were instances in which the usual confusion of state legislatures, combined with the ignorance of their members when confronted with any bill that was not a party measure, played into the hands of reformers.

It enables a small minority of zealous men, backed by a few newspapers, to carry schemes of reform which the majority regard with indifference or hostility. Thus in bodies so depraved as the legislatures of New York and Pennsylvania, bills have lately been passed improving the charters of cities, creating a secret ballot, and even establishing an improved system of appointments to office.

Thus reformers who understood the political game could profit much from the shortcomings of the players. "As the Bible teaches us that the wrath of man shall praise God, the fault of politicians are turned to work for righteousness."[32]

This classic description of pressure group tactics was set in the framework of long-term influences that permeated society. In the past they had been mainly religious, but in the nineteenth century powerful scientific and technological forces had been added. Bryce did not give public health as an example, but its history illustrates the process he described. Medical science revealed hidden dangers, technology suggested how they could be controlled, and regulation followed. In other fields, when a problem was identified, there soon followed a demand that it should be solved by public action. "The sight of preventable evil is painful, and is felt as a reproach. He who preaches patience and reliance upon natural progress is thought callous." The spate of regulatory laws passed by the states proved the point. Some were hasty, some ill-conceived, and some so poorly drafted that their implementation was impossible; but they looked to the future and American legislatures were "serving the world, if not their own citizens ... by providing it with a store of valuable information for its instruction."[33]

For Laski this kind of gradualism was simply a way of ensuring that whatever happened the power of the ruling class would be left intact. In past years there had been ostensible curbs on business, but ways had soon been found to circumvent them or to convert them into new defences for the ruling class. Nothing would serve save a truly radical strategy aimed at transforming "the mores of this vast, sprawling continent." Nor could the venerated Constitution be left untouched because "the whole drive of the constitutional system has been away from majority rule and towards the successive protection of minority interests."[34]

This was a formidable agenda, and neither of the old parties was capable of handling it. A new political movement was necessary to translate endemic class conflict into a program for action, new leadership was demanded, and only the trade unions had the organization, resources, and motivation to provide it. However, once launched, the new party would not remain exclusively proletarian, but would draw upon ideas latent in American civilization, expose the iniquity of capitalism, and gather support in all classes. In time a majority in the whole nation would take power and carry through America's "third great revolution."[35]

To many Americans this was fanciful nonsense. One need not be complacent about the condition of America to argue that the situation he described did not exist. In a friendly but ironic review Mark de Wolfe Howe, a Harvard professor of law, observed that though Laski had recognized "the peculiar effect which American civilization had in breeding complacent optimism," he nevertheless insisted that capitalists "had made life a mean and pitiful thing." In reality "the ugly, or perhaps the pleasant fact, is that the vast body of the American people do not realize that their lives are as shabby as Professor Laski considers them to be," and "obstinately refused to see themselves as the helpless victims of brutal and expiring capitalism."[36]

Men who had labored long in the house of reform could not accept that their work had been in vain or that organized labor could do it better. In a typical comment Donald Richberg, sometime General Counsel of the N.R.A. and before that a lawyer who had represented trade unions many times in court, wrote: "Much as I believe in the sincerity and good intentions of many outstanding leaders of labor, I was deeply disappointed in many of their performances under new responsibility arising out of the N.R.A." New Deal insiders knew how little constructive effort had been made by union leaders, even in such matters as social security and unemployment insurance that closely affected their members. The social legislation of the New Deal had been made for American workers but not by them.[37]

Laski prescribed surgery for ills that many thought were already being successfully treated, and some of the symptoms he described seemed to suggest a different diagnosis. He said that the New Deal had "brought into being a positive federal state," and set trends that were irreversible. No future government would repeal the social security laws, dismantle the Securities and Exchange Commission, or allow unemployment on the scale of the Great Depression. He pressed the need for a new party, but the Democratic party, now reconstructed on a broad social base, already met most of his criteria. It seemed perverse to demand a new start because capitalism survived. As Barry Karl puts it: "To assert that Roosevelt saved American capitalism misses the point entirely ... Most Americans perceived the government itself, not capitalist ideology, as the cause of their problems."[38]

The different interpretations by Bryce and Laski of stability and change in American society raised issues that still perplex and divide. Bryce said that Americans had no idea of the State as "a great moral power, the totality of the wisdom and conscience and force of the people." It had "no more ... title to awe, than a commercial company for working a railroad or a mine." True in the past, said Laski, but now "the era of the positive state had arrived in America as decisively as in Europe."[39]

The idea of the positive state was derived from absolutism, refined by Rousseau and Hegel, turned on its head by Marx, and used by Lenin to create a new social order. Can the term be used in a federal system, with separate powers, and entrusting some policy making to courts and commissions over which the Executive has no control? Neo-marxists have argued that the state must be viewed "as an institution and social actor at the center of attention." They focus on people in the administration who have their own ideas, do not always yield to pressure but often react against it, and have more to do with the shape of legislation than legislators. As two contemporary political theorists explain: "Although the state is just an apparatus of rules, it is itself a major influence on the form that these rules take." However, ability to adjust the rules is not the power to determine strategy, and this "autonomous" state operates within institutional, political, and economic parameters that it has not set and cannot alter. If there is a "positive state" in America, it cannot be described in European terms.[40]

Class and government continue to exercise social science minds. Bryce said there was no governing class in America, and a class that did not govern could not rule. Nor could a governing class emerge without "a revolution in national ideas, and a change in what may be called the chemical composition of the national mind, which is of all things the least likely to arrive."[41]

Laski criticized Bryce for failing to realize that business controlled corrupt politicians, and he borrowed William Allen White's distinction between the "governing classes" and the vested interests or "ruling classes" who "used the bosses but were always careful never to have other than political relations with them." This well-tested relationship between business and bosses provided the model for a class that ruled without governing and imposed, on a national scale, what would later be called "hegemony."[42]

No one today would call America a classless society – in some respects the dividing lines are drawn more clearly than in Europe – but the argument is whether class is the dominant or merely one social fact among many. On the one hand it is argued that hegemony exists though exercised in more subtle way than Laski thought; on the other it is asked why a class possessing such power loses so many political battles.

Class can be entangled with elites. Bryce had no doubt that there were local and occupational elites. There was a "reserve fund of wisdom and strength the country has in ... men who so far from being aristocrats or recluses, are usually the persons whom their native fellow-townsmen best know and most respect as prominent in business and in the profession." Business men were prominent but did not stand alone, and what they did for their communities rather than wealth earned them respect. These were the people who set the tone, took the lead in social or charitable activities, and made the rules for professions. When their interests were at stake they mustered their strength to influence politicians; but their various and often conflicting aims made it difficult if not impossible for them to coalesce into a single national elite. This is the way that Bryce argued the case, but Laski disagreed and since the publication of C. Wright Mills' *Power Elite* it has been hotly contested.[43]

Laski believed that democracy meant the substitution of majority for class rule. Bryce rejected "the doctrine that the mere enjoyment of power fitted large masses of men, any more than individuals or classes, for its exercise." According to his old friend, C. W. Eliot, Bryce "thought the only means of making sure progress in free government ... was practice in local government and in party government. That practice ... must develop skill in public discussion – always in discussion first – but discussion resulting in compromise." In this way democracy "not only taught the Americans to use liberty without abusing it, and how to secure equality; it [had] also taught them fraternity." Reflection and respect for others, even when they were mistaken, made democracy possible; government by the mass would destroy it. This did not mean standing still. Compromise normally meant conceding some points to the minority, and minorities led the world to better things.[44]

This reveals a profound difference in political understanding. Acceptance of majority will (as distinct from giving majorities weight in a system of checks and balances) can be justified either by theoretical certainty or by faith that the mass is possessed of a wisdom denied to minority interests or groups. Laski justified it in both ways. Marxism showed with scientific certainty how a better organization of society could be achieved, but there was also a "real will" that would be revealed once class rule was broken. What the people really wanted was "the promise of America" – they got devices to keep it safe for capital. The true task of politics was to release the real will and act upon the conviction that theory and intuition would then agree.

This was the kind of argument that Bryce, bred in the principles of the Scottish enlightenment, could not accept. He had, said Charles W. Eliot, "an aversion to political action directed by abstract principles, or founded on abstract considerations." The real will, if it existed, was already present in public opinion – as a climate not a storm – and mass votes were easily manipulated by party machines or demagogues cresting waves of emotion.[45]

Laski argued for deconstruction as an essential prelude to reconstruction. Rival candidates and party machines were tacitly allied to give the voters no real choice; education, the press, and often religion conveyed the same message. An edifice of conventional ideas and statutory restraints had to be pulled down before the people could be truly free. Bryce could not accept the idea of moral man in immoral society. Political behavior was conditioned by inherited beliefs, customs, and institutions. It was the good fortune of Americans to have inherited a culture that was, in all its most important features, the best that the world had yet known, and it was their duty to pass on this culture to newcomers and the young so that posterity could enjoy its blessings. As a young man Bryce had written a celebrated study of the Holy Roman Empire, and knew full well what happened when the intellectual core of a great institution lost its hold upon the imagination. A great many things needed doing in America but without conservation disintegration would ensue.

The case of Laski versus Bryce is complete. The jurors are out but the sound of heated exchanges between them can be heard. A hung jury is possible but a majority decision for Bryce is probable.

Notes

The Two Authors

JAMES BRYCE (1838–1922) was the son of a Glasgow schoolmaster and pioneer geologist, grandson of a noted but dissident Presbyterian minister; educated at the High School of Glasgow and at Glasgow and Oxford Universities (Trinity College); a fellow of Oriel College and from 1870 to 1893 professor of Civil Law. Published (1864) *Holy Roman Empire*, a minor classic in historical literature; contributed (1867) to *Essays on Reform;* author of books and articles on a wide variety of subjects.

A Member of Parliament (1880–1907); British ambassador to the United States (1907–1913); the only British statesman honored by a bust in the Capitol (outside the room of the Senate Foreign Relations Committee).

HAROLD JOSEPH LASKI (1893–1950) came from a Polish Jewish family settled in Manchester; educated at Manchester Grammar School and New College, Oxford; taught at McGill (1914–1916), Harvard (1916–1920), and the London School of Economics (1920–1950). A prolific writer on the theory and practice of politics. A leasing member of the Labour party and its chairman in 1945, when he was the subject of gross abuse by the conservative press as a Lenin in waiting (he subsequently sued a newspaper for libel but lost the case). There are many tributes to his attractive personality and his generosity to younger scholars.

Biographical Studies

BRYCE – The standard biography is still that by H. A. L. Fisher (1927) but it contains little of interest on *The American Commonwealth*. Edmund Ions, *James Bryce and American Democracy* (London, 1968) and Hugh Tulloch, *James Bryce's American Commonwealth: The Anglo-American Background* (London, 1988) are both excellent. Tulloch has a very full bibliography of materials on Bryce and America. Robert C. Brooks, ed., *Bryce's American Commonwealth: Fiftieth Anniversary* (New York, 1938), has some good essays on the reception and influence of *The American Commonwealth* but does not do justice to Bryce on public opinion and social institutions.

LASKI – Kingsley Martin, *Harold Laski* (London, 1953) and Herbert A. Deane, *The Political Ideas of Harold Laski* (New York, 1955); Granville Eastwood, *Harold Laski* (London, 1972); Isaac Kramnick and Barry Sherman, *Harold Laski: A Life on the Left* (London, 1993); Michael Newman, *Harold Laski: A Political Biography* (London, 1993).

Notes on the text

In these notes all references to *The American Commonwealth* are given as *Bryce* and all references to *The American Democracy* as *Laski*. This avoids frequent repetition of the full titles or "ibid" and also emphasizes the adversarial theme of this paper.

1. *Laski, 16.*
2. Hugh Tulloch lists 54 Americans consulted by Bryce when preparing *The American Commonwealth (James Bryce's American Commonwealth*, 234– 242). In many cases their comments have not survived or are represented by single letters; probably many comments were made on marked proofs. Thomas M. Cooley was exceptional in keeping a full record of what he wrote and this is with his papers in the Bentley Library of the University of Michigan.
3. Laski acknowledged help from 20 Americans but as much of the writing was done during the war recent communication with them must have been limited. Of particular interest is his acknowledgement of "the magnanimity with which the late Franklin D. Roosevelt allowed me to see the working of the presidential system from within."
4. *Bryce*, vol. 2, 833; *Laski*, 725.
5. *Bryce*, vol. 2, 872; *Laski*, 3.
6. London School of Economics, Laski Papers, Laski to B. W. Huebsch, November 4, 1940, March 27, 1943; *Laski*, 3. The 1943 letter also throws light on his mood when writing *Laski*: The immediate aftermath of the war would be grim "but then there will come phase when the young people get their breath, and I think a new and bigger 1848 will sweep the five continents. I've learned a good deal I hope, above all learned to respect the ordinary people and to be quite certain that bourgeois civilization has passed its peak."
7. *Bryce*, vol. 1, 227; vol. 2, 21, 284, 360, 869.
8. *Laski*, 418.
9. *Bryce*, vol 2, 589–591, 613.
10. *Bryce*, vol. 2, 851–852; *Laski*, 250, 259.
11. Bodleian Library, Oxford, Bryce Papers (cited hereafter as "Bryce Papers"), Bryce to Mrs. Whitman, April 25, 1889.
12. *The Nineteenth Century* 25 (January 1889): 140–148; *Macmillan's Magazine* 59 (February 1889): 241–253; Bryce Papers, Thayer to Bryce, January 5, 1889; Abbott to Bryce ... Jesse Macy, a friend from Grinnell College, Iowa, who later edited the abridged edition, wrote that "It is made a starting point for nearly every discussion on American government" (ibid., November 7, 1889).
13. *New York Times* (June 6, 1948); *[London] Times Literary Supplement* (1949), 164.
14. *Annals of the American Academy of Social and Political Sciences* 259 (September 1948): 155. Rowland Egger in the *American Historical Review* 54: 613–615 also found an "underlying intellectual confusion" because "the facts which he is honest enough to adduce controvert at almost every point the thesis to which he clings." Also "too many important things are left out and too many significant things are brushed off or put in the wrong perspective."

15. *Political Science Quarterly* 63 (1948): 599–601.
16. *Laski*, 416–418.
17. Kingsley Martin, *Harold Laski*, 87–88, 270.
18. *Laski*, 198.
19. *American Political Science Review* 42 (1948): 1211–1213.
20. *Laski*, 235; Katie Louchheim, ed., *Making the New Deal: The New Dealers Speak* (Cambridge, Massachusetts, 1983), 88 – interview with Charles H. Horsky.
21. *Bryce*, vol. 1, 1; vol. 2, 871.
22. Foreword to D. W. Brogan, *The American Political System* (London, 1933), 16. He also noted the emergence in America of "all the typical phenomena of European life" including a hereditary leisured class, a middle class "whose access to favoured positions is becoming increasingly stereotyped," and "a characteristic proletariat in the cities."
23. *Laski*, 748.
24. *Laski*, 50–51, 725.
25. *Bryce*, vol. 2., Ch. 85 *passim* (quotation is at 349), 28. It has been suggested that Bryce misunderstood de Tocqueville and thought that "the tyranny of the majority" applied only to political coercion, but it is clear that he understood very well that "tyranny" included social pressure and ostracism, thought control, and religious sanctions. The "fatalism" of the multitude substituted inward for outward pressure as the principal explanation for conformity.
26. *Bryce*, vol. 2, 673, 693, 694 (and Ch. 106 *passim*).
27. *Laski*, 368.
28. *Laski*, 367–369.
29. Bryce described his chapters on public opinion as "the most difficult but also the most vital part of my task." (*Bryce*, vol. 1, 6). He was disappointed when reviewers misunderstood his purpose. "The chapters in the last three parts of the book were not written as detached essays but as parts of the whole, all connected in my own mind, and intended to make the national character and chief conditions and aspects of American life more intelligible to Europeans." (Bryce Papers, Bryce to Theodore Stanton, September 24, 1889). The misunderstanding was in part his own fault because he provided no overall statement and interrupted the logical sequence with chapters on city rings, Kearneyism, and (in the third edition) the South and future of blacks.
30. *Bryce*, vol. 2, 364.
31. *Bryce*, vol. 2, 278–279.
32. *Bryce*, vol. 1, 547.
33. *Bryce*, vol. 2, 539–540, 545.
34. *Laski*, 114, and see also 189.
35. *Laski*, 259–262. "What is … quite clear is that only the labour movement is in a position to choose the majority principle." (259).
36. *Harvard Law Review* 62 (1948): 341. In 1948 an opinion poll commissioned by UNESCO and carried out by Bernard Benson Inc. asked the question "Which country in the world gives the best chance of living the kind of life you would like to lead?" 96 per cent of the Americans responding put the

United States first (the next highest number putting their own country first was Australia: 83 per cent; in Great Britain only 51 per cent did so). The results are cited by David J. Devine, *The Political Culture of the United States*, 93, from William Buchanan and Hadley Cantrill, *How Nations See Each Other* (Urbana, 1953).

37.   Donald Richberg, *The Rainbow* (New York, 1936).

38.   *Laski*, 98–99; Barry Karl, *The Uneasy State* (Chicago and London, 1983), 153.

39.   *Bryce*, vol. 2, 536; *Laski*, 77.

40.   Theda Skocpol et al., eds., *Bringing the State Back In* (New York, 1985); Alan Hamlin and Philip Pettit, eds., *The Good Polity: Normative Analysis of the State* (Oxford, 1989). This is not the place to enter upon the hotly disputed question "What is the State?" For a survey of Marxist theories see Martin Carnoy, *The State and Political Theory* (Princeton, 1984) and for a recent and different analysis see Timothy Mitchell, "The Limits of the State: Beyond Statist Approaches and their Critics," *American Political Science Review* 85, no. 1 (March 1991): 77–96.

41.   *Bryce*, vol. 2, 865–866. "In Europe there has always been a governing class, a set of persons ... to whom has been left the making of public opinion together with the conduct of administration and the occupancy of places in the legislature." There was no such class in the United States (ibid., 268).

42.   *Laski*, 161. For other accounts of business political power see 50, 223, 389. "The business man dominates American civilization. His function is so to organize American society that he has the freest possible run of profitable adventure ... That is why he controls the state power." (389).

43.   *Bryce*, vol. 2, 334, 364.

44.   *Proceedings of the Massachusetts Historical Society* 55 (1921–1922): 204; *Bryce*, vol. 2, 604. This does not mean that Bryce despised the opinion of ordinary people. On the contrary, when a moral issue was clearly presented (as in 1860) the majority choose wisely and "nearly all great political and social causes have made their way first among the middle or humbler classes." (352). New ideas "come from lofty and piercing minds," the response comes most readily from those without an economic stake in the existing order, but the quality of the response depends upon their understanding of basic American principle – an understanding not possessed by "ignorant masses."

45.   Eliot's comment as in note 44.

5

The Exceptionalist Syndrome in U.S. Continental and Overseas Expansionism

Serge Ricard

The Founding Fathers were keenly aware of the historic role bestowed on them. Were they not the descendants of the builders of a New Jerusalem – created in the New World according to God's plan? It was tempting to attribute to divine providence their successful, and novel, assertion of the principle of self-determination. Implementing the Lockean concept of government by the consent of the governed was but another version of God's kingdom on earth, revised by Hobbes, Locke, Montesquieu and Rousseau: a deist republic, with a providential destiny and a universal mission.[1] If the United States could stand as a shining example, a torchlight, for mankind, as Thomas Paine claimed, then it followed that the American model deserved to be exported and even imposed on populations that might be temporarily insensitive – out of sheer ignorance – to the lure of the philosophy of the Century of Enlightenment.[2] The brand of republican messianism that was to be invoked to justify later territorial aggrandizements was derived from the above postulate of American uniqueness; but it rested on an irreducible contradiction that would forever vitiate U.S. foreign policy: the basic incompatibility of the exceptionalist claim with political messianism, of singularity with universalism.[3]

This fundamental ambiguity largely accounts for the incoherence and the inconsistencies of the American diplomatic tradition. The United States needed to preserve its primeval purity through isolation – from Europe, essentially; but the missionary spirit demanded intervention on behalf of freedom, to promote it or defend it in other parts of the continent or the world; in addition, the American model alone allegedly had universal value, but was at the same time deemed useless to any other people, for its application required qualities possessed by the Americans alone.[4] In order to overcome this antagonism there would seem to be no solution other than a benevolent trusteeship, paternalism in the interest of peoples yet unready for democracy – in whom would be inculcated, as a preliminary step, those virtues that were intrinsically American. The preservation – first on the continent, then in the hemisphere, and ultimately the world – of an order favorable to U.S. interests, as well as the imperialistic means employed to achieve it, thereby found a convenient justification – based, what is more, on an unassailable motivation: altruism.

This approach was to enable the United States to surmount another fundamental contradiction: to reconcile its expansionist goals and practice with its anti-imperialist principles. For the patriots of 1776 derived their nationalism from the right of a culturally homogeneous people to self-determination and independence. Revolution was justified whenever a government trampled that inalienable, God-given, "natural" right.[5] But a people's claim to self-determination precluded its subjugating others; the cult of freedom was incompatible with "the passion for conquest," as John Jay, president of the Continental Congress, would peremptorily declare.[6] A century of conquering republicanism on the North American continent would belie that virtuous profession of faith. To escape from a disturbing antinomy that subverted the revolutionary ideals and moral claims of the patriots and of the Founding Fathers, all that was needed was the elabo-ration of an anti-colonial expansionist doctrine, the combining of Empire with Liberty: exceptionalism and universalism made it possible to appeal to a higher law – superior to morality and international law. Did not the American experience, by virtue of its uniqueness, deserve to be guided by atypical principles and judged according to its own criteria? Yet, originally, not all revolutionaries favored expansion. During the Philadelphia Conven-tion the small states expressed their fears of seeing their representation dwindle with the admission of future states. Some delegates also worried about an "unpredictable West" that might disrupt an initially balanced Union and deprive the East of its political and economic supremacy, for the interior, the back country, was known to be more radical than the Atlantic seaboard, while emigration of all the oppressed of the world to the American asylum might lead to the foundation of rival states.[7]

The U.S. justificative rhetoric throughout its continental expansion would be clothed in various garbs and invoke a diversity of principles – all tailored to meet the same end. Albert K. Weinberg has superbly analyzed them in *Manifest Destiny: A Study of Nationalist Expansionism in American History*: natural law, geographical predestination, the right to ownership of the land, the extension of the area of freedom, manifest destiny, the mission of regeneration, natural growth, political gravitation[8] – an extraordinary ideological cocktail concocted to assist an exceptional, and manifest, destiny. Originally defensive, the expansionist arguments soon took up an aggressive coloration: the initial legitimate reaction of self-defense against powerful and ambitious neighbors was soon followed, after two or three decades, by an unbridled territorial growth.

As early as the revolutionary period, the vagueness and flexibility of the concept of natural law allowed for the assertion of a right to security as pretext for territorial aggrandizement, like the projected invasion of Canada, conquest thus being viewed as a defensive measure.[9] After signing the Treaty of 1783 the young republic undertook to secure from Spain a right of navigation on the Mississippi – a departure from existing interna-tional law. Ironically, after acquiring the lower Mississippi valley Jefferson became aware of the benefits of an exclusive use by a nation of its territorial waters and opposed the suggestion of an exchange of Louisiana for the Floridas, for Spain might in her turn claim a "natural" right of navigation. A further inconsistency might be pointed out: in the 1820s the United States claimed access to the Saint Lawrence in the name of natural law.[10]

Spain's concessions of 1795 failed to satisfy the Americans. The cession of Louisiana to France worried them, so much so that Jefferson, of all people, even considered "marry[ing] ... to the British fleet and nation" to offset French influence in the New World. For if distance safely made France a "natural friend," proximity was likely to turn into an enemy a nation well-known for "the impetuosity of her temper, the energy and restlessness of her character."[11] The third president then went on to advocate the application to his country of a different code of natural law on account of its geographical peculiarities.[12] The American nation allegedly had a right of ownership over the whole Mississippi delta; and Spain could not possibly do away with this contiguous territory without consulting her, could not, in other words, inflict upon the United States a dangerous neighbor without its consent[13] – to say nothing of the right to the pursuit of happiness, transcending all others, by which the young republic could determine and control the future of North America.[14] The Louisiana Purchase removed the French thorn from the American side but compelled the United States to a political-philosophical about-face. The interests of the Louisianans who spurned the blessings of American democracy became subservient to U.S. self-interest. The principle of the consent of the governed applied only when the said governed were politically mature, as the Filipinos would find out a century later.

Once the right to protect oneself from potentially dangerous neighbors was put forward as the fundamental justification of territorial expansion, there was no limit to the number of possible corollaries – like the legitimate extension of "natural" borders.[15] Nature and Providence were happily married to beget a wonder child: geographical predestination, fed on the marvelous alibi of territorial contiguity. By that token the Floridas, Texas, the Rockies, the Pacific coast and even the isthmus of Panama could be claimed, and Cuba, the West Indies and Hawaii become "natural appendages"[16] of the North American continent. As noted by Albert K. Weinberg, the theory of territorial contiguity eventually committed geographical suicide with the acquisition of the Philippines; it did not survive the acrobatic splits imposed on it by the victory of Manila Bay and the 1898 treaty of Paris – despite Albert Beveridge's ingenious rhetoric: "Oceans make them contiguous.... Our navy will make them contiguous."[17]

Indeed, the expansionists would never lack ingenuity. In the decade preceding the Civil War, geography would find an ally in biology with the pseudo-scientific argument of natural growth. Nation-states, like all living organisms, needed to grow and fortify themselves; failure to respect that law of nature led to withering and death. America's exceptional vitality therefore demanded that full scope be given to it.[18] Such anatomical analogies – which were by no means novel, witness Plato, Cicero, Machiavelli, Hobbes – anticipated similar neo-Darwinist claims. As early as the 1850s land hunger pointed to such insular preys as Cuba, as evidenced by the Ostend Manifesto, and Hawaii, the United States' new Far West, while extension north and south continued to tempt expansionists, as testified by a persistent interest in Canada and various adventurers' schemes in Central America.[19]

Much has been made of the extraordinary success of the "manifest destiny" idea in the 1840s – a phrase seemingly coined by the journalist-diplomat John L. O'Sullivan and used apropos of the annexation of Texas and the acquisition of Oregon.[20] O'Sullivan, after all, was merely applying new words to an old tune. From its origins the history of the United States had been an exercise in manifest destiny, an illustration of its irresistible growth, sanctioned by Providence. Such a concept was bound to win over all classes of society to expansion, from the humble pioneer to the big businessman; and to obtain their enthusiastic and unflagging support, for it satisfied everyone's interests.[21] Besides, the concept of manifest destiny allowed for an a-juridical approach to expansion: legal objections could be brushed aside in the name of ethical considerations that transcended them. This well-nigh amounted to reviving the Puritan postulate of divine election.[22] Yet, the U.S. predilection for extra-legal justifications, for dialectical cavorting and juggling, did not exclude occasional juridical hair-splitting when dealing with Great Britain or the Latin American republics.[23]

Similarly with the Indian question cynicism and hypocrisy merged to generate continuous juridical and moral contortions, of which the removal of the sedentary Cherokee during the Jacksonian period remains the most striking illustration. Dispossessing the savages of their land had been declared legitimate on the part of civilized Christian nations as early as the fifteenth century. The *vacuum domicilium* or *territoria nullius* theory, as expounded by John Wycliff, would become the legal foundation of the colonial powers' right of conquest and of the New England colonists' title to the Indians' lands.[24] Biblical sanction would also be sought, however dubious the interpretation: the agriculturist had a stronger claim than the hunter, the land belonged to the tiller of the soil, not to the nomad.[25] Later, theological justifications would be supplemented by more secular variations on utilitarian themes: in the name of progress it was out of the question to allow a few hundred savage tribes to use vast expanses of land that could feed millions of civilized people.[26] The idea that such waste was intolerable, contrary to reason and to be rights of mankind, proved immensely attractive in the nineteenth century; one finds it penned in almost identical terms by William Henry Harrison, first governor of the Territory of Indiana at the beginning of the century, or by John W. Burgess and Theodore Roosevelt at the end.[27]

Among the justifications advanced in support of expansion, political duty and mission were no less popular: the spread of republicanism, democratic messianism in other words, seemed to resuscitate the old revolutionary ideal, as during the War with Mexico of 1846–1848 which saw American troops enter the Mexican capital and public opinion clamor for the annexation of all Mexico.[28] Expansionism would henceforward hark back to the political and institutional proselytizing of the Founding Fathers. Yet, ironically, freedom would no longer be promoted through example, but imposed by force, just as Napoleon's armies had warred throughout Europe on behalf of the principles of 1789.[29] It should be noted, however, that the expansionists of 1776 and 1787 thought of enlarging the Union by the peopling of allegedly vacant lands, not of liberating oppressed peoples. Whereas their adversaries would gladly have limited it, the crusaders of democracy in the 1840s were bent on "extending the area of freedom," clearly for the sole benefit of the American people, to Texas, Oregon and Mexico – which to southern expansionists manifestly meant extending the area of slavery.[30] Interestingly, with regard to the sense of mission, the debate of half a century later over the annexation of the Philippines – which Dewey's fleet had rendered contiguous – duplicated in many ways the rhetoric of the all-Mexico movement. It gave an unmistakable impression of *déjà vu* with the paternalistic advocacy of the benevolent teaching of democracy to politically immature, if not helpless, barbarians.

All in all, the birth and early development of the United States was to generate two traditions: missionary republicanism, a strong and enduring one, and anti-imperialism, a more uncertain and ambiguous tradition. As examples of the latter, there was the fear of some patriots that enlarging the "sphere," i.e. empire, would result in the breakup of the Union or, later, the objections raised against absorbing alien populations that would be impervious to Americanization – at the time of the Louisiana Purchase and the creation of the Territory of Orleans, then during the War with Mexico – or have a corrupting influence on American institutions – as in the disputed Oregon country.[31] In fact, at an early date, racism, or more exactly, ethnocentrism, was in many respects the common denominator for both expansionists and anti-expansionists, just as it underlay both the pro- and anti-slavery arguments. The great debate of 1898–1900 over the wisdom of acquiring a remote far eastern archipelago and of subjugating its savage denizens – America's new Indians[32] – would reveal the same racialist convergence of imperialists and anti-imperialists. The melting-pot oratory notwithstanding, the theme of ethnic homogeneity undeniably runs as a constant through the whole of American history.[33]

The rhetorical paraphernalia of expansionism was enriched in the post-Civil War years with yet another excuse, the theory of "political gravitation,"[34] an anticipation of the protectorate policy of the early twentieth century which irresistibly suggests the modern notion of satellite-states. The American way of life was so attractive that it would inevitably win over neighboring peoples, who would spontaneously ask for annexation, the United States acting in the Western Hemisphere as a sort of irresistible political-economic magnet. The Danish Virgin Islands, Cuba, Santo Domingo, Hawaii, Canada and

Mexico, to name but a few, were all so many ripe plums ready to fall in the American lap. Ironically, U.S. hegemony in the Western Hemisphere would eventually produce repulsion rather than attraction by engendering anti-American sentiment, in Latin America particularly.

Last but not least, the evolution of the Monroe Doctrine throughout the nineteenth century – up to the Roosevelt Corollary – similarly reflected the expansionist momentum. The doctrine and its corollary can be viewed as the geopolitical expression of two of the myths that most influenced U.S. diplomacy: exceptionalism and universalism. The warning addressed by James Monroe and John Quincy Adams to the European powers was prompted by the desire to preserve the republican Americas from contamination by an adverse political system. It was a statement of ideological incompatibility and of pan-American solidarity against monarchical Europe. It was also a demand for the reciprocity of non-interventionism.[35] The least one can say is that the fifth president's pronouncement did not worry the Old World unduly, most understandably since the continental powers had no plans in November and December 1823 for reconquering the lost Spanish colonies.[36] The doctrine was then laid to rest for two decades until Polk reactivated it in December 1845 by proclaiming the United States' opposition not only to colonization and reconquest by Europe, but also to any cession of American territory to a European power.[37] The Civil War years saw the consolidation of the doctrine into diplomatic dogma with William Seward's repeated protests against France's ambitions in Mexico and Spain's reoccupation of Santo Domingo, and Grant's and Hamilton Fish's insistence on the no-transfer principle.[38] In later years the ever-increasing interest in an isthmian canal would lead to the gradual substitution of the Monroe Doctrine for international law in the Western Hemisphere.[39] By 1895 the doctrine had become the affirmation of U.S. preeminence in the New World – the outcome of the Venezuelan Crisis being evidence that Great Britain, despite the irritation of the Foreign Office, tacitly approved of that supremacy.[40]

Exceptionalism and universalism finally triumphed with the proclamation and application of the Roosevelt Corollary to the Monroe Doctrine which explicitly turned the Caribbean into the United States' backyard:

> Chronic wrongdoing, or an impotence which results in a general loosening of the ties of civilized society, may in America, as elsewhere, ultimately require intervention by some civilized nation, and in the Western Hemisphere the adherence of the United States to the Monroe Doctrine may force the United States, however reluctantly, in flagrant cases of such wrongdoing or impotence, to the exercise of an international police power.[41]

As a matter of fact, in his annual message of December 1904 Theodore Roosevelt enunciated not a corollary to the Monroe Doctrine but a wholly new diplomatic tenet: the United States was to act as policeman of the Western Hemisphere; it was to put to use the right of interference it continued to deny the European powers.[42] Of course, U.S. interventionism had been at work in Latin America long before the 1904 pronouncement that was to legitimize it. But the great North American republic for the first time, as the 26th president was well aware, was then strong enough to monopolize interference in the New World; not only did it evince industrial and agricultural might but it had acceded to world power status in 1898 at the close of a splendidly profitable little war. This new condition called for a new diplomacy, especially in that part of the globe where the United States was predestined by geography to play a leading role. Monroe's "doctrine" had a weakness: nowhere was U.S. preeminence clearly stated. A "corollary" was to remedy that unfortunate omission and give the hitherto defensive dictum a markedly aggressive coloration.

The catalyst of that drastic mutation was no other than the isthmian canal. Ulysses S. Grant's dream of an American waterway built with American money and exclusively controlled by the United States had by 1904 become a reality thanks to the controversial acquisition of the Canal Zone. Roosevelt had "taken" Panama the year before. It was out of the question to tolerate more European interventions in the Caribbean;[43] the protection of the approaches of the future canal, the defense, in other words, of the Panamanian lifeline, demanded that the latter be turned into an American lake.[44] Notwithstanding its official repudiation at the 1933 pan-American conference the Roosevelt Corollary to the Monroe Doctrine remained in force unofficially. Walter LaFeber remarks that "it is the Roosevelt Doctrine, not Monroe's, that Dulles, Acheson, Johnson, Reagan, and Weinberger had in mind when they justified unilateral U.S. intervention in the internal affairs of Latin American States."[45]

The old frontiers had been territorial; some of the new ones were too. But on the whole the new frontiers of the early twentieth century were to be those of an informal empire, illustrated by the protectorate policy implemented in Cuba, Santo Domingo, Nicaragua, Haiti, etcetera, and especially in Panama where American exceptionalism and the United States' alleged "mandate from civilization" would justify the Rooseveltian disregard of Columbian sovereignty.[46] Colonialism in the Philippines would turn out to be, indeed, an atypical experience – which does not invalidate the imperialist label, as some historians like to believe.[47] The new empire and the new diplomacy reflected the new geopolitical situation: the United States was on the road to world power. The old sense of mission was present in the insistence on America's civilizing duty. Conveniently buttressed by the perennial belief in American exceptionalism, this early-twentieth-century avatar of universalism then combined with the theme of law and order applied to a hemisphere, and soon to be applied on a world scale.

Notes

1. Cf. Elise Marienstras, *Les Mythes fondateurs de la nation américaine: essai sur le discours idéologique aux États-Unis à l'époque de l'indépendance (1763–1800)* (Paris: François Maspero, 1976), 90–91, 95–98, 108–116, and *Nous, le Peuple: les origines du nationalisme américain* (Paris: Gallimard-N.R.F., 1988), 339–345, 351–354; William Appleman Williams, *America Confronts a Revolutionary World: 1776–1976* (New York: William Morrow, 1976), 27.
2. Cf. Marienstras, *Mythes fondateurs*, 108–110, 315; Thomas Paine, *Le Sens commun (Common Sense)*, introd. and trans. by Bernard Vincent (Paris: Aubier-Coll. bilingue, 1983), 54, 90–91, 98–101.
3. Cf. Marienstras, *Mythes fondateurs*, 90, 340.
4. Cf. Gouverneur Morris to William Carmichael, July 4, 1789: "They want an American Constitution with the Exception of a King instead of a President, without reflecting that they have not American Citizens to support that Constitution ..." Gouverneur Morris, *A Diary of the French Revolution*, ed. Beatrix Cary Davenport, 2 vols. (London: Harrap, 1939), I, 136.
5. Albert K. Weinberg, *Manifest Destiny: A Study of Nationalist Expansionism in American History* (1935; Chicago: Quadrangle-Encounter Paperbacks, 1963), 12–16.
6. Ibid., 19.
7. Daniel J. Boorstin, *The Americans*, 3 vols. (New York: Random-Vintage, 1958–1973), II, *The National Experience*, 264–265; Gérard Hugues, *Coup d'Etat à Philadephie?* (Aix-en-Provence: Publications de l'Université de Provence, 1989), 96–97; Jared Sparks, *The Life of Gouverneur Morris, with Selections from his Correspondence and Miscellaneous Papers; Detailing Events in the American Revolution, the French Revolution, and in the Political History of the United States*, 3 vols. (Boston: Gray and Bowen, 1832), I, 104–105, 224–225. Gouverneur Morris would embrace expansionism at the end of his life.
8. Weinberg, 11, 43, 72, 100, 130, 160, 190, 224, *passim*.
9. A much-practiced brand of defensive imperialism, as attested by world history, ancient and modern ...
10. Weinberg, 22–23, 25–26.
11. Thomas Jefferson to Robert R. Livingston, April 18, 1802. Andrew A. Lipscomb and Albert E. Bergh, eds., *The Writings of Thomas Jefferson*, 20 vols. (Washington, D.C.: Thomas Jefferson Memorial Association, 1903–1905), X , 312–315. This important document is quoted in Thomas G. Paterson, ed., *Major Problems in American Foreign Policy: Documents and Essays, Volume I: To 1914*, 2nd ed. (1978; Lexington, Massachusetts: Heath, 1984), 112–113. On the Louisiana Purchase, see Alexander DeConde, *This Affair of Louisiana* (New York: Scribner's, 1976).
12. Weinberg, 29.
13. Cf. Weinberg, 29–30, quoting Gouverneur Morris.
14. Weinberg, 31.
15. Ibid., 44–45.
16. John Quincy Adams quoted in Weinberg, 49, 65.
17. Albert J. Beveridge, *The Meaning of the Times* (Indianapolis: Bobbs-Merrill, 1908), 52. This clever over-stretching of the expansionist point is to be found in a famous speech, "The March of the Flag," which opened the Indiana Republicans' election campaign on September 16, 1898. This

imperialist manifesto enjoyed fairly widespread popularity and distribution between 1898 and 1900. Beveridge's argument equally applied, of course, to Hawaii, Puerto Rico and Cuba.

18.   Weinberg, 196–217.
19.   Ibid., 192–193, 202, 210–212, 214–215, 217–223.
20.   Julius W. Pratt, "The Origin of 'Manifest Destiny,'" *American Historical Review* 32 (1927): 795–798.
21.   Frederick Merk, *Manifest Destiny and Mission in American History: A Reinterpretation* (1963; New York: Random-Vintage, 1966), disagrees: the American nation – despite the expansionist fever of 1846 and 1898 – was basically altruistic. On the causes of that fever, see also Norman A. Graebner, *Empire on the Pacific: A Study in American Continental Expansion*, (repr. ed., 1955; Santa Barbara, California: ABC-Clio, 1983).
22.   Weinberg, 130–140.
23.   Ibid., 152–159.
24.   On this little-known justification of colonization, see Jean-Pierre Martin, "Philosophie et théologie chez Roger Williams (1606–1683)," diss., Université de Paris IV, 1976, 3 vols., I, 239–242. Also Nelcya Delanoë, *L'Entaille rouge: terres indiennes et démocratie américaine* (Paris: François Maspero, 1982), 31–67.
25.   Weinberg, 74–76; Delanoë, 30.
26.   Weinberg, 77–78.
27.   Cf. Weinberg, 92; Thomas F. Gosset, *Race: The History of an Idea in America* (1963; New York: Schocken Books, 1965), 112–113; Theodore Roosevelt, *The Works of Theodore Roosevelt*, ed. Hermann Hagedorn, National Edition, 20 vols. (New York: Scribner's, 1926), IX, *The Winning of the West*, 56–57.
28.   Merk, 107–143.
29.   Weinberg, 11–12, 100, 102–103.
30.   Ibid., 109, 115.
31.   Ibid., 104–105, 109–112; Boorstin, *The Americans*, II, *The National Experience*, 268.
32.   On the similarities between continental and overseas expansion, see my "Uplifting the Barbarians: Imperialism and the Frontier Outlook in the 1890s and 1900s," *Les Américains et les autres*, Actes du G.R.E.N.A. (Aix-en-Provence: Publications de l'Université de Provence, 1982), 131–148.
33.   On racial and cultural exclusivism, notably the puritan legacy and the ideology of the Century of Enlightenment, see for example Jean-Pierre Martin, "Les sources de l'anthropologie esclavagiste: le XVIIIe siècle français," *Une Institution particulière: aspects de l'esclavage aux Etats-Unis*, travaux et textes rassemblés par Jean-Pierre Martin et Serge Ricard (Aix-en-Provence: Publications de l'Université de Provence, 1986), 9–19; Marienstras, *Mythes fondateurs*, 157–176; Martin, *Le Puritanisme américain en Nouvelle-Angleterre (1620–1693)* (Bordeaux: Presses Universitaires de Bordeaux, 1989), 54–56; Gossett, 18–26; Merk, 108, 157–159, 161–163, 192; Weinberg, 160–189; Pierre Lépinasse, "Anti-esclavagisme et abolitionnisme," *Institution particulière*, ed. Martin and Ricard, 69–95; Serge Ricard, "Cautious Radicalism in the Early Republic: Thomas Jefferson and Slavery," ibid., 21–32.
34.   See Weinberg, ch. 8, "Political Gravitation," 224–251.
35.   Dexter Perkins, *A History of the Monroe Doctrine*, new rev. ed. (1941; Boston: Little, Brown, 1963), 5–6, 21–33.

36. Ibid., 50–60.

37. Ibid., 80.

38. Ibid., 155–156.

39. Ibid., 159–168.

40. Ibid., 173–191; Walter LaFeber, *The New Empire: An Interpretation of American Expansion, 1860–1898* (1963; Ithaca, New York: Cornell University Press Paperbacks, 1987), 242–283.

41. The Big Stick in a nutshell… Theodore Roosevelt, *Presidential Addresses and State Papers*, Homeward Bound Edition, 8 vols. (New York: The Review of Reviews Co., 1910), III, 176–177.

42. Cf. Thomas A. Bailey, *A Diplomatic History of the American People*, 9th ed. (1940; Englewood Cliffs, New Jersey: Prentice, 1974), 505: "In brief, the Monroe Doctrine, which was originally designed to prevent intervention by the European powers, would be used to justify intervention by the United States."

43. Perkins, 168–170, notes the annoyance those frequent resorts to coercion caused in the State Department during the last quarter of the nineteenth century.

44. See, for example, his annual message of December 5, 1905: "That our rights and interests are deeply concerned in the maintenance of the Doctrine is so clear as hardly to need argument. This is especially true in view of the construction of the Panama Canal. As a mere matter of self-defence we must exercise a close watch over the approaches to this canal; and this means that we must be thoroughly alive to our interests in the Caribbean Sea." Theodore Roosevelt, *Presidential Addresses*, IV, 603.

45. Walter LaFeber, "The Evolution of the Monroe Doctrine from Monroe to Reagan," *Redefining the Past: Essays in Diplomatic History in Honor of William Appleman Williams*, ed. Lloyd C. Gardner (Corvallis: Oregon State University Press, 1986), 139–140.

46. Theodore Roosevelt's most complete and cogent – albeit disputable – exposition of his Panamanian policy is to be found in his annual messages to Congress of December 7, 1903 and January 4, 1904, and in his autobiography of 1913. Cf. Roosevelt, *Presidential Addresses*, II, 692–757; *An Autobiography* (1913; New York: Da Capo Press Paperbacks, 1985), 526–543.

47. For the most thorough examination to-date of historiographical confusion and warfare over the issue of U.S. imperialism, see Edward P. Crapol, "Coming to Terms with Empire: The Historiography of Late-Nineteenth-Century American Foreign Relations," *Diplomatic History* 16 no. 4 (Fall 1992): 573–597. For a criticism of "objectivism" and "anti-revisionist revisionism," see my "Expansionists and Anti-Expansionists of 1898: The Unfinished Debate," *An American Empire: Expansionist Cultures and Policies, 1881–1917*, ed. Serge Ricard (Aix-en-Provence: Publications de l'Université de Provence, 1990), 59–67; "Countering Counter-Revisionism: The Fraudulent Legend of American Non-Imperialism at the Turn of the 19th Century in Recent Historiography," paper read at the annual meeting of the Society for Historians of American Foreign Relations, June 19–22, 1991, Washington, D.C., and *Théodore Roosevelt: principes et pratique d'une politique étrangère* (Aix-en-Provence: Publications de l'Université de Provence, 1991), 4–21 – from which much of the material for the present essay is derived.

6

In the Name of Anglo-Saxondom, For Empire and For Democracy: The Anglo-American Discourse, 1880–1920

Anna Maria Martellone

Some may wonder at the expression "Anglo-Saxondom" in the title of this paper. Why "Anglo-Saxondom" rather than the better known idiom "Anglo-Saxonism?" Years ago, while searching the stacks of the Harvard Library for literature on the conceptualizations of Anglo-Saxonism in the nineteenth century I came across a rather sumptuous journal bearing the title *The Anglo-Saxon Review*.[1] It was a quarterly miscellany, edited by Lady Randolph Spencer Churchill, and it came as no surprise that the wife of the Tory Democrat Lord Randolph Churchill, himself a supporter of racial and imperialistic nationalism, should have an interest in a journal whose very title evoked visions of imperial expansion in the name of Anglo-Saxon racial superiority. What struck me was the fact that the journal in question appeared to be conceived as a joint Anglo-American venture (the publisher of the first issue was listed as John Linn, London and New York, it was copyrighted in the United States, and printed in England) and that its first issue was published in June 1899, just when the victorious conclusion of the Spanish-American War had launched the United States on the international scene and in the imperialistic arena. The 1890s were also the years of the Anglo-American rapprochement; while there are thorough studies of the international occurrences that brought the two English-speaking countries closer than they had been for over a century,[2] there is not much on the ideological elaboration of the rapprochement in the two countries. The existing studies[3] duly emphasize the role of Anglo-Saxon solidarity, but I was especially interested in ascertaining whether the outburst of Anglo-Saxonism generated by the new imperial course of the United States and the resumption of imperialistic expansion on the part of Great Britain after the anti-imperialist utterances of Gladstone, had been carried on under the general insignia of the old Teutonism, so dear to Henry Baxter Adams in America and to Edward Freeman in England, or whether new international circumstances had induced the supporters of Anglo-Saxonism to leave behind the Teutons and to restrict themselves within the shores of the British Isles and of the North-American subcontinent.

I had long been studying Anglo-Saxonism. What had started as an interest tangential to my studies of immigration in the United States, had over time turned into an extended research project on the construction of national identity in the United States from the early Republic to the 1920s. By the time I discovered *The Anglo-Saxon Review* on the shelves of Widener Library I well knew that Anglo-Saxonism, far from being a coherent ideology, had painted itself in many hues, fulfilling different aims at different times, in England as well as in America. In seventeenth-century England it had been exalted as the pillar of "English liberties" vindicated against the "Norman Yoke";[4] in the early American Republic the myth of an ancient Saxon democracy had been one of the ingredients of American political culture;[5] in the course of the nineteenth century it enjoyed wide currency both in America and England.[6] For all its inconsistencies, Anglo-Saxonism "features prominently in the literature of the Empire," and besides being relevant to debates on relations with other European powers and on tensions within the British Isles, characterizes English as well as American discourse on Anglo-American relations.[7]

By the last decade of the nineteenth century, however, the meaning of Anglo-Saxonism underwent a shift both in England and the United States; what for over two centuries had been an exaltation of Teutonic origins and institutions common to all the peoples that could boast of Nordic stock – Englishmen, Americans, Netherlanders, Scandinavians, and Germans alike – became a less encompassing glorification of the Anglo-Saxon "race" limited to English and Americans. The Anglo-Saxonism of Herbert Baxter Adams, John W. Burgess and a host of American historians and political scientists, who had all studied in Germany, had been fabricated on German models of historical inquiry and comparative philology; it had also been widely influenced by the English Teutonists Freeman, Stubbs, John Seeley, Froude, and especially John Green, whose *Short History of the English People* (1874) was enormously popular. Opinions did vary as to the degree of racial kinship now surviving between the Anglo-Saxons and the Teutons, but Victorian historians and social commentators as well as American Anglo-Saxonists had agreed in exalting the common Teutonic stock of all freedom loving Northern European peoples and the Teutonic origins of Anglo-Saxon moral virtues and democratic institutions.[8] The unpleasant accident of the Norman invasion of England, which inconveniently contradicted the claim to uninterrupted Anglo-Saxon purity of blood, was sidestepped by bringing William the Conqueror into the ample Teutonic fold:

There has been no extensive ethnic superimposition among the Anglo-Saxons in England or America ... the Saxons ... under their chieftains Hengest and Horsa, and the Norman hordes under William the Conqueror were Teutonic peoples of the same blood as the early Britons of pre-Roman days ... Hence, English blood is more nearly pure than any blood in Europe, except that of the Scandinavians.[9]

In the words of Edmond Demolins, the French author of a book on Anglo-Saxon superiority that was immediately translated into English, "the Normans were but improved Danes."[10] An article in *The North American Review* which appeared in 1851, shortly after the Mexican War had demonstrated the existence of a Manifest Destiny for the American nation, depicts the relationship between ancient Teutons and Saxons as follows:

> We are the most mixed race that ever existed; and yet the admixture of other races has never been such as to weaken or impoverish the original Saxon stock; – on the contrary, it has infused into it new life and energy. We believe that the Teutonic race excels all others in the possession of these traits of character; and that the Saxons are preeminent or typical for possessing them in a higher degree than any other members of that race.[11]

That some scholars found the great Teuton ancestors a little dumb, that some thought that their intellect might have been somewhat inferior to that of other peoples, put no obstacle to proudly claiming the descent of anything that was good in Anglo-Saxon institutions and mores from a Teutonic germ. In the words of Henry Cabot Lodge, who had studied the legal institutions of the Anglo-Saxons

> the extreme clumsiness of the Anglo-Saxon mind is apparent to anyone who has closely studied their early legal history: and this mental awkwardness led them to cling to their primitive ideas, with a tenacity unequalled except among the Scandinavian races, by the kindred continental tribes.[12]

Better to be uncouth and free than cultured and enslaved like the Latin peoples. The Norman invasion was a fortunate event for the development of the Anglo-Saxons, "otherwise the physical in their civilization would have overborne the intellectual and esthetic; and they would have been of a nature though strong, yet too coarse and uncultivated for the highest eminence in an enlightened period."[13]

At some point in the late 1890s, at the time of the Anglo-American rapprochement and of English and American difficulties with Germany, the revered Teutons seem to have all but disappeared from the horizon of former Teuton-loving Anglo-Saxonists, who instead now cultivated Anglo-Saxonism in a less Pan-Teutonic form. It is quite true that in the nineties Frederick Jackson Turner's frontier thesis dismantled the "germ theory" of the Teutonic origins of American democracy and made it inapplicable in historical writing. But what I want to discuss here is not historiography *strictu sensu*, but rather the uses of Anglo-Saxonism in public discourse; and it is my contention that the probable reason for the disappearance of Teutonism from political rhetoric both in the United States and in England was that Germany had become a potential enemy for both countries.

The events leading to the Anglo-American rapprochement and to fear of Germany are quite clear, but less clear are the stages of the change in the Anglo-American discourse on respective national identities and of the waning of Teutonism in favor of a more limited Anglo-Saxonism. A review that styled itself "Anglo-Saxon" and that so obviously aimed at reaching an audience on both sides of the Ocean, would probably provide a good insight into the conceptual changes Anglo-Saxonism had undergone in both countries. The contents of this journal, clearly a rather expensive product printed on good paper and provided with luxurious bindings, were preeminently literary and somewhat *recherchés*, featuring short stories by Henry James and poetry by Swinburne, but also an article on "England and America: Strangers Yet," another on Spain in the aftermath of the Cuban War, and still another on "Past and Future in South Africa." A few issues also carried an "Impressions and Opinions" section, a commentary on contemporary events largely devoted to singing the praises of Englishmen and of the British Empire. On the whole, its coverage of Imperial England was more extensive than that of the United States: yet it was here that I first encountered the expression "Anglo-Saxondom" applied to the two countries, two distinct political entities joined in the superior moral mission of building empires by virtue of their common Anglo-Saxon inheritance of democracy and their special Anglo-Saxon gift for self-government.

Whereas Anglo-Saxonism had been a concept stressing common origins and institutions of Nordic peoples vaguely defined as Teutons, an identity mark for nationality, a designation of ethnic origins, Anglo-Saxondom, it seemed, referred to the political sovereignty of states – Great Britain and the United States – bent on expanding the boundaries of their domains, the boundaries, in fact, of an "Anglo-Saxondom" that was ruled by Anglo-Saxons but might encompass peoples of diverse ethnic origins brought together under the superior institutions of Anglo-Saxon democracy. The context of the term "Anglo-Saxondom" contained several other intriguing points:

> In the politics of the hour Imperialism is still dominant. Anglo-Saxondom is occupied with its relations to the external world. It looks outwards instead of within ... Imperialism is just now on its trial. Every political tendency must be judged by the manner in which it answers, not merely to the needs, but also to the aspirations, of its age. It is only a rather shallow opinion which attempts to divorce morality from politics – particularly among the Anglo-Saxon peoples, at the bottom of whose consciousness lies a deep ethical and religious sentiment ... If Imperialism is to vindicate itself, it must do so by satisfying this instinct. It cannot be accepted merely because it helps, or is expected to help, our commerce, or because it gratifies our pride of race ... What is to be the outcome of British and American expansion, besides painting a large part of the world with our colors? ... In America, the question is asked with more insistent heart-

searching than in England, because the responsibilities of Empire are coming suddenly and consciously upon the newer country, whereas in the other they have been accumulating gradually for a century and a half. Still in both nations there is the same desire to find a justification by works for the enlargement of dominion. It is this circumstance which goes some way to explain that sudden passion for Mr. Rudyard Kipling and his writings, into which the English countries have recently plunged ... Another aspect of the same truth was put in "The White Man's Burden," which roused the United States to a ferment of enthusiasm ... When Mr. Kipling talks about the "White Man" he sees the term, inaccurately enough, to express the Anglo-Saxon population, English, American, and Colonial. If the white man's business is "to stay the savage wars of peace," to bid sickness and famine cease, to turn "the silent sullen peoples" into civilized human beings, and generally to make the world a better place, ... the domination of the larger part of the non-Aryan world by the English-speaking nations may be defended by the benefits it confers ...[14]

The article ends with the rejection of the diplomacy of the "Concert of Europe" and a warm endorsement of the notion of arbitration, which is said to be "an Anglo-Saxon idea." As one can see, the emphasis is on the "ethical" qualities of the Anglo-Saxons that guide their expansion and make it a duty (typical and not new the recourse to the image of "The White Man's Burden") and not a pleasurable option. There is, side by side with the use of the expression "Anglo-Saxondom," the idea that the Anglo-Saxon population includes, besides the Americans, the Colonial peoples. Together with the use of the term "Anglo-Saxondom," the article thus implies that the expression Anglo-Saxon was no longer bound by ethnicity but extended to the alien peoples inhabiting the new domains of English and American Anglo-Saxons.

I then took up the study of this change and of the historical Anglo-American setting within which it had occurred. The notions of Empire and Democracy seemed kindred subjects to study, since the extension of the boundaries of Anglo-Saxondom could not be separated from the ethical obligation of bringing higher forms of civilization to peoples that had not been endowed by the Creator with the Anglo-Saxon blessings of self-government, liberalism and parliamentary democracy. I should perhaps repeat and emphasize that all my previous work had been centered on emigration to the United States from the 1880s, and related problems of cultural and political assimilation of immigrants, ethnic boundaries, national self-identity. I was of course interested in a change in the meaning of Anglo-Saxonism, in its extension beyond ethnic boundaries, and this just at the time when in the United States the Anglo-Saxonist impact was leading to restrictions aimed at limiting the entry of non Anglo-Saxon peoples.[15] The theme of the discarding of ethnic boundaries also seemed related to the transition from Teutonism to a brand of Anglo-Saxonism that hinged on

Great Britain and the United States and depended on political assumptions (democracy, arbitration) that left Germany out of the new discourse.

I have not found many instances of the use of the term "Anglo-Saxondom," but the change in the meaning of "Anglo-Saxon" from diffusely Teutonic to Anglo-American with the exclusion of Germany and the inclusion of the colonial peoples – all the "English-speaking peoples," thus making language the real melting-pot of races[16] – is evident in most of the literature of the period. Some authors are even aware of the changed significance of the expression and of its relation to the progress of imperialism. Thus they write that the entry of the United States into a "new area of foreign conquest" will bring about a novel impetus to that extension of Anglo-Saxon civilization to other peoples "for which the mother country alone has been in modern times so conspicuous."[17] Anglo-Saxondom will encompass more and more peoples who have not a drop of Anglo-Saxon blood in their veins. Even now,

> Individuals are not unfrequently met with bearing unquestionably English names and English ... in their language, their ideas, ideals and general mental culture ... whose swarthy complexion, raven hair, deep dark irides and general aquilinity of physiognomy cannot but suggest ... the presence of a predominant strain of Italian, Levantine or Oriental blood, though the subject himself may be quite unaware of it, if not disposed to conceal, any such factor in his make up.[18]

If this spreading of Anglo-Saxon civilization to alien people was true of the English Empire, it was even more evident in "the great Western Republic," that "separated offshoot" of England, with its millions of foreign immigrants. All in all, the term Anglo-Saxon practically ceases to be a race designation and it stands rather for a civilization, "for ideas and institutions, originating indeed with a certain ethnic type of mankind, but no longer its exclusive property."[19]

In this revised form of Anglo-Saxonism, diversity of race could not prevent anyone from subscribing to the Anglo-Saxon values and thus become an Anglo-Saxon through assimilation: so long as one was a British subject or an American citizen, one could be ascribed among the Anglo-Saxons, whatever one's racial stock. Any student of immigration and ethnicity in the United States would recognize in these assumptions the optimistic facet of the assimilationist and Americanizing view; but it is well-known how the tale ended, and that eventually the optimistic, assimilationist facet of Anglo-Saxonism gave way to the denial that the absorbing qualities of the Anglo-Saxon were infinite, that any newcomer could be brought into the mainstream of Anglo-Saxondom, a denial that paved the way for the restriction of immigration based on ethnic discrimination.

But at the time, Anglo-Saxonism looked outward to the endless expansionistic possibilities of Great Britain and the kindred "great Western Republic." Elaborations on Anglo-Saxony or Anglo-Saxondom abound, both in England and the United States, from the 1880s well into the first two decades of our century,[20] and resume shortly before World War II. They go through a variety of shades of meaning that would be too long to list; I shall only touch upon the most relevant. Anglo-Saxons spread around the world because "the most powerful organic instincts drive them forth, and wherever they spread they carry their own ideals" which are based "on the independence and self-determination of the individual."[21] Furthermore,"the disposition to work hard and to face difficulties with single-handed bravery has come more easily to the Anglo-Saxon than to the others because his moral nature is in a high state of development"[22] and that is why they succeed:

> hundreds of thousand of peons throughout England and America, men and women with the true Saxon suspicion of a theory, as such, and the morose Saxon difficulty in welcoming a general idea are moved in all their sentiments ... by this conviction, that it is because they are such a moral people that material success has been given to them in greater measure than has fallen to the share of other modern peoples ... They believe that they have a covenant with the Deity, and all the privileges and also all the obligations that go with the position – all this favor having come to them through their merits of good principle and acceptable conduct.[23]

The implications of being a people endowed with superior morality are easy to deduce: go forth and redeem peoples of inferior moral quality who have no covenant with the divinity,[24] bring them into the blessed condition of Anglo-Saxondom. Social Darwinism helped the notion of racial superiority, but it is the "commanding sense of right or wrong" and his "instinct for governing" that make the Anglo-Saxon the truly imperial race.[25]

By the end of the century, both the imperial and civilizing destiny of Anglo-Saxonism triumphant and the presence of significant blood ties required that England and the United States join forces in a bond that could no longer be denied. Some emphasized the kinship of blood, others pointed to political requirements. In a novel written shortly after the Spanish-American War, the author introduces a Russian character, who says:

> For years, in fact, since the American-Spanish War of 1898, England and America have been bound together by a sentimental semi-alliance. They have acted so often together since that time when danger threatened either one, that we in Russia know or feel sure that should Great Britain resist our program eastward, and need help, the Americans would possibly hang in the wind for a while, but in the end, with their absurdly sentimental cry 'Blood is thicker than water' would join the English."[26]

Others, although not disclaiming Anglo-Saxon ties, were more inclined to reflect on the political feasibility of an alliance. Brooks Adams pointed to the necessity of Anglo-American solidarity in 1898, when, commenting on

the Spanish-American War, he noted that the rising German might was a
threat to England. The support of the United States was vital to England in
the event of an attack by a continental coalition led by Germany. Thus
Great Britain, he believed,

> may ... be not inaptly described as a fortified outpost of the Anglo-Saxon
> race, overlooking the eastern continent and resting upon America ... But,
> if the United States is essential to England, England is essential to the
> United States, in the face of enemies who fear and hate us, and who, but
> for her, would already have fleets upon our shores.[27]

The naval strength of England had a strong appeal, needless to say, for
Admiral Mahan, the theorist of the strategic importance of sea power, who
in 1894 wrote an essay on the "Possibilities of an Anglo-American Reunion"
where he argued the opportunity of a strong Anglo-American union from
the geographical position of the two countries, both dependent upon the
sea.[28]

In the new century, the metamorphosis of Anglo-Saxonism from a racial
to a linguistic conception that could be applied also to people of different
origins who spoke English and lived under Anglo-Saxon institutions, is
reflected in the occasional use of the expression "English-speaking peoples"
in lieu of "Anglo-Saxon," which became more frequent with the approach
and then the outbreak of World War I and was to continue even after the
war.[29]

The idea was also broached that the United States should join with Great
Britain and the peoples of the Dominions and of the British Empire in
forming a great Pan-Anglian Union.[30] It is not quite clear in the literature of
the early twentieth century whether this Union should take the form of a
binding alliance or of a real federation of free states. Some stated that the
United States would consider the idea of joining with England for the
purpose of defining a common international policy only after the transformation of the British Empire into a Commonwealth of free nations.[31] Some
American commentators on current events insisted that the United States
should be the natural site of any future Pan-Anglian Federation. The seat of
empire had been moving West ever since the thirteen English colonies had
become a new nation: already the white population of the British Empire
was only a little more than one-half of that of the United State.[32] As the
change of the British Dominions into a Commonwealth of free nations
approached, the idea of a Pan-Anglian federation gained more supporters.

The advent of Pan-Anglism marked the end of Teutonism: even if a union
of all peoples with Teutonic roots "was bruited now and then by individual
scholars and publicists, and such expansive statesmen as Cecil Rhodes,
Joseph Chamberlain, and Theodore Roosevelt,"[33] the concept of common
descent from the ancient Teutons vanished. Preoccupied with the progress
and threat of modern Germany, English and Americans increasingly

concentrated on the high mission of the modern Pan-Angles. Germans, for their part, had been busy developing an aggressive brand of Pan-Germanism that focussed on the high mission of German-speaking people wherever they lived. A Pan-German League (*Allgemeiner Deutscher Verband*) was founded in 1890 "to support and aid German endeavors in all lands where members of the German people must struggle to retain their individuality" and "to promote an energetic German policy of might in Europe and overseas; above all, to carry forward the German colonial movement to tangible results."[34] Thus Teutonism was torn asunder by the pull of different nationalisms and contrasting political alignments, and turned into Pan-Anglism at one end of the political spectrum and Pan-Germanism at the other.[35] The scene was being set for the clash of powers of World War I "and in 1917 the final alignment of forces would cause no surprise."[36]

The growing apprehensions about Germany found their way into much of the literature on current public affairs, often taking the form of a comparison between different ways of going about the business of building colonies. The fears kindled by German expansion overseas should have been assuaged by reflecting, as did the Frenchman Demolins, that while the Anglo-Saxons were undoubtedly "an absorbing race," capable of moulding in its own cast the peoples it conquered, and therefore destined to fruitful expansion, the Germans let themselves be absorbed by the local elements wherever they went[37] and thus did not create new markets for their industrial products. Private initiative and self-government were the great boon of the Anglo-Saxon, a gift that he carried to other people wherever he founded colonies.[38]

Here we come to the last item of my paper, the Anglo-Saxon commitment to individual initiative in economics and to self-government through representation in politics, in one word to the Anglo-American notion of democracy. "There is no democracy in Germany as we have it here in America," it was affirmed when war had already broken out in Europe.[39] Germany suffered from over legislation, statism and government-controlled economy. Yet, the rise of Russia and Japan to the status of great powers, might have caused Anglo-Saxonists and Pan-Angles alike to view with less apprehension the growth of the German empire. In fact, antagonism toward Germany might have seemed justified were it not for the fear of those other two powers. In the case of threats by peoples belonging to civilizations so different from the Anglo-Saxon, such as the Slav and the Asiatic, Germany would seem a "natural and civilization ally." Thoughts of the Yellow Peril brought vividly back to mind the common roots of Germans and Anglo-Saxons, for "German blood has enriched ours for fifteen hundred years," just as Pan-Angle ideals of religious and political freedom and Pan-Angle language and laws had originated in Germany.[40] If the Pan-Angles were united and strong, Germany would no longer be a source of danger to them; rather, it could become a political ally, "a buffer state for the Pan-Angles against Russia."[41] The foreign affairs editorialist of the London *Times* had

expressed a similar view on an alliance with Germany at a meeting of the
Victorian Club in 1903, in dealing with the menace of Russia on the northern
frontier of India:

> There is only one nation in Europe which can be utilized as a make-
> weight against Russia and that is Germany, and we have encouraged
> Germany to acquire an interest in the continent of Asia, and to put
> money into new railways through Asia Minor, which will eventually make
> a big southern railway line, connecting Asia with Europe. In such case ...
> we must work in with Germany as part of our general policy ...[42]

For all the difference in the systems of government, for all the vaunted
Anglo-Saxon love for democracy, constitutional rights, individualism, and
for all the deprecated German statism and authoritarianism, establishing a
community of interests with Germany still seemed attractive to sectors of
Anglo-American public opinion preoccupied with the growing presence of
Russia, Japan and China on the international scene. In the light of
Germany's potential role as a bulwark against Russia, her total defeat in the
coming war seemed as much of a calamity as her victory for the Pan-
Anglian,[43] because "the German point of view would be intolerable to a
Pan-Angle, but there is no reason for assuming that this bureaucratic
country may not develop a truly representative form of government."[44]

While I leave for another occasion the discussion of the somewhat
prophetic ring of these words, certainly not if applied to the defeated and
humiliated Germany that emerged from World War I but to developments
subsequent to World War II, I would like to conclude this paper with some
short remarks on Anglo-Saxonism.

It seems incontestable that this "invention" of national identity had
acquired in the second half of the nineteenth century a racial content, and a
strongly racist potential. It was the ethnic mixture existing in Great Britain's
Dominions and Empire that prevented this identity mark, concocted from
facts and legends, from serving as an unfailing racial discriminant. In the
United States, matters were different. The diplomatic rapprochement with
England, the entrance of the United States on the international scene, and
the gradual renouncing of isolationism, led the United States to an
expansionist foreign policy that implied the acceptance of the possibility of
performing a "civilizing," anglo-saxonizing mission toward peoples of different biological descent (the debates whether the Constitution followed
the flag are an indication of contrasting views on this question). In internal
matters, there was much less faith in the "absorbing" quality of the Anglo-
Saxon. After the 1880s, the growing inflow of immigrants from Latin and
Slavic countries led to nativism and to an adherence to the racial significance of Anglo-Saxonism, that became a banner for restrictionism. The
Quota Acts of the 1920s bore the imprint of a belief that biological descent
posed an insurmountable obstacle to the integration of peoples from alien

stocks into the national American fabric, which had been woven by people of Nordic descent. It took over forty years to abolish the quota system and even longer to rediscuss questions of national identity.

The dangers of potentially racist notions of national identity are best of all exemplified by the developments of Pan-Germanism. Both Pan-Germanism and Anglo-Saxonism, later called Pan-Anglism, have been said to be nationalistic offshoots of Teutonism.[45] They followed, however, different roads. The one which led from Pan-Germanism to Nazist racism has been described by George Mosse, and it is almost impossible to add new insights to his masterful book.[46] I shall only emphasize one point: Anglo-Saxonism, both in England and in the United States, can be traced back to roots that lie in the exaltation of Saxon liberties in seventeenth-century England and in the presumed existence of an "ancient Constitution." As such, its origins were politico-institutional. The real question was not national identity, since England was unquestionably a nation state, but the limits of the king's prerogative versus the ancient (Saxon) rights of Parliament. In Germany, from the very start the recourse to the ancient tribal virtues of the Germans exalted by Tacitus did not focus on institutions and rights but on the search for a *Volkgeist* that transcended the reality of political fragmentation of the German cultural nation. German philology added to the search for the *Volk* the dimension of Aryanism. This added component introduced into the potentially racist mixture of Teutonism that most fearful ingredient, purity of blood. That Anglo-Saxonism did not follow the same path was due to the different political contexts in which English and American nationalisms developed and, to a large but as yet indeterminable extent, to that conceptual change from Anglo-Saxonism to Anglo-Saxondom, to "English-speaking peoples" and eventually to Pan-Anglism which I have tried to describe in this paper. For this salutary transformation, Great Britain and the United States could perhaps thank that "true Saxon suspicion of a theory" that was indeed an important component of their national character, their attachment to the liberal political tradition, and above all that "admixture of peoples" that lived within the expanded boundaries of Anglo-Saxondom.

Notes

1. *The Anglo Saxon Review: A Quarterly Miscellany*, vols. 1–10 (June 1899–September 1901).

2. See especially Lionel Gelber, *The Rise of Anglo-American Friendship. A Study in World Politics, 1898–1906* (New York: Oxford University Press, 1938; repr. Hamden, Connecticut: Archon Books, 1966); H.C. Allen, *Great Britain and the United States. A History of Anglo- American Relations (1783–1952)* (New York: St. Martin's Press, 1955); Samuel F. Bemis, *The United States as a World Power. A Diplomatic History, 1900–1955* (New York: Holt, 1955).

3. Stuart Anderson, *Race and Rapprochement: Anglo-Saxonism and Anglo-*

94 REFLECTIONS ON AMERICAN EXCEPTIONALISM

American Relations, 1895–1904 (Rutherford, New Jersey: Fairleigh Dickinson University Press and London-Toronto: Associated University Presses, 1981); Michael Hunt, *Ideology and U.S. Foreign Policy* (New Haven and London: Yale University Press, 1987); Serge Ricard and Hélène Christol, eds., *Anglo-Saxonism in U.S. Foreign Policy: The Diplomacy of Imperialism, 1899–1919* (Université de Provence, 1991).

4. John Hare, *St. Edward's Ghost: or, Anti-Normanism* (London, 1667); Asa Briggs, *Saxons, Normans and Victorians* (London: The Hastings and Bexhill Branch of the Historical Association, 1966); Christopher Hill, "The Norman Yoke," *Puritanism and Revolution: Studies in the Interpretation of the English Revolution of the 17th Century* (London: Secker & Warburg, 1958); Ibid., *Intellectual Origins of the English Revolution* (Oxford: Oxford University Press – Clarendon Press, 1965); Richard T. Vann, "The Free Anglo-Saxons: A Historical Myth," *Journal of the History of Ideas* 19 (June, 1958): 259–272.

5. Bernard Bailyn, *The Ideological Origins of the American Revolution* (Cambridge, Massachusetts: Harvard University Press – Belknap Press, 1967); Gordon S. Wood, *The Creation of the American Republic, 1776–1787* (Chapel Hill: University of North Carolina Press, 1969). In Italian, see my essay "Il mito della democrazia sassone nella cultura politica americana," in Anna Maria Martellone, Elisabetta Vezzosi, eds., *Fra Toscana e Stati Uniti. Il discorso politico nell'età della Costituzione Americana* (Firenze: Olschki, 1989): 71–85.

6. Thomas F. Gossett, *Race: The History of an Idea in America* (New York: Schocken Books, 1968[2]) (1963: Southern Methodist University Press, Dallas, Texas); Reginald Horsman, "Origins of Racial Anglo-Saxonism in Great Britain Before 1850," *Journal of the History of Ideas* 37 (July–September 1976): 387–410; Ibid., *Race and Manifest Destiny: The Origins of American Racial Anglo-Saxonism* (Cambridge, Massachusetts and London: Harvard University Press, 1981).

7. Michael D. Biddiss, *Images of Race* (New York: Holmes & Meier, 1979), 27.

8. W. Stull Holt, ed., *Historical Scholarship in the United States, 1876–1901, as Revealed in the Correspondence of Herbert Baxter Adams* (Baltimore, Maryland: The Johns Hopkins Press, 1938; repr. Westport, Connecticut, 1970); Biddis, *Images of Race*; Gossett, *Race*; John Higham, *Strangers in the Land: Patterns of American Nativism* (New Brunswick, New Jersey: Rutgers University Press, 1955; repr. New York: Atheneum, 1963); Edward N. Saveth, *American Historians and European Immigrants, 1875–1925* (New York: Russell, 1965[2]) (1948); Anna Maria Martellone, "Il modello tedesco nelle Università americane: Herbert Baxter Adams e John W. Burgess," in *Tiziano Bonazzi (a cura di), Potere e nuova razionalità: alle origini delle scienze della società e dello stato in Germania e negli Stati Uniti,* (Bologna: Clueb, 1982), 103–134.

9. C. Brooke-Cunningham, *Anglo-Saxon Unity, and Other Essays* (London: Selwin and Blount, 1925), 140–141.

10. Edmond Demolins, *Anglo Saxon Superiority: To What It Is Due*, English translation by Louis Bert-Lavigne (*A quoi tient la superiorité des Anglo-Saxons*, (Paris: Firmin Didot, 1897), (New York: R.F. Fenno & Co., s.d.), xiv.

11. "The Anglo-Saxon Race," in *North American Review* (1851): 42.

12. In Henry Adams, *Essays in Anglo-Saxon Law* (Boston, 1876), 55.

13. Dexter A. Hawkins, *Anglo-Saxon Race: Its History, Character, and Destiny. An Address Before the Syracuse University at Commencement, June 21, 1875* (New York: Nelson & Phillips, 1875), 18.

14. *The Anglo-Saxon Review*, 1 (June 1899): 244–245.

15. Barbara M. Solomon, *Ancestors and Immigrants: A Changing New England Tradition* (Cambridge, Massachusetts: Harvard University Press, 1956); Gossett, *Race*.

16. William S. Howe, *War and Progress; The Growth of the World Influence of the Anglo-Saxon* (Boston: L. Phillips, 1918), 15. It was thought that the melting-pot theory as such was not sound and that it would take two or three thousand years before it worked out, see Brooke Cunningham, *Anglo-Saxon Unity*, 102.

17. Frederick Chapman, "The Changed Significance of 'Anglo-Saxon,'" in *Education* 20 (February 1900): 364–369.

18. Ibid., 367.

19. Ibid., 368.

20. The interest in Anglo-Saxonism among the general public at the turn of the century was such that the Librarian of the Library of Congress decided to answer the many written queries on the subject by printing a list of selected books and articles, see U.S. Library of Congress, *Select List of References on Anglo-Saxon Interests*, compiled under the direction of Appleton P.C. Griffin (Washington: Government Printing Office, 1903); U.S. Library of Congress, *Select List of References on Anglo-Saxon Interests*, compiled under the direction of Appleton P. C. Griffin (Washington: Government Printing Office, 1906). The first list comprised about twenty books published in the United States and Great Britain as well as ninety two articles which had appeared in important periodicals (almost all American); the enlarged edition of 1906 listed forty one more books and 114 articles.

21. Aline Gorren, *Anglo-Saxons and Others* (New York: Charles Scribner's Sons, 1900), 2.

22. Ibid., 6.

23. Ibid., 8–9.

24. Ernest L. Tuveson, *The Redeemer Nation. The Idea of America's Millennial Role* (Chicago: University of Chicago Press, 1968).

25. Russell Thayer, *England and America. Speech of the Hon. M.Russell Thayer, at the dinner given May 27, 1898, by Citizens of Philadelphia to Captain Robert C. Clipperton*, 8.

26. Benjamin Rush Davenport, *Anglo-Saxons, Onward! A Romance of the Future* (Cleveland, Ohio: O. Hubbel Publishers, 1898), 13.

27. Brooks Adams, "The Spanish War and the Equilibrium of the World," in *Forum* 25 (August, 1898): 641–650, here 644–645.

28. Quoted in George L. Beer, *The English-Speaking Peoples* (New York, 1917), vii.

29. Hugh Chisholm, *Anglo-American Relations vis-a-vis the other great Powers. An Address Given by Mr. H.C. of the London Times, Editor of the Encyclopedia Britannica, at a Special Meeting of the Victorian Club, on January 20, 1903* (1903); Sinclair Kennedy, *The Pan-Angles. A Consideration of the Federation of the Seven English-Speaking Nations* (London-Bombay-Calcutta-Madras:

Longmans, Green & Co, 1914); Darwin P. Kingsley, *The United English Nations* (Burlington, Vermont, 1916); W. H. Gardiner, *The Solidarity of English-Speaking Sea Power* (1919); John Randolph Dos Passos, *The Anglo-Saxon Century and the Unification of the English-Speaking Peoples* (New York and London: G. P. Putnam's Sons, 1903); Wilbur Thirkield, *The English-Speaking Peoples Will They Fail in Their Mission to the World* (New York, Cincinnati: The Abingdon Press, 1926); F. H. Bentley, *The English Speaking Peoples in the Post-War World* (Atlantic Foundation, 1943). See also the *Bulletins of the American English-Speaking Union* (1920–1924). The Union was incorporated in the United States in 1920 and it worked in close connection with the English-Speaking Union of the British Commonwealth.

30. Kennedy, *The Pan-Angles*.
31. George Burton Adams, *The British Empire, and a League of Peace*, (New Haven, Connecticut: The Harty Musch Press, 1917).
32. Kingsley, *The United English Nations*, 5, 20.
33. Carlton J. H. Hayes, *A Generation of Materialism, 1871–1900* (New York: Harper & Row, 1963 (1941), 275. Hayes makes useful remarks on the variety of "Pan" movements of the period, 275–277.
34. Quoted in Hayes, *A Generation of Materialism*, 276.
35. Ibid., 275.
36. Gelber, *The Rise of Anglo-American Friendship*, 135.
37. Demolins, *Anglo Saxon Superiority*, xxix.
38. Ibid., xxx.
39. John L. Brandt, *Anglo-Saxon Supremacy; or, Race Contributions to Civilization … with an Introduction by James W. Lee* (Boston: R. G. Badger, 1915), 83
40. Kennedy, *The Pan-Angles*, 154.
41. Ibid., 155–156.
42. Chisholm, *Anglo-American Relations*, 10.
43. Kennedy, *The Pan-Angles*, 155.
44. Loc. cit.
45. Hayes, *A Generation of Materialism*, 275–277.
46. George L. Mosse, *The Crisis of German Ideology: Intellectual Origins of the Third Reich* (New York: Grosset & Dunlap, 1964).

7

Democracy Goes Imperial: Spanish Views of American Policy in 1898

Sylvia L. Hilton

Immediately after the war of 1898 leaders in all spheres of Spanish life tried to justify their attitudes and actions during the crisis. Spanish historians until very recently have not made many serious attempts to overcome the tendency to write judgemental works, which attribute responsibilities for the "disaster." This paper will review recent Spanish contributions to the historiography of the 1898 crisis.

The Spanish Government: Foreign and Colonial Policies

The chronic constitutional and administrative problems of Spanish political life in the 19th century are universally recognized by Spanish historians as a grave weakness which, together with the economic and cultural back-wardness of Spain in comparison with other European powers and the United States, adversely affected foreign and colonial policies. There was a general subordination of foreign and colonial policies to internal problems, and a lack of political direction and of continuity, both in programmes of naval construction and modernization and in the much-needed reforms of the army.

Warnings were not lacking regarding foreign threats to Spanish overseas possessions, but the government was either unwilling or unable to react and plan adequately. Elizalde stresses that domestic problems determined the total absence of an effective policy in the Pacific, a key area of late-nineteenth-century imperialist rivalries for coaling stations, naval bases, raw materials, markets and colonies. Spain's only aim was to conserve her possessions of the Philippine, Mariana, Caroline and Palaos Islands.

Spain should have been alerted to imperialist aspirations in the Pacific by the German attempt to control the Carolines in 1885. Another warning, a clear prelude to the Spanish-American conflict of 1898, occurred in the late 1880s and early 1890s when Spanish authorities clashed with the natives of Ponape (present Pohnpei, Caroline Islands), influenced by American Methodist missionaries.

Robles underlines that all Spanish political parties supported the nineteenth-century policy of isolation, and that this left Spain friendless and defenseless in the face of colonial rebellions and international aggressions. However, Olivié feels it is unfair to blame the government for Spanish international isolation and a predominantly defensive policy. He argues that there was no real alternative because no other nation was at all interested in an alliance with Spain. Nevertheless, he does feel that the government could have effectively checked American expansion if it had enacted timely reforms in the Spanish colonial regime.

The United States and the Cuban War of 1895

No doubts are entertained by most Spanish authors about the fact that the United States harbored a desire to annex or otherwise control Cuba, as well as to bring the Caribbean and Central America under American influence, long before the 1890s.

The activities of Narciso López in 1848–1851 have been studied by Saiz who analyzes them in the context of proslavery ideology and support for American annexation of Cuba and by Manzano, who traces the echo of his expeditions in the New York press, while Robles examines the diplomatic aspects of American interest in Cuba and Latin America in the 1880s and 1890s. However, Navarro and Serrano give far more long-term importance to the internal evolution of Cuban and Spanish affairs, giving the impression that American intervention was, in the definitive analysis, of secondary relevance in the protracted story of Cuban independence.

American moral and material support to the Cuban rebels of 1895, in the form of favorable press coverage, money and supplies, usually figures prominently in Spanish accounts. Robles explains that part of the reason for Weyler's unpopular concentration policy was to prevent any support on land for rebel expeditions organized in the United States, and analyzes in detail the diplomatic exchanges in which the Spanish government defended itself against increasingly incisive American accusations of inhumanity and devastation in repressing the Cuban rebellion. He pays particular attention to the difficulties, inherent and perceived, in the American offers to send aid to suffering Cuban civilians and in the activities of Clara Barton, president of the American Red Cross.

Robles also gives importance to the role played by American Masonic organizations, which undermined Catholicism while supporting political separatism in Cuba through its Cuban affiliates. By contrast, Ayala finds no evidence that the Masonic lodges of Spanish obedience in Puerto Rico were at all involved in separatist movements. He does not, however, exclude possible separatist activities of the rival lodges of Cuban-United States origin. For his part, Andrés-Gallego studies the role of Masonic groups in the independence of the Philippines.

Serrano Suárez briefly studies Cuban emigrations to Key West and Tampa, where tobacco factories afforded not only a source of income but places to meet and to hold public readings and debates on revolutionary ideas and tactics, and where many Cuban revolutionary newspapers were published. He points out that Cuban exiles in New York were more strongly inclined to support United States annexation of Cuba, an idea that Martí feared could seriously weaken the independence movement.

Reformists in Spain and moderates in Cuba had long proposed the establishment of Cuban autonomy, an idea that United States governments had repeatedly supported. However, Navarro holds that home rule had no chance of succeeding after 1895 because the Cuban insurgents wanted nothing short of total independence while Unionists and Peninsular Spaniards, as well as the army, rejected the reforms. Calleja concurs, stressing that the military situation in Cuba was deplorable, which made the "do-or-die" attitude of conservative forces all the more absurd.

Domingo offers new data on the participation of Spaniards in the Cuban Army of Liberation. She has so far identified 473 men who joined the Cuban ranks. The great majority were simple soldiers, and considerable numbers were single, farmers, and Canary Islanders.

The Spanish Army

The Spanish Army was antiquated, inefficient, costly, unfairly recruited, poorly trained, badly fed and paid except in the higher ranks, had far too many officers, and wielded far too much political power. Salas Larrazábal agrees that the Army was badly in need of reforms and suffered from internal divisions, but adds that the Army, though not so affected by technological and industrial factors as the Navy, was equally afflicted by political and administrative problems.

Fernández Muñiz studies the system of recruitment of reinforcements for the Spanish army in Cuba, which contemporaries like Pi y Margall denounced because it affected poor families which were unable to pay the 2,000 pesetas to avoid service overseas. This system was frequently criticized in the opposition press throughout the war, but with particular bitterness from the middle of 1896. As a consequence of the social injustice and great dangers of military service overseas, Serrano has documented a growing tendency in the years 1895–1899 to go missing in order to evade service or to desert. Pérez García offers information about the military veterinarians sent to Cuba between 1887 and 1898, together with some data on regulations and the system of drawing lots to cover vacancies.

From the late 1880s the government, casting about for ways to make economies, proposed to cut military expenditures. This led to an intense controversy in which military hierarchies blindly clung to their autonomy and budgets, rejecting all criticism, in turn severely criticizing the political class, and warning of the dangers of leaving Spain with insufficient defensive resources, not only in the event of direct aggression but even to maintain with dignity Spanish neutrality. No-one seriously offered a constructive, cooperative plan for structural reform, and the debate, full of personal insults, sarcasms and threats, was not only sterile but created a climate which prevented any calm, practical discussion of policies and budget management.

This attitude can still be traced in contemporary Spanish historiography. The version of the Cuban war given by Salas Carmena, for example, indiscriminately praises all military personnel while condemning the government and politicians in general, the lack of resources, and the press.

The Spanish Navy and Merchant Marine

Spanish naval historians also commonly seek political factors to explain the inadequate growth of Spanish naval power. These include the channeling of funds away from the Navy into more short-term political schemes, frequent changes of posts among Spanish naval officers, and a widespread ignorance among politicians of maritime affairs. Vega feels that political changes adversely affected the necessary continuity of naval construction plans because liberal politicians preferred to give contracts to national shipbuilders, even though they were slower and more expensive, while conservatives sought to acquire ships quickly and as cheaply as possible, even if it meant taking business to foreign firms. Also often mentioned is the discriminatory treatment received by naval personnel in comparison with the Army.

Salas Larrazábal underscores the absence of a global political and strategic plan, which he feels was the responsibility of the government, but he also concedes that naval and military officers were in positions of political authority and therefore were largely responsible for shortcomings in Spanish defense policies. He suggests, in fact, that despite evident weaknesses, Spain had sufficient resources to create and maintain naval and military forces which could have effectively dissuaded the United States from intervening in Spanish colonial affairs. Spanish naval inferiority in comparison with American forces in the years leading up to the war is often stressed in the light of the rapid, costly and controversial changes in naval construction and warfare brought about by advances in the use of iron and steel, steam power, magnetism, electricity, and modern explosives.

Parliamentary approval in 1887 of a program of naval construction, sponsored by Rodríguez Arias, is usually put forward as a step in the right direction, but most authors lament the inadequacy of funds, of technological and industrial resources, of political commitment, and of overall planning, all of which caused delays and frustrated the plan.

Llorca, however, contends that the program was controversial, and even if it had been fully developed the outcome of the 1898 conflict would not have been substantially affected because Spanish planning had not solved the problems of phasing out "floating scrapiron," homogenizing the Navy, and above all ensuring that Spanish ships could count on several coaling stations en route to the Caribbean and the Philippines.

Rodríguez González, Vega and Téllez explain that the Spanish plan, inspired by the doctrines of the French *Jeune Ecole* to concentrate on building large but swift armed cruisers backed up by torpedo boats, contrasted with the American preference for the more traditional and slower armoured battleships. But whereas Salas Larrazábal, Vega and Téllez consider that the Spanish plan was a mistake, for cruisers could not confront battleships, Rodríguez holds that this difference in conception made it extremely difficult to discern which of the two forces was the stronger, at least on paper. In support of this view he cites several foreign and Spanish authorities that expressed their opinion in 1895–1898 that the Spanish and American navies were of similar strength.

Téllez points out the need for a more careful assessment of comparative naval power. Incorrect classification of ships provides inexact quantitative data, while qualitative aspects such as the real operational situation of ships seriously affected actual naval strengths.

The inferior strength of the Spanish fleets at the moment of truth is not generally disputed, and most authors offer a long list of factors – political, administrative, economic, technological, strategic, and social – to explain this fact, and in the process, seem to support the notion that Spanish defeat was rooted in grave structural deficiencies and therefore entirely inevitable. Téllez goes so far as to say that even if Spain had had the right naval strategy and built battleships in the 1890s, the inauguration of the era of the dreadnought in 1905 would have sealed the fate of unsolved colonial problems.

Vega concludes his detailed technical description of Spanish and American naval forces between 1865 and 1898 with the consideration that fundamental differences are discernible only in the 1890s, not before, and that the three factors which gave decisive superiority to the United States were a strong national industry, a sense of purpose inherent in Mahan's doctrine, and the decision to concentrate on armored battleships.

By contrast, Rodríguez González points out that the exact timing of the conflict was disadvantageous to Spain because only a few months later her Navy would have been very much stronger as ships in the final stages of construction or under repairs became available for active service. He stresses that Spanish ships were not antiquated and of scarce military value, as has often been stated, but that they had been severely punished by years of hard service in campaigns in Cuba and diverse places in the Pacific, a point with which Llorca concurs.

In this generally negative assessment of the Spanish Navy, whether the focus is long-term or short-term, Spanish sailors and naval officers are not only spared any criticism but are praised for their dedication, professionalism, discipline, zeal, efficiency despite material failings, and heroism. The accusation made in 1898 that Spanish sailors were incompetent and even cowardly is rejected as the result of confused public opinion, misinformed by an irresponsible or malicious press.

Nevertheless, Vega, although attempting to praise the naval engineers on Spanish ships at the end of the nineteenth century, ends up showing that they were inadequately trained, with very little theoretical schooling; they were treated badly by other naval officers, their work load on board was extenuating and increasingly complex, and their insufficient numbers made it necessary to employ engineers of unproven qualifications from the merchant marine. For their part Salas Larrazábal and Téllez concede that Spanish naval officers contributed to the strategic mistakes made in global design of naval policy, and also committed tactical errors during the actual combat phase of the conflict.

The end of protectionism of the Spanish shipbuilding industry in 1868–1869 led to a rapid increase of steamships in the Spanish merchant marine but, as Llorca points out, they were of foreign construction and this definitively established Spanish dependence on foreign expertise and resources.

Nevertheless, the substantial maritime resources in private hands were valuable aids to Spanish naval and military operations in times of crisis. The role of the Transatlantic Company in transporting troops and supplies, in repeatedly breaking through the American blockade of Cuba, and in repatriating Spanish troops after the war have been afforded some attention although Martín Berrio concludes the merchant marine "was employed with incredible ineptness," without giving any clue as to how its use could have been improved.

The Spanish Press and Public Opinion

According to Núñez Spanish anarchist newspapers manifested indecisive and ambiguous attitudes about the Cuban war. They felt they should not support the rebellion which, after all, sought only political independence and would, in fact, only replace one set of capitalist exploiters by another equally oppressive for the Cuban proletariat. They argued that bourgeois patriotism, whether Spanish or Cuban, was of no interest to the working class.

Some Spanish anarchists did, however, sympathize with the rebels, or at least with the idea of armed rebellion, and gradually moved nearer the opinion which was expressed in Spanish-language papers published in Tampa and New York that Cuban separatism was only the beginning of a popular movement which would evolve into a full-blown social revolution. On the whole, though, American aid to the Cuban rebellion was bitterly resented, and gave rise to the generalized use of the image of a pig in the Spanish press to represent the dirty conduct of the United States. Likewise, when American military intervention seemed imminent the Spanish press in 1898 is generally recognized to have become irrationally and irresponsibly belligerent, patriotic and optimistic about the victorious outcome of an armed conflict.

Bolado and Serrano analyze Spanish press coverage of the Cuban war in the context of Spanish political rivalries. The liberal opposition press accused the Cánovas government of yielding dishonorably to Yankee pressures, which forced conservative newspapers to hotly deny any defeatism or weakness in the face of American demands. As a result there was very little press support for a practical, conciliatory policy, and the sense of offended national honor grew irresistibly in the face of repeated American interference in Cuba, considered not as a colony but as part of Spanish national territory. Only *The Socialist* remained steadfastly pacifist throughout the crisis. The Spanish Socialist Workers' Party, in fact, managed to overcome its internal divisions by late 1897 and launch a national campaign designed to tap popular hostility against the war, which, although it did not affect the course of the crisis, did afford the Socialists considerable political credit in post-war years.

By contrast, ultra-conservative Carlists maintained throughout their belligerent, imperialist rhetoric, while left-wing Republicans (except Pi y Margall) thought that, by adopting a patriotic attitude in support of Spanish pacification and conservation of Cuba in the face of insurgency and American intervention, they would be in a better position to take over the government in the event of a foreseeable disaster and collapse of the monarchy. Catalonian and Basque businessmen also supported the government's policy in Cuba because they feared losing their commercial privileges, but Catalonian and Basque regionalists opposed the war on the grounds that it represented central government oppression of their respective nationalities.

Sevilla analyzes Andalusian press coverage of American intervention in Cuba, and finds that newspapers of different ideological profiles tended to criticize the United States at all stages of the crisis. Early opinions warned against American interests in the island, denouncing their support of Cuban insurgency, but did not quite believe that the government would go as far as to intervene directly in what was considered an internal matter of the Spanish monarchy. At the start of the war American military power was universally scorned and, when the Spanish defeat became evident, the United States was condemned for abandoning its national principles of freedom and democracy to become an imperial power. However, the Andalusian press was apparently unaware of the growth and scope of American imperialist aspirations until the war was almost over.

Whereas some authors have maintained that the press was misinformed about respective naval strengths, Vega contends that this was not so and categorically states that complete and correct information about both the Spanish and the American navies was available. Rodríguez González also insists that naval affairs had long been a pet subject of the press and that it gave ample proof of access to the best sources of information. Its sudden change of attitude on the eve of the war must, he feels, be put down to an emotional, patriotic reaction in the face of unwarranted aggression, and bearing in mind that Spanish naval inferiority was not so evident at the time as it became in hindsight.

For his part, Rivadulla questions the degree to which the imperialist discourse penetrated in Spanish mentality in the 1890s. On this subject,

Robles repeatedly states that belligerently patriotic military opinion was a grave obstacle to the government's desperate efforts to avoid a war with the United States. Hernández Sánchez-Barba claims that conflicts with Germany and Morocco in 1885 and 1893 sparked off popular patriotism in Spain, despite the negative image of an army used by the government to repress regionalist and working class movements, while Schulze agrees that the Spanish press reflected an emotional popular bellicosity when Spain and Germany clashed over possession of the Carolines. Robles also affirms that the Spanish patriotic response in 1898 to imminent war with the United States was unanimous, except for the Stock Exchange. Serrano, too, speaks of Spanish "Jingoism," and the very decisive role played by the Catholic Church in favor of the maintenance of the existing colonial order, supporting, if necessary, the recourse to war. Ruiz Sánchez uncritically summarizes the ideas of the archbishop of Seville, Marcelo Spínola, as intensely patriotic, belligerent, anti-American, anti-Protestant, and anti-Masonic.

However heavy Spanish losses in the Cuban war, the result not only of military actions but of tropical diseases, unsanitary conditions, and malnutrition, produced such a degree of exhaustion in Spanish opinion by 1898 that, according to Elorza, many were relieved by the prospect of American intervention because it would end the war and, with it, Spanish frustration; at the same time it would save Spanish honor since defeat by a stronger foe would be acceptable, even if painful.

Arcas studies the social complexities of the crisis, explaining that McKinley's April 11 message to Congress sparked off a patriotic demonstration in Malaga, initiated by students and urban middle class representatives and directed against the American Consulate. However the popular classes soon swelled the numbers of the demonstrators and began to vent their accumulated anger and frustration against property and symbols of the established social and political order in Spain. In this process, the patriotic and anti-American elements faded.

Finally, Serrano, Andrés, Sevilla and Lasa say there is some evidence that the government misread the national mood, and that a large sector of Spanish society wanted peace at any price, but did not express their opinions for fear of being labeled antipatriotic.

The Growth of American Imperialism
in the Caribbean and the Pacific

The beginnings of American economic imperialism are often presented by Spanish historians as background and not as causes of the war. Companys and Allende, in fact, claim that American mercantile, industrial and financial interests in Cuba were much less to blame than the Jingoes active in politics, the press and the armed forces. By contrast, Morales Padrón contends that American economic imperialism was indeed the predominant factor behind the urge to obtain bases and markets in Cuba, Latin America and the Far

East. Rivadulla also gives great importance to American economic expansion and the demand for active government protection of private property interests abroad as powerful stimuli tothe emergence in the 1890s of American political interventionism in world affairs.

Robles also stresses the growth of militarism as a key factor in American expansionism in the 1890s. He sees the imposition of United States hegemony in the world as a political project designed to strengthen national cohesion in the face of internal tensions resulting from the massive immigration of new and varied (non-Anglo-Saxon, non-Protestant) ethnic groups, the end of the continental "frontier," and lingering resentments rooted in the war of secession.

Robles, Bolado, and Navarro make it clear that the United States could not be indifferent to political unrest and insurgency in Cuba, because the Cuban struggle for independence adversely affected legitimate American economic interests in the island. Spanish and American tariff agreements resulted in the United States absorbing 85% of Cuban production and, in particular, almost the entire sugar and molasses production in the 1880s and 1890s, while Cuba was also an important market for American exports. The United States was then, according to Lasa, Cuba's "commercial metropolis."

The economic depression of 1893 in the United States and the new tariff on imported sugar caused the price of sugar to fall drastically, fomenting unemployment and discontent in Cuba which in turn facilitated the 1895 uprising. On the other hand, the 1895 war not only played havoc with production and trade, but also destroyed valuable American properties and put American lives at risk. Lasa makes an interesting contribution to this subject by analyzing in detail the conflicting commercial interests of the United States, Cuba and Catalonian businessmen.

The 1893 depression also lent force to the idea that the United States must compete with other nations for world markets, at a time when Asia was the most coveted prize. Togores, therefore, feels that the traditional Spanish interpretation of American imperialism in 1898, which gives preeminence to the Cuban crisis, must be revised in order to give full recognition to both Spanish and United States interests in the Pacific.

Only a few Spanish historians give attention to the commercial and strategic value of China and the different archipelagos of the Pacific, and Rivadulla calls the Philippine problem the "Cinderella" of Spanish historiography on the 1898 war, but Togores, Allende and Elizalde suggest that Roosevelt's preparation of Dewey's fleet well before April of 1898 clearly shows that the acquisition of the Philippines was not an improvisation but a goal of prime importance in American imperialist plans. The intervention in Cuba was, therefore, to be the pretext for a much more ambitious imperial expansion.

Several authors have recently focused on American missionary and strategic interests in the Carolines. Elizalde particularly studies American conflicts with Spanish authorities in the island of Kusaie (present Kosrae).

Her main theme is that the crisis of 1898 was not so much a bilateral – Spanish-American – conflict, as the culmination of a period of intense imperialist, expansionist rivalries and of pressures for colonial redistribution, in which other important actors were Britain, Germany, France, and Japan, with minor Russian and Dutch interests. For his part Robles studies in detail the activities of American Methodist missionaries in the Caroline Islands, in the context of native unrest after the Spanish occupation of these islands in 1885 and the diplomatic protests made by the United States government to Spanish authorities in defense of American citizens and property in this archipelago.

Rodao also pays special attention to American interest in the island of Pohnpei. Methodist missionaries cultivated the friendship of the native elite, and lent moral support to native rebels. Rebel leader Henry Nanpei was a Protestant, educated in the United States. The "yellow" press accused Spain of being cruel towards the islanders, envious of Methodist success, and of using "ignorant and sensual" Tagalo sailors as troops. In general, American press coverage of Spanish American conflicts in Pohnpei was much more effective, both in the United States and in Spain, than the Spanish effort. American ships often visited the island (some bringing arms to the rebels), while the constant pressure exerted by American reports and diplomatic notes on the situation severely taxed the Spanish capacity to respond. Spanish authority in Pohnpei was ineffectual, while divisions within the Spanish government weakened its handling of American demands. Authorities in Manila and the Ministry of Overseas Provinces were much less conciliatory than the Ministry of State. In short, Rodao finds many similarities between the Spanish-American conflict in Pohnpei and the crisis of 1898, stressing the overwhelming American capacity to employ varied human and material resources in pursuit of established and potential interests.

Nevertheless, despite evidence to the contrary, Torre and Togores hold that the Spanish government did not perceive the strength of United states imperial aspirations, and was unaware of the American threat to Spanish possessions in the Pacific.

American Public Opinion and the Press

Navarro dispassionately recognizes that, at least at first, American public opinion was divided on the Cuban issue. Some remembered the United States' own struggle for independence and republicanism and sympathized with the Cuban people's fight, while others shuddered at the memory of the Haitian revolution and disliked what they saw as a predominantly Negro rebellion, with little possibility of establishing a viable government, and the wanton destruction of private property.

On the contrary, Companys says that American public opinion was wholly sympathetic to the Cuban rebels from the start. Serrano even concedes that the denunciation of "Spanish barbarism" in Cuba was some-times justified and inspired by sincere humanitarianism.

However most Spanish authors are quick to lay part of the blame for the outbreak of war on the intense campaign waged by the American press, particularly by William Hearst in the *New York Journal* and Joseph Pulitzer in the *New York World*. They condemned the harsh policies and methods of general Weyler in Cuba and all things Spanish, prematurely pronounced the failure of Cuban home rule inaugurated in January of 1898, and irre-sponsibly reported the sinking of the *Maine*. In this, Spanish historians follow the oft-repeated traditional interpretation of many American authors. However, González López-Briones seeks to test this view by analyzing six Indiana newspapers. She concludes that they did not run sensationalist and belligerent articles merely to increase sales, as Hearst and Pulitzer did, but they did cover Cuban affairs on a daily basis, stressing United States economic and strategic interests in the Caribbean, pro-pounding ideas connected with humanitarianism, Social Darwinism, the Monroe Doctrine and Manifest Destiny, favoring Cuban revolutionary propaganda, and giving a negative image of Spain, all of which predisposed public opinion towards American intervention and war with Spain.

Most Spanish authors link the American press to the development of widespread approval of a policy of imperialist expansionism (Jingoism), but the exact nature of this linkage tends to be obscure since, on the one hand, American ambitions in the Caribbean and the Pacific are held to result from economic interests, ideological factors, and political designs conceived and pursued long before 1898, in which case the press would merely be reflecting established American opinion, and on the other hand the press is deemed to have deliberately, cynically and maliciously spawned and cultivated an otherwise weak public demand for American intervention.

What is most perturbing in this subject is the affirmation, implicit in most authors and explicit in Companys, that the American people were naive, ignorant about other nations, ready to believe anything the press affirmed, unable to discern frauds, contradictions and ulterior motives in "yellow" articles, and had an extremely short memory, even when a rival paper denounced a deception.

Allende and Elizalde say there was indeed popular support for an expansionist policy, but not before the 1890s. Companys concludes that public opinion was deceived and mobilized by the sensationalist press, and that this public opinion exerted pressure on the government, but he also says that the government was largely responsible for the belligerent state of mind of the American people. Both Allende and Olivié suggest that McKinley and the Republicans had included Manifest Destiny and the conquest of Cuba in their electoral campaign and had acted accordingly, but then hold that the President was driven to intervention and war by public opinion. This imprecision in the relationship between public opinion, the press, and politics is not, however, a failing exclusive to Spanish historiography, as Louis Perez so ably shows in his analysis of the matter in American works.

The obtention by questionable means and the publication on 9th February 1898 in the *New York Journal* of a private letter written by Spain's ambassador in the United States, Enrique Dupuy de Lôme, together with inflammatory headlines and commentary about the unfortunate diplomat's unflattering opinions of president McKinley and his lack of confidence in the success of peace negotiations with the Cuban rebels, is often cited as proof of Hearst's bad faith. Companys is sympathetic towards Dupuy, and repeatedly disqualifies the American press as immoral, cynical, hypocritical, and belligerent, while noting that no spokesman from the McKinley administration attempted to defuse the situation. Only the diplomatic corps in Washington spoke up to defend freedom of expression in private correspondence. This minor incident gains prominence in explanations of the immediate causes of the war between the United States and Spain because it occurred only 6 days before the explosion of the *Maine*, another incident considered to have been irresponsibly manipulated by the "yellow" press.

Once the war began, Morales Padrón comments bitingly on the frenetic celebration in the American press of the victory at Cavite, even though hardly anyone in the United States knew where the Philippines were.

International Reactions

It is generally felt that American expansionist impulses were long held in check by Great Britain and France but that the shifting balance of power and new interests inhibited European opposition to American moves towards the end of the nineteenth century. Britain feared growing German and Russian power, and also wanted to establish a more cordial relationship with the United States in order to protect her valuable American trade and to consolidate her influence in China. Therefore Britain was inclined to let the United States extend its influence in the Caribbean and Central America. The other European powers for their part were reluctant to intervene without Britain.

Torre analyzes the British posture in depth, evaluating British interests in the Mediterranean (above all, Gibraltar), the Caribbean and the Pacific (particularly China), and seeking to explain the Spanish attempt to obtain British aid in the crisis of 1898. Spain tried to convert her colonial problem into a matter of international concern, in the hope that a coalition led by Britain would check the American bid to become an imperial power. Contrary to some views Torre finds no evidence that Britain prevented the formation of a European coalition hostile to American expansionism, although Lord Salisbury's government clearly showed a desire to maintain Anglo-American relations as cordial as possible. The British interpretation of neutrality was favorable to the United States, and Salisbury's "dying nations" speech reflected his acquiescence in the post-war redistribution of

Spanish colonial possessions to the United States and Germany, as long as British imperial interests were protected. She shows that Britain was willing to contemplate American acquisition of the Philippines, but would have insisted on buying them herself rather than permit any other power to control them.

Sarabia and Hernández Sandoica point out that Torre's interpretation is one of a number of recent Spanish works which reject traditional separations of European or "continental" issues from colonial or "overseas" issues in Spanish historiography, in favor of a more correct global view of Spain's role in world history and of the international context of the crisis of 1898. The seminal Spanish works for this new international focus of the 1898 crisis are those of Pabón and Jover. Similarly, Níguez and Fernández Aponte also develop the theme that the crisis of 1898 was not simply a conflict between Spain and the United States, but a problem of colonial redistribution involving all the powers, old and new, declining and growing, in a context of Darwinist ideas applied to imperial expansion.

For her part, García Sanz studies Italian reactions to Spain's plight, pointing out that while Italy had no special interest in the Caribbean it was concerned that Spain might be forced to make concessions in the Mediterranean and North Africa which could well affect Italian positions in these areas. The Italian perception of the crisis was that the Cuban separatists had ample justification for repudiating Spanish rule. Nevertheless, the Italian government maintained a sympathetic attitude towards Spain, while firmly refusing to lend any strong diplomatic support. Finally, Morales Padrón contends that American imperialist interventions in Chile, Brasil and Venezuela in the 1890s encouraged the growth of pan-Hispanic sentiments in opposition to the perceived Anglo-Saxon prepotence.

United States Government Policy

Theodore Roosevelt is invariably portrayed as an ardent imperialist and impatient interventionist in the Cuban crisis, duly noting the web of influences between Roosevelt and others of like mind – naval historian Alfred Mahan, Under-Secretary of State William R. Day, Senator Henry Cabot Lodge, Admiral George Dewey – and his relationship with Long and McKinley. He is described as being picturesque and dangerous, lacking in scruples, immoral, and a bold opportunist.

Companys, Robles and Bolado are also at pains to show that Consul Lee, who sympathized with the Cuban revolution and favored annexation, deliberately contributed to the growing diplomatic tension on the eve of the war by sending uniformly pessimistic and alarmist reports and by demanding the presence of an American warship in Havana. Calleja describes Lee as being "of excitable character and an eternal supporter of American intervention in Cuba." By contrast, Secretary of the Navy John D. Long, is more palatable to Spanish authors, who see him as more of a pacifist.

American political involvement in Cuban affairs is also admitted by
Padrón and Navarro to have been propitiated by delegations of different
Cuban interest groups, which constantly sought American support for their
own particular ends, while Martín Berrio, for his part, mentions Puerto
Ricans who were in favor of annexation of their island to the United States,
and particularly describes the role of Dr. Julio J. Henna, who offered
information and aid to Lodge, Roosevelt and McKinley in the event of an
American occupation of Puerto Rico.

Cleveland is usually presented by Spanish historians such as Companys as
a strong figure, as is his Spanish counterpart, Cánovas. Most Spanish
authors admit that the policies followed by Cleveland and Olney were
reasonable and consistent enough, declaring American neutrality, plus
American support for a political reform which would bring home rule and
permanent stability to Cuba, despite growing fears that neither Spain nor
the Cuban rebels would be able in the short term to pacify the island. They
do, however, draw attention to the different attitude expressed by the
United States Congress, which in early 1896 pressed for the recognition of
Cuban rebels as belligerents, and consistently favored Cuban independence.

However, other Spanish historians do not concur with this view,
affirming instead that the United States always coveted Cuba and that
Cleveland's manifestations to the contrary were hypocritical. Robles, for
example, says that the Spanish government should have realized that the
electoral defeat of the Democrats in November 1894 would lead Cleveland
to try and distract both Congress and the masses by adopting a more
aggressive foreign policy, in order to regain popularity. Similarly, Morales
Padrón, Salas Larrazábal, and Lasa maintain that McKinley and so-called
imperialist Republicans were, in fact, merely following policy lines
previously defined by Cleveland and Olney.

McKinley's role in the crisis causes Spanish historians some trouble, as it
does their American colleagues. Vega and Togores see him as a pacifist,
pushed into war against his will. Alonso, Robles and Navarro seem to accept
that McKinley remained basically respectful of Spanish sovereignty, neither
showing excessive impatience nor making deliberately belligerent demands,
until the explosion of the *Maine*.

Ñíguez, Companys and Allende agree with Jesús Pabón's opinion that
McKinley was a weak man, with no clear idea of foreign policy, easily swayed
by public opinion, and incapable of avoiding the war, as was his liberal Spanish
opponent, Sagasta. However, Companys also claims, without specifically
accusing the president of duplicity, that all the public posturing and diplomatic
language affirming United States neutrality and friendship contradicted the
evidence of orders and movements of naval forces which denoted the true
belligerency of McKinley's administration in late 1897 and the first weeks
of 1898. Sevilla, Calleja, Bolado and Lasa also suggest that McKinley's
apparent prudence masked his true aggressiveness and the fact that he was
determined to go to war against Spain, and annex or at least occupy Cuba.

Navarro carefully points out that McKinley refused to support Estrada Palma's plan to buy Cuban independence: he refused to recognize the rebel government and at the same time denied any intention of annexing Cuba. These stances and events up to the incorporation of the Platt Amendment in the Cuban constitution lead Navarro to conclude that McKinley's rejection of continued Spanish colonial rule, of full Cuban independence, and of annexation by the United States, left only one alternative: a nominally independent Cuba which in fact would be a colony of the United States.

The *Maine*

The inauguration of the new autonomous Cuban government sparked off violent unrest among Havana's more conservative elements, moving consul Lee to repeat a previous request for the presence of a warship to give some measure of protection or reassurance to American citizens in the city. Accordingly the armoured warship *Maine* entered Havana port on January 25, ostensibly on a courtesy visit of goodwill, but without waiting for Spanish acquiescence.

Calleja describes the battleship in detail, pointing out that it was probably the biggest warship ever to anchor at Havana, and suggesting that its presence was at best a provocation, an opinion with which several other authors concur. Morales Padrón goes further and states that the presence of the *Maine* was meant to impress Spain with American naval power, to encourage the Cuban rebels in their intransigence, to annoy the opposition to the reform, to demoralize moderate elements, and to ensure the failure of Cuban autonomy. Martín Berrio, by contrast, is willing to concede that the visit of the ship was a gesture of friendship.

The explosion of the American ship on the night of February 15, with the loss of 266 American lives, could not possibly have been in Spain's interest and Company explains that the Spanish and Cuban character make it impossible to believe that they could have kept secret the preparations necessary for such a crime. Calleja and Companys stress that many Americans were at first inclined to believe it was an accident, which is Companys' own conclusion. However, the "yellow" press almost immediately accused the Spaniards of using a mine or a torpedo to sink the ship. The official report of the United States commission lent credence to this idea by concluding that an external explosion had caused the internal detonation of the explosives carried by the *Maine*, but Calleja points out weaknesses in the investigation, stressing the American refusal to allow Spanish engineers to cooperate in the inspection of the ship. Prominent in the traditional historiography of the crisis the sinking of the *Maine* still looms large in some Spanish versions, mainly with a view to exposing American bad faith, and/or the inevitability of the war from this point, but other historians such as Navarro give only slight attention to the incident.

Very few American historiographical publications find their way into

Spanish translations, but Rickover's report on the results of his 1976 investigation into the causes of the explosion of the *Maine* was an exception because of his conclusion that it was an accident produced within the ship, and therefore not imputable to criminal negligence or malicious intent on the part of the Spanish (or indeed, American) authorities. Calleja summarizes Rickover's findings, but then goes on to show that the subject has not yet been exhausted.

He notes that John F. Tarpey expressed in 1988 the opinion, shared by many American naval officers, that the *Maine* was sunk by a Spanish mine, but he himself seems inclined to support the theory recently put forward by Navarro Custín that the ship was sunk by a mine invented and designed by the Peruvian engineer Federico Blume during Peru's conflicts with Chile in the 1870s and 1880s. The commander in chief of the Cuban Army of Liberation, Máximo Gómez, met Blume on his 1887 trip to Peru, after which Blume began to show an interest in the Cuban cause. He gave copies of all his work on naval warfare to the Cuban agent Arístides Agüero, who in turn sent the information to the Cuban nationalists in New York. This group, in close collaboration with Italian anarchists residing in the United States, is singled out as being responsible for planting the mine, stressing that the Cuban army was not part of the plot.

The United States Moves towards War with Spain

Morales Padrón pulls no punches and speaks of American bad faith, perfidy, and the use of false pretexts to justify military intervention. He and Bolado accuse McKinley of failing to give moral support to the new Cuban autonomous regime, because its success was not in American interests. Robles also speaks of American arbitrariness, prepotence and faithlessness in this phase, when the Spanish government made every possible effort to reach a peaceful solution.

After the destruction of the *Maine*, and a last offer to buy Cuba in March, McKinley is generally portrayed as moving deliberately towards direct military intervention in the island. His obtention of fifty million dollars from Congress, his orders to the American Navy, his steadfast refusal to recognize Cuban independence, and his peremptory demands of March 27 that Spain abandon the policy of concentration, send relief supplies to the suffering Cuban population, guarantee full home rule, and declare an immediate and unilateral armistice are all interpreted as proof of his intention to intervene. However it is also suggested that McKinley was merely responding to the increased pressures of the "yellow" press and popular clamour for war after the sinking of the *Maine*.

The fact is that, except in a few cases, Spanish historians struggle unhappily with McKinley's attitudes and actions in 1898. Companys, for example, depicts the president's initial reaction as agonizingly anxious, and states that McKinley was both weak and indecisive, was afraid of making his actions too transparent, tried to disguise his true plans, and did not permit the press to alter his handling of affairs: contradictions which seem typical of the lack of a firm judgement on the president's role in the crisis. In the middle of March, Day told Polo, Dupuy's substitute in Washington, that the United States wanted neither war nor possession of Cuba, but Companys is unconvinced, says the words did not match government actions, and credits the McKinley administration with not being so naive as to confess its plans. Finally, he suggests that the United States, having failed to persuade Spain to yield sovereignty over Cuba, was determined to eliminate Spain and exercise some form of control over the island itself. For his part, Robles dedicates a well documented monograph to the attempts to prevent American intervention in Cuba through the mediation of Pope Leon XIII in late March–early April.

Naturally most Spanish historians are at pains to explain that Sagasta's government finally complied with all American demands, but conclude that no concessions would have satisfied McKinley at this stage because he was determined to intervene. Salas Larrazábal and Allende even suggest that American demands became so unreasonable, precisely because of the Spanish inclination to make concessions which might have brought lasting peace to Cuba, a development which was not in the interest of the United States. In his April 11 message to Congress, McKinley did not give due credit to Spanish concessions, and instead sought authorization to use force. McKinley's insinuation that the United States would intervene, if the unilaterally declared Spanish cease-fire failed to bring peace to Cuba, could only be interpreted as an invitation to the independentist rebels to resist.

Morales Padrón is extremely negative in his judgement of McKinley's actions: "The President showed perfidy in dealing with the matter of the *Maine*; malice in ignoring <Spanish> orders ending concentration; inaccuracy in affirming that pacification by force was the only solution; premeditation in not informing Congress of the armistice ... and in seeking permission, not to support the pacification, but to provoke a war; tendentious hypocrisy in ignoring political changes brought about by the new liberal government ...; and treachery in not recognizing either the belligerency or the independence of Cuba, alleging that the Cuban government did not meet the requirements for recognition." (129–130).

Companys and Navarro also point out that some members of both Congress and the American public were surprised and indignant when they discovered that McKinley had never in fact asked Spain to recognize Cuban independence. But, on the whole, Spanish authors devote little attention either to American anti-expansionist opinion, or for that matter, to Spanish Jingoist opinion.

At this stage, or as soon as hostilities began, Spanish historians also tend to start using the term "Yankee" where they previously used "North American" or "United States."

McKinley's ultimatum of April 20, demanding that Spain grant Cuban independence or face direct American intervention, was frustrated by the

Spanish decision to break off diplomatic relations on the 21st. On the 23rd McKinley ordered the naval blockade of Cuba. Rodríguez González suggests that the U.S. forced the onset of the war when it did, and in fact initiated hostilities prematurely, in order to take advantage of the temporary material and strategic weakness of the Spanish Navy.

The Spanish Decision to Fight

Spain declared war on the United States on April 24, in answer to McKinley's ultimatum of 20th and the initiation of the Cuban blockade on the 23rd. The American government's bad faith is underscored by its declaration of war on the 25th, made retroactive to cover hostilities committed since the 21st. Torre maintains that Sagasta's government based its decisions on two misconceptions about international realities: the belief that the interests of other European powers coincided with those of Spain, and the belief that those interests would mobilize European opposition against American expansion. Robles, Serrano and Companys underscore the influence of military opinion on the Spanish government.

One widely-held view of the Spanish decision to fight in 1898 is that Sagasta's government went to war knowing that Spain would be defeated. This interpretation states that to back down without a fight would have provoked a global institutional crisis threatening the monarchy, in view of the government's belief that neither public opinion nor the military and naval hierarchies would have accepted the honorability or the wisdom of such a decision. Serrano and Torre go so far as to argue that Sagasta's government was relieved by American intervention because Spain could not win the war against Cuban rebels, and her predominant ideology prohibited yielding to demands for independence or the sale of the island. A quick defeat by overwhelmingly superior American forces would cut the Gordian knot, and save Spanish honor, together with the throne.

The Spanish army in Cuba was very numerous and well seasoned, and could be expected to resist strongly American attempts to occupy the island, with the resultant heavy military and civilian losses. Therefore the only hope to curtail the conflict and minimize Spanish losses was to choose to confront the American Navy, knowing that Spanish naval forces were inferior, and expecting a quick end to hostilities.

However, Rodríguez González questions some of this. He explains that Cuban dependence on imported foodstuffs and other supplies meant that the island could be forced to surrender by a tight naval blockade, but not before having subjected the civilian population and the army to great suffering. The Cuban economy was, of course, based on the production of sugar and tobacco. The traditional dependence on imported foods had become even greater as a result of the recent policy of concentration of the rural population and the guerrilla practice of burning crops. The United States would not want to risk sustaining heavy losses by engaging the formidable Spanish army in the island, but Spanish military strategy would be severely taxed by having to keep alert to that possibility, while at the same time preventing Cuban guerrillas (foreseeably supplied and supported by American ships) from establishing control over large areas of the island.

The only real hope of a Spanish victory lay, then, in breaking the American blockade, and that demanded a naval war. According to Rodríguez González this was the correct conclusion from the perspective of strategic imperatives and not a "lesser evil" imposed by political necessity. However, regarding the definitive decision to actually wage the war on these terms, he maintains that Sagasta's government was not properly informed of the very real Spanish naval inferiority in April of 1898, while the deficiencies of the American Navy were overestimated.

For this misinformation Rodríguez González squarely blames Spanish naval authorities. Vice-Admiral Beránger, Rear-Admiral Bermejo, and in fact 14 of the 18 government advisors on Naval Affairs consulted in April professed to believe (either sincerely or out of a sense of patriotic duty) that Spain could win a maritime war against the United States. Salas Larrazábal, too, draws attention to the absurd attitudes of certain naval officers in positions of authority, while Blanco tries to justify them by saying that they were not given time to consider their votes, and in any case were unfit for such a responsibility because of their advanced age.

Dissident voices were not lacking, of course. Cervera and the officers of his fleet flatly stated their belief that defeat was certain, while four of the naval advisors consulted by minister Bermejo expressed their doubts by suggesting that Cervera's fleet should not be deployed until it could be repaired, fully manned and fitted out, and reinforced by other ships. However these opinions were in the minority and were not made public.

Sagasta, then, according to this view, had some reason to believe that a successful naval war was possible. The government was not unaware that Cervera's fleet was not at present strong enough to face the American forces, Theoretically the fleet was composed of three armored battleships, ten large cruisers, six destroyers, and at least three armed torpedo boats, but in fact at the end of April Cervera had only four cruisers and three destroyers in active service. Nevertheless, the initial plan was to avoid an all-out engagement and to threaten American trade and towns on the East coast. The objectives were to divide American naval forces with a view to easing the blockade of Cuba, and to cause as much havoc as possible with American trade until such time as Spain's full naval power could be brought to bear. For this reason the fleet was to make its base in San Juan de Puerto Rico, not in a Cuban port.

Morales Padrón suggests that Sagasta and Minister of the Navy Bermejo must be held responsible for ordering Cervera's fleet to go to the defense of Cuba, though he concedes that they reconsidered the decision and sent a second telegram (which arrived too late) authorizing him to return at his discretion rather than risk losing the fleet.

In any case the sense of impending doom floats over many versions of this phase of the conflict and the Spanish government's decision to fight. Navarro sees Sagasta as resisting the role of resigned victim of an expoliation with little real hope of success.

The War: Naval Operations

Given the extreme brevity of the war between Spain and the United States, and the resounding defeat of Spanish naval forces, many Spanish historians have sought to evaluate and explain respective naval strengths and weaknesses.

Téllez presents, with little critical analysis, the explanations offered after the war by Spanish naval officers. All deplored Spanish naval weakness, blamed the government for the disaster, accused the press of ignorance in naval matters and of creating a false optimism in public opinion, and affirmed that the Navy knew it would be defeated but accepted the sacrifice in silence out of a sense of duty.

With regard to the Pacific Blanco maintains the traditional version of totally inadequate Spanish defenses: Cavite was a useless naval base; the Navy pressed for a base at Subig, but the plan was frustrated by government indecisiveness and the provincial egoism of Manila residents who feared losing the capital; Montojo's fleet was small, so antiquated as to be almost useless, and its artillery did not have the range to cause Dewey's ships any damage; defense afforded by coast artillery and mines at Subig was entirely unsatisfactory, forcing Montojo to return to Cavite; Captain General Agustín forbade Montojo to try and take the fleet elsewhere; Dewey's superiority converted the battle into mere target practise for the Americans.

However, according to Rodríguez González, Spanish and American forces were reasonably balanced. To be sure, Dewey's fleet was made up of more modern ships of greater military potential, but Montojo's fleet was not as old and useless as has sometimes been maintained, and, whereas Dewey was operating 7,000 nautical miles from his nearest West coast bases, Montojo could expect to improve his defense by the intelligent use of submarine mines and coastal batteries.

In the actual course of events, however, Dewey received aid from the British colony of Hong Kong (in violation of official British neutrality), while Spanish mines were prevented from arriving and coast artillery was ineptly placed. Even so, Rodríguez González insists that the battle of Cavite was not such a rotund, unilateral defeat as has been suggested.

In the Caribbean the destruction of Cervera's fleet has tended to over-shadow minor operations carried out by Manterola's forces based in Puerto Rico. Rodríguez González analyzes these actions, using primary archival and periodical sources. He gives a detailed description of the components of Manterola's fleet, leaving little doubt regarding its extreme weakness, not because of age but as a result of the punishing work done since the beginning of the Cuban war in 1895. Nevertheless, after describing actions in Havana, Cardenas, Caibarien, Nuevitas, Nipe, Cienfuegos, Casilda, Manzanillo, Santiago and Guantanamo, he concludes that this fleet managed to distract large enemy forces from the Cuban blockade, while protecting both Spanish coasts and merchant ships trying to get through the blockade, and preventing enemy contacts with Cuban rebels. Most of its battles and skirmishes with American ships ended inconclusively: defeats were offset by a few victories and, overall, it inflicted more damage and losses on the enemy than the fleets of Montojo and Cervera, while most of the vessels lost were scuttled by the Spaniards themselves, with little loss of life.

Spanish successes in naval operations during the war are also mentioned by Larrazábel, Bisquets, Blanco and Cervera. Admiral Cervera clearly stated that his fleet would be defeated if sent to face the American forces in the Caribbean, and he proposed to concentrate on the defense of the Canary Islands and the Peninsula itself. Most Spanish historians consider Cervera's assessment of the situation as correct. Alvarez disagrees; but his only argument is that Spanish naval inferiority, though manifest, was not sufficient justification to evade an encounter with the American fleet. He also criticizes Cervera for not attempting to reach Havana, either from Curacao or after recoaling at Santiago.

The bottling up of Cervera's fleet in Santiago de Cuba was an unforeseen circumstance, not part of the Spanish war plan. Cervera's refusal to consider Bustamante's advice to leave the port immediately, as soon as the danger became apparent and before the blockade was complete, is put forward as a grave error of judgement by Alvarez and Rodríguez González, as is his later refusal to attempt a surprise nocturnal flight in different directions, also suggested by Bustamante, in the hope of saving at least some of his ships. Blanco, by contrast, offers some justification of Cervera's decision.

When the Spanish ships finally sailed, one by one and in broad daylight, the American advantage was by all accounts overwhelming. Alvarez believes that Cervera should have sent the destroyers first, and both he and Blanco suggest that the fleet should have sailed at night. Even so, Rodríguez González and Vega record that the manoevres and marksmanship of the Americans were only mediocre, and that Spanish artillerymen were more successful than is generally credited, although their missiles were too light to cause serious damage.

Blanco and Navarro make brief but damning commentaries on the Spanish decision to order Cervera to sail from the port of Santiago. Spanish losses (at least 264, perhaps as many as 350 dead, many injured and taken prisoners, all ships sunk) were not necessary to demonstrate American superiority, particularly since Montojo's defeat at Cavite. For his part, Morales Padrón chooses to find solace in the honorable treatment given to Cervera by the American Navy. Bordeje deals with the subject of the Spanish Navy in the political debate which ensued after the war.

The War: Military Operations

Navarro dedicates very little attention to the military phase of Cuban independence, but he does find space to portray Calixto García's little army as hungry, nearly naked and lacking in military supplies, while the American expeditionary army is described as improvised, indisciplined and under incompetent commanders. Roosevelt's Rough Riders are mentioned only to dismiss them as "picturesque."

Morales Padrón draws attention to the disdainful attitude of the American Army towards the rebel Calixto García and his predominantly Negro forces, adding that "the victors were more favorably inclined towards their chivalrous Spanish enemies than towards their Cuban allies" (p. 132).

National pride demands that narrations of the war record the military virtues and qualities of the Spanish Army, not just despite its ultimate defeat but precisely because of it. Usually present in Spanish versions, then, are the more than 1,300 American losses in the assaults on El Caney and San Juan, defended by only 1,000 Spanish soldiers; the heroic professionalism of Colonel Federico Escario, who brought a column of 3,700 men from Manzanillo to relieve Santiago, fighting off thirty guerrilla attacks on the way.

Several studies focus on the experiences of individual participants in the war. Martínez concentrates on the battle of Las Lomas de San Juan, paying special attention to the role of naval captain Bustamante. Paz Sánchez offers a brief biography of Antonio Serra Orts, who served in the Spanish army in Cuba from 1875 to 1878, from 1886 to 1892, and again from 1895 to the end of the war. He fought in the battle of Loma Ayua, which took place the day after Spain and the United States had signed the peace agreement (August 12). Serra's later writings show him to have been very critical of Spanish politicians from a "regenerationist" standpoint, a reaction he shared with many Spaniards after 1898. Santos offers a biographical study of Juan Espinosa, while Serrano Monteavaro does the same for Fernando Villaamil, both Spanish heroes of the Cuban war.

Cervera calls attention to the war in Puerto Rico, which he considers has been insufficiently studied. He condemns Sampson's decision to bombard San Juan, and comments that the Spanish defense was more efficient than might be expected. Morales Padrón shows his disgust at General Miles' invasion of Puerto Rico on July 25 by pointing out that this island had not rebelled against Spanish rule, and stating that American motives have never been clarified. Other authors also insist on the nonexistence of any serious political unrest in Puerto Rico, affirming that this island's separation from Spain was attributable solely to American expansionism and McKinley's use of force.

For his part, Martín Berrio describes the nineteen-day campaign in Puerto Rico as a model of civilized, modern and humanitarian war. He gives succinct information about the military and naval defenses of the island, with little commentary but suggests a serious lack of adequate artillery.

Between the statement that nobody in Puerto Rico wanted the American invasion and descriptions of the enthusiastic welcome accorded to the triumphant American troops, the only explanation given is that the loss of Cervera's fleet demoralized the population at large, although some evidence is offered of the existence of separatist sentiments in the island.

Puerto Ricans, says Fernández Aponte, were astonished, both by the fact of the American invasion and by the immense material wealth displayed. For some, she says, these circumstances briefly represented a promise of economic and political progress for Puerto Rico, and explained the jubilation which, however, soon changed to dismay.

The heroic Spanish defense of Baler against the Philippine rebels is the subject of a detailed study by Ortiz Armengol. Based largely on primary sources written by Lieutenant Saturnino Martín Cerezo, Friar Félix Minaya, Manuel Sastrón and Manuel Quezón, but giving evidence of familiarity with American and Philippine historiography, the article carefully recounts "the most brilliant military page of the entire war." Ortiz feels that the close relations between the United States and the Philippines in the twentieth century caused their war of 1899–1902 to be largely forgotten in historical works, but notes a growing interest in the subject since the Vietnam war. He himself suggests, as does Tormo, that Philippine and American losses in that war, though disputed, were probably much greater than those sustained by Spain and the Philippines in 1898–1899.

Pozuelo succinctly recounts the American occupation of Guam in June of 1898, stressing not the almost total lack of defenses on the island but the power and the planning manifested by the United States. She also points out the geographical value of Guam in connection with the American project to establish a trans-Atlantic cable from San Francisco to Honolulu and Manila.

Hernández García contributes data on defense measures taken in 1898 in the Canary Islands, whose strategic value led many to fear an American invasion. Article IX of the treaty of Paris defines Spanish subjects as those born in the Peninsula, giving rise to curious questions about the status of people born in the Canary and Balearic Islands, and the North African possessions, and the possible deliberate American desire to consider them as non-Spanish.

The Peace

On July 26 Spain requested the opening of peace talks, and on August 12 the armistice was agreed. This was, by all accounts, very painful for the Spanish government because Puerto Rico and Manila were still in Spanish control, and the army in Cuba had not been defeated, but most authors recognize the powerful reasons for a rapid Spanish surrender. The peace negotiations were not easy, and the treaty of Paris was not signed until 10th December.

In the meantime the Cuban Army of Liberation was not allowed to enter Santiago, and no Cuban, Puerto Rican or Philippine representative participated in the negotiations. This fact is often underscored with a view to showing that McKinley had no real respect for the rights of the people whose national destiny was being debated.

However, Torre and Allende follow "orthodox" American historiography in maintaining that American imperialism in the Caribbean, and specially in the Pacific, was a consequence, and not the cause, of the way the crisis developed (unexpectedly easy and resounding naval victories, European willingness to contemplate both the defeat of Spain and the redistribution of her colonies and the ascent of the United States to the rank of great power).

Therefore Torre states that McKinley's expansionist aspirations in the Pacific crystallized, in fact, only after the battle of Cavite and during the peace negotiations between August and December. Sevilla and Allende also subscribe to the notion that McKinley's demands were not premeditated but grew as a result of Spain's collapse as an imperial power, while Elizalde is inclined to think, on the contrary, that the American decision to take over the Philippines was taken long before the war broke out.

It is generally felt that there were, in fact, no real negotiations, because the Spaniards were given no options in view of the American threat to renew hostilities if Spain refused to hand over the entire Philippine archipelago and take responsibility for the huge Cuban public debt. Predictably, Morales Padrón is severely critical of McKinley's attitude during this period, maintaining that bad faith and force were the overriding vehicles of his impositions, which not only surprised the Spanish government (which still hoped to save all or most of the Philippines), but also divided the American delegation in Paris, and mobilized anti-imperialist opinion in the United States. Togores also sees the President now as frankly avid of colonies, once he has yielded to imperialist pressures and total Spanish defeat is evident. Finally Spain was forced to give up Cuba, Puerto Rico, the Philippines and Guam.

The rapid establishment between 1899 and 1903 of American economic domination of Cuba is often carefully and critically noted, as are the manoevres to frustrate Cuban political independence, which, though not entirely successful, left the new nation still very far from the goal of full sovereignty. Fernández Aponte stresses that the change of sovereignty in Puerto Rico was totally unexpected, illegal and traumatic for the people of this island. She says that Puerto Rico had not sought independence from Spain, but that events of 1898 forced its people to consider their options. In this process, widespread admiration for American economic and constitutional advances vied with the profound sense of Puerto Rican identity. The widely-held view that the United States did not originally intend to take over the Philippines, but was encouraged to do so by Great Britain, whose government feared the islands might fall into German hands, is questioned by Togores, who argues that the United States was a far greater threat to British interests in the Pacific than Germany, but that Lord Salisbury's government had no choice in the matter.

The notion expressed by McKinley that the United States acquired the Philippines in order to take Christianity and civilization to the natives is dismissed as absurd by Padrón and Togores. American financial and military leaders were fully aware of the golden opportunity to obtain an insuperable base in the Pacific at very low cost, and no consideration was afforded Filipino demands for independence. However, Allende points out that the American conflict with Spain in 1898 was really only the beginning of a long struggle in the Philippines, which did not end till 1916, on the eve of American intervention in World War I.

The initial results of the Spanish-American war of 1898 inevitably sparked off a scramble for remaining Spanish possessions in the Pacific. Elizalde analyzes the attitudes of the great imperialist powers in connection with the sale of the Caroline, Marianas (except Guam, already ceded to the United States) and Palaos Islands to Germany in 1898–1899. She notes that American interest in acquiring possessions in the Carolines was very strong during the negotiations of late 1898, but that both the United States and Britain recognized the need to compensate Germany, whose hopes of acquiring all or some of the Philippine Islands were frustrated by Anglo-American opposition.

Finally, because the two Philippine Islands of Sibutú and Cagayán de Joló (Sulu) were not expressly ceded to the United States in the treaty of Paris, their occupation by American troops in 1899 was protested by the Spanish government, and this attracted the attention of Great Britain and Germany. The United States claimed that they had meant to obtain the entire archipelago in the 1898 treaty, but eventually (November 7, 1900) agreed to give Spain $100,000 for the two islands. Togores feels that this epilogue to the crisis clearly confirms his thesis that the Pacific and the Far East were of far greater importance in American imperial plans than is generally reflected in traditional Spanish historiography.

Another epilogue examined by Torre concerns Spain's reorientation of foreign policy, already begun during the peace negotiations of 1898, with a view to obtaining international protection for the Spanish territories of the Canary and Balear Islands, and the two North African possessions of Ceuta and Melilla.

Spanish Perception of the War of 1898

The word that is most extensively used in Spanish historiography in connection with the 1898 war is still "disaster," often with a capital D. Other terms commonly used to describe Spanish sentiments and perception of the war are "catastrophe," "humiliation," "calamity," "tragedy," "holocaust." The war is seen as precipitating the end of the Spanish Empire, not only because of the loss of Spain's last colonial possessions, but because it brought about the destruction of Spanish naval power and spelled the end of Spain's relevance as an international power.

By contrast, Companys concedes that Cuba was a liability whose loss could only benefit Spain, and that even if home rule had succeeded for a while, eventual total independence was inevitable. Serrano seems to concur with this view when he points out that the political and military disaster of 1898 was partially compensated by a relative economic expansion, one of the reasons being the repatriation and investment in Spain of capital accumulated in the ex-Spanish colonies.

Ñíguez also sees some beneficial consequences of the crisis: Spain was forced to review its foreign policy with a view to protecting true national interests; regionalism and socialism gained ground; Joaquín Costa's regenerationism inspired the middle classes to seek the Europeanization of Spain; the intellectual generation of 1898 gave Spain a second literary golden age and criticized Spanish officialdom which had for so long hidden and oppressed the "real" Spain. These views echo that of philosopher Ramiro de Maéztu, who in 1897 foresaw the "disaster" but welcomed it if it led to a self-analysis of Spain's problems.

Alonso mentions these same processes, but is not so sure they were beneficial. He argues that Spanish losses (in lives, ships, war material, economic cost of mobilization, colonial markets) were not, in fact, so great as to explain the profound national demoralization which ensued after 1898, but that the Spanish reaction to the defeat was really the expression of an immense psychological and moral need to break with the Restoration years (1874–1902), which came to be associated with the political, military, economic, and cultural decadence of Spain. However, the Army and the Navy in particular, he believes, served as scapegoats, and the legitimate military concerns of Spain were not afforded the attention they required after the war. Serrano also doubts any real benefits ensuing as a result of the crisis. He notes that military pressures on Spain's political life did not fade after the war, although the ideas of national identity and unity were severely weakened, both by the disaster and by the social gains of regionalism and socialism, and he feels that the "regenerationist" movement did not have the necessary focus to succeed. Serrano and Allende nevertheless agree with Alonso that the material consequences of the war were much less important, both for Spain and the United States, than its ideological and symbolic consequences. Rivadulla draws attention to the selectiveness of Spanish historical memory, which has given preeminence to Cuba in the crisis of 1898. The loss of Cuba, then, was, and to a large extent still is, considered emblematic of the end-of-the-century domestic, colonial and international crisis of Spain.

Spanish interpretations today of American policy in 1898 show the same diversity of opinions that characterizes most modern historiography. Where some see only premeditation at all stages, others concede that the McKinley administration was on occasions reacting to unforeseen circumstances and was caught up in an on-going process of redistribution of imperialist power in the world. The idea, expressed by Henry Cabot Lodge in 1900, that 1898 marked the definitive emergence of the United States as a world power, is still very much in evidence in Spanish historiography, but the ideological repercussions in the United States itself have received very little attention so far. Allende does mention that the "splendid little war" was of immense importance because it produced a cathartic identity crisis among many American intellectuals, but he does not offer an analysis or evaluation of the psychological impact of the war in the United States. Spanish historians have, perhaps inevitably, been primarily concerned with Spain.

Crisis of 1898: Spanish Bibliography 1980–1992

"Acuerdo hispano-norteamericano para la evacuación final de Cuba e islas adyacentes, de 16 de noviembre de 1898." *Revista de Historia Militar* 32 (1988): 214–219.

ALONSO BAQUER, Miguel. "La Guerra Hispanoamericana de 1898 y sus efectos sobre las instituciones militares españolas." *Revista de Historia Militar* 27 (1983): 127–151.

ALVAREZ ARENAS, Eliseo. "Lo naval en el noventa y ocho." *La marina ante el 98. Génesis y desarrollo de un conflicto. VI Jornadas de Historia Marítima.* 2 vols. Madrid: Cuadernos Monográficos del Instituto de Historia y Cultura Naval, n. 11, 1990. 2: 71–108.

ALLENDE SALAZAR Y VALDES, José Manuel. "La clase política norteamericana ante la guerra del 98." *La marina ante el 98. Génesis*, 1990, 2: 59–70.

ANDRES-GALLEGO, José. *Regeneracionismo y crisis del 98.* Madrid: Cuadernos Historia 16, núm. 30, 1985.

——. "El papel de la masonería en la Independencia filipina." *La marina ante el 98. Génesis*, 1990, 2: 45–58.

ANTA FELEZ, José Luis. "La guerra hispano-americana: introducción bibliográfica." *Aportes. Revista de Historia del Siglo XIX* 7 (marzo 1988): 66–69. (Very incomplete; many errors).

ARCAS CUBERO, Fernando. "Málaga en el 98. Repercusiones sociales de la guerra hispano-cubano-norteamericana." *Baética. Estudios de Arte, Geografía e Historia* 12 (1989): 281–298.

AYALA PEREZ, José Antonio. "La masonería de obediencia española ante el conflicto colonial puertorriqueño." *Brócar. Cuadernos de Investigación Histórica* 17 (diciembre 1991): 21–36.

BLANCO NUÑEZ, José. "De Cavite a Santiago." *La marina ante el 98. Génesis*, 1990, 2: 7–20.

BOLADO ARGUELLO, Nieves. *La independencia de Cuba y la prensa: apuntes para la historia.* Torrelavega (Bilbao): Ayuntamiento de Torrelavega, Artes Gráficos Quinzaños, 1991.

BORDEJE MORENCOS, Fernando de. "La Armada en el debate político de la postguerra." *La marina ante el 98. Génesis*, 1990, 2: 153–167.

BUSQUETS I VILANOVA, Camil. "La *Transatlántica* y la crisis del 98." *Revista General de Marina* 216 (marzo 1989): 295–302.

CALLEJA LEAL, Guillermo G. "La voladura del Maine." *Revista de Historia Militar* 34 (1990): 161–196.

Castilla y América en las publicaciones de la Armada. II Jornadas de Historiografía. 2 vols. Madrid: Cuadernos Monográficos del Instituto de Historia y Cultura Naval, n. 13 y 14, 1991.

CERVERA PERY, José. "Marinos españoles en su protagonismo histórico." *La marina ante el 98. Antecedentes de un conflicto. V Jornadas de Historia Marítima.* Madrid: Cuadernos Monográficos del Instituto de Historia y Cultura Naval, n. 8, 1990. 49–74.

——. "La guerra olvidada de Puerto Rico." *La marina ante el 98. Génesis*, 1990, 2: 143–152.

COMPANYS MONCLUS, Julián. "La carta de Dupuy de Lome." *Boletín de la Real Academia de la Historia* 184 (septiembre–diciembre 1987): 465–481.

——. "Los orígenes de la prensa "amarilla" y su relación con la insurrección cubana de 1895." *Boletín de la Real Academia de la Historia* 185 (mayo–agosto 1988): 327–346.

——. *La diplomacia norteamericana en torno al 98.* Barcelona: Universidad de Barcelona, 1989. (Thesis in microfiche, 244).

——. *De la explosión del Maine a la ruptura de relaciones diplomáticas entre Estados Unidos y España (1898).* Lleida: Universitat de Barcelona, 1989.

——. *España en 1898: entre la diplomacia y la guerra.* Prólogo de C. Seco Serrano. Madrid, 1992.

DOMINGO ACEBRON, María Dolores. "La participación de españoles en el ejército libertador en Cuba, 1895–1898." *Revista de Indias* 52 (mayo–diciembre 1992): 349–364.

ELIZALDE PEREZ-GRUESO, María Dolores. "Una visión historiográfica de las coordenadas internacionales del Pacífico español, 1875–1899." *Revista de Indias* 49 (1989): 845–862.

——. "La venta de las islas Carolinas, un nuevo hito en el 98 español." *Estudios históricos. Homenaje a los profesores José María Jover Zamora y Vicente Palacio Atard.* 2 vols. Madrid: Universidad Complutense de Madrid, Departamento de Historia Contemporánea, 1990. 1: 361–380.

——. "Las grandes potencias y el Pacífico español: los intentos de los países hegemónicos en la colonia de las islas Carolinas." *Revista de Estudios del Pacífico* 1 (julio–diciembre 1991): 65–82.

——. *España en el Pacífico. La colonia de las Islas Carolinas, 1885–1899. Un modelo colonial en el contexto internacional del imperialismo.* Madrid: Consejo Superior de Investigaciones Científicas, 1992.

ELORZA, Antonio. "Con la marcha de Cádiz: imágenes españolas de la guerra de independencia cubana." *Estudios de Historia Social* 44–47 (1988): 327–386.

España y el Pacífico. II Jornadas Pacífico-Filipinas. Madrid: Agencia Española de Cooperación Internacional, 1989.

Estudios históricos. Homenaje a los profesores José María Jover Zamora y Vicente Palacio Atard. 2 vols. Madrid: Universidad Complutense de Madrid, Departamento de Historia Contemporánea, 1990.

Extremo Oriente Ibérico. (Actas del primer Simposium Internacional: El Extremo Oriente Ibérico, Madrid, 7–10 noviembre 1988). Investigaciones históricas, metodología y estado de la cuestión. Madrid: Agencia Española de Cooperación

Internacional, Consejo Superior de Investigaciones Científicas, 1989.

FERNANDEZ APONTE, Irene. *El cambio de soberanía en Puerto Rico. Otro '98.* Madrid: Editorial Mapfre, 1992. (Puertorican author).

GARCIA SANZ, Fernando. "El contexto internacional de la guerra de Cuba: la percepción italiana del 98 español." *Estudios de Historia Social* 44–47 (1988): 295–310.

GONZALEZ ECHEGARAY, Rafael. "La última compañía de Filipinas." *Revista General de Marina* 201 (agosto 1981): 47–60.

GONZALEZ LOPEZ-BRIONES, Carmen. "The Indiana Press and the Coming of the Spanish-American War, 1895–1898." *Atlantis. Revista de la Asociación Espanola de Estudios Anglo-Norteamericanos* 12 (1990): 165–176.

HERNANDEZ GARCIA, Julio. *La invasión frustrada de los EE.UU. a Canarias en 1898. El "tributo en sangre" de 1678–1778.* Santa Cruz de Tenerife: Centro de la Cultura Popular Canaria, 1984.

HERNANDEZ RUIGOMEZ, Almudena. "El 98 americano en la Historiografía Naval." *Castilla y América en las publicaciones de la Armada. II Jornadas de Historiografía.* 2 vols. Madrid: Cuadernos Monográficos del Instituto de Historia y Cultura Naval, n. 13 y 14, 1991. 1: 17–38.

HERNANDEZ SANCHEZ-BARBA, Mario; MALAGON, Javier, and LEAL SPENGLER, Eusebio. "Presencia, conflictos y relaciones con los Estados Unidos de América. La crisis del 98. La Institución Libre de Enseñanza." *Iberoamérica, una comunidad.* 2 vols. Madrid: Ediciones de Cultura Hispánica, 1989. 2: 713–725.

HERNANDEZ SANDOICA, Elena. "La cuestión cubana y sus implicaciones internacionales." *Hispania. Revista Espanola de Historia* 49 (1989): 343–354.

JOHNSON, Lyman L. "Presidential Leadership in Foreign Affairs: McKinley's Role in the Spanish-American War." *Boletín Americanista* 28 (1986): 55–74.

JOVER ZAMORA, José María. *1898. Teoría y práctica de la redistribución colonial.* Madrid: Fundación Universitaria Española, 1979.

La marina ante el 98. Antecedentes de un conflicto. V Jornadas de Historia Marítima. Madrid: Cuadernos Monográficos del Instituto de Historia y Cultura Naval, n. 8, 1990.

La marina ante el 98. Génesis y desarrollo de un conflicto. VI Jornadas de Historia Marítima. 2 vols. Madrid: Cuadernos Monográficos del Instituto de Historia y Cultura Naval, n. 11, 1990.

LASA AYESTARAN, Eugenio. "La burguesía catalana hace un siglo: de la conquista del mercado colonial a la pérdida del Imperio." *Trienio. Ilustración y Liberalismo. Revista de Historia* 18 (noviembre 1991): 109–148.

LLORCA BAUS, Carlos. "La marina mercante y el papel de la Transatlántica en Ultramar." *La marina ante el 98. Antecedentes,* 1990, 109–118.

MANZANO, Cristina. "Las expediciones de Narciso López a través de la prensa de Nueva York." *Trienio. Ilustración y Liberalismo. Revista de Historia* 16 (noviembre 1990): 53–102.

MARTIN BERRIO, Raúl. "1898: Intervencionismo militar de los EE.UU. sobre Puerto Rico y Cuba." *Quinto Centenario* 16 (1990): 253–269.

MARTIN CEREZO, Saturnino. *La pérdida de Filipinas.* Edición de Juan Batista. Madrid: Historia 16, 1992.

MARTINEZ VALVERDE, Carlos. "Las lomas de San Juan de Santiago de Cuba, y el capitán de navío Bustamante." *Revista General de Marina* 213 (agosto–septiembre 1987): 161–169.

MATEU Y LLOPIS, Felipe. "El 98 en mi memoria." *Haciendo historia: Homenaje al profesor Carlos Seco.* Madrid: Facultad de Ciencia de la Información de la Universidad Complutense, and Facultad de Geografía e Historia de la Universidad de Barcelona, 1989. 409–416.

MORALES PADRON, Francisco. *Historia de unas relaciones difíciles: EE.UU. – América española.* Sevilla: Universidad de Sevilla, 1987.

NARANJO OROVIO, Consuelo. "Repercusiones de la guerra de 1898 en la vida política cubana." *La marina ante el 98. Génesis,* 1990, 2: 109–126.

NAVARRO CUSTIN, Jorge. "Nuevas Inces en torno a la voladura del Maine." *Diario de las Américas,* Miami, II, Fibrero 1988.

NAVARRO GARCIA, Luis. *La independencia de Cuba.* Madrid: Editorial Mapfre, 1992.

NUÑEZ FLORENCIO, Rafael. "El presupuesto de la paz: una polémica entre civiles y militares en la España finisecular." *Hispania. Revista Espanola de Historia* 49 (enero–abril 1989): 197–234.

——. "Los anarquistas españoles y americanos ante la guerra de Cuba." *Hispania. Revista Espanola de Historia* 51 (septiembre–diciembre 1991): 1077–1092.

ÑIGUEZ BERNAL, Antonio. "Las relaciones políticas económicas y culturales entre España y los Estados Unidos en los siglos XIX y XX." *Quinto Centenario* 12 (1987): 71–134.

OLIVIE, Fernando. *La herencia de un imperio roto.* Madrid: Editorial Mapfre, 1992.

ORTIZ ARMENGOL, Pedro. "La defensa de la posición de Baler (Jn. 1898–Jn. 1899). Una aproximación a la guerra de las Filipinas." *Revista de Historia Militar* 34 (1990): 83–178.

PABON, Jesús. *El 98, acontecimiento internacional.* Madrid: Ministerio de Asuntos Exteriores, 1952, repr. in *Días de Ayer.* Barcelona: Alpha, 1963. 139–95.

PASTRANA, Apolinar. "Los franciscanos en el Bicol durante la revolución filipina de 1898." *Archivo Ibero-Americano* 51 (enero–junio 1991): 217–319.

PAZ SANCHEZ, Manuel de. "Antonio Serra Orts (1856–1926): el último combatiente español en la guerra hispano-cubano- norteamericana." *Cuadernos de Investigación Histórica* 13 (1990): 103–124.

——. "La muerte de José Martí: un debate historiográfico." *Brócar. Cuadernos de Investigación Histórica* 17 (diciembre 1991): 7–19.

PAZOS, Pío A. de. *Héroes de Filipinas.* Madrid: Servicio de Publicaciones del Estado Mayor del Ejército, 1985.

PÉREZ, Louis. "The Meaning of the Maine: Causation and the Historigraphy of the Spanish-American War". *Pacific Historical Review* 58 (August 1989): 293–322.

PEREZ GARCIA, José Manuel. "Los veterinarios militares en el ejército de Cuba (1887–1898). Aportación a la historia del cuerpo de veterinaria militar. Los ejércitos de la emancipación." *Temas de Historia Militar. Segundo Congreso de Historia Militar, Zaragoza, 1988.* 3 vols. Madrid, Servivio de Publicaciones del Estado Mayor del Ejército, 1988. 3: 441–455.

POZUELO MASCARAGUE, Belén. "El final de la presencia española en las islas Marianas, 1898–1899." *España y el Pacífic* (1989): 169–180.

RICKOVER, H.G. *Cómo fue hundido el acorazado "Maine".* Madrid: Editorial Naval, 1985.

RIVADULLA BARRIENTOS, Daniel. "El "98" español y sus fuentes: los fondos sobre Filipinas del Archivo General del Palacio Real (Madrid)." *Extremo Oriente*, 1989, 183–202.

ROBLES MUÑOZ, Cristóbal. "Los Metodistas Americanos en Las Carolinas. Un litigio de soberanía con los Estados Unidos." *Missionalia Hispanica* 42 (julio–diciembre 1985): 337–367.

——. "1898: la batalla por la paz. La mediación de León XIII entre España y Estados Unidos." *Revista de Indias* 46 (enero–junio 1986): 247–296.

——. "Guerra y población civil: los reconcentrados." *La marina ante el 98. Génesis*, 1990, 21–44.

——. "La lucha de los independentistas cubanos y las relaciones de España con los Estados Unidos." *Hispania. Revista Espanola de Historia* 50 (1990): 159–202.

——. *1898: Diplomacia y opinión*. Madrid: Consejo Superior de Investigaciones Científicas, 1991.

RODAO GARCIA, Florentino. "Conflictos con Estados Unidos en Ponapé: preludio para 1898." *Estudios sobre Filipinas y las islas del Pacífico*. Madrid: Asociación Española de Estudios del Pacífico, 1989. 97–102.

RODRIGUEZ GONZALEZ, Agustín R. "Operaciones menores en Cuba, 1898." *Revista de Historia Naval* 3 (1985): 125–146.

——. "El peligro amarillo en el Pacífico español, 1880–1898." *España y el Pacífico*, 1989, 201–226.

——. "Balances navales, estrategias y decisiones políticas en la guerra de 1898." *Estudios históricos. Homenaje*, 1990, 1: 633–653.

RUIZ SANCHEZ, José Leonardo. "La mitra sevillana y el desastre del 98: el patriotismo de don Marcelo Spínola." *Temas*, 1988, 3: 491–505.

SAIZ PASTOR, Candelaria. "Narciso López y el anexionismo en Cuba. En torno a la ideología de los propietarios de esclavos." *Anuario de Estudios Americanos* 43 (1986): 441–468.

SALAS CARMENA, Delfín. *La guerra de Cuba, 1898*. Madrid: Aldaba Ediciones, 1989.

SALAS LARRAZABAL, Ramón. "Las últimas guerras coloniales." *Temas*, 1988, 1: 569–612.

SANTOS MIÑON, Francisco J. *Juan Espinosa Tudela, laureado zapador de la guerra de Cuba (1878–1924)*. Ronda: Caja de Ahorros de Ronda, 1990.

SARABIA LOPEZ, María del Pilar. "Notas en torno al problema de la neutralidad británica durante la guerra hispano-americana de 1898." *Quinto Centenario* 11 (1986): 157–162.

SERRANO, Carlos. "Prófugos y desertores en la guerra de Cuba." *Estudios de Historia Social* 22 (julio–diciembre 1982): 253–278.

——. *Final del Imperio. España, 1895–1898*. Madrid: Siglo XXI, 1984.

——. "1898. España en cuestión." *Estudios de Historia Social* 44–47 (1988): 387–393.

SERRANO MONTEAVARO, Miguel Angel. *Fernando Villaamil. Una vida entre la mar y el dolor: la guerra de Cuba*. Cádiz: Asamblea Amistosa Literaria, 1989.

——. "La política norteamericana en relación con Cuba." *La marina ante el 98. Antecedentes*, 1990, 27–47.

SERRANO SUAREZ, Fernando. "Notas para un estudio de la prensa revolucionaria cubana en el exilio, 1878–1887." *Aportes. Revista de Historia del Siglo XIX* 7 (marzo 1988): 28–43.

SEVILLA Y SOLER, Rosario. "La intervención norteamericana en Cuba y la opinión pública andaluza." *Anuario de Estudios Americanos* 43 (1986): 469–516.

TELLEZ MOLINA, Antonio. "La Marina de Guerra española frente al desastre del 98: una aproximación al testimonio de sus combatientes." *Revue de Historia Naval* 8 (1990): 39–50.

——. "Reflexiones en torno a la situación de la Armada española hacia 1898." *Revue de Historia Naval* 10 (1992): 55–68.

Temas de Historia Militar. Segundo Congreso de Historia Militar, Zaragoza, 1988. 3 vols. Madrid, Servivio de Publicaciones del Estado Mayor del Ejército, 1988.

TOGORES SANCHEZ, Luis Eugenio. "Imperialismo, relaciones internacionales y derecho internacional en Extremo Oriente (Filipinas), 1830–1898/1914." *Quinto Centenario* 16 (1990): 141–172.

——. "España y la expansión de los EE.UU. en el Pacífico. (De la guerra hispano-americana de 1898 y la pérdida de Filipinas, al pleito por Sibutó y Cagayán de Joló)." *Estudios históricos. Homenaje*, 1990, 1: 655–676.

TORMO SANZ, Leandro. "Repercusiones de la guerra de 1898 en Filipinas." *La marina ante el 98. Génesis*, 1990, 2: 127–142.

TORRE DEL RIO, Rosario de la. *La neutralidad británica en la guerra hispano-norteamericana de 1898.* Thesis. Madrid: Universidad Complutense, Departamento de Historia Contemporánea, 1985.

——. "La crisis de 1898 y el problema de la garantía exterior." *Historia. Revisat Espanola de Historia* 46 (1986): 115–164.

——. *Inglaterra y España en 1898.* Madrid: EUDEMA, Ediciones de la Universidad Complutense de Madrid, 1988. (This is practically the same as her thesis, read in 1983, published in 1985, without the documentary appendices).

——. "Los acuerdos anglo-hispano-franceses de 1907: una larga negociación en la estela del 98." *Cuadernos de la Escuela Diplomática* 1 (junio 1988): 81–104.

——. "Filipinas y el reparto de Extremo Oriente en la crisis de 1898." *Extremo Oriente*, 1989, 509–522.

TUÑON DE LARA, Manuel, and ANDRES-GALLEGO, José. *El desastre del 98.* Madrid: Cuadernos Historia 16, núm. 30, 1985.

VEGA BLASCO, Antonio de la. "Programas y efectivos navales españoles y norteamericanos (1865–1898)." *La marina ante el 98. Antecedentes*, 1990, 77–108.

——. "Los Maquinistas del 98." *Revista de Historia Naval* 9 (1991): 43–54.

VOLTES BOU, Pedro. "Nuevo análisis de los antecedentes de la guerra de 1898." *Cuadernos de Economía* 11 (mayo–agosto 1983): 313–353.

8

World War One and Wilsonian Exceptionalism: The Dual Response of the Italian Masses and Leaders to the American Message

Daniela Rossini

Woodrow Wilson's belief in American exceptionalism profoundly influenced his approach to foreign affairs. It was reflected in the position of "associated" power he struggled to maintain for his country throughout the war and in the arbiter status he advocated at Versailles for his country and for himself. In fact, since this faith in the uniqueness of the United States was coupled with an equally strong faith in his own uniqueness, the president came to see himself as the spokesman not only of the American people, but of all the peoples of the world. He developed, as Schulte Nordholt observed, "the myth of the good people whose rulers are evil ..."[1] From that basic source came both the good and bad aspects of Wilsonian foreign policy: on one hand, the mass appeal of his political message, essential to master a modern war; on the other hand, the self-righteous attitude and the disregard for political dialogue the American president often showed in his relations with other countries' representatives. As Walter Lippmann caustically observed in 1919: "We never negotiated but simply enunciated."[2]

Wilson's policy towards Italy contains both the bright and the dark aspects of his approach to foreign policy. In Italy especially Wilson revealed himself as a great propagandist of the world war: in a very short time, through an effective combination of idealistic utterances and pervasive propaganda campaign throughout Italy, he became an idol of the Italian masses. However, he was unable to exploit the amazing popularity achieved during the war to work out a satisfying compromise with Italy at Versailles; the war leader could not become a constructive peace diplomat.

Wilson's exceptionalism, superb in war propaganda at home and abroad, was lacking in the realm of political dialogue and compromise. Elsewhere, I have characterized Wilson's policy towards Italy in the following terms:

- successful propaganda;

- weak political analysis;

- absence of diplomacy.

129

Let us explore these three basic aspects of Wilson's policy towards Italy at the end of World War I, together with the dual response of Italians to his message. And, since the success of the American propaganda campaign in Italy in 1918 can be better understood by contrasting it with the ignorance and distrust for the United States prevalent in Italy before that year, we can begin with this topic.

Italian Ignorance of the United States before 1917

Before the war, Italy and the United States had moved in different and reciprocally isolated spheres of influence. Italy's recent industrial take-off, in particular, had taken place under the aegis of Germany, while most Italian intellectuals were attracted by French and German culture. Very few of them, for example, were fluent in English. Americans living in Italy were often puzzled by the ignorance of the present-day United States they found among the Italian upper classes. Ambassador Nelson Page, for example, remarked:

> In the first place, there was almost universal ignorance of America ... and this ignorance was quite equalled by their indifference. Academically, it was known that there were two American Continents, and that therein were regions of immense extent and fertility ... But how they compared with each other, Italians generally knew little and care little. They were recognized as a good field for exploitation by their emigrant class, and the Italians were content to leave it at that.[3]

In short, the cultured Italian elites were strongly Europe-centered, ignorant of and indifferent to what was happening on the other side of the Atlantic.

In particular, the United States was beyond the political horizon of most Italian leaders. Generally, well-informed political observers considered the United States a distant country, whose impact on Europe's balance of power was negligible. Even in January 1918, nine months after the American entrance into the war, America hardly existed for Sidney Sonnino, foreign minister and symbol of the Italian war. Of the changes revolutionizing the world, Sonnino said to the American ambassador: "I shall not see them. I am too old."[4]

Ignorance and indifference were often combined with distrust. Like its European partners, Italy viewed America's long neutrality as a selfish choice made by a country interested only in exploiting the war as a source of enormous profits. In the closing days of 1916, most Italian newspapers bitterly criticized Wilson's appeal to the belligerents as a "mercantile document," one that might be expected from America. The United States was commonly considered an egoistic, money-oriented society, spiritually very distant from the European mentality.[5]

Co-belligerency did not reduce the Italian-American cultural gap. In fact, the United States, much more acquainted with Italy's major European allies, France and Great Britain, was emotionally focused on the struggle against German autocracy and had few antagonistic feelings for the Hapsburg Empire. Moreover, most American political observers were inclined to consider Italy a half-hearted and opportunistic ally, whose appetites in the Adriatic were essentially imperialistic. The result was that the United States initially declared war only against Germany, concentrated its army on the French front and declared war against the Austrian Empire only at the very end of 1917. The exact opposite could be said for Italy. Towards Germany, the "big brother" of her recent industrialization, Italy had little hostility. Italy's significant enemy was Austria, and Italian propaganda described the war as the last war of the Risorgimento, aimed at redeeming Italian territories still under Austrian rule. As a result, Italy declared war on Germany only in the summer of 1916. Therefore, for almost the entire duration of the war, the two nations kept fighting two parallel wars. In many respects, as Stuart Hughes put it, they were "allies-by-accident."[6]

However, there was a portion of Italian society that knew the United States. This was the emigrant class. Ambassador Page observed in 1916: "The common country folks know more of us than any other class does through the great body of emigrants."[7] In fact, beginning in the last decades of the nineteenth century, for the poorest country people, especially in southern Italy, emigration to America had become the only alternative to an impossible life. Emigrants' tales had alimented the popular myth of America as the land of freedom, democracy and plenty. In 1918 Antonio Gramsci accurately pointed out the "messianic" expectations of the Italian populace with respect to America's entrance into the war. It was the same attitude as the prospective emigrant had towards America as the promised land.[8]

With respect to the United States, therefore, two opposite social attitudes, strongly differentiated by class, existed in Italy.[9] Inter-class miscommunication allowed the longstanding survival of such a dualism. Then the war amplified it: the sympathetic attitude of Italian lower classes eventually flowed into the Wilsonian myth, whereas the ruling class's lack of awareness frequently turned into an open refusal of the American democratic message. Only at the very end of the war, after the rout of Caporetto, did Italian leaders change their attitude towards their powerful ally, at least on the surface.

The Turning Point of the Italian War: Caporetto

In the last days of October 1917, a forceful offensive by the Austrian army broke through Italian lines near the small town of Caporetto. The Italian retreat lasted for more than two weeks, until a new front was organized along the Piave River. At that point the entire region of Friuli and eastern part of Veneto was in Austrian hands, and the loss in men, equipment and supplies had severely undermined Italy's military power. Both Italian and

Allied leaders feared that Italy could collapse completely and follow the path of Bolshevik Russia to military paralysis and social revolution. According to many observers, including the American ambassador, the failure at Caporetto was largely the result of the effective propaganda waged among the troops by enemy agents, along with Vatican and socialist pacifists. In their view, it was a case of collective treason because the weary Italian soldiers just stopped fighting and disbanded.[10]

More than the American intervention of the previous April, the rout at Caporetto marked the turning point of the Italian war. Domestically, it forced the Italian ruling class to become aware of the perils of the nation's old-fashioned leadership. The defeat demonstrated that it was impossible to lead a mass army only through iron discipline; both troops and civilians needed ideals to motivate them. Another lesson was that the split between the ruling minorities and the people had to be closed to avoid military collapse and social uprising. Abruptly, in the closing months of 1917, Italian leaders had come to realize the vital importance of the new techniques of mass propaganda.

Internationally, Caporetto prompted the U.S. declaration of war on the Austro-Hungarian Empire, along with a vast involvement in Italy of American relief and propaganda apparatus. However, despite the persistent pressure from Italian leaders and American representatives in Italy, Washington did not respond to the Italian crisis by sending fighting troops. During the entire war Wilson concentrated America's Expeditionary Force on the French front. Even in the summer of 1918, when the American Army numbered millions of men, the United States sent Italy only Red Cross ambulances – c.f. Hemingway's novel[11] – publicity agents and a small number of soldiers who mostly toured Italy for propaganda purposes. The twofold response of sending material aid and propaganda allowed America's leaders to assist their distant ally in surviving what was essentially interpreted as a morale crisis, without becoming too involved in a questionable war.

Thus in 1918, Italian and American leaders found common ground in the need to propagandize the disaffected people of Italy, postponing to a quieter future the discussion of their conflicting war aims. The Italian ruling class quickly discovered the appeal that Wilson and the American myth had for ordinary Italians, and they exploited that appeal to achieve consensus and to stimulate military resistance. At the end of 1917, the Wilson myth was the only one capable of balancing the rising myth of Lenin. Thus, numerous local and national committees started to disseminate Wilsonian ideas among Italian soldiers and civilians. Even Italian conservatives, frightened by the spectre of a Bolshevik revolution, temporarily borrowed Wilson's powerful slogans. For almost a year different elements of Italian society, some sincerely others opportunistically, adopted the Wilson creed.

Therefore, in 1918 the Italian public at large, the press and the politicians became increasingly interested in their powerful ally. In no more than a year, the distant and mistrusted partner became the symbol of liberty and democracy for which the European masses were fighting.[12] This phenome-non, though partially spontaneous, was to a large extent the creation of a new force that was emerging in those days: propaganda.

The American Propaganda Campaign in Italy in 1917–1918

Propaganda was the salient feature of American activities in Italy during the last year of World War I. "The present crisis," Ambassador Page cabled in November 1917, "calls imperatively for efficient propaganda on our part."[13] The echo of Wilson's words in the Italian mass media were but a part of it, the other being the effective propaganda action very rapidly undertaken after Caporetto. The American campaign covered all the Italian territory. Its main arms were the activities of the American Red Cross, the Young Men's Christian Association (YMCA) and the Italian branch of Creel's Committee on Public Information (CPI). Also important were the American embassy's activities and new involvement in Italian political life.

The khaki uniform of the American army became popular in Italy not through the presence of combat units but via the officials of the American Red Cross and the YMCA. Throughout Italy, they became the visible representatives of a mythic America and its concern for the common man. It is difficult to overestimate the propaganda impact of these two humanitarian organizations on the lower strata of Italian society.

The American Red Cross arrived in Italy in November 1917, just after Caporetto. Despite the fact that its primary task was to provide medical assistance, the Red Cross became fully involved in propaganda. Indeed its officials considered themselves an integral part of the U.S. war effort. It was not by chance that they wore, in Italy as elsewhere, the uniform of the regular American troops. In Italy, they felt it their responsibility to carry not only material relief, but also Wilson's gospel to the discouraged masses. "The Red Cross is doing a great work here," Ambassador Page wrote to Wilson in January 1918, "and it has, as far as it goes, undoubtedly, an excellent effect as propaganda."[14]

At its peak, the organization's workforce in Italy included 949 American and some 1,000 Italians. The general headquarters was a seven-story building in downtown Rome. The country was divided into sixteen regional districts, each under a Red Cross delegate. Each district had offices in the provincial capital, a storehouse, and an efficient system of transportation to bring material aid and the message from America to the most remote village of the region.[15] The Red Cross's abundant aid gave the astonished Italians the impression that the organization had unlimited funds and the capacity to accomplish most any goal – an impression that corresponded with the mythical image of America as the land of plenty.

Relief for wounded and sick soldiers was but a small part of the organization's activity. Its primary mission was to invest Italian society with heart, will, and commitment. Accordingly, the American Red Cross spread its activity throughout Italy, from the front in the Alps to Sicily. Only 10% of Red Cross's aid went to soldiers at the front. Most of it was distributed to needy families, orphans and refugees.[16] The Red Cross was there to heal not only the combatants' wounds, but also to minister to the "wounds of the spirit" of the Italian people.[17] Its main target was to fortify the "home front," combating want and discontent through material relief and propaganda. Good examples of the Red Cross efforts were the frequent campaigns of money distribution to the poorest families of Italian soldiers: in the only campaign of April 1918, for example, the Red Cross distributed 6,431,000 lire, benefiting 290,000 families in 7,051 different towns and villages of Italy.[18]

Red Cross officers were careful to exploit the aid's propaganda value. All of them received generous propaganda materials, together with instructions about how to make their activity more productive from the propaganda standpoint. In a short while, Red Cross posts became centers of relief radiating the American message. Even the ambulances, before reaching the front, paraded in towns along the way.[19]

State and local public authorities, eventually aware of the need to maintain the morale of the troops and civilians, helped the Red Cross workers to get the maximum results from their propaganda activities:

> Generally [the Red Cross delegate] was met at the city gates by the Mayor, the town doctor, the parish priest, and other dignitaries, and a large crowd of people, and escorted to the city hall, showered with flowers and notes of welcome, while the band played and barefooted children ran ahead waving American flags. Then in the public square the delegate would deliver his message, the Mayor and the Prefect respond, and the meeting turn into an enthusiastic patriotic rally.[20]

Sometimes, in country villages the popular response took on religious overtones. In the town of Nuoro in Sardinia, for example:

> The distribution of garments took place, but this had to be temporarily interrupted, for the town had organized a religious procession in our honor. It was a most interesting sight. The children from the Red Cross colony with large American flags insisted on heading the procession, marching before the priests and the celebrants and a life-sized image of the Virgin, waving the Stars and Stripes. It made the picture rather incongruous, but was a pretty sight.[21]

The simple country folk, until then forgotten by Italian leaders, were the main focus of the American Red Cross campaign. They reacted most gratefully to the unexpected aid of this faraway country, already known to them from the tales of emigrants. In fact, it was immediately apparent that the success of the Red Cross among the Italian people was due not only to abundant aid, but also to the Italians' identification of the Red Cross with a mythical, generous and bountiful America. "Everywhere in Italy," Red

Cross delegates noticed, "America is known at first hand and admired as a land of power and plenty and loved as a land of freedom."[22] The Red Cross's propaganda effort simply tossed seeds onto already fertilized ground.

Likewise, the Young Men's Christian Association was an integral part of the American expeditionary force in Europe. In fact, as soon as the United States declared war against Germany, the YMCA Secretary General, John R. Mott, put the Association's services at the disposal of the government and took on the task of providing soldiers with recreational material and moral support. Since its contribution to the war effort was aimed at sustaining the troops' morale, the YMCA, more than any other institution, integrated its relief work with the diffusion of the American message.

In Italy, the YMCA concentrated its humanitarian activities on soldiers, both in the war zone and behind the lines. At the front, in particular, it provided recreational activities to help the fighting men endure their hardships. To this end, the YMCA took over the management of a system of both permanent and mobile centers of recreation, called "soldiers' houses," *case del soldato*. Furthermore, the YMCA agents created and managed relief stations, *posti di ristoro*, in major Italian railway stations and towns, and regularly visited hospitals and refugee and prison camps.

From January 1918 until the end of the war, the YMCA manned a total of approximately two hundred soldiers' houses. These included a range of buildings, from huts in the snowy mountains to country villas and town hotels requisitioned by the Italian army and put to the use of the "Y" and its soldier guests.[23] By the end of 1918, there were about 270 YMCA secretaries in Italy, along with around 1,500 Italian employees. Actually the organization was understaffed and not able to satisfy the increasing demands from the front and the rear areas. The urgent request for personnel and supplies provided the dominant theme of the early YMCA reports to Washington. In many ways, the cooperation of the Italian officers enabled the Americans to expand their productive capacity.

Italian officers valued the service rendered by the YMCA secretaries, who were able not only to spread good cheer and renewed confidence among the weary troops but also to cooperate with the army propaganda office and to speak frequently to soldiers close to the front lines. In tense situations along the front, the "Y" men had close rapport with the troops. From the beginning, Italians responded warmly to the activities of the "Y" and welcomed these representatives of the fabled United States.[24]

Last, but not least, in April 1918 the Committee on Public Information (CPI) established a branch office in Rome. With keen realism and sensitive attention to the importance of American public opinion, President Wilson established the CPI, a censorship and propaganda organization, a few days after intervention. George Creel was appointed as its chairman.[25] Within months, the new organization mushroomed into a gigantic advertising agency, whose dimensions were not equalled until the rise of the mass propaganda machines of the European dictatorships of the thirties. The

CPI employed about 150,000 paid and volunteer workers and exploited all means of propaganda. Abroad, as Creel remarked, the CPI carried "the Gospel of Americanism to Every Corner of the Globe."[26] It tried "to 'sell' America to the World. ... to bring home to them the meaning of American life, the purposes of America, our hopes and our ambitions."[27]

Charles Merriam, a University of Chicago professor of social science and a progressive Republican activist, became chief of the Rome Office. His resounding title of "High Commissioner for Italy" and his view that he was a personal emissary of the Federal government greatly disturbed Ambassador Page, but gave him access to Italian political circles.[28] Propaganda was not a part-time occupation for Merriam but his only absorbing duty. In a short time, he became an energetic directing force behind America's propaganda campaign in Italy.

The CPI staff in Italy of some fifty people was organized in four departments: the Department of the Press, the Department of Speakers, the Department of Pictures and the Film Bureau. A few statistics give an idea of the scope of CPI's activities in Italy. The News Department reached several hundred newspapers scattered throughout Italy. The Photographic Division alone distributed over 4.5 million postcards, more than 320,000 booklets containing extracts of President Wilson's speeches, 200,000 American paper flags, besides President Wilson's posters, war posters, bowpins, ribbons, buttons and American flags. The Department of Speakers alone estimated that in three months it had an aggregate audience of five million people.[29] The Film Bureau exploited the new medium of moving pictures, powerful especially among illiterate people.[30]

With its skilled enthusiastic staff and ample propaganda material, the CPI effectively carried out Creel's program of "mass education in Italy."[31] Sharing the basic belief of other Americans in Italy about the nature of the Italian collapse and the purpose of their intervention in Italian affairs,[32] CPI agents focused their efforts at spreading the news of America's extensive war preparations and of its democratic war aims among a people "largely uninformed, and in general...highly skeptical."[33] In a few months, they had launched a mass campaign, aimed, like those of the American Red Cross and the YMCA, at the common people, rather than the political or social elite. As a result, in 1918 the Fourth of July was celebrated in many Italian towns with considerable enthusiasm.[34] Later, in January 1919, the triumphal reception the Italian masses gave to Wilson demonstrated that the American propaganda campaign in Italy had succeeded.

Every American who worked in Italy in those years was struck by the rise of the Wilsonian myth among the masses.[35] Many of them borrowed images and terms from religion to describe the Italian people's attitude towards the United States and Wilson. The American consul at Venice, for example, observed that "Italy sees in America a kind of embodiment of Divine Providence...,"[36] while Arthur Bennington of the CPI reported about "Wilson being looked upon as almost God."[37] Norval Richardson of the

American embassy of Rome remembered a personal experience of his, when he was brought by a friend to see a sort of altar with lighted candles made by Italian soldiers in front of a large poster of President Wilson.[38] By the end of 1918, many representatives of the ruling class had much the same reverential, almost religious, attitude toward Wilson. A senator from Sicily, for example, vividly confessed to Richardson:

> I think of him [Wilson] as something remote, set apart from the rest of us, not a man of actual flesh and blood, but some one with only a mind and a voice that rings across the world from some far-distant Olympus. Do you know, I am almost afraid to see him. I am afraid he will be just like all the rest of us.[39]

Of course, such reports encouraged Wilson's confidence in his power over the Italian people and probably accentuated his tendency to disregard the national leaders as unrepresentative of the country.

The American Embassy of Rome in 1917–1919

The war transformed the American embassy of Rome from a quiet and peripheral post into a bustling one. America's intervention and the rout of Caporetto plunged the embassy's few employees into hectic work.[40]

Thomas Nelson Page, a Virginian gentleman and writer, was the American ambassador to Italy throughout the war. He was one of the most acute and sensitive observers of the gap between Italians and Americans and of the cross-cultural miscommunication it generated. From the beginning of his appointment, he tried to "bridge this sea of mutual misunderstanding and ignorance"[41] dividing the two countries and kept fighting the mounting tide of wartime oppositions up until the disappointing conclusion of the Peace Conference, after which he retired with bitterness.

As soon as the United States entered the war, Page directed his actions toward stimulating American propaganda in Italy and bettering the quality of American political intelligence about Italy. In April 1917, he created an Intelligence Office at the embassy, under the direction of Gino Speranza, a skilled Italian-American journalist who had been working in Rome since 1915. For more than two years Speranza wrote daily and weekly reports on the political, military and economic trends of the Italian war. His detailed and lucid analyses contained many insights into the Italian political situation.

The embassy in Rome was the first American organization given the challenge of coping with the Caporetto crisis. Using its established Relief Clearing House, the embassy passed on the initial aid from the American Red Cross. It also housed, before the arrival of the CPI, the first tiny publicity office, under the direction of John Hearley, a United Press journalist. Probably the greatest success of Page's early propaganda work was enlisting as a speaker Fiorello LaGuardia, who was in Italy at the end of 1917 as an officer of the American aviation training camp of Foggia. In his politics and in his personal life LaGuardia was exactly the kind of successful, integrated and democratic Italian-American pleasing to Italian masses at that moment. His extensive speaking campaign ranged far and wide.[42] However, the best propaganda, Page continuously reiterated in his letters to Washington, would have been to send a contingent of American soldiers to the Italian front: "such a detachment of troops would be worth more than fifty years of diplomacy." Even a small group of soldiers with a flag would produce an effect which would "last for generations."[43] Washington never responded to his pressure, with the single exception of a regiment sent to Italy in July 1918.

From 1917 Ambassador Page worked under exceedingly difficult conditions. Sonnino's secretive and distrustful attitude was matched by Wilson's indifference. As a result, rarely were Page's words listened to on both sides of the Atlantic. Like most of the American ambassadors at that time, he was not a career diplomat, having obtained his ambassadorship as a reward for his support during Wilson's first presidential campaign. Neither Wilson nor his close advisors, like Colonel Edward House and George Creel, considered him a reliable source of information or a proper vehicle for Wilson's plans abroad. With a few exceptions, they disregarded the services of American diplomats everywhere.[44]

The result of this situation was that the embassy's reports did not help to develop American policy towards Italy in the period 1917–1919. In particular, not one of Speranza's political reports found its way to Wilson's experts on Italy. Afterwards, at Paris, the reports from the embassy of Rome were overlooked because considered too sympathetic to Italian positions.[45]

As far as the Italian-American cultural gap was concerned, Page's observations deserved greater attention. Throughout his stay in Italy he sympathized with the Italian people and gained a basic understanding of the Italian situation, which, had it become the basis for policy, would have better reflected reality than the antiseptic reports written by Wilson's "experts" in far off America. Page never failed to take into consideration the intensely emotional components of the Italian war, offering a precise picture of Italy's socially differentiated attitude toward the United States.

American Political Intelligence of Italy

Secretary of State Robert Lansing was sensitive to Ambassador Page's words. Under the pressure of Page's letters, in three critical moments in 1918 Lansing endeavored to change Wilson's attitude towards Italy by revealing the destabilizing consequences of the lack of a political dialogue.[46] Unfortunately, Wilson did not listen to him. Routine rather than political intelligence was the State Department's main charge in Wilson's foreign policy.

The American president preferred to base his policy toward Italy on the activity of two novel institutions which were his own wartime creatures, the CPI and the Inquiry. Mainly because of the State Department's marginal role in policy formulation, the Inquiry, a body of around 130 experts, mainly university professors, became Wilson's main foreign-policy consultant organization.[47]

Previous work has revealed the important role the Inquiry played in shaping American policy towards Italy.[48] Its experts concentrated their efforts on the strategic and economic aspects of the disputed Italian boundaries, overlooking the vital political and emotional implications of the Italian war. In particular, Wilson's foreign-policy experts had scant contact with the Department of State and none with the American Intelligence Service based in Rome. Not one of the embassy's daily and weekly political reports was present among the hundreds of reports received at the Inquiry from all around the world to help Wilson's experts derive their conclusions. In all likelihood, Inquiry officials were unaware that such reports existed, since in 1918 they incorrectly located Gino Speranza in New York, when in fact he had left that city in the summer of 1915.[49]

Curiously, the only scholar charged officially with the study of Italy at the Inquiry was William Lunt, who was not an expert on Italy at all. He was a professor of English Medieval History at Cornell University, who had gained some knowledge of the Italian language through his early studies of Anglo-papal relations during the medieval period. He produced one long report focused on the linguistic boundaries of "The Italian Tyrol." He went to Paris as the only expert on Italy within the American peace delegation.

Wilson's reliance on the Inquiry's experts was apparent in the ringing appeal he made to them on his way to Paris: "Tell me what's right and I'll fight for it," he said. "Give me a guaranteed position."[50] Actually, this was one of the main problems of the American negotiating position at Paris. Both Wilson and his expert advisers assumed that a "guaranteed position" could be taken in international affairs. While Wilson was partially blinded by his almost religious feeling of mission, the Inquiry's engineers were blinded by the aura of science. They believed they possessed the particular skills, detachment and moral insight needed to promote the right reforms of the world society. In this reductionist frame of mind, Italy came to assume the part of "evil" and, as always, compromise between good and evil is not possible.

Thus, at Paris, Wilson's intransigence and moralism were nurtured by the narrow views of the Inquiry's territorial experts. Instead of receding, the Italian-American rift was growing during negotiations. The final attitude of the Inquiry's territorial experts towards Italy is well expressed in the letter they wrote to Wilson in April 1919, urging him not to yield to the "infamous" Italian requests.[51] This letter prompted the outbreak of the Adriatic crisis. Ambassador Page, relegated to the frustrating role of mere spectator, bitterly commented:

[Wilson's] geographical boundary experts ..., while undoubtedly wholly honest, seem to have entirely overlooked ... the most essential factor: the human. They have reported on figures and geographic facts, but have neglected, apparently, the weightier matters – the passions of peoples, and especially the passion of the Italian people ...[52]

The idea of basing the final decision on which may hang the peace of the world on the reports of geographical experts, and of leaving out the fundamental sentiments of peoples is erroneous, and can only lead to failure.[53]

In conclusion, Wilson's propaganda was effective and powerful. But American political intelligence about Italy was poor, and diplomatic action was almost absent. Information coming from Italy flowed to different bodies that were only loosely connected. In particular, of the three organizations dealing with the political situation in Italy – the State Department, the Committee on Public Information and the Inquiry –, the State Department was increasingly relegated to a secondary position. In the vacuum that was left the CPI undertook propaganda, while the Inquiry wrote scholarly reports on the "scientific" aspects of the Adriatic Question.

Conclusions: Limits of Wilson's Policy Towards Italy

We have seen the basic reasons for Wilson's popularity among the Italian masses at the end of World War I. The Wilson myth was rooted in an earlier myth of America that flourished in the flows of mass emigration. It was something like an oral tradition of the Italian lower classes, very different from the ignorance and distrust of the United States so common among the upper classes. By the end of the war the Wilsonian creed had emerged as a response to the lack of national ideals among the Italian people at large, filling a need which the old-fashioned ruling class had been unable to meet. Wilsonianism accompanied the entrance of the Italian masses to the political stage, proving to be the only ideology capable of stemming the contemporaneous diffusion of the myth of Lenin.

Wilson's popularity was strongly enhanced by the pervasive propaganda campaign promoted by the Wilson administration in Italy in 1918. It was one of the first such campaigns to which Italians were subjected. Its features showed the strong connection between realism and idealism that characterized Wilson's New Diplomacy.

After the rout of Caporetto, the Italian leaders abruptly discovered the power of the American and Wilsonian myths over the Italian masses and adopted Wilson's democratic slogans in their own propaganda activity. Legions of *petit bourgeois* spread this new credo across the country, finding in this apostolic effort a new, rewarding social and political role. For different reasons, by the end of 1918 many sectors of Italian society seemed open to a dialogue with the new world power.

The fiasco of Wilson's direct appeal to the Italian people in April 1919, which disrupted Italian-American negotiations at Paris, illustrated the limits of Wilson's overall attitude towards Italy. Italians, despite their early almost religious devotion to Wilson, would not tolerate his open disregard for their national leaders; at the outbreak of the April crisis, they rallied around their representatives. The public reaction – one might say overreaction – to Wilson's betrayal deepened the Italian-American rift.

How was it that Wilson, despite his enormous popularity, obtained such meagre results from the Italian-American negotiations at Paris? No doubt Wilson's foreign policy, superb in its enunciation of general principles and war aims, lacked the more prosaic arts of dialogue and compromise. The limits of a Wilsonian approach became apparent during the peace negotiations, when good political intelligence of Italy and strong contacts with Italian political parties and leaders would have paid handsome dividends. But Wilson never tried to build political alliances with Italian political leaders who shared his ideas and approach. Instead, he scorned politicians of every persuasion, whether part of the government or the opposition. Lacking respect for Italian leaders, he snubbed, for example, the repeated efforts of Francesco Nitti, future premier of the Italian government, to make contact with him.[54] Particularly in the case of Italy, the American president remained self-righteously committed to a crude distinction between peoples and governments. As he said to his technical advisers in a confidential speech on the ship that was bringing the American delegation to Paris: European leaders "do not represent their own peoples," while Americans "would be the only disinterested people at the peace conference."[55]

Wilson's belief that the United States was the herald of a "new standard of international morality"[56] was shared by most American negotiators and political observers. Wilson and most Americans also consistently undervalued the Italian political establishment. American envoys to Italy, official and unofficial, frequently urged Wilson to bypass Italian political representatives and to reach the Italian people directly.[57] Given this frame of mind, political dialogue between equals was almost impossible. This was perhaps the most important consequence of American exceptionalism. The result was that, after two years of intense and emotional contacts, Italy and the United States – each in a period of instability – once again found themselves separated and moving in different directions: the United States toward isolationism; Italy toward its historic encounter with fascism.

Notes

1. J. W. Schulte Nordholt, *Woodrow Wilson: A Life for World Peace* (Berkeley: University of California Press, 1991), 183.
2. Lippmann to Frankfurter, July 28, 1919, *Lippmann Papers*, Manuscripts and Archives Division, Yale University Library, New Haven, Connecticut.
3. T. N. Page, *Italy and the World War* (London, 1921), 142–143. Thomas Nelson Page was the American ambassador to Italy throughout the war.
4. F. Colgate Speranza, ed., *The Diary of Gino Speranza. Italy 1915–19* (New York: Columbia University Press, 1941), vol. 2, 126.
5. In January 1917, Nelson Page sent the Department of State a translation of

an article just published in a leading Italian newspaper, which commented on Wilson's recent note to belligerents: "The note of President Wilson was the proof of the immesurable [sic] spiritual distance which separates his particular mentality from the European mentality, and the impossibility of the comprehension of one by the other. Should one from Pekin [sic], after having slept for seven centuries in Confucianism, awaken unexpectedly today, he would have judged with not less accuracy and nearness of time and space as to European affairs. The South American Republics though indeed infinitely less advanced ... are, on the other hand, infinitely less Chinese than President Wilson ...," "The Two Americas," *La Tribuna*, January 5, 1917, article enclosed in the letter from Page to Lansing, January 6, 1917, Doc. No. 763.72/3163, Department of State, *Records of the Department of State Relating to World War I and Its Termination, 1914–29*, Record Group 59, M 367, National Archives, Washington, D.C. See also *La Tribuna*, December 24 and 25, 1916; and *Il Corriere della Sera*, December 24, 1916.

6.   H. Stuart Hughes, *The United States and Italy* (Cambridge: Harvard University Press, 1965), 7.

7.   Page to House, February 1, 1916, *House Papers*, Manuscripts and Archives Division, Yale University Library, New Haven, Connecticut.

8.   A. Gramsci, "Wilson e i Socialisti," *Il Grido del Popolo*, October 12, 1918, republished in *Scritti Giovanili 1914–1918* (Torino: Einaudi, 1958), 318.

9.   The massive phenomenon of Italian emigration to the United States also produced negative side-effects. It is true that in the long run it brought the two nations closer together, but in the short run it also generated new prejudices and stereotypes. In the United States, the growing tide of anti-Italian feeling was replacing the idyllic image of Italy created by the cultured travellers of an earlier period. In Italy, the emergence of the negative American attitude towards Italian immigrants and the mounting requests to close off frontiers was forming a different image of America as a racist, selfish and money-oriented society. On the dual image of Italy present among the American public, see J. A. DeConde, *Half Bitter, Half Sweet. An Excursion into Italian-American History* (New York: Charles Scribner's Sons, 1971); A. W. Salomone, "The Nineteenth Century Discovery of Italy: An Essay in American Cultural History. Prolegomena to a Historiographical Problem," *The American Historical Review* 73, no. 5 (June 1968): 1359–1391; J. P. Diggins, *Mussolini and Fascism, the View from America* (Princeton University Press, 1972), 5–21; and H. Stuart Hughes, *The United States and Italy*, 3–13.

10. The commander-in-chief of the Italian army, Luigi Cadorna, was the first to call Caporetto a "military strike;" see the letter from Cadorna to Orlando of November 2, 1917, as quoted in Luigi Cadorna, *La guerra alla fronte italiana* (Milano, 1921), vol. 2, 214.

11. E. Hemingway, *A Farewell to Arms* (London: The Albatross, 1947).

12. As Nelson Page noted, already in the spring of 1918, "The United States was the country best known to the body of Italians, – especially those of south Italy – and was greatly respected and appreciated. At first this appreciation was only of America's power, but later the spirit in which the United States entered the war came to be generally recognized, and this had an effect on the Italian spirit itself." [T. Hinckley], "Quarterly Report No. 2:

Italy, April 1, 1918 – June 30, 1918," enclosed in the letter from Page to Lansing, July 30, 1918, Doc. No. 865.00/70, Department of State, *Records Relating to Internal Affairs of Italy, 1910–29*, Record Group 59, M 527, National Archives, Washington, D.C.

13. Page to Lansing, November 14, 1917, *House Papers*.

14. Page to Wilson, January 29, 1918, Series 2: Correspondence, *Wilson Papers*, Library of Congress, Washington, D.C.

15. George M. Trevelyan, the well-known British historian, who was the Commandant of the First Ambulance Section of the British Red Cross at the Italian front from June 1915 to November 1918, remembered in his memoirs: "The Americans ... devoted themselves with characteristic energy, publicity, and largeness of scope, to fortifying the 'home front.' The American Red Cross did fine ambulance work at the front; but it did not confine itself to the sick and wounded there, or even to the refugees, but also pursued an intensive cultivation of the towns and villages of the north, centre, and south, combating want and discontent, the enemy garrison which always threatened the rear of the Italian army. Above all, the soldiers' families, with their insufficient separation allowances, received in every village of the Peninsula the aid of the American Red Cross, a fact which reacted most favourably on the tone of the army at the front," G. M. Trevelyan, *Scenes from Italy's War* (London: Jack, 1919), 199–200.

16. From November 1917 to June 1919, the total expenses of the American Red Cross Commission to Italy were almost 115 million lire, divided as follows: Civil Affairs 64.7%; Military Affairs 10.2%; Medical Affairs 13.2%; Tuberculosis Division 3%; Administrative Bureau 7.7%; Miscellaneous 1.1%. The Department of Civil Affairs made funds available for relief of refugees (33.1%), relief of Italian soldiers' families (22.1%), children's work (17.3%), *ouvroirs* (15.9%); see C. M. Bakewell, *The Story of the American Red Cross in Italy* (New York: McMillan, 1920), appendix 1, 209.

17. Bakewell, *The Story*, 36.

18. Ibid., 60.

19. Dos Passos, the American novelist who was in Italy as a volunteer ambulance driver, remembered: "The Italians were trying to boost public morale which had hit bottom after their smashing defeat at Caporetto. A great deal was made of our entrance into Ventimiglia. The newspapers tried to give the impression that our little Section 1 was the vanguard of a great American army. We were greeted by crowds and flagwaving and singing school-children. People pitched flowers and oranges into the ambulances." He was very disappointed with the Red Cross' "ornamental" role: "[Two Red Cross majors] rubbed me the wrong way by declaring in a fit of winey candor that we were at the Italian front only as a propaganda gesture to help keep the Italians in the war. I knew that well enough ... What I liked to think I was doing was dragging the poor wounded wops out from under fire, not jollying them into dying in a war that didn't concern them." John Dos Passos, *The Best of Times: An Informal Memoir* (New York: New American Library, 1966), 59, 63.

20. Bakewell, *The Story*, 58–59.

21. Ibid., 154. Similar descriptions of the enthusiastic reception the Red Cross

delegates were given in remote southern villages of Italy are contained in the cables sent by local police offices to the Ministero dell' Interno. Among many others, a cable from Avigliano (Potenza, Basilicata), for example, said: "*Oggi ore 10 iniziativa questo prosindaco imponente corteo con musica bandiere autorita' civili militari ecclesiastiche rappresentanze sodalizi popolari popolane recaronsi ricevere porte abitato membri croce rossa americana qui giunti da Potenza stop fra applausi entusiastici giunsesi municipio ove commissione lascio' lire dodicimila distribuirsi famiglie povere militari combattenti. Furono pronunciati discorsi inneggianti vittoria fratellanza italo americana dopo di che fu riaccompagnata estremo abitato sempre applaudita al suono inno nazionale americano stop*," Tenente Carabinieri Carini to Ministero Interno, April 12, 1918, Ministero Interno, *Direzione Generale Pubblica Sicurezza, Affari Generali e Riservati, Cat. A5G: Prima Guerra Mondiale*, Archivio Centrale dello Stato (Rome, Italy), fasc. 66, sf. 1.

22. Bakewell, *The Story*, 57.
23. A YMCA report from the front zone described a typical *casa*: "Over the entrance the crossed colours of Italy and America; the interior attractive and cosy, with 150 good books, a phonograph, and excellent discs, a piano, a fine little stage for concerts and other programs. Outside a small garden and a court for volley ball, basket ball, *boccie*, and other games. From manoeuvres on the high mountains nearby, the soldiers came down by teleferica in the evenings to the comfort of this home-like resort and to frequent concerts by professional musicians. From 5:30 till 9:30 the *casa* belonged to the men. At 9:30 they must give way to the officers, who enjoyed equally the only available resort," Olin D. Wannamaker, *With Italy in Her Final War of Liberation. A Story of the "Y" on the Italian Front* (New York: Fleming H. Revell Co., 1923), 204–205.
24. Olin D. Wannamaker, "Relief for Italy," *The New Republic*, November 16, 1918.
25. On the Creel's activity as chairman of the CPI see: James Mock and Cedric Larson, *Words that Won the War* (Princeton, New Jersey: Princeton University Press, 1939), 3–74; George Creel's books: *How We Advertised America* (New York: Harper, 1920), and *Rebel at Large. Recollections of Fifty Crowded Years* (New York: Putnam's Sons, 1947), 156–222; Frank L. Mott, *American Journalism. A History of Newspapers in the United States through 250 Years, 1690 to 1940* (New York: McMillan, 1941), 625–627; and Lee W. Huebner, "The Discovery of Propaganda. Changing Attitudes Toward Public Communication in America 1900–1930," unpublished dissertation 1968, Harvard University Archives, Cambridge, Massachusetts, 114–185.
26. The subtitle of the George Creel's book, *How We Advertised America*, is "The First Telling of the Amazing Story of the Committee on Public Information that Carried the Gospel of Americanism to Every Corner of the Globe."
27. George Creel, "Public Opinion in War Time," *The Annals*, 78 (July 1918): 189–190.
28. "He [Merriam] gives himself the title of 'High Commissioner' and his manner and actions are such as to convey the impression to the Italians that he is a kind of secret special plenipotentiary having extraordinary powers in Washington. He has made considerable personal impression in Rome owing

to his pretentions and his large appropriations," Rickley to Creel, October 2, 1918, *Committee on Public Information Papers*, box 20-17-A1, National Archives, Washington, D.C. See also: Karl D. Barry, *Charles E. Merriam and the Study of Politics* (Chicago and London: University of Chicago Press, 1974), 89–95.

29.   George Creel, *Complete Report of the Chairman of the Committee on Public Information, 1917: 1918: 1919* (Washington: Government Printing Office, 1920), 192–193.

30.   C. E. Merriam, "American Publicity in Italy," *The American Political Science Review*, 13, no. 4 (November 1919): 546–553.

31.   Ibid., 191.

32.   "What [in early 1918] made the situation still more serious – Merriam observed – was the fact that the Italian defeat at Caporetto had been caused to a large extent by enemy propaganda," moreover "the combination of Giolittians, Socialists powerful in rural as in urban districts, and underground business interests, was a powerful one, and made itself felt in weakening the war will of Italy," Charles Merriam, "American Publicity in Italy," 542–543.

33.   Ibid., 544.

34.   See *Il Corriere della Sera*, July 5, 1918 and *Il Messaggero*, July 4, 1918.

35.   "... the popularity of President Wilson ... is so great as to be positively astounding. Scarcely a shop of any importance but has its photograph, home made drawings, or rudely sculptured bust of the President displayed in its windows. The American flag is everywhere seen. ... the propaganda material disseminated by this office [the CPI] is in evidence everywhere...," report by K. Moses to J. H. Hearley, Rome, n.d. [but November – December 1918], box 20-B3, *Committee on Public information Papers*.

36.   Harvey B. Carroll, Jr., "Why half a million American soldiers are immediately needed on the Italian front," September 17, 1918, Doc. No. 763.72/11898, *Records of the Department of State Relating to World War I and its Termination, 1914–29*.

37.   Report by A. Bennington, Rome, November 30, 1918, box 20-B3, *Committee on Public Information Papers*.

38.   "I doubt very much if anywhere else in the world President Wilson achieved quite the same exalted position that he did in Italy towards the end of 1918; it was a short-lived popularity – it disappeared almost entirely a few weeks after the Peace Conference had been in session – but it was tremendous while it existed. At that time you could not go anywhere in Rome without finding a life-sized portrait of President Wilson – furnished wholesale by the Bureau of Public Information ... Signor Vovro Veelson ... was indisputably the man of the hour ... a religious significance quickly developed about his name ... I had no idea of the extent of this religious attitude until one of my friends, an Italian soldier, asked me to go with him to one of the barracks and witness a scene that he felt sure would amaze me. As a matter of fact, what he showed me did exceed anything I had heard of pertaining to the Wilson cult. We arrived at the barracks at dusk and were shown down a long corridor, at the end of which a sort of altar had been made of a box covered with a white cloth. Over this hung a large poster of President Wilson. Just below the picture were four lighted candles; and kneeling before this

temporary altar were several soldiers ... I heard later that this poster had been hung in many shrines throughout the country districts of Italy, where mothers and wives constantly brought candles and flowers and prayed for their sons and husbands at the Front ..." N. Richardson, *My Diplomatic Education* (New York: Dodd Mead and Co., 1923), 179–181.

39. Ibid., 196.
40. Indeed, the number of political dispatches transmitted from the embassy to the State Department in the fall of 1917 equalled the total number for the several years preceding it, see roll no. 4: "Political Affairs," *Records of the Department of State Relating to Internal Affairs of Italy, 1910–29.*
41. F. Colgate Speranza, ed., *The Diary of Gino Speranza*, vol. 2, 25.
42. "'La Guardia is more popular here than if he were an Italian Deputy,' exclaimed one Italian cabinet member. 'I love him like a brother.' He combines 'in his own person American strength and Latin geniality. In fact, forming a link between the two races,'" Arthur Mann, *La Guardia. A Fighter Against His Times, 1882–1933* (Philadelphia and New York: J.B. Lippincott, 1959), 90.
43. Page to [House], n.d. [but November 1917], Miscellaneous n.d., *T.N Page Papers*, Duke University Library, Durham, North Carolina); and Page to Wilson, January 15, 1918, *Wilson Papers*.
44. As Walter Lippmann sarcastically commented in 1919: "The truth is that our embassies were either telegraph or passport stations ... as independent sources of information they did not, with one or two exceptions, exist. The proof of this assertion is that the President did not use them. It never occurred to him to use his diplomatic service where matters of high policy were concerned. It never occurred to him to inform his diplomatic service as to what he was about. Mr. Creel's agent might know, or pretend to know; some other agent sent from Washington might know some scrap of policy, but the very last place to discover American policy was an American Embassy. ... Mr. Wilson acted through other agencies, informed himself from other sources, and acted independently. The [State] Department, divorced from responsibility, lacked all incentive, and so it creaked along out of contact with American diplomacy, a mere instrument of diplomatic formality," Walter Lippmann, "For a Department of State," *The New Republic*, September 17, 1919.
45. John W. Gould, "Italy and the United States, 1914–1918: Background to Confrontation," unpublished dissertation, Yale University 1969, 376.
46. In January, after the Fourteen Points' Message, Lansing stressed the perils hidden in the Italian feeling of being misunderstood and discriminated against by the Allied countries. In May, in Lansing's mind, Italy should be the first beneficiary of the new American policy openly aimed at the dismemberment of the Hapsburg Empire. Finally, in October, Lansing urged a political overture towards Italy, which was to be reinforced by the sending of American troops to the Italian front. See Lansing to Wilson, January 25, 1918, *The Lansing Papers, 1914–20* (Washington: Government Printing Office, 1939), vol. 2, 89–90; my paper, "Wilson e il patto di Londra nel 1917–18," *Storia Contemporanea*, 22, no. 3 (June 1991): 501–502; Lansing to Page, May 11, 1918, *Papers Relating to the Foreign Relations of the U.S.,*

1918, suppl. 1, vol. 1 (Washington: Government Printing Office, 1933), 803; and Lansing to Wilson, October 19, 1918, Doc. No. 763.72.119/2223, R. 385, *Records of the Department of State Relating to World War I and Its Termination 1914–29*.

47. President Wilson created it a few months after intervention and placed it under the supervision of Colonel House, his influential, unofficial advisor, who was said to be the real Secretary of State during Wilson's administration. The Inquiry's staff played an important role both in the drafting of the Fourteen Points and in the Paris peace negotiations.

48. See Daniela Rossini, *L'America riscopre l'Italia. L'Inquiry di Wilson e le origini della Questione Adriatica, 1917–1919* (Rome: Edizioni Associate, 1992).

49. "Confidential Memorandum of Persons Having Information in Regard to Special Subjects," arrived at the Inquiry on January 28, 1918. Doc. No. 991, *Records of the Inquiry*, National Archives, Washington, D.C.

50. D. H. Miller, *My Diary at the Conference at Paris*, 21 vols. (Washington, D.C.: privately printed, 1928), vol. 1, 373.

51. "Never in his career did the President have presented to him such an opportunity to strike a death blow to the discredited methods of old-world diplomacy. ... To the President is given the rare privilege of going down in history as the statesman who destroyed, by a clear-cut decision against an infamous arrangement, the last vestige of the old order," letter from I. Bowman, W. E. Lunt, C. Day, D. W. Johnson, C. Seymour and A. A. Young to Wilson, April 17, 1919, in Baker R. S., *W. Wilson and the World Settlement* (Garden City, New York, 1923), vol. 3, 278–279.

52. Page to House, May 26, 1919, Selected Correspondence, *House Papers*.

53. Page to White, June 2, 1919, Diplomatic Papers, 1919, *T. N. Page Papers*.

54. Alberto Monticone, *Nitti e la grande guerra (1914–1918)* (Milan, 1961), 59 and after; F. Barbagallo, *Francesco S. Nitti*, (Turin, 1984), 189–199 and 222–227.

55. David Hunter Miller, *My Diary at the Conference at Paris*, vol. 1, 370.

56. Letter from Johnson to House, April 26, 1920, *House Papers*.

57. For example, in a report to House on the Italian situation, R. S. Baker, future official biographer of Wilson, quoting an article of *The Nation*, noted: "Mr. Wilson may have to come out and appeal to the scores of millions who accept his leadership against the trusts and the cabinets who reject it," Baker to House, December 6, 1918, *House Papers*. Merriam, on the other hand, in a report on "Democratic Ideals" in Italy referred that "A high official of the Italian Government said to me in effect: The European governments are willing to take American men her money, her munitions, her food, her moral support through the preaching of democracy and universal peace; but in the end at the peace settlement they expect to have their way. They are willing to allow us to talk democracy as a war measure, but they intend to have 'no nonsense' in the finish. ... He said, however, that the President could make peace terms on his own basis, that is on a democratic basis, but that he would have to go over the heads of the governments representatives and appeal to their people," [C. Merriam], "Democratic Ideals," s. d. [prob. summer 1918], *Committee on Public Information Papers*, box 20-B2. The possibility of a President Wilson's direct appeal to the Italian people was up in the air long before he actually made it.

9

The Principle of Self-Determination of Nations and American Policy in the Region of the Former Yugoslavia from Wilson to Roosevelt

Ivan Čizmić

In a speech before the Peace League in Washington May 27, 1916, about the foundations for lasting peace in Europe President Woodrow Wilson stressed that America's neutrality did not mean disregard for events in Europe. He agreed with the principles of protection for small States, freedom and the right to self-determination for all, even small States, and unequivocally stated that: "... each people has the right to choose the sovereignty under which it is to live."[1] Not long after Wilson's speech the American ambassador in Vienna, F. Penfield, reported to Washington about reactions to it in Vienna. Penfield said that the government in Austria supported peace, but military circles wished for war until victory. One of the reasons for this was that certain circles feared that President Wilson would not be an effective mediator who would represent the interests of a Monarchy embracing ten different nations. Wilson's belief of the natural right of all peoples to govern themselves was not acceptable to a Monarchy which ruled over different peoples.[2]

On December 26, 1916 the German government, with the agreement of its allies, forwarded a proposal to the Antanta powers for direct talks on neutral territory between all warring sides in an attempt to exchange attitudes to peace. In the meantime, on December 18, 1916, President Wilson sent his own peace proposal to the warring sides. In a response to these initiatives the Allies sent a note on January 10, 1917 in which amongst other things they sought the liberation of Czechoslovaks, Poles, Serbs and Slavs.[3]

South Slav emigrants from Austro-Hungaria who gathered in the Yugoslav Committee in London followed President Wilson's speeches with great interest. The President of the Yugoslav Committee, A. Trumbić turned to the Yugoslav National Council in Washington[4] with a letter alerting them of the necessity of forwarding despatches and manifestoes to the American government. In the letter Trumbić writes:

We've turned great attention to Wilson ... because in his message to the Senate he stressed some principles which were almost written for us and are to be our moral support in the struggle for freedom from Austro-Hungaria and in the struggle against the appetites of our neighbours abroad and finally because I am under the impression the Union is looking for ways to enter the conflict so as to have the right to partake in future congresses between warring powers when it comes to brokering peace. We can be pleased with this because at the congress the Union will bring its democratic outlook about freedom and it will increase the importance of those elements which not only defend freedom for small nations but will disenable the old politics of violence over the small which Wilson has openly branded.[5]

On April 6, 1917 the United States declared war with Germany. In Wilson's declaration of war he said: "We will fight for that which is held in the depths of our souls, for democracy, so that all those who are oppressed can raise their voice and choose their government; for freedom of small nations, for the universal dignity of rights, that the alliance of free nations ensure peace and survival for peoples and make freedom govern the world in its universal and absolute form."[6]

Political statements made by President Wilson about the just resolution of political problems in Europe on the principle of self-determination of peoples had a fundamental meaning for the South Slavs in Austro-Hungaria and was a moral support for their own national aspirations. It was only in the first half of May that the Secretary of State Robert Lansing asked the head of the Near Eastern Division of the State Department, Albert H. Putney, to study the Yugoslav problem and submit a solution. Putney, former Dean of the Illinois College of Law and author of several books on international finance, had at the time close relations with a Czech, Charles Pergler, and with the Serbian Minister Ljubo Mihailović. He was the first of the State Department high officials to take an interest in the "Slav" problem. At Lansing's request on May 26, 1917 he prepared a memorandum "Nationalistic Aspiration in the Near East." This memorandum was lost in the State Department and on June 1 Putney was asked to supplement it with suggestions on reaching a peace settlement "along nationalistic lines."

The Supplement had seven headings: (1) The Yugo-Slav Question; (2) Poland; (3) Bohemia; (4) Russia; (5) Rumania; (6) Turkey; (7) Persia. In the introduction Putney stresses: "The most immediate cause of the present war was the irreconcilable conflict between nationalistic aspirations of the South Slavs and the dynastic interests of the House of Habsburg."

Putney examines three solutions within the framework of the Yugoslav question: (a) incorporation of all Yugoslavs in the Habsburg Empire; (b) return to the *status quo ante*, and (c) creation of an independent Yugoslav state. Putney rejected the first two solutions and accepted the third. According to Putney the Yugoslav state would include Serbs and Croats but not the Slovenes, whose historical bonds with Austria were too old to disrupt, and because the Slovenes were separated from the Serbs and Croats by linguistic differences. With regard to Rijeka and Trieste Putney says that they naturally belonged to Italy but Rijeka should remain in Austria as its only access to the sea. Putney concluded his recommendation with the following: "The three most numerous subject races of the Near East at present are the Poles, the Serbo-Croats, and the Bohemians. It is entirely practicable to give complete political independence to each of these races. The creation of these three Slav states would be a death blow to Germany's dreams of *Drang nach Osten*."

Lansing never gave Putney's recommendation to President Wilson, who at the time thought differently about solving the Slav problem in Austro-Hungaria. However, the memorandum is significant in that it shows that Lansing envisaged the possibility of solving the Slav problem according to the principle of nationality.[7]

Even though the State Department showed some interest in the Slavs in Austro-Hungaria, their desires for the Allies to recognize their right to self-determination and separation from Austro-Hungaria were not accepted by the Allies at the beginning of 1918. Lloyd George's speech of January 6 and Wilson's fourteen points of January 10 seemed to thwart all their efforts for freedom. In point 10 Wilson stated: "… The peoples of Austro-Hungaria which we wish to see preserved and ensured, need to be given the freest possibility for autonomous development." In other words Wilson did not support independence for the Slav peoples in Austro-Hungaria but rather he took the stance that, once some territorial concessions had been given to Serbia, Rumania and Italy, the Monarchy should be preserved and its peoples ensured free and democratic development within its borders.

At the beginning of 1918 the Kingdom of Serbia did not unconditionally support the unification of South Slavs into one state. Even when a Serbian mission visited the USA in January 1918, in a speech given by its leader M. Vesnić before the American Congress it was evident that Serbia was not prepared to support Yugoslav unity at all costs as Vesnić expressed solidarity with the political program set out in the fourteen points. By the same token the Serbian Premier Nikola Pašić, in a note dated January 17 to the Allied governments, and in response to Lloyd George's speech of January 6, asked that the issue of Bosnia-Herzegovina be considered as well as the significance of this problem with regard to Serbia. In a letter which Pašić wrote to his ambassador in Washington, Ljubo Mihajlović on January 22, Pašić demanded that he investigate the American government's view of Serbia's pretensions to Bosnia-Herzegovina.[8]

Another Balkan problem emerged for American policy in the first months of 1918. This was the diplomatic activity of Montenegro's King Nikola who was attempting to convince the USA to recognize Montenegro as an ally. Seeing the discord in the Yugoslav line during the sessions of the Rome Conference the American ambassador in Rome, Thomas Page, sent a report to Washington in which amongst other things he wrote that there were no Montenegrins at the conference "thanks to the Yugoslav discord and jealousy." On May 7, 1918 Page informed Wilson that during his stay in Rome King Nikola called him and told him that the Montenegrin people held their hopes in America as the embodiment of freedom and democracy. Nikola requested the ambassador to recommend Montenegro and himself to President Wilson and he stressed "that his country consigned itself to America." Page responded that America and Wilson had great affinity and respect for all free people and that he would relay the conversation to Wilson; however, the final stance on the Montenegrin issue could be made only by the American government. Nikola gave Page a list of Montenegro's demands which the ambassador relayed to Wilson. Page asked the king whether he was satisfied in France to which he replied: "There is a lot of Serbs around me there, and the Serbs don't like me. They despise my country and wish to absorb it." The king also informed the ambassador that he had directed his representative to Washington.[9]

King Nikola's activities were felt in America immediately after the United States had entered the war. The king welcomed this decision by the American government and its people and turned to the government with a plea for a loan of ten million francs. Furthermore, in the beginning of October 1917 he began the process of opening a Montenegrin Embassy in Washington; this was approved by the American government.

In his fourteen points Wilson recognized the right to renew Montenegro. King Nikola nominated Gvozdenović as the Montenegrin ambassador to Washington in July 1918 and he in turn was received by President Wilson on September 20. Gvozdenović gave the following statement to the American press: "Small and oppressed states look to victory for the USA as a guarantee for their salvation … Montenegro which is the smallest among the allies … expects freedom from its reputable allies."[10]

Gvozdenović's arrival stimulated the American press to write a series of articles on the Montenegrin question. The *Washington Star* for example, on November 3, 1918 wrote: "The aspirations of Montenegro are the same as those of other nations of the same race, to become part of the Yugoslav confederation, whilst preserving its autonomy, independence and tradition."[11]

The Serbian government through its ambassador in Washington opposed the opening of the Montenegrin Embassy. On October 5 Vesnić informed Mihajlović from Paris that the American government had approved the opening of the Montenegrin Embassy and sent him a list of names which King Nikola had submitted. On October 24 Pašić requested his ambassador to Washington to prevent the nomination of Petar Plemenac as the Montenegrin ambassador and to discredit him both as an individual and as a politician.

After attempts to divide Austro-Hungaria from Germany had fallen through and following a report which was sent to Washington on May 16 by Pleasant Stowell, the American ambassador in Switzerland, in which he recommended a more decisive attitude towards Austro-Hungaria and for the preparation of plans to divide the Monarchy, Washington came to believe that the destruction of Austro-Hungaria needed to be a main aim for

America as this would contribute to a quicker end to the war.[12] This is why Lansing could continue with the initiative to resolve the Yugoslav question which he had started over a year ago. In fact before Stowell's suggestion, that means on May 10, 1918, Lansing in a memorandum had warned President Wilson about the problem which had arisen because Austro-Hungaria had not been separated from Germany, as well as other important political factors which resulted from the conference of oppressed peoples held in Rome. Lansing posed an alternative in this memorandum: Whether to continue to support the existence of Austro-Hungaria within its existing borders, or to assist the process towards the disintegration of the Monarchy and then trying to influence unification for each of its individual components on the basis of self-determination of nations. Lansing questioned: "Do we need to encourage such a movement in Austro-Hungaria, giving support to the peoples who seek independence? Will we wait or will we disencourage them?" In his memorandum Lansing individually listed Yugoslavia, Czechoslovakia and Rumania as states which sought freedom.

After Lansing's memorandum Wilson decided upon liberation and self-determination for oppressed nations, and with that American policy took on a concrete new and decisive direction. Wilson and Lansing took to this policy by informing the Allied governments who offered a considerable amount of opposition. France and England hesitated to specify their viewpoint on Austro-Hungaria while Italy recommended caution, especially with regard to the Yugoslavs, in order for this issue not to cause discord amongst the Allies. The Serbian government also asked for an explanation, via their ambassador, of the new American policy.

Fearing that the hesitative attitude of the Allies, especially Italy, and that Serbia's intervention would dishearten Wilson, Lansing on May 21 submitted a new memorandum. He informed the president of Page's report according to which Italy was in favor of the independence or at least self-determination of Czechoslovakia but was not favorable towards the Yugoslavs because of their ties with Serbia, whose ambitions and demands clashed with those of Italy with regard to the Adriatic coastline. Lansing emphasized that Italy's belief that the Serbs and the Yugoslavs would fall under the control of Austria, was without foundation.

> Knowing their motives will we listen to Italy and withhold any assistance to the South Slavs? Will the possible dissension that may arise in the Austrian Empire be of value to the awakening sense of hope in these peoples for independence even when this would not perhaps be in tune with the ambitious expectations held by Italy with regard to the east coast of the Adriatic? I believe that the Yugoslavs are adequately developed as a nation and have the right to self-determination and this right must be recognized except in the case where this would hamper their political development. This amounts to whether we will listen to Italy or recognize the justice in the Yugoslav wishes for a nationalistic existence

not allowing Italy's extreme demands for territory which is now inhabited by the Yugoslavs. Looking at in on principle, I believe the Yugoslavs and Serbs have the right to support; but looking at it from the point of attaining a victory in the war then the decision is a lot more difficult. I believe however, that it is necessary to make some decision and quickly because if the idea is to awaken the oppressed peoples of Austro-Hungaria then now is the time to do so.[13]

After Lansing's memoranda, and following the conference of oppressed nations in Rome in April 1918, the American government considered that the situation was ripe to offer open support to the struggle for independence of the Slav people in Austro-Hungaria, and that at the same time this would not provoke a reaction by Italy or any other of the Allies. Speaking for his government on May 29 Lansing stated that the United States had followed the conference of oppressed nations in Rome with great interest and that the nationalistic aspirations of Czechoslovakia and the Yugoslavs for free-dom were looked at with serious affinity. That same day Lansing sent a message to Ambassador Page in Rome along with this text and requested he give the Italian foreign minister an explanation how this statement could be of double interest for the Czechs and Yugoslavs as well as the Allies, and Italy in particular, because it would encourage the South Slav and Czech migrants in the USA to offer huge aid to the American government to fill the ranks of the Czech Legion in Italy with new units and would stimulate the Czechs and Yugoslavs in the Austro-Hungarian army to desert.[14]

In September 1918 the Austro-Hungarian foreign minister Otokar Czerin attempted to attain a distinct peace for Austro-Hungaria with the aim of saving the Monarchy. In keeping with these initiatives, the Austro-Hungarian government via the Swedish Ambassador W. Ekongren on October 4 forwarded to the American government a peace offer in which, amongst other things, it offered autonomy for the Slavs. Lansing rejected the offer noting that the American government had also "recognized fully the right for the Yugoslav nationalistic aspirations for freedom."[15] This statement represented America's final stance on the Yugoslav issue and put an end to all other combinations for a solution within the framework of Austro-Hungaria. At the time the State Department had high hopes for the Slav movement in Austro-Hungaria and especially for Czech military units in Siberia, and so on June 28 the American government issued a new statement:

Ever since this government on May 29 issued a statement which refers to the nationalistic aspirations of the Czechs and Yugoslavs for freedom, German and Austrian officials and their sympathizers have tried to misinterpret and distort the clear meaning of that statement. So that there can be no misunderstanding about its meaning the State Secretary has today expressly announced the American government's viewpoint that all branches of the Slav races need to be totally liberated from German and Austrian rule.[16]

However, the problems for the South Slavs were far from solved. On August 19 Lansing informed Wilson that Austro-Hungaria needed to be destroyed but he was not sure that full recognition should be given to the Czechs as yet because this would disturb the South Slavs if they were not to be recognized as well. Lansing said that as far as the Yugoslavs were concerned the difficulty was in: "as is known, Italy's jealousy and Serbia's wishes to absorb the Yugoslavs rather than enter into a federation with them and this shows us that we need to be patient in making political decisions." On September 2 Wilson responded and told Lansing that Czechoslovakia needed to be recognized. He did not mention the Yugoslavs. This in reality meant that the South Slavic question had still not been resolved but that the American government was waiting to see what decision would be brought forward by Italy, the Serbian government and the Yugoslav Committee in London.[17] The State Department rejected the Serbian Premiere N. Pašić's request of June 28 that Serbia be given the right to liberate the Yugoslavs, which would have meant absorption of Austro-Hungarian Yugoslavs into a Serbian state.

The work of the conference towards a truce in Paris was a great trial for Austro-Hungarian Yugoslavs. At a meeting of the Executive War Council held in Paris on October 31, 1918, it was made possible for Italy to occupy the western sections of the Monarchy. This enabled Italy to occupy virtually the entire Croatian coast including the city of Rijeka. The Serbian representative in Paris, M. Vesnić did not defend the Yugoslavs' interests decisively enough. On the other hand the Italians led a very strong propaganda campaign in order to win over public opinion in Allied countries. This is why the Italian ambassador to Washington, Macchi di Cellere, at the beginning of 1919 requested his government to open its own information centres in New York and Washington. When these centres were to be officially opened a special Italian mission headed by Pietro Tozzi arrived in the United States. The result of this action was that at the beginning of 1919 a majority of the American press wrote in favor of Italy's pretensions for the east Adriatic coast.

In the first few months of 1919 the Italian migrant press was dominated by the question of Italy's right to Rijeka. They conveyed articles from the press in Italy, and "Italy's Sons" and "The Association of Italian Irredentists" asked their members to send petitions to the American delegates in Paris in support of Italy's demands. When it was established that Wilson favored the Yugoslav demands for the Adriatic, the "Association of Italian Irredentists" warned him that it was strategically necessary for Italy to control the Adriatic, while the *Il Carrocio* newspaper alerted Italian migrants to oppose Wilson's proposal. The American-Italian Congressman Fiorello La Guardia stated that there were differences between Czechoslovakia, which was fighting alongside the Allies, and the Yugoslavs who were against them. The Italian Ambassador Di Cellere on February 13, 1919 told the *World* newspaper that: "the former Austrian ruler Carl in a speech once said that the real and effective force in his army was the Croatian element because the

Croats were his only soldiers that showed any military spirit."[18] This statement was intended to arouse discomfort amongst the Americans against Croatian pretensions toward the Adriatic. A letter which Senator Henry Lodge sent the Italian community in Boston in March 1919 certainly enhanced the Italian propaganda. In the letter Lodge noted: "Italy is looking at Rijeka as did our forefathers at our states when they saw the Mississippi river, holding that if any nation wished to invade the mouth of the Mississippi they would be considered an enemy to the United States."[19] An Illinois senator also stated that: "Rijeka is Italian by blood, language and tradition so Italy's demands to establish natural ties between Rijeka and its mother country were totally justifiable."[20]

The president of the Yugoslav Committee in London, A. Trumbić, turned to the Yugoslav National Council in Washington on October 30, 1918 and asked them to request the U.S. government for fifty thousand soldiers with the aim of occupying strategic points in Dalmatia, Istria, Kranjska, Croatia and Slavonia. He was afraid that these contestable regions would not be occupied by the Serbian or Italian armies and that this would affect the development of the political situation. When representatives of the Committee, N. Grškovič and A. Hinkovič, talked about this matter with the Assistant Secretary of State Phillips he asked them why the Yugoslav Committee had such an aversion to Serbian occupation. He was informed that occupation would favor greater Serbian aspirations, and that Austro-Hungarian Yugoslavs could never accept a Greater Serbia which would from the very beginning undoubtedly carry the seeds of civil war and would be detrimental to world peace. Phillips agreed with the Council representatives and emphasized that there were no obstacles to the Yugoslav Committee's recognition in as much as the Committee first came to an agreement with the Serbian government. Phillips forwarded Trumbić's proposal along with his own letter of explanation to Lansing. However, Lansing took no action in this regard. It was far too late for any American military intervention because Colonel House had already accepted Austria's peace conditions concerning Austro-Hungaria. Apart from that Lansing knew that Wilson did not look favorably at using American troops to occupy territory of the former Austro-Hungarian empire. Nor did Baker from the war ministry. Apparently the Office of War Information believed that Austro-Hungarian territories should be occupied by Allied armies in an attempt to thwart Bolshevism from spreading.

However, despite Wilson and Baker's negative stance it appears that there were certain individuals in the American government who believed that Trumbić's proposal should be adopted. This is seen in a telegram which Grškovič sent Trumbić on October 31 in which he specifically stated that Phillips showed special interest in American troops occupying some of these territories. In the telegram it is noted: "If the cease-fire is concluded with Austria the American troops situated on the Italian front could be used for occupation."[21] It never came to occupation. It is necessary to point out that until 1920 Trumbić regarded the presence of American troops as a guarantee which ensured Yugoslav territories. Trumbić used an official of the Yugoslav Relief for this purpose. At the end of 1919 he met in Paris with this representative, Predović, after returning from the United States. In Washington Predović met with Secretary of the Navy Daniels and in Trumbić's name asked that steps be taken with the government which would prevent the American navy from being withdrawn from the Adriatic because if this was done the Italians could occupy the whole of Dalmatia.[22]

Wilson was opposed to the occupation of Austro-Hungarian lands for the same reasons as his opposition to intervention in Russia: "On principle and for the sake of incalculable difficulties keep hands off the pieces of Austro-Hungaria and reduce outside intervention to a minimum." On November 11 the State Department issued a statement that in future the United States would not meddle in the problem of Rijeka nor the Adriatic question because there were other problems that the American government needed to resolve. With this statement American politicians ceased to be involved in the Adriatic debate.[23]

At the end of 1918 and in 1919 the State Department was fully aware of all the problems surrounding Yugoslavia's unity and had serious criticisms of Italian policies towards the Adriatic issue but even more so against the imperialist aspirations of the Kingdom of Serbia. As an example there is the case when J. Simić, Serbia's ambassador in Washington, on October 22, 1918 informed the Serbian government that official American circles believed that there was disorder in the Serbian parliament. Even though the Americans did not want to interfere with the internal affairs of Allied countries the internal situation nevertheless affected policy. They were, said Simić, by their outlook and education very sensitive to parliamentary rule and a negative attitude to a particular country could affect that entire land which is dependent on America.

Simić said that the State Department, which was always in favor of Yugoslavia's unification, received the November 1, 1918 Proclamation of the establishment of the Kingdom of Serbs, Croats and Slovenes, with great reserve. The American press did nevertheless print news of the proclamation and excerpts from it but without any comment or special attention. Simić noted that this, "according to our people, great historical event did not receive the best reception in American circles and the press need not draw us to the conclusion that America opposes it. Almost the entire political public as well as government circles are sympathetic to the unification of our people. But despite all this favor and sympathies particularly to the Serbian people there still exists a certain lack of confidence ... the belief that we at home do not respect a parliamentary regime has taken on an even stronger hold and this negatively influences all national activities even those to do with the economic renewal of our country."[24]

A lack of confidence in the Yugoslav state continued in the American State Department the entire time between the two world wars. American

politicians and the American public considered Yugoslavia to be an unsuc-
cessful or "artificial compilation" resulting from the Treaty of Versailles.[25]
Nevertheless, in 1941 the American president and government sharply
condemned the aggression of the Axis powers towards the Kingdom of
Yugoslavia. Immediately after the attack on Yugoslavia in April 1941,
President Franklin D. Roosevelt and Secretary of State Cordell Hull
decided to offer moral and material help to Yugoslavia.[26] That same year on
November 11, President Roosevelt sent a letter to a Yugoslav government
delegation which had visited the United States stating that the Kingdom of
Yugoslavia was of vital interest to the defense of the United States.

In July 1942 the Yugoslav King Peter visited the United States and was
received by President Roosevelt and Winston Churchill, who at that time
was also in the United States. Roosevelt and Churchill declared on this
occasion that their governments wanted the restoration of a Yugoslavia that
was "stable internally and not undermined by national conflicts."[27]

At a meeting of the representatives of American South Slavs in
September 1942, at the Office of War Information at the State Department,
Assistant Secretary of State Adolf Berle explained the position of the
American government toward Yugoslavia and toward other friendly and
Allied states. He said that the United States of America recognized
Yugoslavia as a state and as an ally in the war against the Axis powers, and
America would extend every possible moral and material help.

> All three Yugoslav people in Yugoslavia are participating in the resistance
> to Hitler and Mussolini, as well as to their vassals Pavelić and Nedić, and
> our duty is to support all of the Yugoslav peoples and to extend help to all
> those elements that wherever and however contribute to the defeat of our
> common enemy. The American government does not want to become
> involved in the internal differences or views of particular parties or
> individuals on the future organization of the government in Yugoslavia,
> nor do Americans want to try to influence in any respect how that
> government will be organized, even though clearly there are different
> ideas and different opinions on the matter. But the duty of us Americans
> is not to worry now, at this moment, about these things or to waste
> energy on them. Our true, only, and main obligation is to overcome
> Hitler and his allies, and all other matters must be subordinated to that
> end. Every quarrel and every disturbance of the peace among Americans
> in relation to questions of differences in the old country, which concerns
> those nations and which they themselves must organize, weakens our
> effort and is of use to our enemies.[28]

Berle's exposition best shows the true idea behind America's support for
the Yugoslav state. The main reason was of a practical nature. America
wanted to have yet another ally in its battle against the Axis powers. The
true relationship of American policy towards Yugoslavia, that means
whether that state should be preserved after the war in its present form, was

a much more complicated question and required a much deeper analysis.

In his book *Seven Decisions That Shaped History* the Under Secretary of State Sumner Welles focused on some of President Roosevelt's political views regarding events in the Balkan regions. Welles noted that Roosevelt showed a tendency to choose principled solutions for problems which were difficult to resolve due to their origins and nature. He believed that many territorial conflicts in Europe could be solved by plebiscite. He had considerable faith in plebiscites as an universal remedy, considering this more efficient than the general principle of self-determination which for instance Woodrow Wilson favored. Welles refers to one night when he spoke to Roosevelt for well over an hour about the desirability of using plebiscites to settle once and for all the friction between the Serbs, the Croats and the Slovenes which had so burdened Yugoslavia as an independent state. He did not show concern for the harm that would be done to the national economies of all three peoples should they decide to become independent entities. Nor did he show much concern for the impoverishment that had spread over most of the Danube basin after the Treaty of Versailles had dissolved the Austro-Hungarian Empire and the economic federation the Empire represented. Welles stressed that Roosevelt had a strong sense of justice and responded instinctively to a freely held plebiscite as a means of preventing the subjugation of national minorities. According to Welles however, Roosevelt failed to take into account the very practical consideration that the further fractionization which he proposed would mean an increase in economic maladjustments which were one of the chief causes for Europe's woes during the years between the two world wars.[29]

Welles not only wrote about Roosevelt's political meditations in his book but rather also indicated where Roosevelt's practical political steps were heading.

At the beginning of the war there were quite serious misunderstandings between Roosevelt and Winston Churchill. A little more light is shed on this matter in a memorandum dated July 8, 1941 which Assistant Secretary of State Berle sent from London to Roosevelt. Berle warned Roosevelt that it was evident that preliminary commitments for the post-war settlement of Europe were already made, mostly in London. Berle asked Roosevelt whether he was aware of these because it was not clear whether the State Department was being kept informed. Some settlements had been indicated to Berle by the British while others had been just heard about. Berle proposed to Roosevelt that from time to time he would send him information as to the post-war commitments in Europe as he heard of them.[30]

Berle reminded Roosevelt that at Versailles President Wilson was seriously handicapped by commitments made to which he was not a party and of which he was not always informed. Berle therefore mentioned to Roosevelt that he had suggested to Under Secretary of State Sumner Welles that America indicate that it could not be bound by any commitments to which it had not definitely assented. When Berle referred to commitments for post-war Europe he first meant the alleged turning over of Trieste to Yugoslavia.[31] Roosevelt was quite disturbed by Berle's memorandum and gave a sharp warning to Churchill. After Welles had agreed with its contents, Roosevelt sent the following letter to Churchill on July 14, 1941:

> I know you will not mind my mentioning to you a matter which is not in any way serious at this time but which might cause unpleasant repercussions over here later on. I refer to rumors which of course are nothing more nor less than rumors regarding trades or deals which the British Government is alleged to be making with some of the occupied nations. As for example the crazy story that you have promised to set up Yugoslavia again as it formerly existed and the other story that you had promised Trieste to Yugoslavia.
>
> In certain racial groups in this country there is of course enthusiastic approval for such promises in relation to postwar commitments, but on the other hand there is dissension and argument among other groups such as the Czechs and Slovaks and among the Walloons and Flemish.
>
> You will of course remember that back in early 1919 there was serious trouble over actual and alleged promises to the Italians and to others.
>
> It seems to me that it is much too early for any of us to make any commitments for the very good reason that both Britain and the United States want assurance of future peace by disarming all troublemakers and secondly by considering the possibility of reviving small states in the interest of harmony even if this has to be accomplished through plebiscite methods. The plebiscite was on the whole one of the few successful outcomes of the Versailles Treaty and it may be possible for us to extend the idea by suggesting in some cases preliminary plebiscites to be followed a good deal later on by second or even third plebiscites. For example, none of us know at the present time whether it is advisable in the interest of quiet conditions to keep the Croats away from the throats of the Serbs and vice versa.
>
> I am inclined to think that an overall statement on your part would be useful at this time, making it clear that no postwar peace commitments as to territories, populations, or economies have been given. I could then back up your statement in very strong terms.[32]

President Roosevelt was opposed to discussion of future borders and post-war commitments ahead of time. The Wilson experience with secret treaties was much on his mind. And most of these commitments were being made in London. Berle mentions those which had come to the attention of the State Department. Along with the question of Trieste going to Yugoslavia there was talk of Moscow's demand to establish national committees of Polish, Czech and Yugoslav nationals as the nucleus of a postwar federation. Russia then uncompromisingly insisted on recognition of Russian title to the Baltic states to which the British were sympathetic.[33]

Churchill did not reply to Roosevelt's suggestion of public statements that no commitments had been made about the European post-war order. An explanation can be found in a diary note made by Antony Eden on July 21 after Harry Hopkins, Roosevelt's special advisor, had been to London: "Winston was clearly not interested in the peace and Hopkins therefore had been told to speak urgently to me. I explained our position, and that I was as eager to keep my hands free as anybody, but the spectacle of an American President talking at large on European frontiers chilled me with Wilsonian memories."[34]

In a speech to the International Student's Congress in Washington, President Roosevelt said that the "living spirit of the struggle" was in Norway, Czechoslovakia, Poland, Serbia and Greece.[35] Roosevelt did not use the word Yugoslavia because in May 1944, Churchill was already to make the suggestion of dividing the Yugoslav state into its composite parts. In a letter sent to Churchill, dated May 18, Roosevelt among other things noted:

> Incidentally, do you remember my telling you over a year ago of my talk with Peter in which I discussed the possibility of three nations in place of the one, he to be the head of a reconstituted Serbia? This created no excitement on his part or that of Purić.
> The King, with real fire in his eyes, remarked that he was a Serb. I think that you and I should bear some such possibility in mind in case the new government does not work out. Personally I would rather have a Yugoslavia, but three separate states with separate governments in a Balkan confederation might solve many problems.[36]

When Antony Eden visited the United States in March 1943, Sumner Welles informed him of Roosevelt's speculations for solving the Yugoslav question. Eden emphasized that the view of his government was that the reconstitution of the former Yugoslavia was desirable. Welles answered that this coincided with his own judgement although it should be clear that President Roosevelt favored determination by the Croatians and the Slovenes of their own future destiny through a plebiscite. Welles stressed that the most salutary objective in eastern Europe would be amalgamation rather than partition, and the President's objective could be satisfied if both the Croats and the Slovenes were to obtain complete autonomy through the Yugoslav federative system.[37]

Consideration for the future of Yugoslavia was present amongst London's political circles as well. During a visit by the Yugoslav Ambassador Fotić to the State Department he informed Welles of the latest thoughts in London which worried his exiled government. According to Fotić some members of the British government opposed the reconstruction of Yugoslavia and favored its splitting up according to ethnic criteria, after which they could be included as part of a Danubian federation. Fotić stressed to Welles that he believed the Croat-Serb difficulties could be ironed out. All members of the Yugoslav Government in London considered that Yugoslavia should be reconstituted in such a way that the Slovenes, the Croats and the Serbs would have joint national defence and foreign relations while they would be independent in all other matters.[38]

In the meantime the Yugoslav government in London issued its own official announcement in which it stressed that the Yugoslav people themselves would decide their own future. The government's statement noted that the era of centralism had passed and that the future lay in a federation which would permit the Serbs, Croats and Slovenes to collaborate with each other without it being at the expense of any other of the nations.[39]

In Moscow there was also talk of whether to renew Yugoslavia and in what form. In 1944 Marshall Tolbuhin secretly sent a delegation to Zagreb where they met with the head of the Independent State of Croatia, Ante Pavelić. They relayed a message from Stalin by which the Soviet Union would recognize Croatia under one condition: if it were to establish itself under a communist order. Pavelić rejected this.[40] Stalin's offer was congruous to his proposal forwarded to Averell Harriman, Roosevelt's close advisor: "At this point Stalin made the surprising suggestion that five or six Allied divisions might be transferred from the Italian front to Dalmatia for an advance on Zagreb, the capital of Croatia, and then join forces with the Red Army in southeastern Austria." Stalin suggested that this operation be carried out in the Spring of 1944, but as is well known this event never took place.[41]

Debates about the future of Yugoslavia were largely animated by controversial news items about the war happening in the Yugoslav region. American politicians were under the impression that the civil war in the Yugoslav region was a war between the Serbs and Croats, or at least that it was inspired by the Serb-Croat conflict. Even though these evaluations were not entirely correct, they were the basis for most of America's political ideas towards Yugoslavia. Thinking about how to consolidate the political situation in south eastern Europe Adolf Berle primarily sought a solution to end the civil war between the Croats and Serbs, the Partisans and the Yugoslav government in London, and revolutionaries stimulated by Russia and by Serbian nationalists.[42]

When the Soviet ambassador in London cautioned the British government that the Soviets had their own interest in the Adriatic, Berle commented: "There is of course the Communist Manifesto already promulgated in Greece, and the active Communist-led Partisan movement in Croatia."[43]

The State Department was concerned with the dimensions the civil war in Yugoslavia had taken on where "the Croat-Serb civil war is reflected in quarrels in the Yugoslav communities everywhere in the world, notably the United States and South America."[44] When the American government despatched its military mission to the Partisans, Berle commented: "... but this whole Tito business worries me. There are still six million Serbs, and Tito's genial observation that he will come to an understanding with them by invading Serbia and settling their hash looks to me more like a civil war than anything else."[45] Berle continued to warn that American policies had to take account of any possible repercussions: "But if the British and the

Soviets elect to work out their difficulties in Yugoslavia by sacrificing the Serbian population which revolted and fought the Germans at our insistence the least we can do is make it clear that this is their work and not ours."[46]

Draza Mihailović the leader of the Chetniks did not find many sympathizers of other ethnic background for his movement. The conflict between the Partisans and the Chetniks was interpreted in America in many different ways: 1. As a Serbo-Croatian conflict; 2. As Serbian imperialism; 3. As a counterpart of the Spanish Civil War, with reactionary elements (the Chetniks) suppressing the liberals (the Partisans).[47]

Berle believed that Mihailović enjoyed British sympathies whilst the Partisans were supported by the Russians.[48] When Churchill began to favor Tito, he persuaded Roosevelt to follow him. According to Churchill, supporting Mihailović would mean conducting a civil war.[49] However, when in the summer of 1944 Churchill agreed with the Russians to divide influence in the Balkans, Roosevelt strongly protested.[50] The Americans found it hard to decide whom to give their support to, whether to the Partisans or the Chetniks because of the sympathy the Serbs enjoyed among American politicians. When the Americans wanted to send a military mission to Mihailović's headquarters, Churchill sharply remanded Roosevelt: "If, at this very time, an American mission arrives at Mihailović's headquarters, it will show throughout the Balkans a complete contrariety of action between Britain and the United States. The Russians will certainly throw all their weight on Tito's side, which we are backing to the full."[51]

Secretary of State Cordell Hull had defined the broad American policy toward Yugoslavia when he stated on December 9, 1943 to newspapermen that the United States would help both the Partisans and General Draza Mihailović's forces. The basic goal of U.S. aid to Yugoslavia was a pragmatic one: to unite all groups, whatever their political ideas, in the struggle against the Germans. The American government recognized the king and the Yugoslav government in Cairo as the legitimate representative of Yugoslavia in general questions of military strategy, but the success of the Yugoslav National Liberation Army (NOVJ) was of immense usefulness to the anti-Hitler coalition. The final organization of the state and the political system in Yugoslavia was a matter that the Yugoslavs would themselves decide in the future. In the first months of 1944, the American government and the governments of Great Britain and the USSR diverged somewhat in their attitude toward events in Yugoslavia. The American government was willing to protect the Chetnik movement and the interests of King Peter and his government. On April 14, 1944 Edward Stettinius, the director of the Lend Lease Administration, arrived in London with instructions from President Roosevelt to work out a joint Allied policy toward Yugoslavia. Stettinius's talks in London ended in favor of international affirmation of the Partisans' war of national liberation.[52]

Taking sides with Tito, Churchill nevertheless found himself in two minds. In a letter to Roosevelt he wrote with concern: "We do not know what will happen in the Serbian part of Yugoslavia. Mihajlović certainly holds a power-ful position locally as Commander in Chief, and it does not follow that his ceasing to be Minister of War will rob him of his influence. We cannot predict what he will do. There is also a very large body, amounting perhaps to 200.000 of Serbian peasant proprietary who are anti-German but strongly Serbian and who naturally hold the views of a peasants' ownership community."[53]

American policy towards the events in Yugoslavia was put to another test when the Yugoslav Ambassador Konstantin Fotić was recalled from Washington. The British informed Berle of this on October 15, highlight-ing that in London Fotić was considered to be the symbol of the pan-Serb movement and that they wanted to remove Fotić because of his oppressive pan-Serb doctrine. Berle informed British Ambassador Campbell that the American government was also concerned about the growth of pan-Serb politics which was mostly being spread from the Yugoslav Embassy. For this reason the State Department sent several sharp protests to Fotić. Berle also informed Campbell about the conflict among Croat immigrants who were supported by American left wingers and Serb immigrants supported by the Yugoslav Embassy.[54]

However, Konstantin Fotić had a considerable number of friends among American politicians and in the State Department itself who favored his political outlook and who did not agree with the decision to recall him. On October 29 Campbell once again visited Berle and insisted that the American government agree to recall Fotić. Berle pointed out to Campbell that Fotić's recall would be received with regret among some Yugoslav circles in the United States and that it would be regarded as definite support for the Partisans in Yugoslavia and Croatian migrants under left wing leadership in the United States; this should be considered by the Foreign Office. Campbell indicated that in London they were aware of the risk involved, however, this was not satisfactory an argument for Berle. He believed the matter needed to be examined by the State Department because recalling Fotić could encourage Croatian Leftists and the Ban of Croatia Ivan Šubašić, who was in the United States to form a Yugoslav National Committee under their own control.[55]

Half way through 1944 Winston Churchill began working systematically on an agreement between the National Committee for the Liberation of Yugoslavia headed by Marshall Tito and the Yugoslav government in London whose president, Ivan Šubašić, had returned to London from the United States. Churchill believed that ideological differences would not hamper the agreement. During a meeting in Naples on August 13 Churchill later wrote that "Tito assured me that, as he had stated publicly, he had no desire to introduce the Communist system into Yugoslavia, if only because most European countries after the war would probably be living under a democratic regime ... I asked Tito if he would reaffirm his statement about communism in public, but he did not wish to do this as it might seem to have been forced upon him." Tito's reply evidently satisfied Churchill.[56]

An agreement between Ivan Šubašić and Josip Broz Tito was signed on the island of Vis on June 17, 1944. The agreement aroused a great deal of doubt and mistrust in America. The State Department was receiving news that the agreement caused a lot of opposition among a large section of the Yugoslav government-in-exile while the majority of Serbian ministers believed that the new movement had a strong Croat backing.[57] Even America's military attaché in London forwarded President Roosevelt a message informing him that there could be a lot of problems because Šubašić did not take the Serbian view point into account when resolving the Yugoslav crisis.[58]

By ratifying the Tito-Šubašić Agreement the Allies practically authorized Tito and the Communist Party of Yugoslavia to solve the Yugoslav crisis and determine the future of the Yugoslav nations during the next few decades. However, the fact is, and it can be seen in historical sources, that the Allies, which included American politicians, knew well that the crux of the Yugoslav problem was Serbo-Croatian relations and their national conflicts. In the United States it was well known that the future of the Yugoslav state depended on a solution to the Croatian-Serbian conflict.

Conclusion

Two American presidents, Woodrow Wilson in World War I and Franklin D. Roosevelt in World War II, did not have a defined stance towards a Yugoslav state. By accepting the principle of self-determination as his political motto Wilson supported the nationalistic aspirations of the Austro-Hungarian Slavs, but only through autonomy within the Empire. Wilson supported this solution until virtually just prior to the end of the war. By a secret settlement in 1915, the Kingdom of Italy was promised by the Allies that Dalmatia would be annexed to Istria and that Trieste would go to Italy. The Kingdom of Serbia in principle agreed with the unification of all South Slavs into one state but on condition that unification was achieved under Serbia's leadership, which meant ensuring Serbian supremacy in the future state. Serbia however, showed that it was willing to negotiate with the Allies over territory. It negotiated with Italy over the division of Dalmatia while it demanded the Allies hand over Bosnia and Herzegovina to Serbia. Montenegro which until then had been a sovereign state, was also to become part of the Kingdom of Serbia. On these concrete and unsolvable Balkan problems Woodrow Wilson realized how much his principle of self-determination of peoples was nothing more than political idealism. That is why it seemed easier that the Austro-Hungarian Slavs solve their problems by way of self-determination of nations but within the framework of the Monarchy. Nevertheless, after 1915 American policies had slowly but surely headed in a different direction. This occurred when Robert Lansing replaced William Jennings Bryan as secretary of state. This change in personnel had far reaching repercussions for U.S. foreign policy. With Lansing arriving on the scene the nationalistic aspira-tions of the Yugoslavs found a good spokesman. It was thanks to him that the Austro-Hungarian Ambassador K. Dumba was compelled to leave the

United States in 1915. As early as in 1917 Lansing favored resolving the Yugoslav question outside the framework of Austro-Hungaria, which often caused him to be opposed to Wilson. It needs to be emphasized that Lansing only found out about Wilson's fourteen points one day before they were released. An entire group in the State Department followed Lansing: Richard Crane, Lansing's secretary, William Phillips, Lansing's assistant, Frank Polk and Albert Putney, all supported the idea of resolving the Yugoslav question outside the Monarchy. Wilson's greatest deed is in that, by articulating the principle of self-determination of nations he laid a foundation for a political program which, at least to some extent, allowed Austro-Hungarian Slavs to realize their nationalistic aspirations in the newly created states following World War I. One of these states was Yugoslavia.

Franklin D. Roosevelt did not have much faith in Yugoslavia. In July 1941 he criticized British politicians in London because they were repeating the same political mistakes made in World War I. He believed that the solution to the Yugoslav question lay in a plebiscite by which the South Slavic peoples could freely determine in what form of state they wished to live. Unfortunately few in the State Department or Foreign Office in London supported Roosevelt in this idea. Nevertheless his new ideas were germinating and it came to be believed that Yugoslavia should be a federative or at least a confederative state in which national equality should be guaranteed as well as a democratic way of life for all its peoples. Few considered that Yugoslavia should be disbanded. It needed half a century and the fall of communism to open the way for plebiscites as mechanisms for resolving the problems of the Balkans. Unfortunately the dissolution of this "artificial compilation of Versailles" did not end in a peaceful way but rather the opposite: it was followed by a serious inter-ethnic war.

Notes

1. Albert Shaw, ed., *The Messages and Papers of Woodrow Wilson*, 2 vols. (New York, 1924), vol. 2, 274.
2. U.S. Department of State, *Papers Relating to the Foreign Relations of the United States* [hereafter *FRUS*], *The Lansing Papers 1914–1920* (Washington, 1939), vol. 2, 656.
3. The word "Slavs" is used to mean "Yugoslavs" because Italy was opposed to the use of the latter term. In this paper the expressions "South Slavs" and "Yugoslavs" relate to the South Slavic nations which lived in the Austro-Hungarian Monarchy. Ivan Čizmić, *The Yugoslav Emigrant Movement in the USA and the Creation of the Yugoslav State in 1918* (Zagreb: Institute of Croatian History, 1984), 231.
4. The Yugoslav National Council in Washington represented Yugoslav migrants in the USA who supported the dissolution of Austro-Hungaria and the forming of a Yugoslav state. See: Ivan Čizmić, *The Yugoslav Emigrant Movement*.
5. Archives of the City of Split, Immigrant Collection.
6. *Archives of the Yugoslav National Defence from South America* (Zagreb, 1934–1935), 324.

7.   Victor S. Mamatey, *The United States and East Central Europe* (New Jersey, 1957), 91.
8.   Dragoslav Janković and Bogdan Krizman, *Material on the Creation of the Yugoslav State* (Belgrade, 1964), vol. 1, 44.
9.   *FRUS, The Lansing Papers 1914–1920*, vol. 2, 123.
10. Ministry of Foreign Affairs, Belgrade, Archives of Serbian Ambassador to Washington.
11. Ibid.
12. Ante Smith-Pavelić and Ante Trumbić, *Problems with Croatian-Serbian Relations* (München, 1959), 121.
13. B. Krizman, *American Documents on Italian – Yugoslav Relations in 1918*, "Hrvatsko kolo" (Croatian Circle) (Zagreb, 1953), 229.
14. *FRUS, The Lansing Papers 1914–1920*, vol. 2, 808.
15. *The Yugoslav World*, New York, October 22, 1918, no. 2728.
16. M. Paulova, *The Yugoslav Committee* (Zagreb, 1925), 461.
17. *FRUS, The Lansing Papers 1914–1920*, vol. 2, 142. Among the Diplomatic papers of the Ministry of Foreign Affairs in Belgrade is a report by the Serbian Supreme Commander in Solun of August 17, 1918. In the report it says that the Americans, Major Brener, the military attache with the French-American war commissariat, and Louis Cranton, a Michigan congressman, visited the French command in Bitola. They presented themselves as envoys on behalf of President Wilson and the American government and stated that their aim was to conduct a survey about the Balkan question. In Bitola they met with the Serbian representative with the French command, Simić and asked him: "1. About the nationality of Macedonia; 2. About the future Yugoslav state as well as whether the Serbs had any pretensions of hegemony over the other nations in that state which would be at the expense of general and lasting peace which the Allies and especially America leaned towards. This question was repeated several times; 3. Wouldn't this new state tend to expand towards Greece which in this case is a lot weaker?"
18. Joseph P. O'Grady, *The Immigrants' Influence on Wilson's Peace Policies* (University of Kentucky, 1967), 111; *National Gazette*, New York, February 15, 1919, no. 46.
19. Lodge made his statement in order to win over Italian voters. It nevertheless attracted a lot of public attention. Thomas A. Bailey in *A Diplomatic History of the American People* (New York, 1955), 667, writes: "There were not enough Yugoslav voters in Massachusetts to make it politically profitable for the Senator to admit his error."
20. *The Yugoslav World*, New York, August 8, 1919, no. 2126.
21. Archives of the City of Split, Immigrant Collection.
22. *Croatia*, Calumet, January 1, 1920.
23. Mamatey, *The United States and East Central Europe*, 347.
24. Janković and Krizman, *Material on the Creation of the Yugoslav State*, 725.
25. See: Ivan Čizmić, *Croatians in the Life of the United States of America* (Zagreb: Globus, 1982).
26. *FRUS, 1941* (Washington, 1959), vol. 2, 975; *The Fraternalist*, Pittsburgh, April 9, 1941.
27. Bogdan Radica, "The Work of Croats in the USA During the Last War," *Croatian Review*, Buenos Aires, no. 1 (1957): 55.
28. Roosevelt Study Center Microform Collections, *The Diary of Adolf A. Berle*,

1931–1971, Organization of European Groups in America, July 6, 1942; *The Fraternalist*, September 30, 1942.

29. Sumner Welles, *Seven Decisions That Shaped History* (New York, 1951), 136.
30. Beatrice Bishop Berle and Travis Beal Jacobs, eds., *Navigating the Rapids 1918–1971. From the Papers of Adolf A. Berle* (New York, 1973), 372.
31. Ibid.
32. Francis L. Loewenheim, Harold D. Langley, and Manfred Jonas, eds., *Roosevelt and Churchill. Their Secret Wartime Correspondence* (New York, 1975), 149.
33. Joseph P. Lash, *Roosevelt and Churchill 1939–1941. The Partnership That Saved the West* (New York, 1976), 367.
34. Ibid., 368.
35. Radica, "The Work of Croats in the USA," 57.
36. Loewenheim, *Roosevelt and Churchill*, 498.
37. *FRUS, 1943* (Washington, 1961), vol. 3, 24.
38. Ibid., vol. 2, 1004.
39. Ibid., 1013. American politicians became more and more convinced that the Balkan peoples needed to be given the right to self-determination. So in November 1943, Secretary of the Treasury Henry Morgenthau tried to convince President Roosevelt that the people in the Balkans had the right to their own elected government and that they did not need any kings imposed upon them. This proposal by Morgenthau was not accepted by Roosevelt with enthusiasm because it favored the Monarchy in principle. (*From the Morgenthau Diaries, Years of War 1941–1945* by John M. Blum (Boston, 1967), 169).
40. *Croatian Review*, Buenos Aires, no. 3 (1980): 515.
41. W. Averell Harriman and Elie Abel, *Special Envoy to Churchill and Stalin 1941–1946* (New York, 1975), 379.
42. Berle, *Navigating the Rapids*, 432.
43. Ibid., 440.
44. Roosevelt Study Center Microform Collections, *The Diary of Adolf A. Berle, 1931–1971*, Memorandum for the Secretary, January 13, 1943.
45. Berle, *Navigating the Rapids*, 454.
46. Ibid., 465.
47. *FRUS, 1943*, vol. 2, 996.
48. Berle, *Navigating the Rapids*, 430.
49. *FRUS, 1943*, vol. 2, 997.
50. Loewenheim, *Roosevelt and Churchill*, 62.
51. Ibid., 482.
52. See: Slobodan Nešović, *The Diplomatic Game Around Yugoslavia 1944–1945* (Zagreb, 1977).
53. Loewenheim, *Roosevelt and Churchill*, 497.
54. Roosevelt Study Center Microform Collections, *The Diary of Adolf A. Berle, 1931–1971*, reel 4, 0179.
55. Ibid., reel 4, 0202.
56. Loewenheim, *Roosevelt and Churchill*, 511.
57. *FRUS, 1945* (Washington, 1967), vol. 5, 1192.
58. Roosevelt Study Center Microform Collections, *Map Room Messages of President Roosevelt (1939–1945)*, reel 4.

10

The Myth of America in Poland from the "Empire of Liberty" to the "Empire of Liberation"

Zofia Libiszowska

Like those European nations with no part in overseas expansion, the Poles, too, were not uninterested in developments taking place in the Western Hemisphere. This is confirmed by numerous Polish records containing information about the New World.[1] Educated Poles were aware of the significance of the discovery of America. In their opinion it not only enlarged geographical horizons but also influenced political, socio-economic and religious developments in countries and regions distant from main maritime routes.[2]

During the exploration and conquest of the New World Jagiellonian Poland (1386–1572) emerged as a great continental power with an area amounting to about 900,000 square kilometers. It spread at times from the Baltic to the Black Sea. Danzig (Gdanski in Polish), with its large autonomy within the Polish-Lithuanian Commonwealth, remained the chief harbor on the Baltic for several centuries. It flourished thanks to the protection and generous privileges granted by Polish kings. Sigismund Augustus (1548–1572), a contemporary of the Virgin Queen, loudly proclaimed and adhered to the principle of the freedom of navigation on the high seas – this in spite of the fact that Poland did not have a navy, and Danzig's merchant marine was not equipped for ocean travel and limited its operations to the Baltic and North Seas.[3]

Prior to the American Revolution, Polish public opinion was largely unaffected by the propaganda and rumors about the New World's fantastic riches. Poland was beyond the reach of "the American mirage," a powerful propaganda tool of shipping and colonial companies seeking new settlers. Much more than the New World generally, and Virginia specifically, Polish settlers were attracted by the fertile and largely uninhabited Ukrainian steppes.[4] Any Polish participation in the New World's settlement was of a sporadic and marginal nature only; it included a small group of radical Polish religious dissidents, known as the Polish Brothers (Anti-Trinitarians), who in the seventeenth century joined their Dutch co-believers in America.[5]

Poland herself remained for long a haven for religious refugees. Several hundred thousand Jews lived there, new ones chiefly from Spain and Portugal kept arriving, and they were joined by many religious dissidents from various parts of Europe.

A Polish migratory movement, chiefly for political reasons, only started in the second half of the eighteenth century when Poland-Lithuania was in visible decline. This political emigration, to which in the second half of the nineteenth century was added migration for economic reasons, has never stopped. Hence it is no exaggeration to speak of the Polish diaspora.

The first emigrants from Poland were military officers of noble origin, who volunteered to fight for America's freedom. Two among them – Tadeusz Kosciuszko and Kazimierz Pulaski – served as generals in the Continental Army and became part of the American legend. Pulaski met a heroic death at Savannah, Georgia,[6] and Kosciuszko later served as Poland's supreme leader (naczelnik in Polish) during the anti-Russian uprising of 1794, thus becoming a hero both in the New World and in his native Poland.[7] The names of these two heroes created a bridge between the Polish and American peoples. The term Liberty came to mean much more to them than individual freedom; it signified national independence.

Pulaski, wishing to join the Continental Army, stated: "Il me serait bien doux de vivre libre ou mourir pour la liberté. (It would be sweet for me to live free or die for freedom)." Another Polish volunteer, Lieutenant Colonel Kotkowski, assured Benjamin Franklin, while seeking his recommendation: "I shall find means to join the brave defenders of Liberty, which is dear to all those who know its worth."[8] It was not easy to receive Franklin's recommendation to Washington, but in spite of that some eager enthusiasts succeeded in crossing the ocean to join Pulaski's regiment.

The Polish press reacted vividly to news from America. In reprints in Polish there appeared fragments of the declarations and appeals of the Continental Congress, and characteristic quotations must have stuck in the memory of Polish readers. Citations like "We would rather die than live in slavery," found a particularly warm reception in Poland, because of her specific situation. After the first partition of 1772, Poland-Lithuania was no longer an independent and active participant on the international scene. Her situation was very precarious, future very uncertain, and in addition, Warsaw remained under the control of the Russian embassy. The Poles remained in a subdued mood. Little wonder that news about successes of the Americans, and their determination to fight for full independence, had special meaning in Poland. The poet Kajetan Wegierski, who was the first Polish tourist to visit the United States, in 1783, in a meditating mood compared the decline of Poland to the American triumph: "A nation of three million individuals was able to resist successfully Britain's might, defending united its rights."[9]

The new republican system of government in the New World seemed to be a risky experiment to many, but in Poland, which proudly called herself a republic, headed by elective kings, it was viewed with a sympathetic understanding. "The amount of American freedom," wrote the publisher of a Polish monthly, "cannot be compared with that of any other country. If the Americans have accomplished so much at their birth, they will certainly do substantially more in the future."[10]

The U.S. Constitution and the Bill of Rights served as a model to the authors of the Polish Constitution of May 3 1791. In addition, the two above documents were frequently mentioned in the debates of the Great Diet of 1788–1792.

Accused of links with revolutionary France, Poland succumbed to a Russian invasion of 1792 and was partitioned for the second time one year later. An attempt to save both independence and national dignity under General Kosciuszko in 1794 failed, and Poland was erased from the map of Europe by Russia, Prussia, and Austria one year later. Forcefully incorporated into its three neighbors, the Polish nation never lost faith in recovering its own statehood.

At the end of 1797, after a period of Russian captivity, General Kosciuszko arrived in the United States and was enthusiastically welcomed in Philadelphia. In a dispatch from the French consul the famous hero of the Old and New Worlds was said to be a "Martyr de la Liberté" ("A martyr for freedom").[11] At this time Kosciuszko's friendship deepened with the then vice president, Thomas Jefferson, and this mutual affection resulted in numerous letters exchanged between the two following the general's departure for Europe.[12]

The short-lived Napoleonic period resulted in a Polish awakening, and new hopes for statehood. For the United States this was also a period of great challenges. As a result the country of the initial thirteen states had been transformed into an empire of freedom. The latter kept its gates open to immigration from Europe.

Newcomers from Polish lands were divided into political and economic immigrants. The first large groups represented former Polish insurgents of the November 1830 Uprising in Russian Poland, who found themselves in the Austrian and Prussian partitions, and who, fearing tsarist reprisals, could not return home. Composed of three hundred men and one woman, the above groups, deported from Austria and Prussia, reached the United States one after another in 1834–1835.[13] Because of, among other reasons, protests from the Russian embassy, projects to settle all its members in Illinois, and granting them a region called "Little Poland," never materialized. The Polish refugees found, however, support, sympathy, and assistance in Congress, as well as in intellectual and press circles. "The cause of Poland is closely associated with the cause of mankind," declared a member of Congress, the Honorable Churchill C. Cambreleng. Dr. Samuel Gridley Howe, on his part, stated as follows: "Shall we not say to the persecuted patriots, come here and ye shall find rest; we have lands rich as your own plains; and rivers as broad as your own Vistula, on whose banks you may build a new Warsaw, which the sword of no Suvaroff shall ever reach." On the basis of such statements, conviction grew among the Poles about the generosity of the American people and their staunch devotion to the struggle for freedom and human rights.

Another wave of political refugees appeared in America during the Civil War after the January Insurrection of 1863–1864 in Russian Poland. Many Poles volunteered to fight on the side of the Union; only some (1,000 men) joined the Confederacy. In Europe, Polish lands included, the news about the Civil War and its length and toughness hurt somewhat the idyllic image of a free nation which had been considered to be the model of democracy.[14]

Polish economic immigration ("in search for bread") had a different character. It was divided into two main groups: peasants and workers. Peasants usually arrived in organized groups, originating in closed communities, and from time to time with their own priests. They settled as pioneers in designated territories. The ease with which they were granted land, such a precious commodity for Polish peasants, was the chief reason for emigration from poor and overcrowded Galician and Silesian villages. The first such settlement, founded by peasants from Prussian Silesia, originated in Texas in 1854.[15] It became a model for future colonies.

Prior to the Census of 1910 U.S. statistical forms did not differentiate between nationality and statehood. As between 1795 and 1918 Polish lands belonged to Russia, Prussia, and Austria, no mention of Poles exists in early U.S. statistical data. According to Polish estimates, 2,227,966 persons from Polish lands had settled in America between 1820 and 1914.[16] Most of the new arrivals settled in rapidly growing industrial centers, where they found blue collar work, not infrequently at the bottom of the social ladder. Like Italian immigrants, their Polish counterparts counted on returning home after saving enough in America, but not many did. Those born in the New World gradually adopted the American way of life and value system, though most did not forget their country of origin and preserved, selectively of course, their customs and above all their faith.

Some Polish teachers, journalists, artists, intellectuals, and others also migrated to the New World.[17] Together with Polish priests, such individuals played an important educational, cultural, and civic role, thus establishing a bridge between Europe and America, between Poles and Polish-Americans. Most Polish economic emigrants were not only poor, but illiterate as well: hence the special role of educated Poles (clergy and laymen) in teaching immigrants about America, its freedom, and value system, and, of course, their rich Polish heritage. Gradually, cultural, fraternal, and pro-Polish associations were founded. Polish-Americans cared for the monuments of Poles who participated in the American Revolution and solemnly and enthusiastically celebrated the annual Pulaski Day.

Word War I re-opened the Polish Question.[18] Political leaders immediately engaged in pro-independence activities. At home, Polish public opinion was divided into support for either the Entente or the Central Powers. The belligerents (Imperial Russia on the one hand, Germany and Austria-Hungary on the other) made promises to their Polish subjects. Seven hundred thousand Poles perished on various battlefields of the Great War, not infrequently being forced to fight other ethnic Poles, drafted by the partitioning powers. Polish-Americans behaved patriotically, collecting funds for pro-Polish activities and military units, promoting the Polish Question in America, issuing numerous appeals to ethnic Poles to join

Polish military units and appealing to the American authorities to support Polish national aspirations.[19]

President Woodrow Wilson's decision to declare war against the Central Powers put an end to any hesitations. The Poles in the home country and in the diaspora had not the slightest doubt that America would triumph in the war. In a crusade for freedom and democracy two declarations by Wilson, particularly the famous Fourteen Points, mentioned Poland. Patriotic Poles did not remain idle. One Polish petition, eagerly supported by the Polish-American community, and addressed both to the Department of State and to the president himself, was delivered by the famous pianist and staunch Polish patriot Ignacy Paderewski. Paderewski was subsequently appointed prime minister of a reborn and democratic Poland and also served as one of Poland's chief representatives at the Paris Peace Conference.

The Second Polish Republic did not forget America or Wilson, whose popularity was immense and crossed party lines, as was that of Herbert Hoover through his relief activities. The first diplomatic notes exchanged between Poland and America, which started as early as 1918, confirmed the general belief that the United States was viewed as Poland's important ally and protector.

Under Pilsudski and his successors Poland enjoyed a precarious existence as an independent nation state during the inter-war years, only to be subjected to renewed partition by its powerful neighbours in 1939. From the first day of the invasions in September 1939 Polish public opinion never doubted that the United States would decide the outcome of World War II. Most Poles saw the benevolence of Wilson in Roosevelt. The Poles staunchly believed that America would promptly join France and Britain. Those who maintained such views were not mistaken, though the United States joined the conflict later than expected and the Poles had to live under occupation for over five years.

The victorious Grand Alliance had a decisive say with regard to liberated Poland. As compensation for Poland's former eastern territories she received parts of the Third Reich.[20] Although the country's limited sovereignty and the imposed communist rule represented a bitter pill to proud and freedom-loving Poles, an overwhelming majority of them preserved their faith in America. Among the Poles who, because of their determined anti-communist stand, staunchly rejected the post-1945 reality at home, many were admitted to the United States as displaced persons. They were both civilian and soldiers (Polish military units in the West had amounted to some 200,000 men and women), who willingly or otherwise had moved out of Poland following the invasions of September 1939 and thereafter.

Some forty-five years of the Yalta system strengthened rather than weakened Polish faith in America. Not only did Poland's former communist rulers in the post-1956 period not shun agreements with the United States but also, with the exception of Yugoslavia and Romania, the relations of the Polish People's Republic with America were larger and deeper than those of other members of the Eastern Bloc. Edward Gierek (Poland's leader in 1970–1980) paid an official visit to the United States, and the bi-centennial of the American Constitution in 1987 was celebrated in Poland. Presidents Richard Nixon, Jimmy Carter, and George Bush were warmly and enthusiastically received in Poland.

Young Poles have almost religiously embraced new trends in American culture. Initially U.S. army uniforms (particularly coats) became fashionable, with blue jeans and cowboy hats following suit. American movies attracted many viewers; jazz, rock, and blues music largely triumphed over Polish national dances. Almost all American writers, whose works have been translated into Polish, have enjoyed large circulation and sold exceptionally well. Contrary to various misapprehensions regarding the Sovietization of Polish culture, an Americanization in almost every field began to prevail.

U.S. history, with an emphasis on America as a liberator and a place of freedom, entered Polish educational programs, including higher education. Chairs and centers of American studies were founded. The myth of America has been gradually superseded by the reality of knowledge.

America's bloodless triumph over the USSR led to the political emancipation of Eastern Europe. Now, politically independent and secure, many Poles continue to seek America's umbrella (protection). They count, above all, on substantial economic assistance from a friend given to Poland by Providence.

The American myth in Poland has survived, though in changed circumstances and against a different political backdrop. Myths, it should be explained, are a transformation of reality. The myth formed during the Polish partitions of 1772–1795 and the birth of the first sovereign state in the Western Hemisphere, a country whose chief slogan was liberty, has attracted numerous generations of Poles, and will most likely continue to do so. The words of Kosciuszko, the supreme leader of Poland's uprising of 1794, "[t]he name of America is sacred to me," never lost their true meaning in Poland.

My aim here was to provide an overview of changes in mentality among the Poles with regard to America. From a country of freedom and opportunity to the average Polish immigrant it subsequently evolved into a mighty empire, strong enough and willing to spread freedom and democracy beyond its own borders.

Notes

1. Janusz Tazbir, "The Popular Impact of the Discovery of America in East-Central Europe," *The Polish Review* 37, no. 3 (1992): 263–284; the same, *Rzeczpospolita szlachecka wobec wielkich odkryc* (The Commonwealth of the Gentry and the Great Discoveries) (Warsaw, 1973). See also Romuald Wroblewski, *Znajomosc Ameryki w Polsce okresu Odrodzenia* (Knowledge of America in Renaissance Poland) (Warsaw, 1977).

2.   B. Keckermann, *Brevis Commentatio Nautica*, K. Augustowska ed. (Gdansk, 1992).

3.   For more details, see Remigiusz Bierzanek, *Morze otwarte ze stanowiska prawa miedzynarodowego* (Open Sea in the International Law) (Warsaw, 1960).

4.   For details, see Tazbir, *Rzeczpospolita szlachecka*.

5.   Janusz Tazbir, *Bracia Polscy na wygnaniu* (The Polish Brothers in Exile) (Warsaw: Polish Scientific Publishers, 1977), 150–170.

6.   For detailed information, see Wladyslaw Konopczynski, *Kazimierz Pulaski* (Cracow, 1931); and C. Manning, *Soldier of Liberty Casimir Pulaski* (New York, 1945).

7.   M. Haiman, *Kosciuszko in the American Revolution* (New York, 1946); and, the same, *Kosciuszko the Leader and Exile* (New York, 1946).

8.   Two letters of Lieutenant Colonel Count Kotkowski to Benjamin Franklin of 26 December 1777 and 24 February 1778. See Franklin Papers (Yale University), nos. 1837 and 1885.

9.   Zofia Libiszowska, *Opinia polska wobec Rewolucji Amerykanskiej w XVIII wieku* (Polish Opinion and the American Revolution in the Eighteenth Century) (Lodz, 1962), 116.

10.   Ibid., 124.

11.   Archives des Affaires Étrangères (Paris), États-Unis, vol. 48, 1797, no. 38. Consul Latombe. Philadelphia, le 3 Fructidor, an 6 de la République.

12.   Jefferson to General Horatio Gates, 21 February 1798, about his Polish friend: "He (Kosciuszko) is the purest son of liberty." Gates was also fascinated with Kosciuszko. In his opinion, "Kosciuszko is the only pure republican I ever knew. He is without any dross." Quoted by M. Haiman, *Poland and the American Revolutionary War* (Chicago, 1932), 21.

13.   For more details, see Jerzy Lerski, *A Polish Chapter in Jacksonian America* (Madison, Wisconsin: University of Wisconsin Press, 1958).

14.   For more information, see Joseph W. Wieczerzak, *A Polish Chapter in Civil War America: The Effects of the January Insurrection on American Opinion and Diplomacy* (New York, 1967).

15.   T. Lindsay Baker, *The First Polish-Americans: Silesian Settlements* (College Station, Texas: Texas A&M University Press, 1979).

16.   H. Kubiak, E. Kusielewicz, and T. Gromada eds., *Polonia Amerykanska, prezeszlosc i wspolczesnosc* (Polish-Americans: Past and Present) (Warsaw: Ossolineum, 1988), 40.

17.   For details, see Bogdan Grzelonski, *Do Nowego Jorku, Chicago, i San Francisco. Szkice do biografii polsko-amerykanskich* (To New York, Chicago and San Francisco: Polish-American Biographies) (Warsaw, 1983).

18.   For excellent works relating to the Polish Question during World War I, see Titus Komarnicki, *Rebirth of the Polish Republic* (London: William Heinemann, 1957); and Piotr S. Wandycz, *The United States and Poland* (Cambridge, Massachusetts: Harvard University Press, 1980).

19.   Zofia Libiszowska, "Polish-Americans and Wilson's Polish Policy on the Eve of World War I" (Marseille: University of Marseille, 1985). Proceedings of EAAS Historical Conference, in Rome, in 1984.

20.   For details, see Piotr S. Wandycz, *Polish Diplomacy 1914–1945: Aims and Achievements* (London: School of Slavonic and East European Studies, 1988).

11

The Gulf War and the New World Order: American Exceptionalism Revisited

Pierre Lépinasse

Each in turn all nations have claimed their exceptional virtues or particular situations to justify their attempts at becoming the overruling leaders of a region or a continent. The most egregious case in that respect was that of Rome which over six centuries steadily extended its power around the Mediterranean sea and enforced the famous "Pax Romana" with its legions.

But in 1815, to reverse the situation created by the French Revolutionary and Napoleonic Wars, the Congress that met at Vienna aimed at achieving an international order to wipe out revolutionary ideas and secure a balance of power meant to prevent any recurrence of war. Count Metternich of Austria and Lord Castlereagh of Britain were the architects of the system which they brought all other European countries to accept. With variations it was to last until World War I in 1914.

In the meantime the United States had reached a position of world power, more especially after the splendidly profitable little (Spanish-American) war of 1898. President Woodrow Wilson entered World War I more or less reluctantly, and tried to prevent the return of such a tragedy first by setting forth his Fourteen Points, then with his plan for a League of Nations which was designed to be a forum in which all international disputes could be resolved through negotiations. In a sense this may be viewed as the first American attempt at forging a new world order under an American aegis, but it came to nothing when the Senate, led by Senator Henry Cabot Lodge, refused to ratify both the Versailles Peace Treaty and the Covenant for the creation of the League of Nations in 1919. The United States then receded into political isolationism, while taking up an economic expansion that stopped short with the 1929 Wall Street crash. The ensuing helplessness in the domestic and international areas was not to come to an end until America had become "the arsenal of democracy" before and after it was drawn into World War II.

This war was a boon of sorts for the United States. Protected from any kind of damage by both oceans, its regenerated economy was the means for it to take a leading part during the hostilities and still more importantly in the negotiations that were to prepare both for victory and for the peace settlements. American statesmen recreated the League of Nations according

175

to their own views and under the name of the United Nations Organization (UNO) in 1945. When plans were discussed in the War and Peace Studies Group, one participant, the chief of army intelligence General George V. Strong, had expressed the opinion that the United States "must cultivate a mental view toward world settlement after this war which will enable us to impose our own terms, amounting perhaps to a pax americana."[1] That allusion to the Roman empire suggested that, as a model system imposing its will, it has to be kept in mind for future circumstances. In any case its exceptional role in the war enabled the United States to establish its unique leadership in a war-shattered world. America was the sole superpower left in 1945 because of its strong economic position (at the time it produced 50% of all goods manufactured in the world) and because of its military supremacy with the atom bomb. However not fully aware of this new position, Americans still adhered to the prewar international system in which Britain was considered the policeman of the world.

President Harry S. Truman and his Democratic team had one long-range goal: the prevention of another crash such as that of 1929. Another great depression would endanger the social and political order; the only means to prevent such a possibility was to secure markets for the ever-increasing American production. Already in 1944, Assistant Secretary of State for Economic Affairs Dean Acheson had plainly stated before the House Special Subcommittee on Post War Planning Policy: "We cannot have full employment and prosperity in the United States without foreign markets."[2]

But although the Soviet Union, a bad social model because it had set up a socialist system, was still in the victors' camp it had closed not only its borders to foreign goods but also to those of the East European countries included in the Soviet bloc at the end of the war. The United States had attempted to open the borders, but to no avail.

Early in 1947 war-exhausted Britain had to warn she would withdraw from Greece which she had helped resist the onslaught of Communist-led guerrillas rising against the reactionary Royal government. The United States agreed to step into British shoes in order to stop what was seen as an attempted Communist take-over. So the Truman doctrine was issued in Congress on March 12, 1947 by the president, presented as evidence of American determination to protect freedom threatened with Communist revolution (as in Greece) or aggression (as in Turkey). But few people had paid any attention to President Truman's speech delivered at Baylor University, Waco, Texas, one week earlier, in which he had included among "the objectives of peace and freedom" after World War II, "a third objective ... the re-establishment of world trade," which entailed "bipartisan support for the economic policy of the United States."[3]

These two manifest declarations of the American desire to rule supreme economically as well as politically were naturally followed by the Marshall Plan which was officially designed to bring economic aid to war-shattered European countries. The Soviet Union declined the offer for it would have forced her to indicate the weaker spots of her economy to American business ready to pounce on foreign investments. The Soviet decision was definitively the real beginning of the so-called Cold War – which we need not retrace here in detail.

Suffice it to notice that the United States and its allies felt threatened by Soviet expansion causing the loss of trade markets, when domestic revolutions, assisted by local Communist parties, and the smuggling of Soviet weapons, brought the overthrow of liberal political systems in Europe (as in Czechoslovakia in 1948) and in former European colonies in Asia (attempts in Indochina) and Africa. The last straw came with the Communist takeover of mainland China in October 1949 and the outbreak of the Korean War in June 1950. Both the latter and the French Indochina War persuaded western public opinion that the Soviets were ready to wage war to establish their hegemony; but war was always waged in minor countries by both superpowers and only by proxy.

The United States had come to think that it was invested with a special mission to prevent and even stop the extension of the Soviet system. It sometimes succeeded (for instance Italy, 1948 and Chile, 1973) with American undercover help to threatened countries. In 1954 the United States secretly succeeded the defeated French in Indochina, and sided with the Southern Republic of Vietnam in spite of the stipulations of the 1954 Geneva Accord which had foreseen a reunification of both Vietnams through elections.

To defend South Vietnam President Lyndon B. Johnson plunged his country into a disastrous war: after eight years of fighting, Americans had to accept a cease-fire and withdraw their forces. It had been an utter fiasco, not only militarily, but also politically and for a time ruined American citizens' confidence in their destiny. It did not look so manifest then. After the revelations of the excesses of the intelligence community and the Watergate abuses, Daniel Bell would lament the "End of American Exceptionalism" in 1977.[4]

But there were other far-reaching consequences of those events of the Vietnam War and Watergate: they had brought on a tremendous economic crisis, first of all with a weakening of government finances and of industrial output, and the flight of American corporations to countries with less-costly manpower.

Jimmy Carter's presidency caused fresh worries: American loss of prestige with the protracted imprisonment of the Teheran embassy personnel by the Iranian fundamentalists and the administration's failure to have them freed; then the economic slump and soaring inflation, the apparently easy triumphs of Soviet expansion in Africa and still more in Afghanistan. Hence the extreme-right Republican electoral campaign in 1980 with the slogan of the Committee on the Present Danger (CPD): "Is America No. 2?" The Soviet Union was again supposed to be militarily more powerful and threatening than ever, an argument that seemed to be corroborated by facts. Ronald Reagan was elected to restore America's world position.

Not only did he start a new economic policy by cutting taxes to encourage private investment but also attacked the "evil empire" (the Soviet system) and wanted to roll it back steadfastly into collapse. Hence a tremendous five-year plan for rearmament entailing in September 1980 a $1,500 billion military budget (actually over $2 trillion were spent). That new policy had various consequences. Tax cuts and the build-up of new armed forces primed an industrial development favorable to the higher income levels of the American society, the wealthy, at the expense of the underprivileged who were hit by unemployment and reduced wages. The overall impression, however, was that, thanks to Reagan, the United States had recovered its former prosperity after years of depression and foreign setbacks. It had restored its power in accordance with its exceptional destiny and could again be seen as the true leader of the free world as well as its model.

On the other hand, the military became self-confident again, pampered as they were with higher pay and the supply of "high-tech" weapons. As an answer to the invasion of Afghanistan by Soviet troops – that was exposed as a new proof of Moscow's intentions –, Americans established a chain of Pershing II missiles on launching sites set up in Western Europe against the SS-20 rockets scattered over Eastern Europe and Russia in 1982. Later Reagan was to announce the creation of space-based missile platforms meant to be able to destroy any Soviet nuclear missile fired against the West. Clearly he wanted to engage negotiations with the Soviet Union from renewed strength.

At the same time, the president manifested his determination to oppose the "evil empire" as he called the Soviet bloc from the time of the shooting down of the South Korean 747 airliner on September 1, 1983. A few weeks later, he ordered the landing of a joint task-force on the island of Grenada, in order to eliminate a Communist junta ruling a British Commonwealth territory! The details of the bungled operation were kept secret at the time, only success was emphasized in order to contribute to the erasing of the "Vietnam syndrome" from American minds.

With the armaments build-up Reagan had exerted strong pressure on the Soviet bloc, which could no longer follow the race so easily because of its ever-weakening economy. Moscow stood its ground until 1985 when Mikhaïl Gorbachev succeeded Konstantin Chernenko as Secretary General of the Soviet Union Communist Party on February 11. On April 8, he declared himself ready for an American-Soviet summit and announced that the installation of new SS-20 missiles in Eastern Europe was to be suspended. Decided in July, the meeting was held in Geneva on November 19–21, and was the first of that kind since Carter and Brezhnev had gone to sign the Salt II agreements in Vienna in June 1979. At Geneva general views were exchanged on a future bilateral disarmament to be completed in future meetings. But technical accords were signed: *Business Week* was later to reveal American participation in Soviet key industries such as motor-car making, oil research and drillings; American profits were to be freely taken back to America. That was in compliance with the "Open Door" doctrine and it indicated that future summits would not be to no avail.[5]

They took place as foreseen in Reykjavik (1986), Washington (December 1987), Moscow (May–June 1988). After some misunderstandings and disagreements decisions for a reduction of armaments were reached first in Washington and later in the United Nations General Assembly held in New York, when Gorbachev unilaterally announced a 10% reduction of Soviet armed forces and the withdrawal of ten thousand tanks from Europe. Reagan, his party and Americans could therefore conclude that the president had managed to bring the peaceful surrender of the Soviet Union to the West. The Reagan team was not durably handicapped by the Iran Contra scandal when it exploded in late November 1986, and Vice-President George Bush could be elected to succeed Reagan in 1988.

Although this review might seem wearisome, it is necessary in order to understand George Bush's attitude in the earlier months of his presidency before the outbreak of the Gulf War. The vice-president had centered his electoral campaign on Reagan's foreign policy achievements, and also on the apparent economic recovery with his famous slogan "Read my lips; no new taxes!", perceived by the rich as the assurance that they would keep on getting richer at little or no cost. But, after a year of more popularity than had been enjoyed by the Great Communicator in his first year, Bush was caught up in the consequences of Reagan's financial policy. The federal deficit was ballooning because of the budget deficit caused by huge military expenditures without coverage from tax revenue. As the capital of the debt is never refunded, the debt is only serviced and interests paid to creditors have to be taken from the budget. Under Reagan interest payments kept increasing the federal debt, which was nearing the $4 trillion mark and service over $250 billion a year, an insuperable situation that the Gramm-Rudman-Hollings Act passed in 1985 was designed to remedy: from the fiscal year 1991 (beginning on October 1, 1990) all yearly budget deficits were to be systematically reduced until there would be none left in 1993. If there were no agreement between the president and congress, all expenses above a scheduled figure would be automatically cut.

In the first half of 1990 President Bush could not reach any agreement with the Democratic Congress; he wanted to strike a balance by reducing health expenditures for poorer Americans while also reducing the capital-gains tax in favor of allegedly-investing rich people. Congress wanted none of that, so in June a reluctant Bush had to resort to an increase in existing taxes, thus breaking his campaign pledge and infuriating much of his constituency.

Meanwhile a far more ominous problem was looming. During the Iraqi-Iranian War from 1980 to 1988 the United States had militarily and economically supported Iraq, a country that was seen as the rampart against Komeiny's *shi'ite* threat. Arms were also secretly shipped to Iran with the hope of obtaining as compensation the freedom of the American hostages held in

Lebanon. But at the same time Saddam Hussein was furnished with foodstuffs and industrial equipment he did not have enough money to pay for.

In 1989 and 1990 Saddam Hussein was unmasked as a ruthless dictator cruelly repressing Iraq's Kurdish minority, going as far as gassing civilian populations. The outcry in America led people to ask for an end to American aid (only thought to be agricultural at the time) to Iraq. Congress urged a halt to credit purchases. In April 1990, a delegation of Republican Senators led by Robert Dole met with Hussein in Mossul; they vehemently assured him Bush would not stop the flow of aid, and in late June the President adamantly opposed the end of trade relations with Iraq because this would damage American foreign trade. Hussein must have felt encouraged to have it his own way, and in July he demanded from Kuwait the repudiation of the debt he had incurred to fight the Iranians. Hence a severe dispute developed between the two countries.

But the American administration initially viewed it as a minor problem concerning only the secondary Middle-Eastern countries. On July 25, 1990 American Ambassador April Glaspie saw no reason for Americans to meddle in Arab affairs, and so told Saddam Hussein in a farewell meeting. A few days later, Under Secretary of State Kelly told a Congressional committee that the United States had no cause to intervene in the Middle East, which Saddam Hussein must have interpreted as a green light to go ahead. Iraqi and Kuwaiti delegations met in Saudi Arabia: the latter refused any concession to Saddam Hussein who added new demands: he accused Kuwait of overproducing oil which lowered its price and thus hurt Iraqi trade; and worse, it was pumping oil from Iraqi fields. Doors slammed shut. Incensed, Saddam Hussein ordered the invasion of Kuwait to increase the pressure. It took place on August 1 (August 2 in Washington), and came as a bolt from the blue.

Bush was apparently at a loss to find a response. He must have felt cheated by Hussein while the latter could believe that the President had given the Iraqi a free hand, if not some encouragement. When Bush decided to help the Kuwaitis it may not be irrelevant that he was the former president of the Zapata Overseas Research Corporation, the first to drill Kuwaiti off-shore oil. He may also have found in a major conflict an unexpected opportunity to make American public opinion forget his reneged campaign pledges, a way to recoup American losses in foreign trade, and a means to reaffirm American supremacy through a military victory.

In the first stage he proclaimed only the necessity to restore the "legitimacy of Kuwait," as was expressed in the United Nations Security Council Resolution (No. 660), immediately voted at the urging of the American delegation to lay an embargo on Iraqi trade. Bush sent American troops in order to prevent any further attack by Iraq against its neighbors, first of all Saudi Arabia, under the pretext that oil production and price had to be controlled for the benefit of the Western world. He began assembling a military coalition to protect other Arab countries, and was supported in that by the enthusiastic declarations of Margaret Thatcher who sent a British military force to Arabia. The whole operation was named "Desert Shield" to indicate its defensive aim, and was rallied by Western European governments and Arab countries who feared an Iraqi triumph.

Saddam Hussein must have hoped that his action would receive the massive support of Arabian and other Moslem peoples in the Middle East and Africa and elsewhere in order to hamstring the American-led coalition, which was characterized as the oppressive exploiter of Arabian resources. Even some of his Iraqi domestic adversaries looked towards him as a potential unifier of Arab countries into one nation. Even though his supporters launched huge popular demonstrations in the Middle East and North Africa most governments in those regions were to side with Washington against Iraq. The August 2 Resolution No. 660 taken by the United Nations Security Council had been accepted by the Soviet Union, which ceased to ship any more war equipment to its former ally and customer. On August 10, at an Arab League meeting in Cairo, another resolution condemning Iraq was voted by eleven delegations, only Iraq, Libya, and the PLO voting against, and three countries expressing qualifications. The most spectacular move was the reversal of position taken by Syria, that had only recently been described by the United States and Britain as a terrorist country: Syria jumped on the American band-wagon against Iraq because its leader Hafez Assad was the sworn enemy of Saddam Hussein, both being leaders of the rival Ba'ath party sections in their respective countries. The consequence was the arrival of Egyptian, Moroccan and Syrian troops in Saudi Arabia under General Schwarzkopf, the US commander in chief.

Secretly, supposedly so as not to give intelligence to the Iraqis who were to be led to believe that there would be no hot war, the President assembled an impressive array of military forces. There were some 113,000 Americans by mid-September, far more than was openly announced in order to make public opinion believe there still existed a dangerous possibility of a further attack on unarmed neighbors by Iraq. At the same time the strength of the Iraqi army was grossly exaggerated; it was said to be over one million troops strong, while actually there were only 600,000 with about 300,000 fully trained and reliable soldiers, as future events were to show. Thus Saddam Hussein, no kind ruler, certainly, but rather a cruel dictator, was aggrandized into a demonic new Hitler in order to hint that the new allies were engaged in a new World War II coalition.

Bush's real game at the time can be better seen with hindsight. First of all, in the world arena, especially through the United Nations that he both supported and used, he kept insisting on the international aspect of the action. He did this in order to justify his attitude before the American electors he was then courting in order to persuade them to vote for Republican candidates in the coming mid-term elections. He must have been hoping that the international action would help defuse part of the heat of the controversy between the executive and congress about the not yet voted federal budget.

That he had been trying to fulfil both American plans and personal ambitions became quite clear after those elections. Without consulting Congress, he unilaterally decided to more than double the number of American troops in the Gulf to 400,000 men. Later he pressured the Security Council to pass on November 29 Resolution No. 678 which set an ultimatum for Iraq. If Iraq had not withdrawn from Kuwait on January 15, 1991 "member States cooperating with the government of Kuwait ..." would be allowed "to use all necessary means".

According to the United Nations Charter (Article 43, Paragraph 3), all military operations ordered by the Council should be directed by a joint staff constituted by officers coming from the staffs of the armies of the five permanent members of the Council. Nevertheless, the Americans kept General H. Norman Schwarzkopf, Jr., the American commander in chief, as the sole commanding officer.

As the head of one permanent member of the United Nations Security Council Mikhaïl Gorbachev asked for the constitution of such a general United Nations staff, to no avail. Bush ignored him, for two reasons. The first was the American intention to lead the operation under the cover of the United Nations. The second was the recent helplessness of the Soviet Union. In November 1989, Gorbachev had been forced to give up support to East Germany, and the Berlin Wall had collapsed while Gorbachev had accelerated the departure of the Soviet Army from Eastern Europe. He had serious economic difficulties and he had accepted the first United Nations resolution against Iraq, so he was in no position to stand in the way of American decisions. It must be noted that never during the war did allied troops wear the United Nations blue beret, another sign that the Americans were the leading power even more than during the Korean War.

That the U.S. desire to restore American prestige and leadership after the Vietnam disaster was an important, although perhaps a secondary war aim, became very clear as the way the campaign had been reported was disclosed after it ended. All information was severely censored or screened through either newspapermen's approved pools, or authorized television broadcasts.[6] Obviously the government had heard the protests of the military who .attributed the Vietnam fiasco to alleged media excesses in reporting that war. In this respect both Reagan's landing in Grenada in 1983 and Bush's surprise invasion of Panama to oust its head of state on Christmas 1989 had been rehearsals for the Gulf intervention. The Gulf War was used to reverse the effects of the Vietnam failure in American public opinion and to annihilate bad memories. In early March, on the return of American troops from the Gulf, Bush boasted: "We have kicked the Vietnam syndrome!"

On the other hand Saddam Hussein tried during the war to hit Israel with his Scud missiles, probably designed to produce Israeli reprisals that would have brought Arab coalition members into his camp. But Bush succeeded in both preventing an Israeli response, thus precluding an Arab changing of sides, and then forced Israel to admit American leadership, especially in future negotiations with Arab opponents. Once again, the United States appeared as the sole country able to have such an influence, which was evidence of its exceptional world position.

This was affirmed in another way. The United States made other countries pay part of the American expenditures. Out of an estimated $77 billion total, Saudi Arabia agreed to donate $16 billion, Kuwait $16 billion, the United Arab Emirates $3 billion. Still better in the case of non-participating countries, because their American-inspired post-World War II constitutions forbad participation in foreign interventions, Germany promised to give over $6 billion, and Japan over $10 billion, South Korea added only $385 million. All together, American expenditures were to be reduced by some $36 billion.[7] Did the American Empire have to resort to mercenaries, its very own paid by foreigners, and/or foreign ones from foreign armies? The use of mercenary troops was a tacit admission that the United States was the unquestionable leader of the free world and able to rally its allies. The new world order was taking shape.

This was humorously illustrated by a cartoon published by an American newspaper, in which a GI is shown being interviewed by a television crew with, in the background, a group of military censors dubbed "Pentagon Division of New Manipulation," holding up a prompter's sign to be repeated by the young soldier: "Hi, Mom! We're Number One!" The use of the old CPD slogan of 1980 under the watch of censors is quite telling.[8]

But more than the assertion of the American recovery of its superpower position in the world order, what was hinted at was the peaceful affirmation that the United States was able to lead a coalition and get paid for its efforts, which compensated for temporary economic difficulties.

There was a last and more personal motive for President Bush. The whole operation restored his personal prestige. In March his success gave him the support of 89% of American public opinion, an all-time high which would decline soon enough but he could still think of his re-election in 1992 as a sure thing.

He would fail because of a slow and irrepressible economic downturn. Because of the extensive media reporting of the war a steep fall in advertising started the decline. Moreover, the weakening of the Soviet Union which was to implode into many independent states after August 1991, and the Gulf victory, both entailed a decrease in orders for military equipment, and as a consequence, a reduction in profits and then in employment. In a first stage the Pentagon tried to make up for the coming contraction by selling the expeditionary forces' equipment (tanks, ordnance, ammunition, etc. ...) to the Gulf States allies. The move was contrary to the pre-war decision to reduce armaments in the region; it built them instead, and Stanley Hoffman could sadly warn in the press: "Watch out for a New World Disorder."[9] The slump deteriorated into a recession which Bush did not do much to stop by governmental intervention, true as he was to free enterprise dogmas.

It must be remarked that in 1991 the United States was in the same commanding position as in 1945, perhaps even a better one, since public opinion wanted this dominant position defended. But after the implosion of the Soviet Union the U.S. government still had plenty to worry about. What was to become of the former Soviet nuclear arsenal? Could it be used against any of the free world countries by any one of the newly independent states which had formerly been part of the Soviet Union? Although the Warsaw Pact had already disintegrated the Pentagon still wanted to retain NATO and even extend it to the rest of Europe. An astonishing development was the application by Eastern European leaders in July 1991 for admission into NATO.

In February 1992 the *New York Times* published the Pentagon's new plans for the next ten years. It feared seven potential threats: local conflicts, emerging into major ones such as a renewed attack of North Korea against South Korea, a new attack from a reconstructed Iraq, even finally a new threat from a resurgent Russia against American interests.[10]

Those plans produced less sensation than another Pentagon policy statement that was also revealed by the *New York Times*.[11] It showed the plan designed to keep the United States as the sole superpower. No independent regional association was to be tolerated. In other words, the new world order was to be organized around the United States. The general outcry in world opinion was tentatively defused by the Pentagon which declared that this policy document was only a yet unapproved draft.

Later on, more evidence that such was the U.S. strategy appeared. The chairman of the Joint Chiefs of Staff, General L. Colin Powell, wrote in the 1989–1990 winter issue of *Foreign Affairs* that the United States should lead the world through its armed forces. In his opinion, the extension of NATO to the whole of Europe would be the proper means to achieve security. Although Americans had been dragging their feet for a long time about taking part in the United Nations forces that were trying to bring a halt in the Yugoslavian civil war, they finally accepted that Air Force cargo-freighters drop foodstuffs relief over besieged Bosnian towns, and the United States finally obtained the end of the ban on German foreign military intervention through a decision of the German Constitutional Court.[12] So in the long run, aims and strategy were dictated through NATO direction which might bring about a reinforcement of foreign armies acting by proxy for the new world order, as was first tried during the Gulf War.

One can discover secondary lines of that overall strategy in Africa and again in Iraq. In Somalia rival factions vying to take the place of fallen dictator Siad Barré prevented humanitarian groups from helping the starving civilian populations. Finally, when about to leave the White House, President Bush asked the United Nations Security Council to launch a relief operation which, once approved, took place in December 1992 under the code name "Restore Hope." American marines and a small French force landed in Somalia in front of over two thousand correspondents. They tried to repel Somalian guerrillas and make room for relief operations. But on January 19, 1993 the *Los Angeles Times* published what was possibly the real aim of the action: to explore the reality of oil fields; *a posteriori* this explained why the United Nations force staff was first accommodated in the Comoco Oil Corporation building in Mogadishu! It must be added that again the American and French forces there never wore the blue beret of United Nations contingents. [13] Probably President Bush wanted to make it known that American forces could act for non-military humanitarian motives. In a sense, it was a reversal of the Gulf War.

In early January 1993, the American president accused Saddam Hussein of refusing to comply with United Nations resolutions: the latter was said to have prevented experts from inspecting suspected nuclear facilities, and worse, had sent Iraqi army units into Kuwait in order to retrieve war material abandoned in February 1991. Bush soon unilaterally ordered a fresh series of air bombings. It was later learned that the target was a chemical plant producing for civilian purposes and counted as such by experts. The Iraqi inroads into Kuwait had been allowed by Resolution No. 687 in order for the Iraqis to remove all their materials from their former naval base at Umm al Qasr which was to be occupied by Kuwait on January 15. Although Saddam Hussein was forbidden to repress his minorities, either in Iraqi Kurdistan or South Eastern Iraq near Basrah, no use of United Nations forces and still less the American creations of two "no-fly" zones were authorized. Once again there were distortions of United Nations decisions and a news manipulation. Most probably all those actions were the last propaganda gesticulations of a lame-duck president attempting to go down in history as the true champion of American interests and human rights. [14]

In fact, when all is said and done, the real far-reaching aim behind the military and diplomatic endeavors in recent years has been the recovery of economic supremacy, endangered by the consequences of the Vietnam War and the ballooning federal debt incurred during Reagan's two terms of office. Bush and his associates were simply taking up the "Open Door" policy that dates back to the nineteenth century.

Since 1945 many attempts had already been made to implement such a policy: protectionism was partly the cause of World War II, it was thought in 1947 that a Multilateral Trade Organization (MTO) would ease international exchanges. But the MTO treaty was rejected by Congress as "an infringement of its constitutional mandate to regulate commerce." [15] New international conferences ended with a General Agreement on Tariffs and Trade (GATT) signed in Geneva on October 30, 1947 and enforced as of January 1, 1948. The long range aim was to suppress tariffs and thus to open frontiers to international trade.

A series of trade negotiations took place under the treaty with success (Kennedy Round, 1964–1967; Tokyo Round, 1973–1979). But with world economic difficulties the next Round begun in Punta del Este (hence called the Uruguay Round) was extremely protracted. Starting in September 1986, it broke down in December 1988 because of the American demand that the European Economic Community phased out its subsidies to community agricultural exports as damaging to American exports. However, the United States relented momentarily and gave up its demands for a time when talks were resumed in early March 1989.

But as the American economy continued to deteriorate and, under President Bush the disagreements between the United States and the European Community reappeared, the suppression of Europeans subsidies was again demanded, as well as industrial cooperation and more access to copyrighted productions (films, computer software, etc. ...). Already Congress had adopted a stringent section 301 of a Trade Act to raise tariff barriers on foreign imports. However, American subsidies were never fully taken into account by negotiators. During the 1992 electoral campaign, when President Bush wanted to attract voters, he decided on the sale of a new batch of planes to Taiwan, and then on the construction of twenty B2 bombers which had earlier been eliminated from the budget in order to keep air-industry workers on the payroll. He was trying to take advantage of the victorious coalition set up during the Gulf War in order to recoup American industrial and financial losses.

One might think that the new Democratic President Bill Clinton would have taken another tack: not at all. He wanted to recreate a strong American economy by creating jobs. In his electoral platform published under the title *Putting People First*, there is this rather long but illuminating quotation:

> Because every $1 billion of increased exports will create 20,000 to 30,000 new jobs, we will move aggressively to open foreign markets to quality American goods and services. We will urge our trading partners in Europe and the Pacific to abandon unfair trade subsidies in key sectors as shipping and aerospace – and act swiftly if they fail to respond. To ensure a more level playing field, we will: Pass a stronger, sharper "Super 301" trade bill: if other nations refuse to play by our trade rules, we'll play by theirs. [16]

He was true to his words. In February he demanded the abandonment of European subsidies of Airbus planes which compete with Boeing and McDonald Douglas although so far the European firm had taken only 30% of the whole market. Moreover, President Clinton, like all his predecessors in the White House, simply forgot to mention the "secret" subsidies to American air industries when the government started in 1947 the production of military planes to fight the Soviet "threat": with these subsidies American corporations could develop their technologies to make civilian airlines compete with European ones and weaken them. [17]

As fresh negotiations on agricultural and other products are scheduled, a deadlock is to be feared. Would the economic war ensuing from it come to threaten the new world order prepared and achieved under the leadership of the United States at the time of the Gulf War? In such a case what would remain of American exceptionalism, so often put forward to justify a leadership of the new world order which in fact is nothing but a traditional empire in disguise?

Notes

1. Quoted in Lawrence H. Shoup and William Minter, *Imperial Brain Trust: The Council on Foreign Relations and United States Foreign Policy* (New York and London: Monthly Review Press, 1977), 164.
2. Quoted in William A. Williams, *The Tragedy of American Diplomacy* (New York: Dell Publishing Co., 1972), 236.
3. *Presidential Papers of the Presidents of the United States: Harry S. Truman*, vol. XXXV (Washington, D.C.: Government Printing Office, 1947), 16.
4. Daniel Bell, "The End of American Exceptionalism," in *The American Commonwealth – 1976*, edited by Nathan Glazer and Irving Kristol (New York: Basic books, 1977), 192–224.
5. *Business Week*, January 16, 1986, 6.
6. John R. McArthur, *Second Front: Censorship and Propaganda in the Gulf War* (New York: Hill and Wang, 1992), 146–198.
7. Patrick C. Marshall, "Calculating the Costs of the Gulf War," in *Editorial Research Reports, Congressional Quarterly* 1991 (Washington), 146–155.
8. *International Herald Tribune*, February 27, 1991.
9. Ibid., February 26, 1991.
10. Patrick E. Tyler, "The Seven Deadly Scenarios: Pentagon's Plans for Theoretical But Costly Emergencies," *International Herald Tribune*, February 18, 1992, 1, 4.
11. Tyler, "Pentagon's New World Order: US To Reign Supreme: A Policy to Warn Off Change," ibid., March 9, 1992, 1, 2.
12. Marc Fisher, "Bonn Gets Go-Ahead from High Court for Bosnia Combat Role," ibid., April 9, 1993.
13. Mark Fineman, "After the Marines: 4 U.S. Majors Await Somali Oil Season," as reproduced in the *International Herald Tribune*, January 19, 1993, 2.
14. Alain Gresh, "Les Etats-Unis fortifient leur emprise militaire: Regain d'activisme dans le Golfe," *Le Monde diplomatique*, février 1993, 9; John B. Quigley, "Resolution 688 and the 'No-Fly' Zones," *Lies of Our Times*, May 1993, 17–19.
15. Walter Russell Mead, "Bushism, Found: A Second Term Agenda Hidden in Trade Agreements, *Harper's*, September 1922, 37–45, quotation p. 39.
16. Governor Bill Clinton and Senator Al Gore, *Putting People First: How We Can All Change America* (New York: Random House-Time Books, 1992), 13.
17. On the long-standing policy of governmental public "secret" subsidizing of private production, see notably for the Air Force, the role played by John J. McCone in Laton McCartney, *Friends in High Places: The Bechtel Story: The Most Secret Corporation and How It Engineered The World* (New York: Simon and Schuster, 1988), 94–99. On the recent feud between the United States and the European Community on GATT negotiations, see Marie-France Toinet, "L'Europe désarçonnée par le nouveau protectionnisme américain: le GATT, c'est 'l'Amérique d'abord,'" *Le Monde diplomatique*, avril 1993, 3.

12

Soldiers and Citizens: War and Voting Rights in American History

Manfred Berg

I

Students of the history of universal suffrage cannot escape the observation that many important extensions of the elective franchise have occurred in the aftermath of wars. The large-scale breakthrough of woman suffrage after World War I figures most prominently, but other cases can easily be cited.[1] Despite much empirical research and theorizing about war and social change in general,[2] the reasons for the apparent relationship between war and suffrage have hardly been explored in a broader context. Either the impact of war is simply taken for granted or it is assessed in more or less elusive metaphors.[3] Suffrage extension, the standard accounts could be summarized, is part of the social and political change that nations usually experience in times of war.

Yet the relationship is far from being self-explanatory. There are numerous historical examples when wars did not result in increased democratization and participation. The French woman suffrage movement during World War I, for instance, was almost overconfident that the war would win the vote for French women, but suffered a severe setback when the Third Republic not only continued to deny female suffrage but even embraced outspokenly antifeminist policies after 1918.[4] For the Soviet people victory in the "Great Patriotic War" of 1941–1945 did not bring more freedom and democracy, but was followed by new waves of Stalinist oppression. After all, as Raymond Aron has pointed out, behind the centralization and expansion of state power, which have accompanied modern wars, always looms the danger of the garrison state.[5]

With obviously no historical automatism at work, chronological sequences between wars and suffrage extensions require thorough inquiry into possible causal relationships. Even where the time link appears close, mere coincidence can never be ruled out.[6] To answer the questions if, how, and why wars have influenced the broadening of the electorate, it is necessary to have a theoretical framework of explanatory force and to assess the evidence as to how it matches this framework. The more cases plausibly fit in, the more it is conceivable to come to a few cautious empirical generalizations about the impact of wars on the history of universal suffrage.

The history of suffrage in the United States provides a promising field of investigation, since its intersections with major wars have been particularly frequent and conspicuous.[7] The War of Independence marks the beginning of the abolition of property qualifications, the enfranchisement of black freedmen by the Fifteenth Amendment occurred in the wake of the Civil War, woman suffrage was introduced after World War I, World War II boosted demands by African Americans for the effective protection of their right to vote. Finally, the Voting Rights Act of 1965, which ultimately did away with illegal and pseudo-legal ways of disfranchisement, and the Twenty-sixth Amendment of 1971, which lowered the voting age from twenty-one to eighteen, were both passed while America was fighting the war in Vietnam. While this account certainly falls far short of an "historical law," it appears strong enough to warrant a closer look. Three working hypotheses are suggested as an analytical framework:

1. The *War as a Political Opportunity* Hypothesis.
Since modern wars require the mobilization of societies and the support of populations, it becomes increasingly untenable to deny political rights to those who put their lives on the line or have to make numerous other sacrifices. From the perspective of the underprivileged and disfranchised, war may provide a welcome opportunity to win concessions either by demonstrating their absolute loyalty or by threatening to withhold their support.[8] Correspondingly, military and political leaders have often used the promise of enlarged political freedom and participation to enlist cooperation in the war effort, as German Emperor Wilhelm II tried in 1917 when he promised a reform of the Prussian *Dreiklassenwahlrecht*.[9] Whether elites conceive of the granting of suffrage as a grudgingly accepted necessity or as a well deserved "reward" for sacrifice and patriotism, the crucial point is that their change of mind was brought about by the war. The "good behavior" argument, however, must be consumed with some caution, since it may very well be a rationalization of giving in to political pressure.[10] The interaction between pressures from below and the response of those in power does not follow a uniform pattern and must be carefully scrutinized in each individual case.

2. The *War as a Revolution* Hypothesis.
Modern wars, with their inherent tendency to become total wars,[11] have frequently transformed societies beyond the directions and intentions of the military and political leadership. Nazi leaders, to choose an extreme example, hardly anticipated that the war of imperialist expansion and racial annihilation they started in 1939 would not only lead into total defeat but also amount to a social revolution that in many ways paved the way for a more democratic and equal society in post war Germany.[12] In the *War as a Revolution* perspective, suffrage extension may result either from the social changes and political realignments that occurred during the war, or from a

genuine political revolution as a consequence of war – like the German Revolution of 1918–1919, which at once introduced woman suffrage, proportional representation, and a voting age of twenty years.

3. The *Citizen-Soldier* Hypothesis.

Military service and citizenship, including the right to vote, have been closely wedded in the occidental tradition. The ideal of the citizen-soldier, who fights for his commonwealth when called upon and who has a voice in public affairs, dates back to ancient times and has been heeded time and again from Machiavelli to the English, American, and French Revolutions, and even to the German "Wars of Liberation,"[13] "(T)hat the fulfilment of public duties in the long run will lead to the achievement of public rights," as Otto Hintze stated in his classical *Staatsverfassung und Heeresverfassung* of 1906, and hence universal conscription had to be complemented by universal suffrage, seemed to be of an irresistible logic, even if the Prussian monarchist Hintze himself refused to draw this conclusion.[14] But not everybody became happy with the citizen-soldier ideal. Seeing the citizen perverted, rather than perfected, by the soldier, Arthur Ekirch, the historian of American antimilitarism, viewed it as "one of the paradoxes of modern civilization that the assertion of the rights and liberties of man was followed almost immediately by his regimentation and conscription for military purposes."[15]

In U.S. history, the citizen-soldier ideal became the epitome of a liberal ideology that combined a high esteem for military virtues with a deep mistrust of military professionalism.[16] With peacetime conscription traditionally unpopular and never really imposed,[17] there could be no immediate association between universal conscription and universal suffrage. Yet the link was always palpable, especially for those who were denied the vote. For antebellum free blacks the citizen-soldier ideal in fact became a vicious circle: they were barred from the polls because they were not liable to militia service, and they were excluded from the militia in order to justify their disfranchisement.[18]

Since military service has been a male domain until very recently, the concept of the citizen-soldier posed a particular problem in the quest for woman suffrage. The British *Anti-Suffrage Review* of May 1909 articulated a typical line of argument asserting: "… full power of citizenship cannot be given to a sex which is by nature debarred from some of the crucial duties of citizenship – enforcement of law, of treaties, and of national rights, national defense, and all the rougher work of Empire."[19] To refute this argument, women could either try to dwell on their noncombat contributions to wars, for which they would have ample evidence in due time, or argue, as the American feminist, pacifist, and social reformer Jane Addams did in 1907, that a modern society required many more services from loyal citizens than just military ones – services that women were equally or even better fit to perform than men.[20] The former choice represented a traditional concept of citizenship, the latter its redefinition.

It is important to note that none of the three hypotheses suggested is singular. They all may explain successful quests for inclusion as well as exclusion from the suffrage. Those who lent their loyalty to the losing side, or who belonged to the classes overthrown by a revolution, have often been deprived of their voting rights, as both the loyalists in the American Revolution and officials of the Confederacy after the Civil War experienced when they were temporarily disfranchised after their defeat.[21] And the citizen-soldier ideal could also be used to deny the suffrage to those who allegedly did not contribute to the defense of the nation. Hence it is necessary to go into the historical record of the American wars, enumerated above, to see in what way they were exploited as political opportunities, constituted a revolutionary transformation, or invigorated the citizen-soldier ideal. It is understood, that these three hypotheses are not mutually exclusive, but form an integral explanatory framework that is only separated for analytical reasons. If it is sustained by the empirical evidence the analysis may contribute to a better understanding of how ideological and social forces, created or accelerated by wars, bring about political change.

II

When Thomas Jefferson drafted a constitution for Virginia in 1783, he wanted to exempt militia men from the property qualifications for electors of the House of Representatives, criticizing the "defect" of the 1776 constitution, that it disfranchised the majority of those "who pay [taxes] and fight."[22] Though unsuccessful, the proposal reflected the declining acceptance of the age-old theory that only those with an independent social standing, possibly a freehold, could responsibly participate in public affairs. With the victorious Continental Army and state militias largely made up by the disfranchised lower classes, critics of property qualifications could rightly point out that these soldiers had protected the property of their wealthier fellow-citizens with their lives. Already during the War of Independence there were numerous incidents when landless and often young soldiers or militia men protested their disfranchisement and demanded for themselves the very liberties which they were supposed to defend. A petition of militia privates to the Pennsylvania legislature expressed this new self-consciousness, asserting that "... all Persons (not being Mercenaries) who expose their Lives in Defence of a Country, should be admitted to the Enjoyment of all Rights and Privileges of a Citizen of that Country which they have defended and protected."[23] Such claims were reinforced both by the widespread practice of electing militia officers, and by the observation that many of the well-to-do patriots preferred to hire a poor man or even to send a black slave as a substitute rather than fight for their liberty in person.[24]

Defenders of a property based franchise, however, were unimpressed. To John Adams property remained the very foundation of society, and lowering the property qualifications for voting would only result in a corrupt, irresponsible government.[25] In the conservative view, the duty to fight had nothing to do with the privilege of voting. To extend the latter as a reward for the former seemed an odd idea that was never carried out. Instead, the ranks of the Continental Army and the state militias, which at times suffered from severe manpower shortages, were filled by quite traditional means, using bounties and land grants as incentives for enlistment.[26] That the conferment of land might eventually enable the recipient to meet the property qualifications for voting was hardly a concession to the demand for suffrage. Moreover, fears that the democratic spirit of the soldiers could get out of control[27] were grossly exaggerated. There is no evidence that the demand for suffrage ever led to outright mutiny. The inclination of the men to go home as soon as their terms of enlistment had expired was a much graver problem for maintaining discipline and fighting strength. However, during the crises with France and Britain around the turn of the century, concern over the loyalty of disfranchised soldiers occasionally led to considerations of granting suffrage. During the War of 1812 disfranchised militia men again raised their voices in protest.[28]

The much debated question whether the War of Independence was a revolution in terms of redistribution of property, exchange of political elites, revolutionary ideology and violence, changes of social behavior and so on, need not be discussed here.[29] Suffice to say that in the minds of the contemporaries the Declaration of Independence and the establishment of a republican form of government were certainly conceived of as revolutionary acts. But was there also a revolutionary change in suffrage laws? A closer look hardly warrants Chilton Williamson's assessment of 1960 that "the changes in suffrage made during the Revolution were the most important in the entire history of American suffrage reform."[30] Only Pennsylvania and New Hampshire completely substituted taxpaying for property qualifications, the other states lowered their qualifications at various scales.[31] Religious qualifications practically came to an end, and some states enfranchised free blacks. Robert Dinkin has estimated that the overall electorate in the thirteen states expanded at an average of 10%, from 50–80% of the white male population in the late colonial period to 60–90% by the end of the Revolution[32] – hardly a dramatic upturn. Yet it is also true that the abolition of property qualifications started in 1776, even if it took until the mid-nineteenth century to accomplish this process.[33] Stronger than in the original thirteen states, the egalitarian impact of the Revolution made itself felt in the suffrage laws of the new states that joined the Union after 1790. Of the eleven states accepted until 1821 only two, Louisiana and Ohio, still made the payment of state or county taxes a prerequisite for voting while the rest established white manhood suffrage linked to citizenship, residency, and the minimum age of twenty-one.[34] In this perspective, the Revolution and the foundation of the Republic undoubtedly mark a clear break.

Looking at the suffrage laws at the time of the Revolution the specific impact of the citizen-soldier ideal seems to have been quite limited. Only the 1776 constitution of Connecticut allowed for a direct substitution of the property qualifications or taxpaying requirement by enrollment in the militia and one year of service preceding the election. The Pennsylvania constitution of the same year did not make a clear stipulation, but in its consecutive enumeration of the duty of freemen to serve in the militia and of their right to vote it took the citizen-soldier ideal all but for granted.[35] Yet military service was considered only a substitute. With property qualifications and poll taxes successively lowered or abolished, exemptions for poor soldiers and militia men became unnecessary. The 1821 constitution of New York, where conservatives adamantly fought for retaining a property clause, was the latest instance when a year of militia service or public work was introduced as a substitute for the payment of a property tax. Mississippi had already reversed the ratio in 1817 by making enrollment in the militia the regular requirement for voting, that could be set off by paying taxes.[36]

More important than its immediate effects on suffrage laws was the emergence of the citizen-soldier ideal as a powerful ideological force during the American Revolution. The seventeenth century English Whig ideal of the freeholding militia men as opposed to the mercenary armies of tyrannical monarchs had always been cherished by the American colonists, even if the actual practice in the colonies bore little resemblance to the ideal.[37] But the clashes between the colonials and the British Army, especially the notorious "Boston Massacre" of 1770, reinforced the fear of standing armies as a threat to liberty and revived the republican notion of the citizen-soldier. In 1774–1775 the colonial militias were reorganized, possibly to be "composed of gentlemen, freeholders, and other freemen." The election of officers was supposed to ensure the leadership of the local social elite.[38]

Despite the poor combat performance of militias during the War of Independence, their impact should not be underestimated. John Shy has pointed out that they served as an agency of political mass education, forcing many undecided colonists to take a stand and actively promoting the dissolution of deferential attitudes.[39] Whatever its military value, the citizen-soldier ideal was strengthened by the Revolution and became an important force in the ensuing conflict over the federal constitution. While the Federalists advocated a strong nation-state protected by a professional army against external threats, Anti-Federalists remained deeply suspicious of a standing army and the military powers of the federal government, which not only comprised the right to raise an army but also extended to state militias.[40] Although it paid tribute to the citizen-soldier ideal in the Second Amendment, the Constitution failed to clarify the military obligations of the citizens to the nation just as it failed to establish a uniform national suffrage law. Thus, the two key features of citizenship at the time, military service and the right to vote, basically remained a domain of the states and were not moulded into a complementary concept of universal service and universal suffrage. Nevertheless, with the exceptions of Rhode Island and Virginia,[41] the dual role of soldier and citizen became the uncontested standard for white male Americans, while at the same time it excluded most free blacks and all women. Not until the Civil War, would these groups get a chance to change their inferior status by proving their loyalty and bravery.

III

On the eve of the Civil War, free black males were allowed to vote on equal terms with whites only in five New England states and had to meet a $250 property test in New York. All southern and some northern states, where they originally had been eligible, had disfranchised them, whereas new states usually confined the vote to white male citizens. In its 1857 *Dred Scott vs. Sandford* ruling, the U.S. Supreme Court even denied that blacks, free or unfree, could ever become citizens of the United States.[42] With most Northerners more or less indifferent about slavery, and the South staunchly defending its "peculiar institution," it was virtually inconceivable in 1860 that ten years later all African American men would be enfranchised by the Constitution. Undoubtedly, the roots for such dramatic change are to be found in the Civil War.

For a long time the popular version of the history of black suffrage read that vindictive and opportunistic Radical Republicans had bestowed it on ignorant freedmen to punish the South and to secure the rule of their party. The post-Reconstruction disfranchisement of southern blacks by means of literacy tests, poll taxes, intimidation etcetera then appeared as an understandable effort to "redeem" "home rule."[43] To depict blacks as mere objects, however, ignores that many of them were actively seeking the vote already during the war, insisting they deserved full citizenship for their support in the war effort and that this support would be needed after the war as well. As a petition of Nashville blacks to the Union convention of Tennessee in January 1865 put it: "If we are called on to do military duty against the rebel armies in the field, why should we be denied the privilege of voting against rebel citizens at the ballot-box? The latter is as necessary to save the Government as the former."[44]

The military contribution of black soldiers to the Union victory had indeed been considerable. At least 190,000 African Americans joined the U.S. army during the Civil War, 40,000 of whom lost their lives – a casualty rate 40% higher than among white Union troops, due to inferior equipment and medical care and the brutal treatment in case of capture by Confederates.[45] But despite prejudice and fears in the North that black soldiers would be worthless or dangerous, the African American units generally distinguished themselves in battle.

There is abundant evidence that blacks, both in the North and the South, regarded the war as a unique opportunity to change their lot. Northern free blacks, though barred from the state militias and the army, enthusiastically responded to the outbreak of hostilities, issuing numerous declarations of loyalty and patriotism and offering their services in the field.[46] Yet, their hopes to turn the war into a struggle against slavery and discrimination at first met with a harsh rebuff from most whites. Only when military necessity demanded it were black Americans permitted into the Union army. Ironically, some southern free blacks and slaves also offered to fight for the Confederacy, hoping such proof of loyalty might win them freedom.[47] But since the South had seceded to defend slavery, the idea to arm slaves was anathema. As the military situation became desperate, however, Confederate President Jefferson Davis in March 1865 signed a "Negro Soldier Law," authorizing the enlistment of slaves who eventually might be emancipated by the consent of their owners and the state.[48] This belated and not even half-hearted move could, of course, neither prevent defeat nor win the support of slaves, who had realized long before that their hope for freedom lay with a northern victory and who had joined the Union army in large numbers as soon as they got a chance.

Manifestations of loyalty and demands for citizenship by blacks caused no little embarrassment for the Lincoln administration, which from the beginning of the war had insisted that the fight was about the preservation of the Union and not about the destruction of the South and its "peculiar institution." Since emancipation had only been adopted as a war measure,[49] it was hardly conceivable that citizenship and equality for all African Americans would soon become government policy. Black suffrage, in particular, was most unpopular with white voters in the North, who had almost consistently rejected it in popular referenda before the war.[50] With northern Democrats and the slaveholding border states opposed to emancipation, Lincoln and the Republican Party could not afford public support for a measure widely seen as utterly radical. Only in private would the president consider the vote for "the very intelligent, and especially those who have gallantly fought in our ranks."[51] Even Radical Republicans Senator Wade and Congressman Davis, who introduced a bill to Congress in 1864 providing for much stricter terms of reconstructing rebellious states than Lincoln favored, sacrificed black suffrage to secure a majority.[52]

Radicals, however, were also most aware that acquiescence to racism was no solution to the key question of reconstruction: how could the military victory of the North be transformed into a new political power structure for the southern states that ensured future loyalty to the Union and at the same time represented a republican form of government? As the resentment of large parts of the white population seemed inevitable, it was only natural to embrace the logic, which a convention of Kansas blacks had tried to bring home to their white neighbors as early as 1863, namely, "that it is as necessary to make the black man a voter, as it was to make him a soldier. He was made a soldier to RESTORE the Union. He must be made a voter to preserve it."[53]

The Radical wing of the Republican Party, led by Thaddeus Stevens and Charles Sumner, pursued black suffrage both out of a genuine commitment to civil equality and out of fear that without the voting strength of the loyal freedmen the old southern elite would quickly regain power.[54] Their worst nightmares seemed to become true when Lincoln's successor Andrew Johnson in May 1865 announced his reconstruction plans that would readmit Confederate States into the Union at the mere endorsement of abolition and loyalty oaths by voters, with former officials and rich planters subject to individual presidential pardon. Johnson refused to include black suffrage, because the federal government had no power to interfere with the states' right to regulate voting qualifications, but he also opposed it personally for reasons of racism and political expediency.[55] Without the vote and the help of the federal government, Radicals believed, freedmen would be reduced to quasi slavery again and the entire South would fall under the control of rebels. The election of former Confederate generals to the new state governments and the introduction of the notorious "black codes" only confirmed these apprehensions.

Radical resistance to Presidential Reconstruction could hardly have succeeded if Johnson had not alienated the center majority of Republicans by blocking even moderate measures in favor of freedmen. The president's scrupulous concern for the constitutional rights of the reconstructed states bewildered many of those who initially had backed his plans. After all, the war had not been waged to restore the benefits of the Constitution to rebellious states, but to crush rebellion and to eradicate its roots. The coalition of Radical and Moderate Republicans, formed in 1866 to enact Congressional Reconstruction, was first and foremost based on the conviction that suppression of the rebellion and civil rights for freedmen were inextricably linked.[56]

Facing the prospect of increased congressional representation for a South that was benefiting from the full inclusion of blacks into the reapportionment formula, while barring them from the vote, the majority of Republicans still backed off universal manhood suffrage. The second clause of the Fourteenth Amendment, passed by Congress in June 1866, only reduced the representation of states according to the proportion of disfranchised male citizens – a stipulation, bitterly criticized by Radicals for its implicit acknowledgement of the right of states to racial discriminate in their voting qualifications. But continued defiance from the South, and an uncompromising power struggle with Johnson, eventually persuaded a broad Republican coalition that black suffrage was necessary to secure loyal governments in the South, the civil rights of blacks, and a solid constituency for their party.[57] The Reconstruction Act of 1867 required the enfranchisement of blacks for readmission to the Union, and the Fifteenth Amendment, ratified in 1870, prohibited abridging the right to vote on account of "race, color, or previous condition of servitude".

There can be no doubt that the enthusiasm and loyalty African Americans had shown for the Union both during and after the war critically contributed to their enfranchisement. Radicals, if not committed to a natural rights doctrine, were at least willing to reward their military service, whereas most Moderate and Conservative Republicans and southern Unionists ultimately yielded to the political necessity of counterbalancing the voting strength of former Confederates. Even the bulk of northern voters, while certainly more or less prejudiced against black suffrage, seems to have accepted it as the "lesser evil" to the resurgence of rebellion. As a West Virginia editor had shrewdly observed in 1865: "... abstractly the American people are not in favor of Negroes voting, but as against rebeldom ruling in Congress or even in the South, they are." [58] But the loyalty of African Americans to the Union was not repaid in kind. When Reconstruction came to an end in 1877, the federal government abandoned the protection of the freedmen's civil rights, leaving the southern states free to disfranchise the vast majority of black voters.

To many woman suffragists, the black men's gain seemed to be their loss. Given the close association between the women's movement and abolition-ism, it had only been logical for them to seize the opportunity of the Civil War to foster both causes. During the war, which saw numerous northern women serve as nurses and aids for the newly founded "Sanitary Commis-sion," the cause of abolition was given priority. In 1863, Elisabeth Stanton and Susan B. Anthony, the most conspicuous women leaders, organized the *National Woman's Loyal League* to advocate the passing of the Thirteenth Amendment. [59] With this goal accomplished after the war there were high expectations that male abolitionists would now honor their verbal commit-ment to woman suffrage and make it part of a sweeping post war reform program.

Disappointment was to come soon. The war had just ended when Wendell Phillips, the new president of the *American Antislavery Society* and a Radical Republican, told women suffragists that they would have to be patient for the time being, because: "This hour belongs to the Negro." [60] Convinced that black suffrage was the only reliable safeguard for Recon-struction, Radical Republicans abandoned woman suffrage as a liability which was unbalanced by any possible advantage female voters might offer. From their point of view asking for patience was no betrayal, since the plight of blacks had not ended with slavery and freedmen needed the vote for self-protection much more urgently than did women. [61]

Patience, however, was the last thing Elisabeth Stanton had in mind. She realized the opportunity offered by an amendment to the U.S. constitution. Seeing no conflict between the demand for black and woman suffrage she hoped, in her own famous phrase, "to avail ourselves of the strong arm and the blue uniform of the black soldier to walk in by his side." On the other hand, if the Fourteenth Amendment indeed spelled out the ominous word "male" in its second clause, "it will take us a century at least to get it out." [62] No wonder she and her followers felt bitterly betrayed by the implicit disfranchisement of women in the Fourteenth Amendment and conse-quently severed their ties to former abolitionists. But not all adherents of woman suffrage agreed. When the Fifteenth Amendment again failed to outlaw disfranchisement on account of sex, the ensuing conflict over priority for black manhood suffrage led to an organizational split in the women rights movement. Moreover, the outrage over the enfranchisement of illiterate black men, while educated white women were left in the cold, caused many woman suffragists to adopt a rather blatant white middle class racism that divorced the struggles for equality of the sexes and the races for a long time to come.[63]

Was the Civil War a lost opportunity for women suffrage? Neither the question, if suffragists were betrayed – they surely were – nor the suggestion that the priority of black men had been morally and politically justified,[64] are of much relevance here. Hindsight may well sustain the conclusion that the hope for woman suffrage had been unrealistic because the war had put the freedmen, not women, into the limelight, because the congressional majority had no intention of burdening its agenda with another unpopular emancipatory demand, and because the woman suffrage movement, after all, was still in its beginnings. But observing the completely "unrealistic" ascendance of black males from slaves to freedmen to voters within less than ten years, it is understandable why suffrage activists like Stanton and Anthony desperately tried to seize a chance that might not come again. If they had failed because of their own weakness, the making of a strong and independent women's movement was the obvious consequence to be drawn. In 1870 nobody could possibly foresee that it would take another great war until women suffragists would finally succeed in their quest for their own constitutional amendment.

Even without woman suffrage, the changes brought about by the Civil War may rightly be called "the Second American Revolution."[65] Confederates, in their quest for independence, had claimed the legacy of the American Revolution, while the cruelty and duration of the fight convinced many Northerners, including Lincoln, that slave power was the root cause of this evil, and hence the social fabric of the South had to be destroyed and completely rebuilt. And while later historians, in a conciliatory effort, have played down the uncompromising and revolutionary character of the struggle, modern scholarship, focussing on the black experience, has reemphasized that the Civil War and Reconstruction constituted a true revolution in American history – however, a revolution that remained "unfinished."[66]

The eruption of the sectional conflict also facilitated the shift of abolitionists and Radicals from the fringe to the center of political power. Although they never dominated northern war and Reconstruction politics they were strong enough to carry along Moderates to emancipation and eventually to citizenship for African Americans, including universal manhood suffrage. Radicals like Thaddeus Stevens, Charles Sumner, or Wendell Phillips were never in doubt of the necessity to revolutionize southern society, and were often compared to the leading characters of the French

Revolution. [67] However unwarranted such comparisons may have been, it is indeed hard to imagine the rise of the Radicals if secession and war had been avoided.

But while the years from 1861 to 1877 certainly were a revolutionary experience for blacks, it is questionable whether the introduction of black suffrage in both intention and consequence was a revolutionary measure, as some of its proponents hoped and many critics feared. It has recently been argued, that the Fifteenth Amendment, like the rest of the civil rights legislation during Reconstruction, actually reflected the views of moderate and conservative Republicans who opposed unlimited federal regulations and advocated impartial rather than universal suffrage. [68] Assuming an "original intent" doctrine, such a view implies that most of the later notorious devices for disfranchisement, the poll tax, literacy tests etc., were basically constitutional, if only applied in a color-blind fashion. If this is correct, neither the origins nor the consequences of the Fifteenth Amendment may be called revolutionary. Ironically, this interpretation echoes much of the criticism by Radicals, who asserted that the Amendment neither protected the right to hold office nor closed the many loopholes for ostensibly nonracial suffrage restrictions that were retained in northern states as well. [69] Yet aside from the binding force of "original intent," the obvious compromise character of the Fifteenth Amendment must not be exaggerated. The introduction of black manhood suffrage, after all, was a much more sweeping step towards racial equality than Radicals could have hoped to achieve or Conservatives would have been willing to concede a few years earlier. It certainly was a revolutionary measure from the viewpoint of the white majority in the South and in the North, where voters had overwhelmingly defeated such proposals before and after the war. And while it is true that both Radicals and Moderates viewed the enfranchisement of blacks as the ultimate solution of the "Negro question," which would render prolonged federal intervention obsolete because blacks could protect themselves with the ballot, [70] such an expectation still assumed the inclusion of African Americans into the body politic on an equal footing – a quite revolutionary notion indeed. This, of course, did not happen. Blacks were unable to protect their rights with the vote and eventually lost it, not because of the narrow "original intent" of the Fifteenth Amendment, but because their former allies had either lost power or interest and left them exposed to the gradual "counterrevolution" after 1877.

When blacks began demanding liberty and equality during the Civil War their newly adopted citizen-soldier role formed the cornerstone of their claims and arguments. Pointing to their eagerness to cast their lives into the balance for the Union and to the distinction black troops had won in combat, they felt entitled to nothing less than the same rights white Americans enjoyed. As Frederick Douglass asserted in 1864 the service and bravery of black soldiers had finally laid to rest "this frivolous ... apology for excluding us from the ballot-box." [71] It was not only military performance that qualified them for citizenship, it was also the birth right of native born Americans. "They say that Africa is our country," a black corporal from Ohio fumed in a letter to a newspaper, "I claim this as my native country – the country that gave me birth."[72] That recent immigrants, the proverbial illiterate, drunken Irishman, who did not care about law and order and who rioted when called to duty, should have more right to the franchise than loyal black servicemen, added insult to injury. While the wartime petitions, articles, and letters of African Americans enthusiastically embraced the social and political values of the white society, they bitterly complained their own exclusion from the promise of American liberty. Hence, blacks were not fighting to restore the old Union, Frederick Douglass claimed in 1863, but for a new Union, "… a solidarity of the nation, making every slave free, and every free man a voter."[73]

The struggle for equality took place both within the army, where black soldiers strove for equal pay and the commission of black officers, and within society, where they were seeking full civil rights, including the right to vote and the right to testify in court, both of which were seen as critical instruments for self-protection.[74] The U.S. army organized African Americans on a segregated basis under the name of "United States Colored Troops" and commissioned almost exclusively white officers to lead them. Moreover, blacks received lower pay than whites and were frequently assigned to the most menial work.[75] While protests ultimately achieved equal pay and the commission of at least some black officers, the fundamentally racist hierarchy was hardly challenged. Yet despite all hardships and discrimination, the basic feeling that they were fighting their own cause kept up the spirits of African American soldiers in the Union army.

If their battlefield performance had won them considerable recognition as soldiers by the end of the war, it is doubtful whether this ever translated into full acceptance of black citizenship. When Radical Republican Salmon P. Chase remarked at the end of 1863: "I find, that almost all who are willing to have colored men fight are willing to have them vote,"[76] he referred to the views of his political friends at best. As argued above, loyalty and devotion during wartime helped black men win the vote, but this did not mean their unqualified inclusion into the American citizen-soldier ideal. The numerous suffrage petitions of returning black soldiers fell on deaf ears with their northern "fellow-citizens," who voted down all such proposals after 1865 except for Iowa and Minnesota, and in the South black Union veterans were often brutalized by their defeated enemies.[77] After Reconstruction had been abandoned, the tremendous contribution of black soldiers to the victory of the Union was all but forgotten by most white northerners, who gave reconciliation with the South priority over racial justice.

Blacks, however, did not forget. Whatever sufferings they had endured and whatever disappointments followed, emancipation and pride of victory remained their central Civil War experiences. Enlisting in the U.S. army not only offered fugitive slaves the chance to fight for the freedom of their

families and communities, for many of them the army also served as an
agency of education.[78] Many veterans assumed leadership roles both in
northern and in southern black communities, proliferating ideals of liberty
and equality. The self-esteem as citizen-soldiers that blacks had won in the
Civil War could not prevent disfranchisement, segregation and discrimination, but it remained an important asset in the struggle for equality.

IV

While the majority of African American men had been effectively disfranchised by the turn of the century, the woman suffrage movement had made
at least some progress. Trying to win the vote in as many individual states as
possible until a national constitutional amendment could be secured, it had
had broken ground in the West. In 1914 eleven states, all west of the
Mississippi, granted women full suffrage; in a total of twenty-nine they
enjoyed partial voting rights in school-board elections etcetera.[79] Determined to carry the struggle to a victorious end, Carrie Chapman Catt, the
leader of the *National American Woman Suffrage Association* (NAWSA),
devised a "winning plan" in 1916, which singled out April 1, 1922 as the date
the ratification process of the woman suffrage constitutional amendment
should be completed.[80] Considering that the Tennessee legislature actually
provided the necessary 36th favorable vote for the Nineteenth Amendment
on August 18, 1920, one may ask, if America's involvement in World War I,
except for a minor time gain, had any decisive impact on the achievement of
woman suffrage. To look for a possible impact of the war, however, is not to
belittle the burdens and frustration woman suffragists endured during
decades of struggle.[81]

Due to their close association with pacifism and social reform, woman
suffragists did not welcome the war. But when the United States declared war
on Germany in April 1917, the majority of American women organizations,
like those in all major belligerent countries, joined the national cause. A
Women's Committee, headed by long-time suffragist Dr. Anna Howard
Shaw, was created at the "Council for National Defense" which, however,
remained largely confined to traditional female "volunteer" activities.[82] To
Carrie Chapman Catt, also a Committee member, these activities were first
and foremost part of the suffrage struggle. By showing patriotism and loyalty,
the NAWSA hoped to win President Woodrow Wilson's support for a
constitutional amendment, which he had so far declined as contrary to the
states' right to regulate their voting qualifications.

But not all women suffragists backed this loyalty course. Refusing to be
part of mainstream patriotism the *National Woman's Party* (NWP), led by
Alice Paul, a young intellectual with a Quaker background and close ties to
the British suffrage movement, rather viewed the war as an opportunity to
expose the fundamental contradiction between fighting a war to make the
world "safe for democracy" while denying American women the vote.[83]

Applying the militant strategies learned in Britain, Paul and her followers began picketing the White House, carrying banners that demanded "Democracy at home" and called the President "Kaiser Wilson." Such outspoken "illoyalty" aroused the anger of chauvinist mobs, that started rioting against the picketers, with the police at first standing by and then arresting the suffragists. The NAWSA, seeing its loyalty strategy impaired, not only disavowed the picketing, but also refused to protest the maltreatment of the detained women. Blaming NAWSA for abandoning suffrage work for war work, NWP activists scoffed at its "Look at us, we don't picket – we help the country – please give us the vote" – attitude and demanded the franchise, because the war affected women just as seriously as men and therefore required their consent. [84]

Whether one considers Catt's loyalty course as "realistic" or lacking "moral grounding," because she had been a long-time pacifist, [85] there is no doubt that it succeeded in coopting Wilson in supporting a constitutional amendment. Having restricted his legislative agenda to "war measures," the president privately acknowledged his support for woman suffrage as a war measure as early as May 1917. [86] After the House had passed the Amend-ment in January 1918, Wilson openly joined the suffragist cause when he urged the Senate "that the early adoption of the measure is necessary to the successful prosecution of the war". The day before Carrie Chapman Catt had once again reminded him that all the women who were faithfully doing their duty in the war effort might lose temper if the Amendment failed. [87]

Yet it would be quite simplistic to depict Catt as the mastermind of power broking and Paul as the leader of the lunatic fringe, whose radicalism all but jeopardized success. Militant actions and loyalty were both strategies to exploit the war for the suffrage cause and complemented each other more than the rivals were willing to concede. Not only did NWP's militancy make NAWSA look moderate, so Wilson had a better rationalization for his support, its actions and arguments could also claim credit on their own merits. Police repression, abuse, and prison sentences, although repealed by the end of 1917, against white educated women often with influential social and family ties, caused increasing embarrassment to the administration as did their argument that America could not claim to fight for democracy as long as it deprived women of the vote. In fact, Wilson's address to the Senate made as much of the argument that woman suffrage would be a tangible proof of America's democratic crusade as of the loyalty women had shown in the war effort.

Despite Wilson's support, however, the Amendment fell two votes short of the necessary two-thirds majority in the Senate and failed again in February 1919. [88] Only after the new 66th Congress had convened in May was a positive vote secured. It took more than another year with many dramatically close calls before the ratification by thirty-six states was completed. Apparently, the die hard opponents of woman suffrage, largely made up of brewing interests and southern states' rights advocates, were impressed neither by women's loyalty nor by America's democratic image. But although the crucial votes were taken shortly after the end of World War I, its impact should not be underestimated. Even Alice Paul later acknowledged that Wilson's support had been crucial in converting a sufficient number of legislators to the women's cause.[89] The president's swing from being "a states' rights advocate to a federal amendment evangelist"[90] is hardly conceivable without his own crusade for world democracy and the wartime expansion of federal prerogatives. Moreover, the war clearly effected a change in public opinion. It was in 1917–1918 that woman suffrage referenda first succeeded in northeastern states, most important in New York, and even made first inroads in the solid South.[91] From the contemporary perspective the war opened the road for the constitutional amendment woman suffragists had been seeking for fifty years. By successfully courting and putting pressure on the president, Congress, and state legislatures, they made sure this opportunity would not be missed.

The importance of presidential support becomes even clearer if compared to the disregard, even thinly veiled hostility, the southerner Wilson displayed towards demands for civil rights by African Americans. The day after his Senate address on behalf of the Nineteenth Amendment Wilson received a delegation of black leaders who complained about discrimination and segregation in federal departments. In striking contrast to his bold move toward federal action in favor of woman suffrage, the head of the federal administration bluntly denied his "power to hasten the process," piously consoling his audience that "[h]uman nature doesn't make giant strides in a single generation."[92] In fact, Wilson himself had ordered the racial segregation of federal employees in Washington, D.C. shortly after he took office.[93]

To blacks, loyalty to the national cause was not just an opportunity to win material gains and civil rights but a matter of life and death. Rumors in the South about a German plot to stir racial insurrection only foreshadowed the very real danger of lynching and "race riots."[94] Most African Americans agreed with W. E. B. DuBois that they had to "close ranks" with their white compatriots during wartime. But when black leaders after the war claimed credit for loyalty and cooperation in the war effort a wave of racist violence swept the country as part of the post war hysteria. Instead of being able to dwell on their patriotism, African Americans faced indifferent federal governments and a new heyday of the "Ku Klux Klan."[95]

Although it affected American society and politics, the country's brief involvement in World War I certainly did not bring about any revolutionary changes comparable with the experiences of other belligerent nations. On the contrary, European revolutions during and after the war were so appalling to most Americans that they became almost obsessed with the specter of anarchy and a yearning for "normalcy." The electoral victories of conservative Republicans from 1918 on may even be seen as a mandate

204   REFLECTIONS ON AMERICAN EXCEPTIONALISM

to undo many of the wartime changes, especially the expanded role of the federal government.

Despite apocalyptic visions of disrupted homes and families it would be grossly misconceived to depict the advent of woman suffrage as revolutionary either in its intentions or in its consequences. Making up half of the nation, women quite correctly represented its political attitudes and social values, so woman suffrage, as Judith Shklar has observed, "turned out to be the biggest non-event in our electoral history."[96]

Nor did woman suffragists conceive of themselves as revolutionaries. When Catt in 1917 called the NAWSA "a bourgeois movement with nothing radical about it,"[97] she may have wanted to distance her organization from the "radicals" of the NWP, but she was right nevertheless. Alliances with women trade unions notwithstanding, middle and upper class Wasps made up the leadership and the rank and file of the woman suffrage movement. The "radicals" of the NWP differed in methods and approach, but hardly in social origins and principal aims. Far from trying to revolutionize American society and politics, suffragists sought inclusion into and equality within the system.

Such moderation, particularly the conspicuous silence on the race issue, undoubtedly helped win over majorities of male legislators and voters. In concentrating on "votes for women," suffragists left no doubt that they had no intention of challenging the southern system of racial disfranchisement, thus tacitly excluding most black women. Since parting from the abolitionist movement after the Civil War racist and nativist arguments had frequently been invoked in favor of woman suffrage.[98] Offering votes to counterbalance those of illiterate "negroes" and immigrants the suffrage movement depicted itself as basically conservative. It promised the enactment of moderate progressive social reforms, but it did not challenge the foundations of existing class, race, and even gender relations. Unlike Germany, where the enfranchisement of women resulted from a political revolution in the wake of World War I, American suffragists gained the vote by successfully coopting the support of key leaders in the states, in Congress and in the administration, first of all the president of the United States.

Did women suffragists try to define themselves as citizen-soldiers during World War I and, if so, did they succeed? Reading Wilson's Senate address of September 30, 1918, there seems to be no doubt: "I propose it [woman suffrage] as I would propose to admit soldiers to the suffrage, the men fighting in the field for our liberties and the liberties of the world, were they excluded," the president proclaimed, generously ignoring that the majority of black American soldiers in the American Expeditionary Force (AEF) were indeed excluded from voting.[99] But the relationship between woman suffrage and the citizen-soldier ideal was more complicated than Wilson's statement suggests.

Before World War I suffragists had a hard time with the traditional argument that those who fight shall vote. In an age of militarism, opponents of woman suffrage dwelled heavily on a narrowly constructed "only those who fight shall vote" version of the citizen-soldier ideal. Hence, spokes-women and men for women's rights usually rejected the fateful link between "the ballot and the bullet," arguing that the same logic would disfranchise all men unfit for military service, that women had always been useful in wars, and that modern citizenship should not be based on ancient notions of martial virtues.[100] When war broke out in Europe, Jane Addams and Carrie Chapman Catt founded the "Women's Peace Party," which opposed American involvement out of pacifist conviction and out of fear that it would reinforce male supremacy based on military values.[101]

While Addams remained a pacifist all through the war, Catt could not resist the temptation to join the patriotic bandwagon. However, the suffrage movement did not become militarist. Its activists participated in rather traditional "volunteer" activities like food saving, the promotion of liberty bonds etcetera. Nothing comparable to the small female force in the British army, that actually performed auxiliary military services, existed on the American side. NAWSA's most conspicuous war-related effort was the maintenance of a hospital in France.[102] Whether more militarist organiza-tions, such as the women's section of the *Navy League*, broke much ground for woman suffrage is difficult to assess.[103] But since nobody expected women to fight as combatants, the adoption of an explicitly military posture was not necessary to get credit as citizen-soldiers. It proved much more effective to make visible the war contributions of women in their traditional domestic and public roles. When Wilson finally presented woman suffrage as a "war measure," this move indeed signified the symbolic inclusion of women into the citizen-soldier ideal, regardless.

That symbols meant more than facts is mirrored in the experience of 50,000 African Americans who served in the AEF during World War I. The treatment of black soldiers by the U.S. army cannot be interpreted except as a deliberate effort to exclude these men from the status of citizen-soldiers while making use of their labor.[104] Dreading the vision of armed blacks, the southern states initially resisted their enlistment or conscription, and demanded that all black troops be removed from the South, especially after seventeen whites had been killed by black soldiers in Houston, Texas, who ran amok at the racial harassment they encountered. As a matter of course, African American units were strictly segregated and, reviving the stereotype of their lacking capacity for combat, were mostly employed as stevedores and laborers. Only one single all-black combat division was sent into battle. That the commander-in-chief of the AEF, General Pershing, otherwise jealous to retain full control over his troops, agreed to put four black regiments under French command only confirmed their second-class status. When these troops fought well and received ample praise by their French commanders American officers pressured the French not to "spoil the negroes." More-over, French civilians were constantly warned against black rapists.[105]

Racism was so pervasive in the U.S. army that even the NAACP supported segregated training camps to minimize "racial incidents." But despite ubiquitous discrimination the experience of travelling overseas and taking part in a victorious war effort made many black soldiers think about their inferior status at home. W. E. B. DuBois even attempted to put the race issue on to the agenda of international politics by calling a Pan-African Congress in Paris parallel to the Peace Conference. [106] But America was in no mood to acknowledge the contribution of black soldiers to make the world "safe for democracy" by making them part of democracy at home. Whatever hopes for civil rights and democratic participation World War I had stirred among African Americans were extinguished by a wave of violent racism and the deliberate apathy of federal authorities.

While voting rights remained a dead letter for most black men and women after 1920 the woman suffrage movement managed to rally sufficient political support during the war to secure a constitutional amendment shortly thereafter. Unlike blacks women as a distinct group were never again disfranchised by illegal or pseudo-legal means. The comparison between the success of women, and the failure of African Americans, points to the importance of the response from the power elites to the demands from below. Without even a willingness to take notice on the part of the federal government, neither loyalty nor protests could bring blacks anywhere. The breakthrough to federal support during the war, on the other hand, accounts for the historical significance of World War I for the introduction of woman suffrage. [107]

V

In May 1940, Rayford W. Logan, professor of history at Howard University in Washington, D.C., edited a compilation on the attitude of the southern white press toward black suffrage. After deploring the continued discrimination and disfranchisement of African Americans he reflected on the latest developments in the European war and concluded: "As the United States girds herself for the preservation of Democracy, it might not be a bad idea to have some Democracy to defend." [108] Logan's bitter remark anticipated the paradoxical experience black Americans were about to make in the forthcoming years. Called upon to defend democracy against totalitarian dictatorship and racist oppression they could not escape the contradiction between high ideals and their own deprivation of fundamental democratic rights. By 1940 only 168,888 blacks out of an adult population of more than five million were registered voters in the former Confederate states, where almost three fourths of all African Americans lived. [109] By devices like the poll tax, literacy tests, the white primary or simply by intimidation and violence, the deep South states had all but completely disfranchised their black population.

Having learned their bitter lessons from World War I, African Americans were hardly enthusiastic about American involvement in World War II. Their sensitivity to hypocrisy about freedom and democracy was compounded by the fact that the United States faced a non-white nation as a major adversary. Viewing the war in racial terms, many blacks understandably saw little point in fighting the yellow race to preserve the global supremacy of whites. But the Swedish sociologist Gunnar Myrdal, who made these observations in mid-1942, also noted "the proverbial loyalty" of African Americans to the democratic creed and the constitution. [110] After all, any improvement of their situation rested on the realization of these principles, and could certainly not be expected from a victory of Nazi-Germany or Japanese imperialism.

This time black leaders were pressing their case rather than waiting for gratitude. Before American entry into the war the labor leader A. Phillip Randolph, by threatening President Franklin D. Roosevelt with a protest march on Washington, had forced an executive order prohibiting "discrimination in the employment of workers in defense industries or Government because of race, creed, color, or national origin." [111] Trying to link the war against Nazism to the struggle against racism at home, black opinion adopted the battle cry of "Double Victory" and set out "to persuade, embarrass, compel and shame our government and our nation ... into a more enlightened attitude toward a tenth of its people." [112]

Dwelling on its effects on war morale, NAACP advocated the abolition of the poll tax as a war measure. But, despite support from other civil rights and labor organizations, southern resistance effectively blocked any general legislation. Depending on southern Democrats for the pursuit of his war policies Franklin D. Roosevelt refrained from intervention. [113] In 1944, however, NAACP scored a major judicial victory when the Supreme Court, in its ruling *Smith vs. Allwright*, outlawed the exclusion of blacks from the Democratic primaries – the only elections that really mattered in the one-party South. [114] Since the litigation had been going on for almost twenty years this breakthrough can hardly be attributed to the war. Moreover, *Smith vs. Allwright* stiffened southern defiance which resorted to new devices for disfranchisement like the infamous "understanding clause," that required prospective voters to interpret state constitutions to the satisfaction of registrars. [115]

Whatever impediments white supremacists piled up could not quell the new political self-consciousness many African Americans had developed during the war. Their post-war drive for voter registration, however, often encountered brutal violence in the deep South, including the murder of black veterans. [116] In the face of these events, President Truman was forced to act. In December 1946 he appointed the "President's Committee on Civil Rights," vested with a broad mandate for inquiry and recommendations. The Committee's report, issued in October 1947, was remarkable not only in making numerous practical proposals, including the abolition of the poll tax and other measures to protect the right to vote, but in explicitly accepting both the suffrage as a right of citizenship and the federal government's duty to protect this right. At first, Truman enthusiastically responded to the report and in February 1948 proposed legislation to Congress along the lines of *To Secure These Rights*.[117] Nothing, however, came out of this ambitious program, except the first steps to desegregate the military, enacted by executive order.

Despite his sympathetic rhetoric Truman himself undoubtedly cared more about black votes than about black voting rights. Civil rights never enjoyed a top priority on his agenda, but were subject to party considerations. Facing grim hostility from southern Democrats and conservative Republicans in Congress the president had no intention of jeopardizing foreign aid, defense and social legislation by pushing civil rights, which might split his party and alienate southern white voters.[118] That blacks did not launch a more vocal and effective protest movement certainly had a lot to do with the anti-communist hysteria of the emerging Cold War, which branded all kinds of dissent as illoyalty. Manning Marable has even blamed "moderate" leaders like Randolph and NAACP's Walter White for opportunistically complying with the redbaiting and dissociating themselves from radicals and communists.[119] If an explicitly leftist profile and an allegiance with the American Communist Party, not exactly a mass movement, had been a wise decision is open to debate. The relationship between the Cold War and civil rights is more complex than a mere scapegoat theory suggests.

The emerging ideological conflict with communism initially appeared to offer the opportunity to continue the wartime strategy of pressuring the U.S. government into action by exposing the contrast between its foreign policy rhetoric and the plight of black Americans. To demand free elections in Eastern Europe while denying them to black citizens in the South, black leaders argued, discredited the United States and gave communist propaganda a useful asset.[120] That America had to lend domestic credibility to its crusade for democracy, especially in the competition for the hearts and souls of the new nations of Africa and Asia, consequently became the official position of the Truman administration.[121] Acquiescence in Cold War anti-communism on the part of African American leaders may be seen as another attempt to combine loyalty in international conflicts with the demand for domestic concessions. Whether there was any real alternative to such "opportunism," cannot be discussed here. However, there is no doubt that it failed. Even when black loyalty received official recognition it did not automatically translate into tangible gains. Obviously, more assertive strategies were needed to force the federal government into action.

The creation of the "Fair Employment Practices Committee" by Franklin D. Roosevelt, the *Smith vs. Allwright* decision, and Truman's desegregation order for the armed forces were the only major civil rights achievements of World War II and the post war era. Certainly, the war had not dealt any serious blows to white supremacists who still dominated most southern states and were able to block legislation on the national level. Nevertheless the social and political change the United States experienced during this period did not bypass the right to vote. The number of registered black voters in the South soared dramatically during the 1940s. While their number did not exceed 170,000 in 1940, it had risen to over a million by 1952.[122] In Mississippi, Alabama, Louisiana, and South Carolina, where at the beginning of the decade only 2,000 to 3,000 blacks had been registered, the figures multiplied to 20,000 in Mississippi, 25,600 in Alabama, 80,000 in South Carolina, and 120,000 in Louisiana. Like the upsurge in membership of the NAACP and other civil rights organizations these figures reflect a growing political self-consciousness of African Americans that could not be completely checked either by legal disfranchisement or by violence. Moreover, the mass migration of blacks to northern and western cities had made race a national concern and created a black voter constituency to which politicians had to pay attention.

It is difficult, however, to assess the impact of the World War II on these developments. As early as 1942, Gunnar Myrdal predicted the gradual decline of black disfranchisement because rising levels of education and income would render legal obstacles like the poll tax and literacy tests ineffective, whereas sheer violence would become unacceptable even in the deep South.[123] Yet to assume that the war only accelerated existing trends which sooner or later would have brought about the same results does not provide a satisfactory answer. The end of black disfranchisement did not result from incremental social change but from two decades of struggle following World War II and from vigorous action by the federal government. The upsurge in political consciousness and assertiveness, that made African Americans vote in numbers unprecedented since Reconstruction, justifies calling the 1940s a "watershed in African American history."[124] The question is, if and how this new political consciousness was linked to wartime and to military experiences.

Fighting a war for the protection of freedom that the protectors themselves did not enjoy was a politicizing experience in itself. Although the treatment of black soldiers was generally fairer than in World War I, the U.S. forces basically remained segregated and racist.[125] To be sure, blacks were allowed into more branches, and a considerable number received commission as officers. But the bulk of the roughly one million African American servicemen (and women), half of whom were sent overseas, was employed in all-black transportation and engineering units. The combat troops mostly served in the European theater with great distinction, and in early 1945 the army even began experimenting with integrated units. Stories of black heroism were proudly heeded by African Americans at home and made black leaders press more determinedly for desegregation and an end to discrimination. Such assertiveness, especially when trickling down to the ordinary soldiers, almost inevitably provoked a backlash from white supremacists. Incidents of racial clashes both with civilians and within the army were numerous, and not a few black soldiers in the South confronted the humiliation of being rejected from diners where German POWs were courteously served.

Returning as liberators and victors over a self-styled master-race, many black veterans decided to claim their rights as citizens. Veterans often took the lead in the registration drives, undaunted by threats of violence and encouraging other black men and women of their communities to follow.[126] Without the example of these citizen-soldiers the upswing of black registration after 1945 is hardly conceivable. Courage and perseverance were necessary for white supremacists, far from acknowledging black soldiers as fellow-citizens, sought to restore prewar race relation by all means. "... no Negro is good enough, and no Negro will ever be good enough to participate in making the laws under which the white people in Alabama have to live," a prominent lawyer openly declared; and Mississippi Senator Theodore Bilbo quite frankly advocated violence to prevent blacks from voting.[127] But while ugly incidents when Bilbo's advice was carried out caught public attention and aroused just anger, the many more cases when black veterans actually succeeded in registering, went uncounted. Neither could all African Americans simply be driven away from the registration boards nor were all whites willing to do so. The weakening of disfranchisement that Myrdal had predicted a few years earlier had indeed begun. It may be no unwarranted speculation that the large numbers of self-assertive black veterans helped undermine the resistance of registrars to put African Americans on the rolls.

On the level of federal legislation a color-blind version of the citizen-soldier ideal had received recognition in 1942 when Congress provided absentee ballots and prohibited any poll tax requirement for servicemen.[128] Contrary to custom southern legislators did not filibuster as they did against any general attempts to abolish the poll tax. Since the states were in charge of administering the absentee ballots there was a way to make sure that few black GIs voted. Yet the citizen-soldier ideal got its strongest endorsement after the war from Truman's Committee on Civil Rights which treated suffrage and military service as complementary features of the "Right to Citizenship and its Privileges."[129] The Committee not only condemned racial discrimination in the army but cited the positive experience with integrated troops during the war as evidence for desegregation in other fields. In July 1948, President Truman ordered the desegregation of the armed forces and the creation of a Presidential Committee to implement this policy.[130] Before this bold move Randolph and other black leaders had threatened to launch a massive campaign of civil disobedience if segregation in the military continued. Truman, needing the black vote in the North for re-election, while trying to prevent the bolt of southern Democrats, chose to act on an issue that presented a national civil rights achievement but did not directly touch upon the power structure in the South.

Whereas the efforts to make African Americans first class soldiers clearly were a consequence of World War II it took another twenty years until federal legislation finally and effectively ended racial disfranchisement in the United States. Black leaders had tried to use the war as a political opportunity much more determinedly than in World War I. The southern black population had registered in extraordinary numbers during and after the war, and black veterans had assertively insisted on their citizen-soldier status. President Truman, although more in words than in deeds, took a favorable stand towards civil rights, especially when compared to his World War I predecessor. Even the Cold War, the catch-all explanation for every-thing that went wrong in American post-war politics, had at least an ambivalent impact on the struggle for black rights. To explain why World War II brought such limited progress for African Americans one has to look at the major impediment to desegregation and voting rights: the fierce resistance of the white South. However entrenched the doctrines of white supremacy had become they were still firmly rooted in the majority of the white population and the white political elite of the South. Holding key positions and forming an almost monolithic bloc on race issues southern congressmen were able to forestall all federal legislation interfering with "states' rights." And since the rest of the country tended to consider "the Negro question" a southern problem, African Americans had few allies. World War II, to be sure, created many of the conditions to change this situation, but it did not constitute a breakthrough in race relations. With the hope for inclusion by wartime loyalty once again frustrated, African American leaders came to realize that the system of racial segregation and discrimination had to be challenged more aggressively in order to force the national government and the nation as a whole to respond to their demands.

VI

The ratification of the Twenty-fourth Amendment in 1964, which ultimately outlawed the poll tax, and the "Voting Rights Act" of 1965 allowing federal registrars to supervise registration in precincts with a registration rate lower than 50%, finally cleared the way for an end to racial disfranchisement. Pressured by the civil rights movement, and appalled by the brutal backlash of white supremacists, the Johnson administration and a friendly Congress had taken action to secure the rights of African Americans and to improve their living conditions. [131]

Angry civil rights workers had asked as early as 1963 why the federal government claimed to protect the Vietnamese people from communist aggression, if it could not protect the people in Mississippi from terror-ism, [132] but the Johnson administration had not advocated voting rights of blacks to secure their loyalty for the war in Indochina. Nor did African Americans show their gratitude by enthusiastically fighting for democracy in Vietnam. Most black leaders were critical of the war in varying degrees but African Americans fought in integrated units in Vietnam and were overrepresented in combat forces. In 1967 11% of all U.S. troops in Vietnam were black, but this group accounted for 22.4 % of those killed in action [133]. With no apparent link between the voting rights legislation of 1964–1965 and the beginning of large-scale U.S. involvement in Vietnam, the two events seem to have been merely coincidental.

However, that the lowering of the voting age from twenty-one to eighteen by the Twenty-sixth Amendment in 1971 resulted from the pressure of youthful war opponents, has recently achieved the status of handbook knowledge. [134] There is little evidence for this assertion, as other authors have also noticed. [135] The argument that many of the young soldiers who were drafted and sent to Vietnam could not even vote at best played an auxiliary role for the antiwar movement. In the eyes of those who viewed the war as immoral and oppressive it could hardly be made more acceptable by giving teenage soldiers the vote. The concern was not with disfranchised GIs nor with making the draft more equitable, but with obstructing the war effort. [136] Moreover since age qualifications only disfranchise temporarily, there was little reason for those between eighteen and twenty years of age to organize around a minor issue, if the big issue, the war itself, could not even be expected to be solved by voting.

Instead of resulting from pressures by the disfranchised the lowering of the voting age appears to have been initiated primarily by the political elite itself. A constitutional amendment to reduce the voting age to eighteen had already been introduced during World War II but did not go beyond the Senate Judiciary Committee. In 1963 the reduction of the voting age was recommended by the "President's Commission on Registration and Voting Participation," and by 1968 the presidential platforms of both major parties endorsed the measure, with Democrats favoring a constitutional amendment and Republicans individual state action. [137] Only the latter explicitly referred to the beneficiaries' "service in the nation's defense."

When Senator Mike Mansfield proposed to lower the voting age as part of the extension of the "Voting Rights Act" in 1970, the issue was not desirability but the constitutionality of the procedure. [138] Opponents contested congressional power to reduce the voting age by mere statute and maintained that all federal interference with the states' right to regulate elections had to be codified by a constitutional amendment. Proponents argued that the Fourteenth Amendment covered the measure since the disfranchisement of eighteen-year-olds in contrast to twenty-one-year-olds denied the former equal protection of the law. The conscription of young men below voting age was one important argument in support of the bill, impressively illustrated by Edward Kennedy's statement that 30% of all U.S. forces in Vietnam and a shocking 50% of their casualties were below the age of twenty-one. Even South Vietnam, Kennedy added, had a voting age of eighteen. These facts suggested an urgency that did not tolerate the prolonged ratification process of a constitutional amendment. In a blunt challenge to the states' rights philosophy Senator Mansfield claimed the federal government's right to set the voting age just as "the Federal Government can go down to any state, pick an 18-year-old up by the back of the neck, put him in uniform, send him overseas, and perhaps send him to his death." [139]

As most legislators with constitutional misgivings voted for the extension of the "Voting Rights Act" the lowering of the voting age easily passed

through Congress. President Richard Nixon, though sharing these reservations, signed the bill, but gave advice to the attorney general to clear the way
for judicial review. The subsequent Supreme Court ruling in *Oregon vs.
Mitchell*, however, did not solve the issue, for it upheld the power of
Congress to lower the voting age for federal elections while denying it
for state and local elections. Facing the danger of registration procedures
disrupted by diverging age qualifications, Congress and the states passed the
Twenty-sixth Amendment in record time to ensure the orderly conduct of
the 1972 elections.[140]

The lowering of the voting age can hardly be depicted as a deliberate
attempt of the power elite to secure the loyalty of young Americans for the
war in Vietnam. In 1970–1971 America and its political leaders had long lost
faith in victory. Nobody could be so naive to expect that protesters and draft
resisters would change their mind or that youthful GIs would fight more
enthusiastically because they were granted the vote. In a broader sense,
however, the Twenty-sixth Amendment responded to what policy makers
perceived as a claim for democratization and participation by young people.
The vote, as Senator Moss suggested, offered an opportunity to participate
to the majority of young people who behaved "orderly and responsibly"
instead of rioting in the streets.[141] The near unanimous support for the
Twenty-sixth Amendment was built on its harmlessness. It ostensibly
responded to the wishes of young people and cured an obvious injustice by
synchronizing the age for conscription and for the suffrage, while its effects
on the political system, even on the party balance, were negligible. In the
conspicuous absence of either fervent demands or ardent opposition there
was, of course, nothing revolutionary about lowering the voting age to
eighteen years nor about its consequences. Like all newly enfranchised
groups teenage voters tended to participate below average, and their ballots
seem to have had no distinctive impact.

Although at the center of media interest, the impact of the antiwar
movement on American politics must not be overestimated. In 1968, when
it had reached its zenith, no candidate running on an uncompromising
antiwar platform received more than 0.05% of the popular vote.[142]
Discontent with the war presumably dwelled more on the obvious waste of
lives and money without prospect of victory than on broad moral
condemnation. And avoiding the draft by deferments or going abroad was
much more common than political resistance.[143] Despite its radical rhetoric
and sometimes militant protest, the mass opposition against the Vietnam
War should not be mistaken as revolutionary.

The swift and smooth reduction of the voting age marks the final
breakthrough of a key notion of the citizen-soldier ideal: that military
service gives entitlement to the suffrage and that any violation of this
principle violates the very idea of American democracy. Any "unjustified
[suffrage] discrimination ... undermines the legitimacy of representative
government," Harvard law professor Archibald Cox testified before the

"Senate Subcommittee on Constitutional Rights," but "[t]he exclusion is uniquely bitter when one may be summoned to fight and perhaps to die in defense of a policy he had not even a citizen's indirect voice in making."[144] With the disfranchisement of young soldiers remaining an obvious violation of these principles, legislators were eager to set the record straight. Only a few lonely voices dared to contradict Edward Kennedy's demand "... if young people are old enough to fight, they are old enough to vote." Senators Goldwater and Hruska declared themselves unimpressed by the argument but would vote for the age reduction anyway. And while one opponent pointed to the rejection of the proposal in eleven consecutive state referenda, only Senator Long outrightly argued that eighteen-year-olds, soldiers or not, were not mature enough to vote.[145]

Ironically, the unqualified embrace of the citizen-soldier ideal occurred at a time when the ideal itself was undergoing a profound transformation effected by the Vietnam War. Current research on the antiwar movement within the military claims that "military resistance was truly a mass social movement" representing "an important challenge to existing political and cultural strategies for war-making."[146] Demoralized by elusive, brutal, and racist warfare, up to a quarter of U.S. soldiers in Vietnam actively began obstructing the war effort. Connecting with the protest movements at home, these anti-war soldiers had "transformed the American citizen-soldier into a new, yet characteristically American figure: a new soldier that struggled for peace and political empowerment." To what extent the breakdown of morale among GIs actually translated into political protest and "a revitalized sense of citizenship and activism," may be debatable. But it is obvious that the conferment of voting rights to young soldiers did not have any significant impact on the perception of the war either among soldiers or civilians.

The history of the Twenty-sixth Amendment betrays a reversal of the historical pattern observed in all preceding cases. While the disfranchised usually had looked upon wars as opportunities that could help overcome resistance, there was no resistance to overcome this time. Although little demand was actually articulated political leaders were all but eager to give the vote to young people, invoking a citizen-soldier ideal that had already lost much of its meaning. Neither was it any longer instrumental in gaining political rights nor in enlisting support for the war effort. The reorganization of the U.S. forces into a volunteer professional army after 1973 may be seen as a consequence of this transformation.

The Vietnam War, of course, was also an exception in the sense that Americans were divided over its legitimacy to an unprecedented extent. If the subsequent changes in the citizen-soldier role and in military organization will be permanent, remains to be seen.[147]

VII

The chronological relationship between major wars and the expansion of voting rights in U.S. history is far from coincidental. The three hypotheses of the theoretical framework have indeed displayed considerable explanatory force, although varying from case to case. The following conclusions seem to be warranted by the empirical accounts presented above:

— The suffrage has never been explicitly used as a promise to secure the cooperation of potentially illoyal groups. This may be due to the fact that the United States has never been in a wartime situation when desperate leaders felt compelled to placate discontent and protest by promises of material and political gains. Although far from being a case in point, the reduction of the voting age during the Vietnam War presumably comes closest to this model.

— In contrast, disfranchised groups have always regarded wars as opportunities to advance their cause either by demonstrating their loyalty or by demanding rewards for their cooperation. Woman suffragists were clearly most successful in applying this strategy during World War I, when they managed to link their case with the war effort and to win the support of the president. The protests of disfranchised soldiers and militia men during and after the War of Independence did not exact specific concessions but helped undermine a concept of citizenship exclusively based on property.

The achievement of woman suffrage after World War I indicates that the response from above has perhaps been the crucial variable for success or failure. Significantly, voting rights have never been achieved against the will of institutionalized powers. Except for their brief and shaky alliance with Radical Republicans after the Civil War, African Americans were unable to translate their "proverbial loyalty" into political rights. Both world wars were followed by a racist backlash to crush whatever assertiveness blacks had developed during the war. While the Wilson administration and its Republican successors were indifferent or even hostile to their demands, Roosevelt and Truman showed more sympathy but also did not dare to challenge the white supremacists on whose support they otherwise depended. Only federal laws, Supreme Court rulings, and federal intervention could ultimately do away with disfranchisement and segregation. Ironically, the Vietnam War swiftly undermined the coalition for civil rights and social reform Lyndon B. Johnson had formed in the beginning of his presidency. To stress the key role of authorities does not diminish the struggle of suffrage movements. But it appears instructive to note that the political elite in the case of the Twenty-sixth Amendment enacted enfranchisement it considered necessary and appropriate, without responding to any particular pressures.

Given the unique stability of the American political system, the *War as a Revolution* approach has significant explanatory value only for the enfranchisement of freedmen after the Civil War. Their breathtaking career from slaves to voters was a revolutionary development in itself and also resulted from a number of radical or truly revolutionary changes in American politics and society. The revolution remained "unfinished," however, and in the course of a gradual "counterrevolution," the large majority of African Americans in the South again lost the vote.

Although it dates back much earlier, the citizen-soldier ideal was reinforced and firmly established as an ideological force by the War of Independence. By making martial virtues part of the emerging creed of freedom and democracy, the argument that those who fight for these values are also entitled to their full enjoyment became irresistible. Moreover, the military experience itself obviously contributed to the education of citizen-soldiers, as the example of black veterans after the Civil War and World War II demonstrated. In addition, modern warfare with its necessity of mass mobilization, made it impossible to restrict the status of citizen-soldiers to those in combat but had to include the home front and women in particular. That the privileges of citizenship had to come with its duties became an ideological self-commitment of American democracy, which finally inspired the enfranchisement of teenagers, including soldiers, without much demand from the disfranchised.

The strong relationship between wars and suffrage extension in U.S. history *cannot* be construed to the conclusion that wars have generally advanced the cause of democracy. In focussing on this particular question the many negative impacts of wars on civil rights and democratic participation in American history had to be excluded. However, it seems as if a society which is ideologically committed to democracy, and used to define its involvement in international conflicts as democratic crusades, is especially sensitive to the contradictions woman suffragists exposed in the First and black Americans in the Second World War.

With universal adult suffrage securely established in the United States at last the history of wars as catalysts for voting rights has come to an end with the Vietnam War. Moreover, the introduction of a large professional volunteer army seems to have rendered universal conscription obsolete. But while it is unlikely that America will ever again make disfranchised soldiers fight, the civil rights of soldiers, even professionals, remain a lasting concern in a democratic society.

Notes

1. Woman suffrage was introduced after World War I in the United States, Britain (women of thirty years of age), Canada, Germany, Sweden, the Netherlands, the Soviet Union, the three Baltic states, and the countries of the former Austro-Hungarian empire. France and Italy both introduced woman suffrage immediately after liberation in 1944. Plural voting based on taxpaying and social status also became a casualty of war in various countries. Belgium abolished it shortly after World War I, the infamous

Dreiklassenwahlrecht in Prussia fell in October 1918 as a concession to demands for democratization, and Britain abandoned the last remnants of plural voting, e.g. special constituencies for university graduates, in 1948.

2. Cf. Arthur Marwick, ed., *Total War and Social Change* (New York: St. Martin's Press, 1988), especially Marwick's introduction, x–xxi.

3. In a textbook account of western democracies Harold F. Gosnell, *Democracy. The Threshold of Freedom* (New York: The Ronald Press Company, 1948), 22–25, named war as a major driving force behind suffrage extension but without even indicating why. David M. Kennedy, *Over Here. The First World War and American Society* (Oxford: Oxford University Press, 1980), 284, calls World War I "the final push over the top" for woman suffrage.

4. Stephen C. Hause, "More Minerva than Mars: The French Women's Rights Campaign and the First World War," in Margaret Randolph Higonnet, Jane Jenson et al., eds., *Behind the Lines. Gender and the Two World Wars* (New Haven and London: Yale University Press, 1987), 99–113.

5. Raymond Aron, *The Century of Total Wars* (Westport, Connecticut: Greenwood Press, 1981, repr. of 1954 ed.), 88–90.

6. The introduction of universal manhood suffrage into the constitution of the Northern German Federation in 1867 by Bismarck, shortly after the Prusso-Austrian war, is obviously a case of mere coincidence. The move was meant to deal the liberals a blow and to enlist the support of the rural masses for the monarchy. Considerations of rewarding the soldiers for the recent victories in all likelihood had no part in Bismarck's calculations. For a brief discussion of his motives cf. Peter Steinbach, "Reichstag Elections in the Kaiserreich: The Prospects for Electoral Research in the Interdisciplinary Context" in Larry Eugene Jones and James Retallack, eds., *Elections, Mass Politics, and Social Change in Modern Germany. New Perspectives.* Publications of the German Historical Institute, Washington, D.C. (Cambridge: Cambridge University Press, 1992), 119–146, 131–138.

7. There is no modern overall account of the history of universal suffrage in the United States, presumably due to the much declaimed "compartmentalization" of American historiography, that has carved the topic into a vast bulk of specialized literature. The following essay is designed to explore a more comprehensive and synthetical approach. For an informative overview cf. J. Morgan Kousser, "Suffrage" in Jack P. Greene, ed., *Encyclopedia of American Political History. Studies of the Principal Movements and Ideas*, 3 vols. (New York: Charles Scribner's & Sons, 1984), 3, 1236–1258. A very stimulating essay on the meaning of voting for citizenship is Judith N. Shklar, *American Citizenship. The Quest for Inclusion.* The Tanner Lectures on Human Values (Cambridge, Massachusetts: Harvard University Press, 1991).

8. Marwick, *Total War and Social Change*, xvi, calls this the "participation dimension," but also stresses that it is not an automatism. From a conservative point of view, Tocqueville even argued that the soldiers of democratic armies are especially bellicose, because war offered them an opportunity to enhance their their social and political status. Cf. Alexis de Tocqueville. *Democracy in America. With a New Introduction by Daniel J. Boorstin*, 2 vols. (New York: Vintage Books, 1990), 2, 267.

9.   Cf. Thomas Nipperdey, *Deutsche Geschichte 1866–1918*, 2 vols., 2 *Machtstaat vor der Demokratie* (München: C. H. Beck, 1992), 834ff. The promise, however, was never carried out until very shortly before Germany's defeat and the demise of the Hohenzollern monarchy.

10. Cf. Joan W. Scott, "Rewriting History" in Higonnet *et al.*, *Behind the Lines. Gender and the Two World Wars*, 21–30, 23ff.

11. Cf. Aron, *The Century of Total Wars*, 19. There is of course a continuing debate, if changes were really caused by wars or if they had come anyway. Cf. Marwick, *Total War and Social Change*, *passim*.

12. Cf. Martin Broszat, Klaus-Dietmar Henke und Hans Woller, eds., *Von Stalingrad zur Währungsreform. Zur Sozialgeschichte des Umbruchs in Deutschland* (München: R. Oldenbourg Verlag, 1988), especially the introduction xxv–xlix.

13. Cf. E. S. Staveley, *Greek and Roman Voting and Elections. Aspects of Greek and Roman Life* (Ithaca: Cornell University Press, 1972), 123–129, on the century as the basic unit for voting in the Roman Republic. The soldiers in Cromwell's army who demanded the suffrage, because it would distinguish them from mere mercenaries, became influential role models in the Anglo-American tradition. Chilton Williamson, *American Suffrage. From Property to Democracy, 1760–1860* (Princeton, New Jersey: Princeton University Press, 1960), 63ff. Werner Gembruch, "Zum Verhältnis von Staat und Heer im Zeitalter der Großen Französischen Revolution," in, *Staat und Heer. Ausgewählte historische Studien zum ancien régime, zur Französischen Revolution und zu den Befreiungskriegen*, Historische Studien (Berlin: Duncker & Humblot, 1990), 40, 257–274.

14. Otto Hintze "Staatsverfassung und Heeresverfassung" in ibid., *Staat und Verfassung. Gesammelte Abhandlungen zur Allgemeinen Verfassungsgeschichte* (Göttingen: Vandenhoeck & Ruprecht, 1970), 52–83, 77–79 (quotation translated by M.B.).

15. Arthur A. Ekirch, *The Civilian and the Military. A History of the American Antimilitarist Tradition* (Colorado Springs: Ralph Myles Publisher, 1972), xviff.

16. Cf. Samuel P. Huntington, *The Soldier and the State. The Theory and Politics of Civil-Military Relations* (Cambridge, Massachusetts: The Belknap Press of Harvard University Press, 1957), 143–162, who, like the "consensus school" of the 1950s in general, exaggerated the pervasiveness of liberalism in American life.

17. Only the Selective Service Acts after World War II came close to the principle of universal conscription but met with strong opposition. Ekirch, *The Civilian and the Military*, 277–285, and *passim*.

18. Cf. the 1821 New York constitutional convention in Merrill D. Peterson, ed., *Democracy, Liberty, and Property. The State Constitutional Conventions of the 1820s* (Indianapolis: The Bobbs-Merrill Company, Inc., 1966), 220ff. The delegate R. Clarke rightly pointed to the hypocrisy of the argument, since blacks were not allowed to serve in peacetime but immediately summoned in wartime. In 1834 the state of Tennessee simultaneously disfranchised free blacks and exempted them from the militia. See Kirk H. Porter, *A History of Suffrage in the United States* (Chicago: The University

of Chicago Press, 1918), 80ff, a book generally sympathetic to the disfranchisement of African Americans.

19.   Quoted in Jenny Gould, "Women's Military Services in First World War
        Britain," in Higonnet *et al.*, *Behind the Lines*, 114–125, 117. In the Swiss
        cantons of Appenzell Innerrhoden and Appenzell Ausserrhoden, the last
        European strongholds against woman suffrage, the sword remained the only
        legal token for an exclusively male franchise until 1989. Cf. Thomas
        Wanger, "Männerherrschaft ist Krieg. Waffenkult und politischer
        Frauenausschluß," *L' Homme. Zeitschrift für Feministische Geschicht-
        swissenschaft* 3 (1992): 45–64, 53.

20.   Jane Addams, *Newer Ideals of Peace* (New York: Macmillan, 1907), 180ff.
        In depicting the decision over war and peace as the ancient root of popular
        government, Addams acknowledged the historical dignity of a gender based
        suffrage but suggested, tragically premature, that a modern industrial
        society is beyond the atavisms of tribal warfare.

21.   Cf. Williamson, *American Suffrage*, 115–119. The disfranchisement of
        confederates began in 1864, became a part of the Fourteenth Amendment,
        and was ended by the Amnesty Act of 1872. In response to the draft riots in
        New York during the Civil War, some Republicans also demanded the
        disfranchisement of Northern draft resisters, many of whom were recent
        immigrants from Ireland. John W. Chambers, *To Raise an Army. The Draft
        comes to Modern America* (New York: The Free Press, 1987), 55–59.

22.   Quoted in Willi Paul Adams, *The First American Constitutions. Republican
        Ideology and the Making of the State Constitutions in the Revolutionary Era*
        (Chapel Hill: University of North Carolina Press, 1980), 206ff. On the
        debates over property qualifications for voting during the American
        Revolution cf. ibid., 196–217; Williamson, *American Suffrage*, 92–116.

23.   Quoted in Robert J. Dinkin, *Voting in Revolutionary America. A Study of
        Elections in the Original Thirteen States, 1776–1789*. Contributions in
        American History (Westport, Connecticut: Greenwood Press, 1982), 30.
        On the demands of soldiers and militia men also cf. Williamson, *American
        Suffrage*, 80–82, 102ff, 108ff, 113.

24.   Cf. Walter Millis, *Arms and Men.˙ A Study in American Military History* (New
        Brunswick, New Jersey: Rutgers University Press, 1956), 27–29.

25.   Adams, *The First American Constitutions*, 207f; Williamson, *American
        Suffrage*, 99–101.

26.   Cf. Lawrence D. Cress, *Citizens in arms: the army and the militia in American
        society to the war of 1812*. Studies on armed forces and society (Chapel Hill:
        University of North Carolina Press, 1982), 53–60.

27.   Cf. Williamson, *American Suffrage*, 80.

28.   Cf. ibid., 141, 152 and 227.

29.   Cf. the concise overview in Hans-Christoph Schröder, *Die Amerikanische
        Revolution. Eine Einführung*, Beck'sche Elementarbücher (München: C. H.
        Beck, 1982), 190–202. A recent emphatic defense of the American
        Revolution as being "as radical and as revolutionary as any in history" is
        Gordon S. Wood, *The Radicalism of the American Revolution* (New York:
        Alfred A. Knopf, 1992), 5 (quote).

30.   Williamson, *American Suffrage*, 115ff. In terms of numbers, the enfranchise-

ment of women was certainly the most important, in terms of radicality of change the Fifteenth Amendment seems to be of leading importance.

31. Cf. the survey in Adams, *The First American Constitutions*, 295–307. Georgia in 1777 went farthest in allowing white males "being of any mechanic trade" to vote.

32. Dinkin, *Voting in Revolutionary America*, 39.

33. Cf. ibid., 27–43; Adams, *The First American Constitutions*, 216.

34. Louisiana constitution of 1812, Art. II, Sect. 8; Ohio constitution of 1802, Art. IV, Sect. 1. All references to state constitutions are derived from William F. Swindler, ed., *Sources and Documents of United States Constitutions*, 11 vols. (Dobbs Ferry, New York: Oceana Publications Inc., 1973–1988).

35. Connecticut constitution of 1776, Art. VI, Sect. 2; Pennsylvania constitution of 1776, *Plan or Frame of Government*, Sects. 5 and 6. Sect. 5 also reserved their right to elect their officers.

36. New York constitution of 1821, Art. II, Sect. 1; on the debate in the state convention cf. Peterson, 187–233; Mississippi constitution of 1817, Art. III, Sect. 1.

37. Cf. Cress, *Citizens in arms*, 4–33; Chambers, *To Raise an Army*, 13–19. The militia was mainly a police force, military operations against natives or rival colonial powers were usually conducted by British regulars and long-serving volunteers from the lower social classes. Wealthy Americans could buy themselves out of service.

38. Quotation from the 1774 Maryland convention in Cress, *Citizens in arms*, 49. On the whole subject cf. ibid., 34–50.

39. John Shy, "The American Revolution. The Military Conflict Considered as a Revolutionary War," in Stephen G. Kurtz and James H. Hutson, eds., *Essays on the American Revolution* (Chapel Hill: University of North Carolina Press, 1973), 121–156. Ekirch, *The Civilian and the Military*, 17, even deems the lack of efficiency a price worth paying for the preservation of the ideal of civil liberty.

40. Art. I, Sect. 8 of the Constitution. Cf. Hamilton's defense of these powers, Alexander Hamilton, James Madison and John Jay, *The Federalist Papers*, New American Library (New York: Mentor Books, 1961), *Federalist*, 24–29, 157–187. On the whole complex cf. Cress, *Citizens in arms*, 73–109. On the military stipulations of the Constitution also cf. Chambers, *To Raise an Army*, 25–29.

41. In the Virginia convention of 1829–1830, the *Non-Freeholders' Memorial* still had to complain that if landless citizens "have been ignominiously driven from the polls, in times of peace, they have at least been generously summoned, in war, to the battle-field." Cf. Peterson, *Democracy, Liberty, and Property*, 383. On the "Dorr War" in Rhode Island cf. Williamson, *American Suffrage*, 242–259.

42. James M. McPherson, *The Negro's Civil War. How American Blacks felt and acted during the War for the Union* (Balantine Books, 1991), 276; John Hope Franklin, *From Slavery to Freedom. A History of Negro Americans* (New York: Alfred A. Knopf, 1980), 162; Don E. Fehrenbacher, *The Dred Scott Case. Its Significance in American Law and Politics* (New York: Oxford University Press, 1978).

43. Cf. Porter, *A History of Suffrage*, 150ff; Gosnell, *Democracy*, 23. On the disfranchisement of blacks cf. J. Morgan Kousser, *The Shaping of Southern Politics. Suffrage Restriction and the Establishment of the One-Party South, 1880–1910.* Yale Historical Publications (New Haven and London: Yale University Press, 1974).

44. Ira Berlin, ed., *Freedom. A Documentary History of Emancipation, 1861–1867. The Black Military Experience* (Cambridge and London: Cambridge University Press, 1982), 812. For more documentation of similar demands cf. ibid., 811–816; McPherson, *The Negro's Civil War*, 275–295; Edwin S. Redkey, ed., *A Grand Army of Black Men. Letters from African American Soldiers in the Union Army, 1861–1865* (Cambridge: Cambridge University Press, 1992), 205–229.

45. Cf. Franklin, *From Slavery to Freedom*, 221–224.

46. Cf. the documentation in McPherson, *The Negro's Civil War*, 19–35.

47. Ibid., 23–24.

48. Ibid., 245–248.

49. James M. McPherson, *The Battle Cry of Freedom. The Civil War Era* (New York: Balantine Books, 1988), 502–507. Eric Foner, *Reconstruction. America's Unfinished Revolution.* The New American Nation Series (New York: Harper & Row, 1988), 1–11, emphasizes the efforts of blacks, free and slave, to turn the war against slavery.

50. Kousser, "Suffrage," 1242. Still in November 1860, the abolition of the $250 property clause for blacks was defeated by a large margin in New York, McPherson, *The Negro's Civil War*, 277.

51. Lincoln to Louisiana governor Michael Hahn in March 1864, quoted in McPherson, *The Battle Cry of Freedom*, 707.

52. Ibid., 708; Foner, *Reconstruction*, 61–62.

53. Quoted in McPherson, *The Negro's Civil War*, 278.

54. On the Radical Republicans cf., Foner, *Reconstruction*, 228–239. My interpretation of political alignments after the Civil War generally follows Foner's magnificent work.

55. Ibid., 178–184.

56. Ibid., 239–251.

57. Ibid., 251–280.

58. Quoted ibid., 227. Although northern voters rejected black suffrage in almost all state referenda, they also consistently backed the politics of Congressional Reconstruction, that ultimately led to universal manhood suffrage.

59. Eleanor Flexner, *Century of Struggle. The Woman' s Rights Movement in the United States* (Cambridge and London: Harvard University Press, 1959), 104–115.

60. Cf. Ellen Carol DuBois, *Feminism and Suffrage. The Emergence of an Independent Women's Movement in America* (Ithaca and London: Cornell University Press, 1978), 55–59, quote 59.

61. Cf. the argument of black leader Frederick Douglass, a long-time supporter of woman suffrage, quoted in Flexner, *Century of Struggle*, 147.

62. Quoted in DuBois, *Feminism and Suffrage*, 60–63.

63. Cf. ibid., 162–202; Foner, *Reconstruction*, 254–256.

222   REFLECTIONS ON AMERICAN EXCEPTIONALISM

64. Cf. the tenor in Flexner, *Century of Struggle*, 147–152; Shklar, *American Citizenship*, 57–61.
65. Charles A. Beard and Mary R. Beard, *The Rise of American Civilization*, vol. 2 (New York: MacMillan, 1927), 52–121, 54.
66. Cf. Lincoln in McPherson, *The Battle Cry of Freedom*, 558. On the changing interpretations of the Civil War cf. Charles Crowe, "Civil War: Meanings and Explanations," in Greene, *Encyclopedia of American Political History*, vol. 1, 251–272. Cf. the subtitle of Foner's book.
67. McPherson, *The Battle Cry of Freedom*, 700–702; Georges Clemenceau, then a newspaper correspondent in the United States, compared Stevens to Robespierre, Foner, *Reconstruction*, 229.
68. Earl M. Maltz, *Civil Rights, the Constitution, and Congress, 1863–1869* (Lawrence: University of Kansas Press, 1990), especially 121–156.
69. Foner, *Reconstruction*, 446–449.
70. Ibid., 278ff.
71. Quoted in McPherson, *The Negro's Civil War*, 290.
72. Quoted in Redkey, *A Grand Army of Black Men*, 209.
73. Address before the American Antislavery Society, quoted in McPherson, *The Negro's Civil War*, 275ff. For more documentation cf. ibid., 275–295 and *passim*, Redkey, *A Grand Army of Black Men*, 208–225 and *passim*; Berlin, *Freedom*, 811–822 and *passim*.
74. Cf. the petition by black Kentucky veterans, that the state denied them the suffrage and the right to testify against white thugs who murder and abuse blacks, Berlin, *Freedom*, 822ff.
75. Cf. Franklin, *From Slavery to Freedom*, 221–224; Berlin, *Freedom*, 1–34. On the protests against unequal pay cf. ibid., 362–405; Redkey, *A Grand Army of Black Men*, 229–248; McPherson, *The Negro's Civil War*, 197–208.
76. Quoted in McPherson, *Battle Cry of Freedom*, 701.
77. Cf. Foner, *Reconstruction*, 222ff. On the violence against black veterans in the South cf. Berlin, *Freedom*, 799–810.
78. Cf. Berlin, *Freedom*, 26–34.
79. Cf. "Woman Suffrage Movement," in L. Sandy Maisel, ed., *Political Parties and Elections in the United States. An Encyclopedia* (New York and London: Garland Publishing, Inc., 1991), vol. 2, 1223–1230.
80. Cf. Flexner, *Century of Struggle*, 289–292.
81. This seems to be an important reason why many authors are reluctant to ascribe major importance to World War I for woman suffrage. Cf. Christine A. Lunardini, *From Equal Suffrage to Equal Rights. Alice Paul and the National Woman's Party, 1910–1928*. The American Social Experience Series (New York: New York University Press, 1986), xiv; Scott, "Rewriting History," in Higonnet *et al.*, *Behind the Lines*, 23–24. Carol Hymowitz and Michaele Weissman, *A History of Women in America* (Toronto and New York: Bantam Books, 1978), 280–284, do not ponder the war at all.
82. Cf. Kennedy, *Over Here*, 286; Flexner, *Century of Struggle*, 289.
83. On Alice Paul and the NWP cf. Lunardini, *From Equal Suffrage to Equal Rights*, especially 104–121; a more sceptical view is Flexner, *Century of Struggle*, 291–298. For the party's impact on modern feminism cf. Nancy F. Cott, *The Grounding of Modern Feminism* (New Haven and London: Yale

University Press, 1987), 53–81.
84. Lunardini, *From Equal Suffrage to Equal Rights*, 110–113.
85. Flexner, *Century of Struggle*, 294; Lunardini, *From Equal Suffrage to Equal Rights*, 113.
86. Lunardini, *From Equal Suffrage to Equal Rights*, 123ff.
87. Wilson's address cf. Arthur S. Link, ed., *The Papers of Woodrow Wilson* (Princeton: Princeton University Press, 1985), vol. 51, 158–161; Catt's letter, ibid., 155–157,
88. On the passing and ratification of the Nineteenth Amendment cf. Flexner, *Century of Struggle*, 319–337.
89. Lunardini, *From Equal Suffrage to Equal Rights*, 149.
90. Ibid., 104ff.
91. Arkansas granted women the vote in primaries. Flexner, *Century of Struggle*, 300–303.
92. Cf. Link, ed., *The Papers of Woodrow Wilson*, vol. 51, 168.
93. Cf. Kennedy, *Over Here*, 281; Franklin, *From Slavery to Freedom*, 324.
94. Cf. Kennedy, *Over Here*, 30ff.
95. Cf. Franklin, *From Slavery to Freedom*, 342–351.
96. Shklar, *American Citizenship*, 60ff.
97. Quoted in Cott, *The Grounding of Modern Feminism*, 60.
98. Cf. Hymowitz and Weissman, *A History of Women in America*, 273–276.
99. Link, ed., *The Papers of Woodrow Wilson*, vol. 51, 160.
100. Cf. Carrie Chapman Catt, ed., *The Ballot and the Bullet* (Philadelphia: Alfred J. Ferris, 1897); Addams, *Newer Ideals of Peace*, 180ff.
101. Cf. the argument in Kennedy, *Over Here*, 30.
102. Cf. Flexner, *Century of Struggle*, 298–300. On the women auxiliary corps in the British army cf. Gould, "Women's Military services in First World War Britain," in Higonnet, *Behind the Lines*, 114–125.
103. Barbara J. Steinson, "Sisters and Soldiers: American Women and the National Service Schools, 1916–1917," *The Historian* 43 (1981): 225–239.
104. Cf. Kennedy, *Over Here*, 158–162; Franklin, *From Slavery to Freedom*, 325–338.
105. Franklin, *From Slavery to Freedom*, 336.
106. Ibid., 338. French premier Clemenceau gave his permission for the enterprise.
107. Lunardini, *From Equal Suffrage to Equal Rights*, xiv, dismisses a crucial impact of the war, because hostilities had almost ended when Wilson made his Senate address.
108. Rayford W. Logan, ed., *The Attitude of the Southern White Press Toward Negro Suffrage* (Washington, D.C.: The Foundation Publishers, 1940), xii.
109. Steven F. Lawson, *Black Ballots. Voting Rights in the South, 1944–1969*. Contemporary American History Series (New York: Columbia University Press, 1976), 134.
110. Gunnar Myrdal, *An American Dilemma. The Negro Problem and Modern Democracy* (New York: Harper & Row, 1962), 1004–1008. The study was first published in 1944, the observations referred to were written in August 1942.
111. Cf. Franklin, *From Slavery to Freedom*, 425–428, 426ff.

112. Quote from the Pittsburgh *Courier*, cf. Richard M. Dalfiume "The 'Forgotten Years' of the Negro Revolution" in Bernard Sternsher, ed., *The Negro in Depression and War: Prelude to Revolution* (Chicago: Quadrangle Books, 1969), 299–320, 303–304.

113. Cf. Lawson, *Black Ballots*, 55–85.

114. Darlene C. Hine, *Black Victory. The Rise and Fall of the White Primary in Texas*. KTO Studies in American History (New York: KTO Press, 1979).

115. The clause was first introduced by Alabama in 1946. Cf. Lawson, *Black Ballots*, 90–93.

116. For acts of violence cf. William H. Chafe, *The Unfinished Journey. America since World War II* (New York: Oxford University Press, 1991), 86–88; William C. Berman, *The Politics of Civil Rights in the Truman Administration* (Ohio University Press, 1970), 41–47; Lawson, *Black Ballots*, 131ff.

117. *To Secure These Rights. The Report of the President's Committee on Civil Rights* (Washington, D.C: Government Printing Office, 1947), especially 32–40, 160–163. *Public Papers of the Presidents of the United States: Harry S. Truman, 1948* (Washington, D.C.: Government Printing Office, 1964), 121–126.

118. Cf. Berman, *The Politics of Civil Rights, passim*; Lawson, *Black Ballots*, 137ff.

119. Manning Marable, *Race, Reform, and Rebellion. The Second Reconstruction in Black America, 1945–1990* (Jackson and London: University Press of Mississippi, 1991), 18–32.

120. Lawson, *Black Ballots*, 122ff.

121. Cf. *Public Papers of the Presidents of the United States: Harry S. Truman, 1947*, 311–313, 479f; ibid., 1948, 121–126; cf. *To Secure These Rights*, 146–148.

122. Cf. Lawson, *Black Ballots*, 134. The figures refer to the former confederate states.

123. Myrdal, *An American Dilemma*, 514ff. The migration process had been underway for more than three decades, ibid., 182–201.

124. Marable, *Race, Reform, and Rebellion*, 14.

125. On the military experience of African Americans in World War II cf. the summary of Franklin, *From Slavery to Freedom*, 428–437.

126. Cf. Lawson, *Black Ballots*, 102ff, 107–109.

127. Ibid., 92, quote 98–101.

128. Ibid., 65–66.

129. *To Secure These Rights*, 32–47, 82–86, 162.

130. Berman, *The Politics of Civil Rights*, 116–118, 97–100.

131. Cf. Lawson, *Black Ballots*, 307–338; on Johnson's "Great Society" cf. Doris Kearns, *Lyndon Johnson and the American Dream* (New York: Harper & Row, 1976).

132. Thomas Powers, *Vietnam: The War at Home. Vietnam and the American People 1964–1968* (Boston: G.K. Hall & Co., 1973), 26.

133. Franklin, *From Slavery to Freedom*, 501–503; Marable, *Race, Reform, and Rebellion*, 99–105, criticizes the reluctance of established civil rights leaders, with the notable exception of Martin Luther King, who became more and more radical as a result of the escalating war.

134. Maisel, ed., *Political Parties*, vol. 2, 1138ff.

135. Shklar, *American Citizenship*, 18.

136. Cf. Powers, *Vietnam*, 229–251.

137. The Vandenberg Amendment of 1942, *Congressional Record* (Washington, D.C.: Government Printing Office), vol. 88, part 6, 8316; *Report of the President's Commission on Registration and Voting Participation* (Government Printing Office, 1963), 43ff; Arthur M. Schlesinger, Jr., ed., *History of American Presidential Elections* (New York: Chelsea House Publishers, 1985), vol. ix, 3776, 3785.

138. Cf. the Senate debates of March 11 and 12, 1970, *Congressional Record*, vol. 116, part 5, 6927–6963, 7005–7009; ibid., part 6, 7093–7122. The debates in the House of June 17, 1970, went along the same lines, ibid., part 15, 20159–20198.

139. Kennedy, ibid., 6931; Mansfield, ibid., part 6, 7009.

140. Cf. *Keesing's Contemporary Archives* 17 (1970): 24071; ibid., 18: 24765.

141. *Congressional Record*, vol. 116, part 5, 6963.

142. Robert A. Diamond, ed., *Congressional Quarterly's Guide to U.S. Elections* (Washington D.C.: Congressional Quarterly, 1985), 365.

143. For a critical view of the antiwar movement and the New Left as aloof radicalism of white middle-class students cf. Kim McQuaid, *The Anxious Years. America in the Vietnam-Watergate Era* (New York: Basic Books, 1989), 129–166.

144. *Congressional Record*, vol. 116, part 5, 6936.

145. Kennedy, ibid., 6931; Goldwater, ibid., 6945; Hruska, ibid., 6952; Holland (D.\Fl.), ibid., 6957; Long, ibid., 7007.

146. I owe the following informations and ideas to Richard Moser of Middle-Tennessee State University, who is currently working on a project on soldier and veteran resistance to the Vietnam War, entitled *From Deference to Defiance*. The quotations are derived from a draft proposal, he has been kind enough to send to me.

147. Chambers, *To Raise an Army*, 258–264, views the reestablishment of compulsory draft registration as an indication of a possible return to a more traditional concept of military service.

13

Nationalism in International Law and Practice

Knud Krakau

Introduction

This paper discusses the changing and ambivalent American attitudes toward, and the impact of American nationalism on, international law. Aspects of American nationalism – which will more or less be taken for granted here – have a considerable impact upon the way the United States approaches, interprets, uses international law. How can it be otherwise? International law is, of course, a national policy instrument while at the same time the world community, including the United States, tries to control the behavior of states and other international actors by means of international law. The national impact upon international law is not uniquely American but, for obvious reasons, the American case matters more than most. "United States" in this discussion refers not only to formal decision-makers but to a broad discourse on issues of international law carried on also by Congress, publicists, international legal scholars, and others.

"International law" is a huge field. This paper deals with but one though centrally important subfield of it: the issue of the licit or illicit use of force. The centrality of this issue – in the sense that all other norms and values depend on it – tends to be ignored in times of peace, while in times of conflict the tendency is to regard it as irrelevant. Yet the issue will not go away. The case of former Yugoslavia is only a particularly brutal one in a chain of hundreds of instances of intra- and inter-state violence since 1945.[1] International law is probably least effective in the war/peace area. For that very reason it is a litmus test which reveals a society's basic attitude with regard to international law generally.

This does not ignore the fact that large areas of international activity are effectively regulated by a continuously growing body of international law. It may occasion controversies about proper interpretation without ever being questioned in principle. Its rules do govern the behavior of international actors if only because they – and this refers in particular to national or international bureaucracies – function on the basis of routinized patterns of behavior and expectations. International law provides such routine orientation in many areas.

The long development of international law on the use of force found its climax in the general prohibition of "the threat or use of force" in Art. 2 (4) of the United Nations Charter. This text was born from the devastations of World War II. There is no room for doubt that the containment and prohibition of force and war was the primary objective which was uppermost in the minds of its founders. That is made emphatically clear – but bears emphasizing in view of recent American arguments – by the very first words of the Charter: "Determined to save succeeding generations from the scourge of war ..." The Charter then repeatedly emphasizes the objective of "peace" – "peace and security, and to ensure, ... , that armed force shall not be used, save in the common interest;" and it states as the Organization's "Purposes ...: 1. To maintain international peace and security, ..." Practically everyone is agreed that this prohibition against the use of force is the core element of contemporary international law whatever its foundation in a technical sense. It can be understood as conventional law: the Charter system is universal; as customary law with the Charter as its universal expression; or as historically developed *ius cogens*. This prohibition is not absolute, however. The Charter itself in Art. 51 recognizes the "inherent right of individual or collective self-defense if an armed attack occurs" and U.N. community action "to maintain or restore international peace and security" (Art. 39 and Chapter VII).

There has developed a protracted debate concerning the textual meaning of such clauses as "if an armed attack occurs" in Art. 51, or "breach of the peace, or act of aggression" in Art. 39. The effect of a strict or loose construction of the rule and/or the exceptions is immediately clear. It has been argued – and widely accepted – that there are certain other exceptions to the rule outside the Charter based on customary law, for example the so-called "humanitarian intervention" for the rescue of immediately endangered nationals (Entebbe-like). The details of this never-ending debate do not concern us here. They do not affect the basic rule structure: the fundamental prohibition against the use of force as the core element of contemporary international law, qualified by certain exceptions designed to meet urgent individual or community claims for protective action.[2]

In what follows are described and analyzed four basic positions which the United States has developed with regard to these basic issues in international law. They are in a way ideal types – enriched, however, by historical material, by political and ideological reality. This approach has one practical consequence: any one of these "types" of international law approaches never represents "the U.S. position." There may be varying positions of relative hegemony of one among them over time. But they all compete with each other all the time.

I   Four Ideal Types

1. *Radical Criticism, or Denial of the Existence or of the Relevance of International Law*

This position is the easiest to identify. Its premises are understandable. It has been a recurrent theme in American history and in times of international crises it usually becomes quite popular. In its view there is hardly such a thing as international law – particularly where it imposes limits on national action presumed to be necessary for national survival, security, and perhaps some other values. International law is at best a playful exercise in intellectual or moral futility, at worst a threat to national existence. Only the "real" factors count in international relations: power and counter power, threat, insecurity. In a decentralized system without reliable community control over violence and compulsory settlement of disputes every state is, alone and by itself, responsible for its own security. Hence, its national interest must be geared to ensuring this security through building power or, where that is lacking, through building coalitions, creating balances of power, etc. International law has no legitimate place here. It certainly does not help provide that security.

This argument is, of course, basically the classical repertoire of the so-called "realist" position developed as coherent theory by Hans-J. Morgenthau or George F. Kennan. Historically it is much older. John Adams and even more so John Quincy Adams can be identified with it as can be the classical unilateralist position of the inter-war period represented, among others, by Senator Borah. More recently it has become part of the creed of the major contemporary variants of conservatism. In these perspectives, international law deserves hardly more than ridicule and contempt. The traditional conservative Robert H. Bork (Reagan's nominee for the Supreme Court) articulated this article of faith, significantly in *The National Interest*: "(I)nternational law about the use of force is not even a piety; it is a net loss for Western democracies … the persistence of the idea that it exists can be pernicious." Because the rules do not "express a preference for freedom over tyranny" but, indeed, try to contain force per se irrespective of the objectives for which it is being used, "(t)his moral equivalence" imposes a "major cost" on the United States when the latter acts morally and tries to restore "freedom over tyranny," because "by eliminating morality from its calculus, international law actually makes moral action appear immoral" i.e. "illegal;" and by the – in Bork's eyes misplaced – emphasis on international law the "President can be … drawn into a legalistic defense of his actions." As if he could have a nobler responsibility than explaining his actions in terms of *generally* accepted standards.[3]

Even more radical are the disappointed liberals turned neo-conservatives. Charles Krauthammer in *The New Republic* reflects on "how fictional is the whole notion of an ordered international system regulated by international law." He refers to Morgenthau's diagnosis that American foreign policy was informed by "a particularly disabling diplomatic disease: legalism." And he concludes: "… the law – international law – is an ass. It has nothing to offer. Foreign policy is best made without it."[4]

2. *Pragmatic-Professional Supporters of International Law*

These more often than not are the craftsmen, the practitioners, international legal scholars – i.e. persons knowledgeable in international law. In the United States these people are often appointed to public positions – the career pattern of "ins and outers": legal advisors to the State Department, ambassadors to the United Nations, etcetera. Great names come to mind: John Bassett Moore, Philip Jessup, Abram Chayes.

Their position is modest and "realistic," much more "realistic" than the "realists" claim for themselves. They do not easily assume that international law *per se* is an effective barrier against inter-state violence. They do, however, posit that it is an important factor in the cost-benefit analysis concerning the use of force by states, always assuming, of course, that there is this kind of rationality. Even in a decentralized and horizontal system international legal rules are more than mere paper. They can be sharpened, and they operate through a continuous and global process of judgments on the part of international organizations or third states concerning the international-law-quality of state behavior. These judgments may be partial and through them the participants pursue their own interests. But, in the long run and given quite frequent historical role reversals (for example the United States and England being alternately belligerents and neutrals) or, in other words, in view of the reciprocity principle, this process brings forth relatively stable and uniform judgments as to what is, and what is not, legal or acceptable behavior. Hence, these patterns of judgment and behavior can also tell us something about future behavior and reactions of the participants in the system. Its function as a neutral referent, or as expression of agreed-upon international behavior patterns, helps explain why law can serve as predictor and hence at least indirectly as regulator of behavior. States and other international actors will therefore take these perspectives into account in their own decision on whether or not to use force. If not from devotion to principle, then at least from considerations of long-term enlightened self-interest and, particularly in view of the principle of reciprocity, they will at least pay attention to the legal argument. Secretary of State Seward's retreat in the *Trent* Affair is an obvious case in point. As Oscar Schachter recently observed: "Neither the United States nor the Soviet Union can realistically consider it in the national interest to recognize the unlimited right of each to use force." And: "Legality matters to them [i.e. to governments], not only as rhetoric to win support, but also as a factor to be taken into account as part of the effort to contain violence and reduce the risks of escalation."[5]

It is these skilled practitioners and craftsmen, people knowledgeable as to how the processes work who, without undue illusions but through their patient daily efforts, perhaps contribute most to making international law part of international reality.

3. *International Law as Part of the American Mission*

It has been part of American political culture for a long time to use legal arguments in political contexts or, rather, to argue politics in legal terms or categories: "Legal thought furnished a context for understanding history and acting upon it."[6] This is an important heritage from the eighteenth century enlightenment, from the emerging fight against colonial rule, domestic revolution, and the constitutional processes in the 1770s and 1780s, i.e. the efforts to constitutionalize political structures and individual rights, to reestablish principles of order after the legal bonds with England had been severed. The answer to this need for a new order in America's external relations was to be found in the law of nations or international law. Writes James Kent in the opening paragraph of his famous and influential *Commentaries on American Law*:

> When the United States ceased to be a part of the British empire … they became subject to that system of rules which reason, morality, and custom had established among the civilized nations of Europe, as their public law. … Faithful observance of this law is essential to national character, and to the happiness of mankind.[7]

If this body of law was to provide security and order in relation to the world, the same idea applied within America. The great political and social issues of the times were perceived and explained in terms of legal concepts and categories. Demands for political change and proposed solutions were articulated as legal claims based on "right reason" or natural law, on common law and acts of Parliament or Royal Charters. This process allowed Americans to build consensus among themselves on revolutionary political demands. The Declaration of Independence was, if anything, a lawyer's brief. In short, law appears as the dominant paradigm of an entire era.

Based on these observations Robert A. Ferguson has recently described and analyzed the period from the 1760s well into the nineteenth century as a "legal culture" which supplanted an earlier culture whose dominant paradigm had been religious. "The lawyer came to replace the minister as the spokesman of American culture." America as a nation, or perhaps it became a nation because it, "defined itself so self-consciously [entirely] through law." Here the legal paradigm and the role of the lawyer have their origin: "The lawyer as the expounder and guardian of republican virtue …"[8] John Adams' dictum – "a government of laws and not of men" – captures that spirit.

A closely related motif behind the call for law probably was the idea of law as protection against violence and chaos, law as a means of overcoming fear and insecurity.[9] Hidden behind the sometimes boisterous and self-congratulatory optimistic outlook of early Americans there was often a very deep-seated anxiety that, after its glorious beginning, the American experiment in large-scale republican government might fail. The experience of insecurity and threat to one's existence, individually within the nation and collectively without, was pervasive. The longevity of the popular myth of the frontier sheriff or judge "who impose hierarchy and decorum on the roughest frontier settlement"[10] testify to this deeply felt need for law as a pacifier. The same held true externally – hence the American insistence on neutrality *rights* which the United States helped to shape through this insistence. It was once remarked: "What does it mean to be an American if not to know that law in fact protects the weak."[11] Tocqueville commented on the American insistence on translating politics into legal terms: "Scarcely any political question arises in the United States that is not resolved, sooner or later, into a judicial question."[12] And this is not surprising, at least from a vantage point some 150 years later, given the uniquely unbroken historical constitutional continuity in America. Any problem, be it federalism or race or voting rights, can be cast in legal-constitutional terms under these conditions.

This aspect of American political and legal culture has profound consequences for the problem of foreign relations and international law. America tends to project its concept of the role of law – which in the process subtly changes into rule of law – upon the world at large. The idea that international law can or should regulate inter-state relations, even if not invented by Americans, gets an additional boost, as it were, from the traditional American sense of mission which incorporates the international-law idea. This mechanism of projection, or missionary ideology, is part of the complex set of forces and ideas associated with the concepts of American "exceptionalism" or "chosen people" which at one point translate into "mission," either by America's mere "conduct and example" (*Federalist no. 1*) or "exemplary" role or by more active modes of behavior. Much has been written on that account.[13]

American missionary ideology has been pronounced dead repeatedly: "We have nothing to teach the world," said George Kennan in 1976, "I emphatically reject the concept of the universality of the American experience ... [it offers no answers to the] problems of human society in the modern age." George Ball commented on President Reagan's address to the British Parliament in 1983 which led to the creation of that strange "National Endowment for Democracy" by saying: "... crusade for democracy ... I thought we had gotten over that a long time ago."[14] But this probably was just another case of premature death pronouncement. There *is* a constant and consistent theme in American public texts from John Winthrop to George Bush or Bill Clinton which does base American identity on what it sees as the universality of its experience and whose core values it then projects abroad. One integral part of the experience which defines collective American identity, as we have seen, is the idea that law or the rule of law are relevant, that power, violence, chaos can be contained through law, federal structures, and the transformation of politics into law. These ideas are then being posited as self-evidently relevant for the essentially chaotic international environment. America projects them abroad and integrates them into the structure and objectives of the American missionary ideology: international law becomes its message.

This idea was beautifully expressed by Supreme Court Justice David Brewer in an address to the American Bar Association in 1895: "The final peace of the world will be wrought out through our profession ... [i.e. the] lawyer ... [The day is coming] when all disputes between nations shall be settled in courts of peace and not by the roar of cannon and waste of blood."[15] The extent to which this strikes us as naive a century later is but a gauge of our loss of faith in anything approaching human progress through the application of the rule of law (*vide* Yugoslavia). One result is the realist position which contemptuously refers to this thinking as the American "international arena as a court of law" ideology.[16]

But historically, these ideas have by no means been only chimeric or other-worldly fantasy. I would call to mind the fairly strong American peace movement which produced the first American Peace Society as early as 1828, local and regional societies even by 1815. They counted strong and influential personalities among their members: Jane Addams, William James, and many others.[17] I shall dwell briefly, however, on two substantive approaches which the peace movement also supported: (quasi-)judicial conflict resolution and international organization.

The first has a long tradition in American foreign relations going back to Jay's Treaty of 1794. It created boards of arbitration in important areas of contention: boundaries and financial claims. They operated quite successfully. The 1871 Treaty of Washington with England provided the basis for settling – peacefully and judicially – many outstanding mutual claims, in particular the Alabama claims resulting from British action during the Civil War, and established the principle of "neutral judges" on the claims commissions. The proceedings led to mutually acceptable and hence pacifying results.[18] Though Secretary Blaine's ambitious project of a general inter-American arbitration treaty – characterized at the First Inter-American Conference in Washington 1889 as a "new Magna Carta" – misfired, the movement for peaceful settlement of disputes through international arbitration picked up momentum. It was inspired by the optimistic expectation at the turn of the century that the future belonged to liberal democracy which, presumably, is structurally peaceful, and by the two Hague Peace Conferences of 1899 and 1907 which themselves were expressions of these beliefs. A beautiful testimony to these convictions was Andrew Carnegie's bequest for the Endowment for International Peace, named after him, which made sure that, "when the establishment of universal peace is attained, ... the revenue shall be devoted to the banishment of the next most degrading evil or evils, the suppression of which would most advance the progress, elevation and happiness of man."[19] These were practically-minded utopians.

During those years, up to and including the tenure of Secretaries of State Bryan, Lansing, and Hughes, the United States concluded several dozen bilateral arbitration agreements, ratifying about two thirds of them. And in 1946 it even accepted the compulsory jurisdiction of the International Court of Justice. Older traditions were then revived by a modern World Peace Through Law Movement, and President Eisenhower stated in 1959 that "the time has come for mankind to make the rule of law in international affairs as normal as it is now in domestic affairs ..." The United States would have to accept occasional disappointments before the ICJ, but it would gain disproportionately more: a world "in which everyone lives at peace under the rule of law."[20]

These positive American efforts in promoting the international rule of law, however, had a powerful negative counterpoint which accompanied them and often proved stronger. That counterpoint might be dismissed as the traditional sovereignty argument, which of course it was, and which was shared by many nations. But we face a specifically American problem here. The United States, for much of its history little dependent on close cooperation with other nations for the realization of what it saw as its vital interests, could long indulge in the rule-of-law mission and yet simultaneously avoid facing the costs involved in its practice, short-term costs at least, which can be counted in terms of qualifications of the sovereignty principle. Instead, America yielded to her anxieties, reservations about, and resistance to the implications of the rule-of-law mission – anxieties growing out of America's tradition of noninvolvement and unilateralism. They led to the rejection of the legal instruments proposed by the United States in the very name of the rule-of-law mission, because upon second thoughts even an ever so slight qualification of the traditional and cherished freedom of action ("sovereignty") appeared unbearable. The primary forum for articulation of this resistance is, of course, the United States Senate. Over and again that resistance was based on considerations and various combinations of national honor: vital interest, independence, territorial integrity, international immunity of the individual states, the principles of George Washington's Farewell Address or the Monroe Doctrine. After four months of debate the Senate rejected the first general arbitration treaty with Great Britain in 1897 on these grounds. Victim of this contradiction was not only the League of Nations but also the separate issue of accepting the jurisdiction of the Permanent Court of International Justice which had not found Wilson's initial support, and even the comparatively innocuous PCIJ power to offer advisory opinions. It fell over a Senate reservation offered by Senator Borah (and behind him John B. Moore) concerning questions "touching any dispute or question in which the United States has or claims an interest."[21] In the same vein, the acceptance of the ICJ jurisdiction was accompanied in 1946 by a strong reservation offered by Senator Connally excepting "matters which are essentially within the domestic jurisdiction of the United States of America as determined by the United States of America" itself – before even that was withdrawn in the wake of the Nicaraguan affair in 1985 (see below). In the 1945 debate the proponents of PCI jurisdiction such as Senator W. Morse, a former law school dean, enthusiastically reaffirmed the rule-of-law mission: the United States should set an example accepting the Court's jurisdiction and thus do "a very great deal in the direction of establishing the rule of law as the governing rule of international relations." Ironically, Connally argued for his reservation which emptied the American acceptance clause of much of its positive effect by couching his narrow unilateralist position in traditionally American universalist ideology: it was necessary, he said, "not ... to surrender the sovereignty or the prestige" of the United States; instead, he continued, "(w)e must preserve it because the best hope of the world lies in the survival of the United States with its concepts of democracy, liberty, freedom, and advancement under its institutions."[22]

The other area where American experience and values have been projected abroad with great consequences is the concept and practice of international organization. Of course, the idea of international organization is not an exclusively American domain. The League of Nations, the United Nations, or the Organization of American States, however, do represent genuinely American political-legal-federal experiences and translate them into universal (hemispheric) models for securing world (regional) peace, with the general prohibition of force and intervention as the center pieces at least of the United Nations and the OAS. The UN Charter preamble opens with these words: "We the Peoples of the United Nations ..." Is all this naive, a utopian vision of a peaceful and better world? Certainly, but, at least, a vision. Even the ever-skeptical George Kennan mused not long ago that Woodrow Wilson "was way ahead of his time in his views about international organization."[23]

4. *The Ideological Instrumentalization of International Law*

An ideology of exceptionalism, chosenness, mission is incompatible with the idea of international law as a system of coordination of equals. Earlier in American history this contradiction was resolved whenever the collective ideological ego found satisfaction in the very rule-of-law mission: The subjection of states to the rule of law liberated them from what was seen as the essentially irrational elements of the European political system: power, violence, war (the "war system") and paved the way for them to pursue another course: that of free choice and rationality or trade and commerce, which were considered synonymous modes of international communication.[24] At the same time this had the effect of subjecting American exceptionalism to the great equalizer: the rule of law.

In the United States, however, this long-range trend has always been considered qualified by a reservation in favor of the use of force, provided, of course, that there were sufficiently worthy causes for it: "some cause," as Wilson would see it, "in which it seems a glory to shed human blood …"[25] Such causes could be, in the American view, the creation or the securing of an international environment propitious to the rule of law itself, and also to other elements of the American credo: democracy, self-determination, individual freedoms, human rights, etcetera.

This approach, then, produces a quite different resolution of the contradiction between the American ideology and the concept of the rule of law, in particular the Charter ban on the use of force. At the center of this change is a dialectical re-interpretation of central elements of international law. The prohibition of the use of force in Art. 2(4) of the UN Charter is being transformed into a vehicle for the violent realization of the contents and objectives of the American missionary ideology. The use of force for *these* benevolent or benign objectives loses its forbidden character; instead, it is being seen, if not as a positive duty under, then at least as being in conformity with the "higher law" of the Charter.[26] This brief analysis here will be elaborated somewhat more fully in a later section dealing with developments under the Reagan and Bush administrations.

II The American Position during the Cold War: Between Radical Criticism and Ideological Instrumentalization

From the earlier historical observations it is already clear that, over time, the United States as a rule did not opt for extreme positions (sections I.1. or 4.) but has tended to oscillate between pragmatism and the rule-of-law mission (I.2. and 3.). The latter, however, has long been accompanied by a counterpoint of theme I.1. All positions are there all the time, but with very different degrees of visibility.

After World War II we first observe a strong preference for the rule-of-law mission, expressed in America's strong stand for international organization either universal, the United Nations, or regional, the Organization of American States, and in the emphatic ban on the use of force.

For decades, the United States made great efforts to have this centerpiece of the international legal postwar order widely respected: the principle of the prohibition of the use of force, Art. 2(4) of the Charter, which leaves room only for certain exceptions circumscribed and defined by law, i.e. the Charter itself or traditional customary law (see introduction above), whatever the boundaries between licit and illicit use of force in the particular case. And there has naturally been much disagreement. The United States has consistently, over the decades, condemned the use of force by its emerging ideological and political foes: the Soviet Union and her allies (North Korea, Hungary, CSSR, Afghanistan); by third world countries struggling for liberation from colonial rule; even occasionally by her allies (Suez). But what about the not so rare cases of the use of force by the United States itself? The United States has consistently tried to explain these uses, and justify them before world audiences, for example the United Nations, in terms of categories of the then existing international law: individual or collective self-defense, defensive support for incumbent governments, humanitarian intervention, etcetera. American presidents and many others have indeed engaged in what Judge Bork contemptuously called "legalistic defense of his actions." These justifications were indeed largely plausible because the major tendency of U.S. policies and strategies since the Truman and Eisenhower Doctrines has been defensive in character – i.e. support of existing regimes and incumbent governments against attempts to change or overthrow them, attempts which often were at least in part externally supported. The plausibility of the American international law argument in this kind of setting derives from the fact that traditional international law allows external help to incumbents, forbids such help to rebel groups and imposes neutrality towards both sides only in situations of fully developed civil war. In other words, international law did favor a *status quo*-oriented American policy. [27]

This deceptively simple scheme, however, lost its operational usefulness in third world revolutionary situations. The Vietnam War was the most spectacular case in point, or, closer to home, El Salvador and Nicaragua. What does "incumbent government," "invitation," the crucial internal-external distinction mean under those conditions? Where draw the line between domestic rebellion and external "aggression?" The United States resorted to sometimes daring interpretations of the various exceptions to the ban on the use of force, for example in Guatemala 1954, Cuba 1961, or Vietnam. But the point is *not* that these actions were or were not necessarily in accord with the U.S. sponsored rule of international law. Some of them obviously and even admittedly were not. The point is, rather, that the United States tried hard, in domestic and international forums, to explain and justify them in terms of this very rule of international law. Hence, even its violation recognized and reaffirmed that rule, to the effect that in the worldwide and long-term process of judgment-formation (see I.2. above) concerning the reach of international law even America's critics could use these actions as confirmation of the principle of the ban on force. Though differing on interpretation, official America and its critics shared at least this common ground.

By contrast, developments in the last phase of the Cold War under Reagan and Bush took a quite different turn, i.e. towards denial of the existence or at least the relevance of international law (position I.1.) or even towards its immediate and unveiled ideological instrumentalization. The context was the "evil empire" dynamic: the re-ideologization of America's foreign policy also affected its approach to international law. In the following sections I shall discuss (1) some indicators for the denial position and (2) three variants of the argumentative process of ideological instrumentalization.

1. *Nonexistence or Irrelevance of International Law*

The questioning of the very existence of international law was exemplified by Charles Krauthammer (see I.1.). Senator Daniel Patrick Moynihan took a somewhat more moderate and critical position. In 1984 he was convinced that official America treated international law as irrelevant to foreign policy decision making. The United States had, as he saw it, "abandoned, for all practical purposes, the concept that international relations ... can and should be governed by a regime of public international law."[28] The noted international lawyer Richard A. Falk phrased the same point with a sense of understatement: America's international behavior in the 1980s was to him an indicator "of the decline in normative restraint."[29]

A number of such indicators can be adduced. They support this interpretation, in particular if read in conjunction with the argument developed in the two following subsections:

— The Iranian hostage affair which incidentally shows that this tendency developed already under Carter though he had other points to his credit, for example the Panama Canal Treaties of 1977. In the complex and hopeless hostage crisis international law counted for little. Until very late in the unfolding of that drama it never occurred to American policy makers how good a case at international law they had. When the case finally was *sub iudice* after the ICJ's unanimous provisional order of December 1979 in favor of the United States, and shortly before its final judgment (presumably also pro United States) the latter did not wait and launched its desperate and aborted rescue operation. It thus lost the chance of mobilizing world opinion, in particular among the hesitant third world nations, and of legalizing individual or collective action under Art. 94(2) of the UN Charter.

— Nicaragua: after substantial violations of international law with regard to Nicaragua, a view held by many American international lawyers the United States withdrew from the Nicaragua case before the ICJ at the moment when Nicaragua's chances to "win" became evident. As a further step the United States withdrew even its qualified submission to the ICJ jurisdiction altogether. The Counselor for Legal Affairs to the U.S. Mission to the United Nations observed in this context that the "process of setting a good example does not yield results" – apparently sufficient reason to withdraw from the World Court – and, he further thought, probably coming closer to the real motive, that obsolete international laws and institutions had far too long inhibited the United States from pursuing its self-interest;[30] The nearly 700 pages-long *Report of the Congressional Committees Investigating the Iran-Contra Affair* apparently does not contain a single reference to international law;[31]

— Refusal to sign the International Convention on the Law of the Seas – after decades of hard work to which the United States had positively contributed;

— The withdrawal, even if only temporarily, from UNESCO, or ILO; the partial non-payment of dues to the United Nations. The well-known columnist George Will probably summed up a widely shared attitude when he observed: "... it is bad enough we pay for the United Nations; surely we do not have to pay attention to it;"[32]

— Finally, in this context one might also mention the kidnapping cases, among them the – as dissenting Justice J. P. Stevens said – "monstrous decision" of the Supreme Court in June 1992, monstrous in view of the nonchalance with which Chief Justice Rehnquist dismissed the international law objections against the criminal trial of an abducted Mexican doctor. Justice Sandra Day O'Connor, also dissenting, saw that result as "disregarding the rule of law that this court has a duty to uphold."[33]

George Will may not be a spokesman for "the United States." All these elements taken together would, however, appear to convey a message to the world: that international law, even if not radically denied, is becoming less relevant for American policy making. In November 1984 the then Secretary of Defense Caspar Weinberger, in an address announced as important, developed certain criteria which would govern the future deployment of American military forces abroad. All the criteria had to do with efficiency and the Vietnam syndrome: the vitality of the interest involved, a positive cost-benefit relation, support by the Congress and public opinion, the will to win, etcetera. Considerations of international law were not among them.[34]

2. Ideological Manipulation of International Law: Textual Reinterpretation

At the same time we can observe a tendency to use international law as an instrument for political-ideological purposes. It is highly visible in the cases of Grenada, Nicaragua, and Panama, i.e. cases with and without cold war elements.

By contrast with the earlier cold war period in its final phase the United States was no longer necessarily a *status quo* power. Even within "its own hemisphere" the United States was confronted with regimes and governments which were dominated by its political-ideological foes (Cuba, Nicaragua), or by what it defined as narco-criminals (Panama). Their common characteristic was that they were not democratic. Their removal became a serious objective of U.S. policy.[35] In all three cases the United States employed varying degrees of force and achieved its aims twice: Grenada and Panama; the regime change in Nicaragua was not of American making.

The United States has publicly presented an international law case for its actions through its authorized representatives before the appropriate forums (United Nations, OAS) and through other participants in the public discourse. They have, on these occasions, duly advanced and discussed all the classical arguments in favor of limited exceptions from the principle of

the ban on the use of force: collective self-defense, humanitarian intervention, invitation, or regional treaty authorization as in the case of Grenada
through the Treaty for the Organization of Eastern Caribbean States
(OECS).[36] These defensive arguments are problematical to say the least,
and have been severely criticized in that same discourse.[37]

But their strength or weakness is not the concern here. The contention is
that the legal battles on these terms have, at least on the side of defenders of
governmental policies, become increasingly ritualistic, an exercise dutifully
performed but without force and conviction. The great energy, enthusiasm,
and intellectual effort which the apologists of governmental policies have
evinced now for a decade or more point another way: the re-legitimization of
force for political-ideological ends. The arguments about the use of force
tend to lose their apologetic and defensive character which is logically
connected with the post-1945 international law structure and its central focus
on the prohibition of force. In that framework, arguing for the use of force
necessarily meant justifying it in terms of exceptions from that rule.[38] What
we witness under the Reagan and Bush administrations is the attempt to cut
loose from its restrictions, to break the taboo which has come to surround the
force issue, to reinstate force as a legitimate policy instrument for political-
ideological objectives and to free it from the "obsolete international laws and
institutions [that] had far too long inhibited the United States from pursuing
its self-interest,"[39] finally to turn international force from its barely tolerated
marginal existence into a "positive good," to borrow from the slavery
discourse, at least in relation to some particularly worthy objectives.[40]

This at first subtle and then quite open shift in argument about force, if
generally accepted, would fundamentally and radically alter the structure
and nature of the system of international law as it has developed since 1945.
To be sure that system was never immune from the intrusion of subjective,
ideological, political considerations into the application and interpretation
of its rules and into the very definition of its basic concepts. This is
demonstrated by the long battles about the definition of concepts such as
armed attack, aggression, intervention, etcetera. But the effects of this
process were contained by the fact that the ban on the use of force and the
reciprocity principle operate objectively and set outer limits upon it. The
new approach, by contrast, makes the subjective-normative element, the
subjective value orientation, its very core or "moving principle" as
Montesquieu termed it. The new approach relegitimizes the use of force
and renders it technically legal when necessary for whatever one state – i.e.
the United States – considers sufficiently worthy objectives. This would
amount to a veritable revolution in international law.[41]

The transforming reasoning evolves on three levels.

(a) The Tu Quoque Argument

The first is a rather pragmatic one, the classical *tu quoque* argument. The
United States refuses to be inhibited by the rule against force, particularly

where this rule forbids support, including force, of rebel movements ("freedom fighters") against established marxist regimes in Latin America. America's adversaries, the United States argues, consistently and success-fully ignore this prohibition. The United States feels therefore unfairly treated by what has been called an "international double standard." It wants to overcome understandable frustration at this situation and reestablish equality of "fighting conditions." It has repeatedly argued along these lines, officially and privately.[42]

(b) Reinterpretation of Art. 2 (4) U.N.Charter

The following arguments were developed in "The Great Debate of the 1980s"[43] and are more important in our context than the argument presented under (a). It is really this line of thought which turns the post-World War II system of international law upside down. To reemphasize: That system's ban against force was its supreme and primary objective, the necessary precondition for the realization of all other values contemplated by the Charter: political self-determination, autonomy, human rights and fundamental freedoms, legal equality among human beings and states, social and economic advancement. But, contrary to the repeated claims of the Reaganites forcefully represented by J. J. Kirkpatrick,[44] democracy per se is not among them. It is for obvious historical reasons that the Charter is not committed to democracy per se, however compatible its basic values are with the Charter. The references in Art. 2 (4) UN Charter to territorial integrity, political independence, and the other "U.N. Purposes" were clearly meant to make the ban as global and encompassing as possible. The American position in 1945 was very specific on that point:

> When the suggestion was made at San Francisco that the words "or in any manner inconsistent with the Purposes of the United Nations" might be read to narrow the scope of Article 2 (4), despite the presumption against armed self-help with which the Charter as a whole is infused, the "United States delegate 'made it clear that the intention of the authors of the original text was to state in the broadest terms an absolute all-inclusive prohibition [against the use of force]; the phrase "or in any other manner" was designed to ensure that there should be no loopholes.'"[45]

And Louis Henkin has strongly restated this point only recently:

> Peace was the paramount value ... [The other Charter] purposes could not justify the use of force ... to achieve them; they would have to be pursued by other means. Peace was more important than progress and ... justice. The purposes of the United Nations could not in fact be achieved by war. War inflicted the greatest injustice, the most serious violations of human rights, and the most violence to self-determination and to economic and social development. War was inherently unjust.[46]

The contemporary American argument, by contrast, inverts the priorities between peace and the other Charter values; and it re-reads the referential clauses in Art. 2(4) as restrictions on the prohibition so as to exempt – *a contrario* – any force for such other "benign Charter Purposes" from the prohibition. As the original Charter priorities which considered peace as a precondition for everything else are being inverted, the use of force comes to be seen not only as not generally illicit; it appears as a "positive good," as technically legal where and insofar as it serves these "benign purposes." Such legitimizing purposes have been variously defined by American decision-makers as securing or restoring political self-determination, majority rule, human rights, or democratic institutions. These decision-makers have not been troubled by the fact that the Charter does not concern itself with "democracy" or "democratic institutions," nor by the assumption that presumably they would have to define the justifying purposes and decide upon appropriate – forceful – action unilaterally, even in the face of broad international opposition. [47]

W. Michael Reisman argues that this "inversion," as he calls it, of the pristine customary or Charter law on the use of force really took place *within* the United Nations over the last decades in relation to what he sees as an evolving new type of "just war" in favor of decolonization, national self-determination, and wars of national liberation. In his view the United States only reenacts what had taken place already long before. In its details his reasoning is highly sophisticated. But eventually it is no more than a complex version of the well-known *tu quoque* argument. [48]

Another way of presenting this idea is the argument that the government of a state that is part of the Inter-American system – where multiple commitments to representative democracy are indeed quite strong, whatever their legal character – and that turns away from this democratic orthodoxy towards a communist-marxist-leninist position, thereby loses its quality as a "legitimate government" and is reduced to a mere *de facto*-government which as such presumably loses the protection of the general ban on force. [49]

Jeane J. Kirkpatrick, as ambassador to the U.N. or just as a particularly articulate spokeswoman for (neo)conservative Reaganite positions, has repeatedly and forcefully argued along these lines. Addressing the U.N. Security Council she explained the Grenada intervention on October 27, 1983, in these terms:

> The prohibitions against the use of force in the UN Charter are contextual, not absolute. They provide ample justification for the use of force against force in pursuit of the other values also inscribed in the charter – freedom, democracy (sic!), peace … this chamber is not incapable of making distinctions between policies which serve those purposes and policies which undermine them. [50]

And similarly before the U.N. General Assembly on the same occasion:

We believe that the use of force by the task force [in Grenada] was lawful
under international law and the UN Charter because it was undertaken
... and carried out in the service of values of the charter, including the
restoration of the rule of law, self-determination, sovereignty, democracy
(sic!), respect for the human rights of the people of Grenada.[51]

Even years later Kirkpatrick insisted that "(t)he Grenada action was a
particularly clear example of the use of force to [besides three other goals]
... create the preconditions for self-government."[52] That may be correct as
a statement of fact but certainly not of law. This position has been severely
criticized within the United States.[53] Nor has it found any substantial
support from other states except perhaps the dubious endorsement from the
OECS states in the Grenada context. Incidentally, Kirkpatrick was talking
about that intervention in Grenada in October 1983 by the OECS states
Antigua and Barbuda, Dominica, St. Lucia, and St. Vincent and the
Grenadines – "supplemented," as the U.S. ambassador to the Permanent
OAS Council put it at the time, "by units from the United States."[54]

The use of force for the "restoration of democracy ..."[55] Lest we forget
one of the "contextual" (Kirkpatrick) dimensions of this undertaking in
Grenada – the political-strategic – I would like to quote Deputy Secretary of
State Dam. In a public address advertised as important he denied that the
United States was imposing "any particular form of government" on the
Grenadians. Instead, he emphasized Grenada's dangerous "ties to Cuba and
the Soviet Union and its abandonment of democracy and poor human rights
record." In his view the United States had consistently "underestimated"
the dangers of Cuban/Soviet activities in the area and of the "Soviet use of
Cuba as a surrogate for the projection of military power in the Caribbean."
But now presumably the United States was determined to prevent this
from happening again. Dam's view, therefore, "that Grenada would have
become a fortified Cuban/Soviet military outpost ... that Grenada could be
used as a staging area for subversion of nearby countries ...,"[56] sounded
particularly ominous.

This should serve as a reminder that the Cold War was, of course, one
strong *motif* for the value-oriented reinterpretation of the law of force. It
was, however, not the only one, as the Panama intervention of December
1989 shows.[57] In regard to the major issue, rationalization of the use of
force, America's explanation and justification of its intervention followed
the by now familiar pattern. President Bush claimed that its purpose was
"to defend democracy in Panama." Anthony d'Amato, a professor of
international law and on the Board of Editors of the *American Journal of
International Law*, has argued that "(t)he invasion of Panama was a lawful
response to tyranny" because "human rights law demands intervention
against tyranny."[58]

The temptation to follow these new developments with regard to
Nicaragua must have been great, and the president and many others gave

way to it consistently over years. It proved to be an intractable case with little hope for success and which continued to build up frustration. The judgment of the International Court of Justice in the Nicaraguan case left the United States in an embarrassing position even though that pronouncement was, in a formal sense, irrelevant for the United States. The ICJ held that there had been no armed attack by Nicaragua against El Salvador and that, consequently, the United States had no right to forcible collective self-defense against Nicaragua to be exercised *in* Nicaragua (mining of its harbors, support for the contras).[59] This reasoning, even if not binding on the United States, left the latter with but two major legal justificatory strategies: it could technically plead if not self-defense then at least "counter-intervention" – in defense of El Salvador – against and in Nicaragua.[60] Or the United States could follow the by now established pattern of the ideological reinterpretation of international law. To a large extent, it chose the latter course.[61]

(c) The "New International Law"

The last approach to be mentioned here has effects which are similar to those described in the previous subsection. It does more, however, than reinterpret texts such as Art. 2(4) and its UN-purpose clause. It "deconstructs" them altogether and, having done so, "reconstructs" an entirely new set of loosely organized and vaguely formulated claims for action or policy guidelines which it then calls "international law." Text, i.e. the international legal norm, is nothing; context is everything. The practitioners of this art purport to distil relevant value policies from the totality of legal norms (texts) such as Art. 2(4) and the entirety of the Charter as well as from what they regard as general contemporary tendencies, relate them to the context of time and place, and reformulate norms (claims) on a highly abstract level making all meanings possible and permissible. The embarrassing or restraining technicalities of norms such as Art. 2(4) are left far behind. The new international law is concerned only with the large issues of humankind: an international legal order and legal norms whose function it is to help realize inclusive values of human dignity, autonomy, self-determination of peoples and individuals, freedom, rights, etcetera. As the UN Charter is largely an outgrowth of American (western) legal and political culture, it is no surprise that practitioners of the new international law discover these values or their specific understanding of them in the Charter system. One may even concede that other cultures similarly find their basic values reflected in it. But what is problematical is that our practitioners take these highly abstract value orientations, about whose general congruence with the Charter system there is no doubt, as practical policy guides and technically permissive rules. While ignoring all rule-specific details, they declare any behavior permissible and legal that, given the circumstances of time and place, "reasonably" contributes to realizing these values. Action which they consider a reasonable step towards increasing the chances for creating an inclusive "minimum world public order" or an "international law of human dignity" is licit. If these were the goals of the new international law in the early 1960s, its representatives now discover, for example in the Grenada/ Nicaragua context, that "the main purpose of contemporary international law ... is ... the enhancement of the ongoing right of peoples to determine their own political destinies ... Article 2(4) is the means."[62]

Apparently it does not trouble them that these issues would have to be decided by national (American) decision-makers. Quite to the contrary, they explicitly reject the idea that the International Court of Justice or the General Assembly might be charged with these decisions because they represent only temporary majorities or are elected by them. These institutions are presumably infected by a "factional spirit" and cannot take cognizance of the great issues.

If anyone had thought that Art. 2(4) had attempted to contain the use of international force it will now be learned that, on the contrary – given the general value-orientations of the Charter, or of the international order of human dignity, or of the ongoing processes of self-determination – that article permits the use of force where it serves to enlarge the sphere of democracy. Why? Because and insofar

> (e)ach application of Art. 2(4) must enhance opportunities for ongoing self-determination [which is] ... the basic policy of contemporary international law ... Art. 2(4) ... must be interpreted in terms of this key postulate ... Though all interventions are lamentable, the fact is that some may serve, in terms of aggregate consequences, to increase the probability of the free choice of peoples about their government and political structure. Others [are] doing exactly the opposite ... The critical question ... is not whether coercion has been applied but whether it has been applied in support of or against community order and basic policies, ... in ways whose net consequences include increased congruence with community goals and minimum order ... the licit community objectives for which coercion may be used [are] the basic and enduring values of contemporary world public order and human dignity.[63]

George Orwell appears to have turned international lawyer. Affinity with literary theory is visible also where the warning against "mechanical" rule application is coupled with the reminder that "(l)egal statements ... are made in a context whose features are part of the expectations of speaker and audience."[64] Who would deny the importance of context? This recalls the often futile, because polemical, battles between interpretevists and noninterpretivists, or "protestant" and "catholic" or similar perspectives regarding interpretation of the American constitution over the last ten or fifteen years.[65]

Naturally, relevant context is necessarily and always part of the complex process of interpretation and rule application, just as is textual exegesis, original intent, evolving purposes, practice accepted as law, doctrine and basic postulates of law.[66] The new international law emphasizes one element – contextual value-orientation – at the expense of all others. And it offers no explanation why the alleged "main purpose of contemporary international law" – i.e. "ongoing self-determination" – should take precedence over the basic ban on force which is generally considered *ius cogens*; it does not explain why, on the contrary, force should be a licit means – decided upon by one international actor – to enforce self-determination within another state actor. In the last analysis this is one more case of the missionary projection of American values abroad. The standard for this kind of "reasonableness" is, as Oscar Schachter describes it, "largely determined by crypto-criteria that reflect particular [that means American] preferences and values."[67]

Yet another constitutional analogy comes to mind which might help explain the projection mechanism. Mr. Justice Stone's famous "Footnote Four" in the Carolene case of 1938[68] laid the basis for the Supreme Court's later jurisprudence which applied standards of "strict" or "heightened scrutiny" (*inter alia*) in areas where the political process as the normal avenue for redress was blocked by defects in this very process itself: such as malapportionment of electoral districts or denial of the right to vote. Here the Supreme Court stepped in, discarding earlier applications of the political question doctrine which had barred it from taking cognizance of these issues. A similar idea is to be found in the international context: the United States must intervene, as the new international lawyers see it, and use force in order to restore the "democratic processes" which totalitarian regimes have denied their peoples. The crucial difference is, of course, that the Supreme Court acts *within* the confines of a constitutional system as one of the constitutionally legitimated powers. With regard to other countries the United States may want to serve the same function as does the Supreme Court domestically: reopening the clogged political veins for the democratic life blood of society. And its action may on occasion objectively have this effect, as perhaps it did in Grenada. But doing so for third countries presupposes a common domestic sphere or a hierarchical relationship which is incompatible with the coordinate state principle of the decentralized international system. Again, the new international law approach shows itself to be a case of missionary nationalism.

It remains to be emphasized that this seemingly poststructuralist-deconstructivist approach is much older than many versions of contemporary literary (or other) poststructuralism.[69] It was initiated as early as 1942 as result of the collaboration between the lawyer Myres S. McDougal and the sociologist Harold D. Lasswell. In the late 1950s and 1960s McDougal, then at Yale Law School, developed this approach into a comprehensive, impressive, and influential *corpus* of doctrine, publications, and academic teaching.[70] He (it) attracted a number of brilliant younger colleagues. One of them was W. Michael Reisman, now also of Yale, author of the analyses quoted above. J.J. Kirkpatrick was strongly influenced by McDougal and collaborated with him.

Impressive and sophisticated as their work is it is characterized by extreme subjectivity. Its deliberate value-orientation or "policy-oriented theory" has always been a defensive-aggressive product of the confrontation with hostile powers organized around antagonistic ideologies during World War II and the Cold War thereafter. As such this "new international law" is clearly a reactive expression of traditional American exceptionalism.

(d) Some Conclusions

All three approaches to international law discussed in this section reflect traditional American missionary universalism, or nationalism. The phenomenon is, however, not new. As John W. Coogan remarked not long ago, Wilson's discriminating application of his neutrality policies – using moral-ideological criteria – helped destroy the war-containing effects of the concept of neutrality which the United States had exerted such great efforts to develop since the eighteenth century.[71] The Kellogg Pact extended this principle of discrimination to the rules of *ius in bello* because it was thought they would unduly benefit the aggressor. A more extreme and generalized variant of this idea is the suggestion that if one state violates a fundamental norm such as the ban on force, *all* other states are free from *all* legal restraints regarding the force issue or, even more extreme, of restraints of any kind *vis-à-vis* the original violator because his prior violation affects the rights of all others, namely, their right to have the rule against force respected. It was not easy to reverse this trend which had strong support in the American international law discourse during the 1920s and through the 1940s. It was more or less overcome only with the Geneva Conventions of 1949.[72] In the more immediate context the positions discussed under II.4. all tend to transform the core rule of contemporary international law or Art. 2 (4) of the Charter system from a barrier against violence into a vehicle for the use of force as a legitimate means for realizing the goals of traditional American universalism abroad. The (re-)ideologization of American foreign policy in the 1980s produces a parallel ideologization of the international law discourse and the erosion of those barriers against international violence which the United States earlier had done so much to build in the name of its own rule-of-law mission. The always frail wall against international violence is being torn down again by the trumpet call of another round of universalism. A whole fleet of more narrowly nationalistic political, strategic, economic (or other) interests may then sail through this gap and claim violence as "legal" means. But what is more fundamentally disturbing is the general inversion of the means-ends relationship. The age-old problem might be described in terms of Weberian *Gesinnungsethik* versus *Verantwortungsethik*. But under conditions of modern technologies of violence and communication there is no room for accepting illegal, coercive, and dangerous means as legal for ends, however laudable, such as "restoration of democratic processes."

Whereas America's rule-of-law mission has long striven to contain international violence the new approaches actually reintroduce a modern ideological concept of "just war." The idea, however, that "'good' or 'just' wars ... waged in a good cause such as democracy or human rights" could be a tolerable exception to the general prohibition against violence would not only "give wide latitude to individual powers to decide on the legitimacy of force."[73] It also forgets that under classical just war doctrine the major *iusta causa* which made a war "just" was a legal injury suffered by the state waging the war to seek legal redress in a decentralized system.[74] There is reason for doubt that these new approaches will lead any closer to a "minimum world public order" or an "international order of human dignity" or whatever the laudable objectives. The net result is far more likely to be more anarchy and chaos, not the least because the subjective unilateralism of these approaches "would authorize **all** states to apply and enforce their particular interpretation of international norms."[75] Where once order and containment of force were at least both a possibility and the explicit objectives of the American rule-of-law mission, under the new dispensation anarchy and violence would seem inevitable and planned integral parts of the system itself.

III   Conclusion: The Future after the End of the Cold War

Will America, after the end of the Cold War, revert to its more traditional centrist positions (I.2. and 3.) in regard to the international law of force? These, it should be recalled, never just disappeared, in spite of the developments described in section II (supra). However, in the broad international law discourse the voices depreciating international law or (mis)using it for political-ideological purposes (I.1. and 4.) were definitely more audible during the later Cold War years.

The end of the Cold War would not *per se* appear to necessitate such a swing of the pendulum back in the centrist direction. That is shown by the Panama intervention. On the other hand, it must be remembered that the "new international law" grew out of a context of high ideological and power-political tension of over half a century. With the disintegration of the major political antagonist, with a definite abatement of the high ideological voltage in the international atmosphere, this specific American international law response loses much of its *raison d'être* and one might expect a de-ideologization in this respect too. Such a tendency could be reinforced by a shift in style and emphasis of a new administration.[76] Its attention – or its nationalism – shifts away from the areas of security, power, and force to the economic issues of international trade etcetera. Hence, international cooperation and deference to the international law of force could conceivably become easier for the United States. The new priorities concern other areas of law.

In Latin America the use of force of the type of the Panama intervention may – if a hundred years' history is any guide[77] – call for a shift in the explanatory focus from the "new international law" paradigm back to traditional American power and spheres-of-influence policies, particularly in the Caribbean "backyard" of the United States. This is no legal excuse. The point is that it allows the United States to deflate its ideologically distorted legal reasoning, to revert to more traditional legal categories as explanatory and justifying criteria, and even to admit as it did in the past their occasional violations. But this very process of arguing legally in international forums might induce the United States to give more attention again to international legal considerations in its decision-making. As the United States faces no more (fewer?) global challenges in Latin America it might feel it can afford to defer to international law in the sense of the pragmatist approach (I.2.) of treating it as relevant. Thus international law may regain its modestly restraining influence. Such a change might also lead the United States to transcend the phase of extreme unilateralism and cooperate with other Latin American states within the OAS, as it did successfully in the late 1950s and early 1960s regarding Cuba and Haiti.

Can similar changes be expected on the global level? The Gulf War does not necessarily, as is often claimed,[78] point that way. To treat it as "just war"[79] would rather indicate the opposite direction. Though the building of the anti-Iraqi coalition certainly was a great diplomatic achievement it is not clear that the war decisions did reflect deference to substantive international law and community decision-making related to it. The basis for action remained unclear. The reference to "Chapter VII of the Charter" in Security Council Resolution 678 of November 29, 1990 is a vague foundation for a decision of such momentous consequences. It "authorizes … to use all necessary means … to restore international peace and security …" Did this indeterminacy reflect a lack of consensus in the Council, or rather the fact that it was being dominated by U.S. unilateralism which used rewards and punishment, very much as a strong leadership might do in the U.S. Congress, in order to cloak its strategic interests? Unilateralism in any case prevailed even more in the implementation phase: the decisions for the war and its mode of conduct were those of the United States plus perhaps its major allies; the UN was, to put it mildly, marginalized.[80] The overriding UN objectives of peace and peaceful conflict resolution might have called for more genuinely multilateral responsibility for peace – including more extended use of nonviolent means such as economic or other sanctions (cf. Articles 41 and 42 of the UN Charter) – as well as for war.

The United Nations and international law did come into play. But reasons for doubt remain. As seen from a United Nations or world community perspective, more authentically multilateral strategies and intra-UN checks and balances would seem to be essential *vis-à-vis* the one preponderant member on whose power the UN security system seems centrally to depend. And if we look at it from the vantage point of the United States it remains uncertain whether the enterprise reflected a greater deference to the substance and processes of international law or, rather, the desire to take advantage of the legitimizing effect of (pseudo-)multilateralism for America's own strategic purposes – whether, in the words of one of the foremost universalists, the United States really acted "not for the extension of power, not for the seizure of territory, and not for the price of oil, but for the defense of world order(,)" because its interests are involved "when acts of aggression occur in distant places."[81]

Notes

1. The United States alone employed its armed forces for political purposes in 215 incidents between 1946 and 1975, see Barry M. Blechman, Stephen S. Kaplan et al., *Force Without War. U.S. Armed Forces as a Political Instrument* (Washington, D.C., 1978), chapt. 2.

2. Cf. recent discussion of these issues by Oscar Schachter, "The Right of States to Use Armed Force," *Michigan Law Review* 82 (1984): 1620–1646; ibid., "Self-Defense and the Rule of Law," *American Journal of International Law* 83 (1989): 259–277; Ian Brownlie, *International Law and the Use of Force by States* (Oxford, 1963), and Brownlie with Robert J. Beck, *International Law and the Use of Force. Beyond the United Nations Charter Paradigm* (Oxford, 1993); Louis Henkin, "Use of Force: Law and U.S. Policy," in Henkin et al., *Right v. Might. International Law and the Use of Force* (New York, London, 1989), 37–69; Edward Gordon, "Article 2(4) in Historical Context," *Yale Journal of International Law* 10 (1985): 271–278.

3. Robert H. Bork "The Limits of 'International law,'" *The National Interest* (Winter 1989/1990): 9–10.

4. Charles Krauthammer, "The Curse of Legalism," *The New Republic*, November 6, 1989, 44, 50.

5. Oscar Schachter, "Self-Defense and the Rule of Law", 266; also ibid., "The Right of States to Use Armed Force", 1623; cf. also the pertinent remark by L. F. E. Goldie: "Obedience to law … is not only a categorical value but also a prudential one" quoted by Daniel Patrick Moynihan, *On the Law of Nations* (Cambridge, Massachusetts, London, 1990), 149.

6. Robert A. Ferguson, *Law and Letters in American Culture* (Cambridge, Massachusetts, London, 1984), 14.

7. James Kent, *Commentaries on American Law*, 4th ed., vol. 1 (New York, 1840), 1. See also Daniel G. Lang, *Foreign Policy in the Early Republic. The Law of Nations and the Balance of Power* (Baton Rouge, Louisiana, London, 1985).

8. Ferguson, *Law and Letters*, 9, 10 and 16, 26, generally Prologue to part 1 and chapt. 1; cf. also Lawrence Friedman, *A History of American Law* (New York, 1973), part 2; Perry Miller, *The Life of the Mind in America from the Revolution to the Civil War* (New York, 1965), particularly Bk. 2: "The Legal Mentality;" Miller, ed., *The Legal Mind in America from Independence to the Civil War* (Garden City, New York, 1962); Peter Charles Hoffer, *Law and People in Colonial America* (Baltimore, London, 1992), x.

9. See for example Max Lerner, "Constitution and Court as Symbols," *Yale Law Journal* 46 (1936/1937): 1290, 1311–1312; Ferguson, *Law and Letters* (note 6), 16, 24, 33.

10. Ferguson, *Law and Letters*, 33.

11. Senator Daniel Patrick Moynihan, *Loyalties* (San Diego, New York, London, 1984), 94.

12. A. de Tocqueville, *Democracy in America*, translated by Phillips Bradley (New York, 1958), vol. 1, chapt.16, 290.

13. But cf. for a recent statement and references to the literature Knud Krakau, "Critical Reflections upon an Old Theme: The Topoi of Chosen People and Mission in American History," in Gustav H. Blanke und K. Krakau, *Mission, Myth, Rhetoric, and Politics in American History*, Working Paper 54/1992, J. F. Kennedy-Institut für Nordamerikastudien, Freie Universität Berlin (Berlin, 1992), 25–39; Ernest Lee Tuveson, *Redeemer Nation. The Idea of America's Millennial Role* (Chicago, London, 1968, repr. 1980); Russel B. Nye, *This Almost Chosen People. Essays in the History of American Ideas* (East Lansing, Michigan, 1966); Kurt R. Spillmann, *Amerikas Ideologie des Friedens. Ursprünge, Formwandlungen und geschichtliche Auswirkungen des amerikanischen Glaubens an den Mythos von einer friedlichen Weltordnung* (Bern, Frankfurt am Main, New York, 1984); James Schlesinger, *America at Century's End* (New York, 1989), chapt. 2: "The American Style in Foreign Policy."

14. Both quoted by Moynihan, *Loyalties*, 74 and 76.

15. Quoted by Thomas M. Franck and Jerome M. Lehrman, "Messianism and Chauvinism in America's Commitment to Peace through Law," in: Lori F. Damrosch, ed., *The International Court of Justice at the Crossroads* (Dobbs Ferry, New York 1987), 3–18, quotation at 6.

16. Krauthammer, "The Curse of Legalism", 44.

17. See for example Merle E. Curti, *Peace or War. The American Struggle, 1636–1936* (Boston, 1959); Lawrence B. Wittner, *Rebels against War. The American Peace Movement, 1933–1983* (Philadelphia, 1984).

18. See the most recent work on the Treaty of Washington, Pia G. Celozzi Baldelli, *Arbitrati e Politica di Potenza. Gli Stati Uniti dopo la Guerra di Secessione* (Rome, 1990); cf. review in *American Historical Review* 97 (1992): 935.

19. In Joseph Frazier Wall, *Andrew Carnegie* (New York, 1970), 898.

20. Quoted by Franck and Lehrman, "Messianism and Chauvinism", 5. See the entire paper by Franck and Lehrman for the above context and the following paragraphs; also Albert B. Hart, "American Ideals of International Relations," *American Journal of International Law* 2 (1907): 624, 633–635.

21. Quoted in Franck - Lehrman, "Messianism and Chauvinism", 13.

22. Both quoted by Franck and Lehrman, "Messianism and Chauvinism", at 15 and 16, respectively.

23. In Hearings before the Senate Committee on Foreign Relations, "The Future of U.S.-Soviet Relations," Spring 1989, quoted by Daniel Patrick Moynihan, *On the Law of Nations* (Cambridge, Massachusetts, London, 1990), 151.

24. See Anatol Rapoport, "Changing Conceptions of War in the United States," in Ken Booth and Moorhead Wright, eds., *American Thinking about War and Peace* (New York, 1978), 59, 61.

25. Wilson in 1916, quoted by Reinhold Niebuhr and Alan Heimert, *A Nation*

So Conceived. Reflections on the History of America from its Early Visions to its Present Power (London, 1963, repr. Westport, Connecticut, 1983), 138.

26. Oscar Schachter also uses this analogy to American constitutional law thinking in his critical appraisal of American international law attitudes, "The Legality of Pro-Democratic Invasion," *American Journal of International Law* 78 (1984): 647–648.

27. A particularly lucid statement on the traditional law on this point is Oscar Schachter, "The Right of States to Use Armed Force": 1620, 1641–1645; also Louis Henkin, "Use of Force: Law and U.S. Policy," in Henkin et al., *Right v. Might. International Law and the Use of Force* (New York, London, 1989), 37–69, at 63–65.

28. Moynihan, *Loyalties*,66, also 83; ibid., *Law of Nations*, 1 and *passim*.

29. Richard A. Falk, "The Decline of Normative Restraint in International Relations," *Yale Journal of International Law* 10 (1985): 263, 265.

30. Quoted in Franck and Lehrman, "Messianism and Chauvinism", 4, and discussion ibid. 17–18; cf. also Moynihan, *Law of Nations*, 143–147.

31. According to Moynihan, *Law of Nations*, 6–7.

32. Quoted by Moynihan, *Loyalties*, 94.

33. Quoted from: "U.S. High Court backs Abductions for Trial," *New York Times*, June 16, 1992: 1:7 and 8.

34. Speech before the National Press Club, *New York Times*, November 29, 1984: A 1:3, A 4:3, A 5.

35. This was ocasionally denied by official spokesmen, but the denial was contradicted by presidential (and other) utterances and by U.S. action. See for a series of declarations to this effect by congressional leaders statement by Paul Reichler at the meeting of the American Society of International Law in 1984, *Proceedings* (1984), 163. Among congressional leaders quoted by Reichler are E. Bowland and Majority Leader James Wright.

36. The argument based on the OECS Treaty is particularly spurious: it vaguely provides for consultation on security issues but certainly does not contemplate such drastic steps as foreign military intervention; see, however, John N. Moore, "Grenada and the International Double Standard," *American Journal of International Law* 78 (1984): 145, 153–159; a rigorous and critical analysis, on the other hand, is Christopher C. Joyner, "Reflections on the Lawfulness of Invasion," ibid. 131, 135–140.

37. See for example statement by nine eminent American international law professors, among them Abram Chayes, Richard Falk, "International Lawlessness in Grenada," in *American Journal of International Law* 78 (1984): 172–175; Detlef F. Vagts, "International Law under Time Pressure: Grading the Grenada Take-Home Examination," ibid. 169–112; Christopher C. Joyner, "Reflections on the Lawfulness of Invasion", ibid. 131–144; Moynihan, *Loyalties*, 93; ibid., *Law of Nations*, 127, 133; at least skeptical Nicholas O. Berry, "The Conflict between United States Intervention and Promoting Democracy in the Third World," *Temple Law Quarterly* 60 (1987): 1015–1020.

38. Against conventional wisdom Eugene V. Rostow still has it the other way round: "Article 2(4) is a derogation of the sovereignty of all states, and a limitation on their historical freedom to use force both for aggression and in

self-defense. As an exception to the normal rule of state sovereignty ..."
Rostow, "The Legality of the International Use of Force by and from
States," *Yale Journal of International Law* 10 (1985): 286, 289. This is histori-
cally correct but not as interpretation of contemporary international law.

39.   See text above with note 30.

40.   This really was the thrust of American actions and their official public
justifications. Such views were explicitly and emphatically expressed over
and again by Jeane J. Kirkpatrick, as member of the Reagan cabinet and
ambassador to the United Nations and later after leaving that position but
still a powerful spokeswoman for these positions, see for example
Kirkpatrick with Allan Gerson, "The Reagan Doctrine, Human Rights, and
International Law," in Louis Henkin et al., *Right v. Might. International Law
and the Use of Force* (New York, London, 1989), 19, 20–24, 30–34;
Kirkpatrick with Carl Gershman, Allan Gerson, Meyers McDougal, "Law
and Reciprocity," *Proceedings of American Society of International Law* (1984):
59–68, also as "The Limits of International Law," in Kirkpatrick, *Legitimacy
and Force*, vol. 1: *Political and Moral Dimensions* (New Brunswick, Oxford,
1988), 241–252, and ibid. *passim*; Kirkpatrick, "The Use of Force in the Law
of Nations," *Yale Journal of International Law* 16 (1991): 580–595. See also
various influential writings by W. Michael Reisman quoted here; John
N. Moore, "Grenada and the International Double Standard," *Amercan
Journal of International Law* 78 (1984): 145–168.

41.   There are few who see this far-reaching consequence, but cf. Franck and
Lehrman, "Messianism and Chauvinism", 4–5; the works by Moynihan
quoted supra.

42.   Jeane J. Kirkpatrick, ambassador to the United Nations, addressing the
American Society of International Law and the International Law Section of
the American Bar Association in April 1984, "Law and Reciprocity" or "The
Limits of International Law" (note 40), 67–68 and 241–243, 251–252,
respectively; ibid. with A. Gerson, "The Reagan Doctrine", 23, 32–34. This
is also the thrust of John N. Moore's long article, "Grenada and the International Double Standard", *American Journal of International Law* 78 (1984):
145–168, in particular 167–168. For a highly sophisticated presentation of
the *tu quoque* argument see W. Michael Reisman, "Old Wine in New
Bottles: The Reagan and Brezhnev Doctrines in Contemporary International Law and Practice," *Yale Journal of International Law* 13 (1988):
171–198, 188 to end. Strongly critical Francis A. Boyle, "Remarks" at panel
on "U.S. Relations with Central American Nations: Legal and Political
Aspects," *Proceedings of American Society of International Law* (1984): 144,
164–165.

43.   David J. Scheffer, "Introduction: The Great Debate of the 1980's," in Louis
Henkin et al., *Right v. Might. International Law and the Use of Force* (New
York, London, 1989), 1.

44.   Jeane J. Kirkpatrick, "The Use of Force in the Law of Nations," *Yale Journal
of International Law* 16 (1991): 591: one if not the overriding "purpose of the
Charter is ... to promote a world order based on democratic values and
practices."

45.   Edward Gordon, "Article 2(4) in Historical Context," *Yale Journal of*

International Law 10 (1985): 276; the quotation is from Ian Brownlie, "The Use of Force in Self-Defense," *British Yearbook of International Law* 37 (1961): 183, 236 note 2.

46. Louis Henkin, "Use of Force", 38–39.

47. This is what David J. Scheffer, "Introduction", 9, 11, calls the neo-realist position. Stuart S. Malawer stresses that the Reagan Administration's legacy "is one of excessive unilateralism with little regard for international law or the future development of the international legal system." See his "Reagan's Law and Foreign Policy, 1981–1987: The 'Reagan Corollary' of International Law," *Harvard International Law Journal* 29 (1988): 85, 108–109.

48. W. Michael Reisman, "Old Wine in New Bottles: The Reagan and Brezhnev Doctrines in Contemporary International Law and Practice," *Yale Journal of International Law* 13 (1988): 171–198.

49. Jeane J. Kirkpatrick and Allan Gerson, "The Reagan Doctrine", 21–23, 30–33.

50. *Department of State Bulletin* (December 1983): 74, 76.

51. *Department of State Bulletin* (December 1983): 77.

52. "The Use of Force in the Law of Nations," *Yale Journal of International Law* 16 (1991): 584.

53. See voices quoted in note 37; Louis Henkin, "Use of Force", 44, 61, 56: "It is not permissible under the Charter to use force to impose or secure democracy; nor does the Charter contain a Monroe Doctrine exception that would permit the U.S. to use force to keep the Western Hemisphere free of communism." Also Edward Gordon, "Article 2(4) and Permissive Pragmatism," *Proceedings of American Society of International Law* (1984): 87, 91–92.

54. Statement by Ambassador Middendorf, October 26, 1983, *Department State Bulletin* (December 1983): 72.

55. The Legal Adviser to the Department of State, Davis R. Robinson in a letter of February 10, 1984, to the American Bar Association, however, reaffirmed traditional American respect for the principle of Art. 2(4), in *American Journal of International Law* 78 (1984): 661–665.

56. Address at Louisville, November 4, 1983, in *Department of State Bulletin* (December 1983): 81–82.

57. See for example Margaret E. Scranton, *The Noriega Years. U.S.-Panamanian Relations 1981–1990* (Boulder, Colorado, London, 1991).

58. President Bush, address December 20, 1989, *Weekly Compilation of Presidential Documents* 25 (1989): 1974; see also documentation in *American Journal of International Law* 84 (1990): 545, 546; Anthony D'Amato, "The Invasion of Panama Was a Lawful Response to Tyranny," ibid. 516, 519. Critical evaluations are Ved P. Nanda, "The Validity of United States Intervention in Panama under International Law," *American Journal of International Law* 84 (1990): 494–503; also Tom J. Farer, "Panama: Beyond the Charter Paradigm," ibid. 503–515.

59. International Court of Justice, Military and Paramilitary Activities in and against Nicaragua (Nicaragua versus United States), Merits. Judgment of June 27, 1986, Paragr. 210–211.

60. See for example John A. Perkins, "The Right of Counterintervention,"

Georgia Journal of International and Comparative Law 17 (1986): 171–227; short but lucid and critical discussion in Oscar Schachter, "The Right of States to Use Armed Force": 1620, 1643–1644; Louis Henkin, "Use of Force", 48–50, 63–65. Defensive of the right to counterintervention, of course, the various writings of J. J. Kirkpatrick, for example "The Use of Force in the Law of Nations," *Yale Journal of International Law* 16 (1991): 589–590.

61.   See for example John N. Moore, "The Secret War in Central America and the Future of World Order," *American Journal of International Law* 80 (1986): 43–127; and critical response by James P. Rowles, "'Secret Wars', Self-Defense and the Charter – A Reply to Professor Moore," ibid. 568–583; all the writings by W. Michael Reisman cited here.

62.   W. Michael Reisman, "Coercion and Self-Determination: Construing Charter Article 2(4)," *American Journal of International Law* 78 (1984): 643.

63.   W. Michael Reisman, "Criteria for Lawful Use of Force in International Law," *Yale Journal of International Law* 10 (1985): 279, 282, 284–285; ibid., "Coercion and Self-Determination" where at 644 he reminds the reader "that norms are instruments devised by human beings to precipitate desired social consequences" – but which ones? This begs the question; ibid., "Old Wine in New Bottles: The Reagan and Brezhnev Doctrines in Contemporary International Law and Practice," *Yale Journal of International Law* 13 (1988): 171–198; ibid., "Article 2(4): The Use of Force in Contemporary International Law," in: *Proceedings of American Society of International Law* (1984): 74, 84–87.

64.   Reisman, "Criteria", 283.

65.   John Hart Ely, *Democracy and Distrust. A Theory of Judicial Review* (Cambridge, Massachusetts, London, 1980), chapt. 1 and *passim*; Sanford Levinson, *Constitutional Faith* (Princeton, 1988), introduction and chapt. 1 through page 37.

66.   See Oscar Schachter, "Self-Defense and the Rule of Law", 259, 274.

67.   See Oscar Schachter's harsh criticism of Reisman's approach, "Self-Defense and the Rule of Law": 274–277, at 275; and ibid., "The Legality of Pro-Democratic Invasion," *American Journal of International Law* 78 (1984): 645, 647–650; ibid., "The Lawful Resort to Unilateral Use of Force," *Yale Journal of International Law* 10 (1985): 291, 293–294; also Ved P. Nanda, "The Validity of United States Intervention in Panama under International Law," *American Journal of International Law* 84 (1990): 494, 498–500.

68.   United States versus Carolene Products Co., 304 United States 144 (1938); text of Note Four printed in Henry A. Abraham, *Freedom and the Court. Civil Rights and Liberties in the United States*, 3rd ed., (New York, Oxford, 1977), 19, for discussion ibid. 17–32.

69.   See for example discussion in Jonathan Culler, *On Deconstruction. Theory and Criticism after Structuralism* (Ithaca, New York, 1982) 22, 85, 120.

70.   That early programmatic article was McDougal and Lasswell, "Legal Education and Public Policy: Professional Training in the Public Interest," *Yale Law Journal* 52 (1942/1943): 203–295; central to the basic concept McDougal, "Law as a Process of Decision: A Policy-Oriented Approach to Legal Study," *Natural Law Forum* 1 (1956): 53. From his major works I

mention only the massive studies McDougal and Associates, *Studies in World Public Order* (New Haven, Connecticut, 1960); with F. P. Feliciano, *Law and Minimum World Public Order. The Legal Regulation of International Coercion* (New Haven, Connecticut, London, 1961), and many others. The present author has once devoted a book chapter to analysis and critique of the McDougal approach, see Knud Krakau, *Missionsbewußtsein und Völkerrechtsdoktrin in den Vereinigten Staaten von Amerika* (Frankfurt M., Berlin, 1967), chapt. 15.

71.   John W. Coogan, *The End of Neutrality. The United States, Britain, and Maritime Rights 1899–1915* (Ithaca, New York, London, 1981), 254–256.

72.   Cf. for a discussion of the neutrality and laws of war issue Knud Krakau, *Missionsbewußtsein und Völkerrechtsdoktrin* (note 70), chapts. 11 and 12; ibid., "Concepts of War and Neutrality: The Impact of American 'Uniqueness' on the Contemporary Debate," *Comparative Law Review* 2 (Poznan, Poland, 1991): 49–56.

73.   Oscar Schachter's criticism of the new "just war" concept, in "The Lawful Resort to Unilateral Use of Force", 291, 294; also Christopher C. Joyner, "Reflections on the Lawfulness of Invasion," *American Journal of International Law* 78 (1984): 131, 143–144; also "Comment" by Robert Rosenstock in "Discussion," *Proceedings of American Society of International Law* (1984): 97.

74.   See a recent statement of the doctrine in Daniel George Lang, *Foreign Policy in the Early Republic. The Law of Nations and the Balance of Power* (Baton Rouge, Louisiana, London, 1985), 48–49, 53–54: "As a rule the internal character of another regime is unacceptable as a basis for a justifiable foreign policy." (54)

75.   Stuart S. Malawer, "Reagan's Law and Foreign Policy, 1981–1987: The 'Reagan Corollary' of International Law," *Harvard International Law Journal* 29 (1988): 108 (my emphasis).

76.   On the nature and effect of dicplomatic style cf. Knud Krakau, "American Foreign Relations. A National Style?," *Diplomatic History* 8 (1984): 253–272.

77.   See for the relevance of this history in this particular context Francis A. Boyle, "Remarks" in session on "U.S. Relations with Central American Nations: Legal and Political Aspects," *Proceedings of American Society of International Law* (1984): 144–148.

78.   See for example statement by (designated) U.S. Ambassador to the UN Madeleine Albright at confirmation hearings before the Senate Committee on Foreign Relations on January 21, 1993, in: 4 *Amerikadienst*, U.S. Embassy Bonn (January 27, 1993), 1–5.

79.   See James Turner Johnson, *Just War and the Gulf War* (Washington, DC, 1991).

80.   See somewhat along these lines the long and richly documented article by Burns H. Weston, "Security Council Resolution 678 and Persian Gulf Decision Making: Precarious Legitimacy," *American Journal of International Law* 85 (1991): 516–535.

81.   W. Michael Reisman, "Some Lessons from Iraq: International Law and Democratic Politics," *Yale Journal of International Law* 16 (1991): 203, 215, 207.

For a complete list of Ryburn
and Keele University Press books in print
please write to Ryburn Distribution
Keele University
Staffordshire ST5 5BG
England